# Practicing Development
# Anthropology

# About the Book and Editor

What is it like to be an anthropologist working in international development? Once objective observers of isolated cultures, many anthropologists today play an active role in affecting social change in Third World countries. Increasingly they are hired by development agencies to help improve health and nutrition, to promote family planning, to increase agricultural productivity, and to expand education and employment opportunities. Given this active involvement and the need to work on multidisciplinary teams, development anthropologists often face challenges and problems that do not exist in traditional anthropology.

Offering candid, first-hand accounts of their field experiences, the contributors discuss the obstacles and opportunities that they have encountered. The short-term overseas assignment presents a special challenge because the anthropologist must observe, evaluate, and make recommendations in the space of a few weeks. Traditional data-gathering methods must often be adapted to meet new needs. The anthropologist may have to mediate between the donor agency, local elites, and intended beneficiaries. The authors explore these and other issues, offering their own solutions. Throughout the book, they emphasize the real contribution the anthropologist can make, and in the final chapter they provide advice on employment and career opportunities in development anthropology.

Edward C. Green is senior research associate for John Short and Associates, Columbia, Maryland.

# Practicing Development Anthropology

edited by
Edward C. Green

Westview Press / Boulder and London

*Westview Special Studies in Applied Anthropology*

This Westview softcover edition was manufactured on our own premises using equipment and methods that allow us to keep even specialized books in stock. It is printed on acid-free paper and bound in softcovers that carry the highest rating of the National Association of State Textbook Administrators, in consultation with the Association of American Publishers and the Book Manufacturers' Institute.

Copyright © 1986 by Westview Press, Inc.

Published in 1986 in the United States of America by Westview Press, Inc.; Frederick A. Praeger, Publisher; 5500 Central Avenue, Boulder, Colorado 80301

Library of Congress Cataloging-in-Publication Data
Practicing development anthropology.
    (Westview special studies in applied anthropology)
    1. Applied anthropology—Case studies.   2. Ethnology—
Field work—Case studies.   3. Technical assistance—
Anthropological aspects—Case studies.   I. Green,
Edward Crocker, 1944-    .   II. Series.
GN397.5.A59   1986      306      86-15745
ISBN 0-8133-7256-9

Composition for this book was created by conversion of the editor's word-processor disks.
This book was produced without formal editing by the publisher.

Printed and bound in the United States of America

The paper used in this publication meets the requirements of the American National Standard for Permanence of Paper for Printed Library Materials Z39.48-1984.

6   5   4   3   2   1

# Contents

# Tables and Figures

# Acknowledgments

I would like to thank Don Messerschmidt, who conceived the idea for the book and did some of the preliminary editing; Sue McLaughlin, my editorial assistant, for her untiring efforts; and Victoria Yogman of Westview for her useful advice.

*Edward C. Green*

# 1

# Themes in the Practice
# of Development Anthropology

### Edward C. Green

Since many of the chapters to follow consist of personal accounts, it may be appropriate to begin the introductory chapter with one of my own. In 1979, when I was a NIMH postdoctoral fellow at Vanderbilt University, I wrote and later published an essay critical of policy analysis. I showed how policy analysts served the interests of an entrenched elite and I set forth an agenda for retooling policy analysis as a potent weapon for grassroots organizations seeking to redress the imbalance of power. I showed the essay to a lawyer acquaintance who directs a citizens action group in Washington. He read it and said, "Great. When do you begin?" I frowned and asked him what he meant. He went on to say that I had identified a problem and proposed a solution in the form of an action program. Surely I meant to do something about it, or why would I have bothered to write the article?

This question forced me to realize how remote direct involvement, let alone advocacy, had become to me during my years as an academic anthropologist. I was forced to admit to myself that I wrote articles of the sort described mostly to advance my academic career. Of course I hoped that my ethnographic or advocacy publications would do some good in the world, but the translation of anthropological findings or insights into any sort of action would have to be left to someone else. As a scientist, especially one reared in the doctrine of cultural relativism, I was above the human fray.

Such a position of neutrality and even aloofness was expressed, in fact prescribed, by Laura Thompson in an article entitled "An Appropriate Role for Postcolonial Applied Anthropologists" (1976). She felt anthropologists should not "assume the part of an administrator, developer, manipulator, 'do-gooder' or missionary." At most, we should provide alternatives to policymakers or whomever, but not go so far as to advocate one or another alternative. The applied or development anthropologist "sets no goals, engineers no solutions, activates no policies" (Thompson, 1976: 5). Part of this argument rests on the possibility that an involved or activist anthropologist would detract from the decision-making abilities of the people he is trying to help.

Positions diametrically opposed to, or at least very different from, Thompson's can be found in the writings of Dell Hymes (1974), Elizabeth Colson (1985), or various proponents of Marxist or radical anthropology, political economy, and applied anthropology including "action anthropology" and development anthropology. All of these call for direct involvement, if not advocacy or activism, on the part of anthropologists. David Spain (1978), reflecting on his own and other anthropologists' experience in Nigeria, advocates what he sees as pragmatic involvement on the part of anthropologists concerned with development. He contends that to call anthropologists' involvement in economic and social development neocolonial is itself "neopaternal" and

> . . . leads to development anthropologists being in the unenviable position of standing on the sidelines, shaking their heads in paternal dismay. It can also lead to the dubious position of knowing that with a little less neutrality and a little more advocacy, disasters could have been averted (Spain, 1978: 26).

Whatever the motives or circumstances that led contributors to this volume into applied work related to international development, it is clear that they felt they could do more by bringing their efforts and skills to bear on the problems of social and economic development than they could by standing on the sidelines and criticizing; that it is worth sacrificing strict scientific neutrality and cultural relativism if the lives of the world's poor majority can be improved; and that development projects and programs informed by anthropology are better to those not so informed.

In his review of the recent growth and expansion of anthropological activities related to development, Hoben (1982: 349) notes that, "Anthropologists working in development have not created an academic subdiscipline, 'development anthropology,' for their work is not characterized by a coherent or distinctive body of theory, concepts, and methods." I think there is now considerable evidence that a subdiscipline has in fact emerged. For example the American Anthropological Association—hardly a forerunner in anything to do with applied anthropology—has published a Training Manual in Development Anthropology (Partridge, 1984). I agree, however, with the rest of Hoben's characterization. Development anthropology is probably not an academic subdiscipline, not only for the reason given but because the scope of applied anthropology in the context of development is such that it cuts across many anthropological and other subdisciplines: public health, nutrition, population, forestry, agronomy, ecology, economics, communications, and marketing, to name but a few. It would be surprising if a coherent body of theory, concepts, or methods could emerge from such diverse fields of study and activity. Another reason the subdiscipline may not be academic is because there has always been tension between branches of a discipline that are more theoretical, "basic," and therefore academic-based, and those that are more applied, operational, client-centered and therefore non-academically based. We may be in a boom period for university-based teaching of development anthropology at present due to diminished career opportunities in academic anthropology and recent expansion of such opportunities in the broad field of development. But development anthropology, like development economics, will probably remain an amorphous, non-academically oriented field and as such will never be regarded as a legitimate academic subdiscipline—at least by traditional academicians.

In the training manual referred to above, Partridge and Warren (1984: 1) define development anthropology as "scientific research with significant applications within the development project cycle. Its objective is to enhance benefits and mitigate negative consequences for the human communities involved in and affected by development efforts." I would argue for a somewhat broader definition. As the contributors to this volume demonstrate, development anthropologists do more than research, even as broadly defined to include information gathering by whatever means. Development anthropologists also learn to operate effectively as members of organizations involved in development work, becoming knowledgable about the "professional culture" of such organizations ". . . and the bureaucratic and political decision-making processes that characterize development assistance programs" (Hoben, 1982: 349–350). Some development anthropologists, such as Greeley in this volume, are primarily managers, administrators, or planners. Others engaged in applied or operations research, such as DiBella, Green, and Rhoades, find that research by itself may have little impact unless research results and implications are communicated—if not argued—to client organizations and host country officials.

For those involved in research, it seems that standard anthropological methods are useful and adaptable to a wide range of information-gathering tasks. Key-informant interviews, participant-observation, open-ended questionnaires, village census, and even material culture assessment are found to work very well in diverse contexts of development work. Fujisaka's team members—economists and botanists—engaged in participant-observation research themselves, although it is not clear where they learned to do this. Groenfeldt developed key informants in banking and loan circles in India in order to obtain sensitive, elusive information. Rhoades and Green both describe using in-depth, key-informant interviewing as an important complement to standard survey research. Several contributors illustrate the community-level focus characteristic of anthropology, whether village (e.g. Groenfeldt) or urban slum (e.g. Mason). Sando and DiBella are among those who relied on the case study approach.

Curry comments on the opportunities for research provided by assignments with development agencies and notes that his consultancy with AID in Niger gave him valuable country experience beyond the village level. At a time when funds for anthropological research from traditional sources are scarce, it is possible to do research in exotic parts of the world with more than adequate funding as well as logistical and manpower support. I would add that working for a development agency helps ensure host country permission to carry out the research, something that cannot be taken for granted in these days of growing nationalism and sensitivity about American researchers poking around in rural areas talking to the poor and dispossessed.

Greeley emphasizes the need for a literature search of published and unpublished sources prior to project design and certainly prior to recommending or designing any research. Although this might seem axiomatic to the university-based, this step is often overlooked by busy development professionals who may feel that something like library research is not really part of their duties—or is too much like a historic or other academic exercise. In my experience, a preliminary literature search seems a natural thing to do for an anthropologist beginning an assignment of any length in a foreign country. A little time spent doing one's "homework" puts the anthropologist in a position of credibility and authority with his colleagues. It may also save time and money and help avoid reinventing the wheel or repeating the mistakes of the past.

In this connection, anthropologists, as "culture experts," are usually expected to have expertise in the culture of the local population ("beneficiaries," in development jargon) involved in a development project. If this is the case, the anthropologist may gain a certain amount of acceptance, credibility, and even leverage with colleagues from other disciplines. Unfortunately the converse is true. If the anthropologist has no experience in the local country, he may find himself in a weak, awkward, and untenable position. The value of his general analytic and research skills may not be as readily apparent to his colleagues as the country expertise they expect the anthropologist to have.

As the case studies that follow illustrate, anthropologists remain essentially and characteristically anthropologists even when working in development jobs. For example, the anthropologist tends to act as a mediator, if not a culture broker, between local populations, donor agency personnel, technical advisors, and host government officials. Robins discusses this in the context of the short-term assignment, and it is equally true of anthropologists on longer-term assignments. Robins also describes a useful "field sense" that anthropologists bring to development, something made up of experience, intuition, common sense, holistic perspective, and intimacy with people that permits complete views of their perceptions, needs, motivations, and lives.

Anthropologists also exhibit a commitment if not preoccupation to data validity or "getting at the truth" that serves them well in development work. In research, it helps avoid the sometimes monumental mistakes sociologists, economists and others may make using "reliable" methods of survey research. Green describes his efforts to complement survey research with validity-sensitive anthropological methods in order to overcome the pitfalls of survey research designed by a culturally-naive outsider, i.e., himself. In the context of the short-term assignment, the anthropologist has to rely heavily on what local "experts" tell him. This is obviously risky since such informants may have biases, blind spots, and "bones to pick" as well as their own perhaps limited perspectives. Concern with data validity plus prior field experience with key-informant interviewing make anthropologists quite adept at sifting through often diverse and conflicting accounts and arriving at a coherent and comprehensive picture not too remote from reality.

Development anthropologists, like their academic counterparts, tend to be defenders and spokesmen of the poor and powerless. This is fortunately true even when the anthropologists are employed by powerful donor agencies, as the contribution by Harrison and Enge attests. In fact it seems likely that the "New Directions" paradigm shift in the U.S. Agency for International Development (USAID), which occurred in the early 1970s as a result of a Congressional mandate (see Robins in this volume), attracted several of the present contributors to AID-sponsored development work in the first place. In addition to greatly expanding employment opportunities for anthropologists by introducing the requirement of a "social soundness analysis" for all AID-sponsored projects, New Directions proved ideologically and methodologically compatible with the training, orientation and practice of anthropology (cf. Hoben, 1982: 357–362). The paradigm shift was away from centrally-planned, top-down, "trickle-down" development to a more beneficiary-centered, grassroots community-participation approach committed to meeting the "basic human needs of the poor"—even the "poorest of the poor." Mason, Robins, and Greeley all mention or discuss New Directions favorably.

New Directions had its critics, however. There were those who argued it was ill-suited to poor areas such as Africa. In particular, New Directions prohibited major infrastructure projects and required recipient countries to finance recurring costs of AID-initiated projects. The problem in Africa, critics contended, is that major infrastructure projects are very much needed to enable Africa to catch up with other regions of the world. Furthermore, capacity for income-generation by African governments is weak, as are the bureaucracies expected to handle project recurrent costs (Copson, et al., 1986).

With the beginning of the first Reagan administration, there has been a further paradigm shift away from New Directions. Accelerated Development, as the new approach is known, emphasizes policy dialogue (a polite term for policy reform), technology transfer, fostering institutional development, and private sector involvement. Since 1982 these have become known as the Four Pillars of AID's development assistance program. The current approach was inspired not only by conservative Republican ideology but by growing frustration on the part of multilateral donor or lending agencies with the pace of economic growth in developing countries. AID's current emphasis is no longer on directly assisting the poor majority by meeting their basic human needs; this approach is viewed by some in the present administration as global welfarism.

Defenders of Accelerated Development claim the approach

. . . is not inconsistent with basic human needs strategies. In their view, inappropriate economic policies in Africa and a pattern of excessive government involvement in national economic life have stifled investment and initiative and themselves become major causes of Africa's poverty. By aiming at policy reform, supporters argue, accelerated development can ease the governmental burden on peasant farmers and other producers and release their productive energies. . . .

Critics, however, see accelerated development strategies as a return to pre-1973 "top-down" philosophies of assistance, which neglected the needs of the poor and tended to benefit those who already enjoyed considerable economic advantage (Copson, et al., 1986: xii–xiii).

Greeley, the only contributor writing as an AID career insider, is also the only one to acknowledge that we are now operating in a post-New Directions era. He tries to think positively about the future role of anthropologists in AID, but even he expresses some doubts. As Hoben (1982: 361) may have been the first to speculate publicly, AID's shift away from concern with the needs of the poor may portend a diminished need for social scientists, especially those champions of the downtrodden, anthropologists. It may be, however, that anthropologists are sufficiently well established within AID that even if their role is diminished in social soundness analysis it may be expanded in other areas of AID activity. Whatever the approach to development, I believe anthropologists continue to have skills valuable to AID; this is no less true in Accelerated Development. For example, both Greeley and I are currently engaged in AID-sponsored activities in Africa's private sector. In my own health and population work, I have been able to expand more conventional definitions of the private health sector to include indigenous health practitioners and traditional leaders. This means being able to go beyond ministry of health personnel and to include the likes of traditional birth attendants, herbalists, and chiefs in the delivery of primary health care services or information. This is certainly the stuff of anthropology and it may well prove a boon to realizing public health goals.

Of course development is broader than AID. There are development anthropologists such as DiBella in this volume who work for private, voluntary organizations (PVOs) and who directly aid the poor in less-developed countries regardless of the development paradigm currently in favor with AID. And although we lack a contribution that discusses the World Bank, Cernea (1985) seems optimistic about the expanding (albeit too slowly) role of social scientists and incorporation of sociological knowledge in World Bank projects. Still, for the American anthropologist working in development, AID is the "biggest game in town" in terms of direct or indirect funding, therefore this agency's philosophy of and approach to development remains centrally important to development anthropologists.

Although the tone of the contributors is basically positive, even enthusiastic, some of the problems encountered by development anthropologists are discussed. For example, anthropologists often have some involvement in project design—usually after basic decisions have already been made—and in later evaluations, but rarely are they involved from beginning to end. [Cernea discusses this problem in the context of World Bank projects (1985: 8).] Rhoades, Mason, Green, Sacherer, and Greeley all refer to this problem, although not all confronted it in their work. Green worked on the implementation phase of a project in Swaziland that had had the benefit of good social soundness inputs in its design. Greeley, as a regional anthropologist for AID in Africa and later as a project officer in Kenya, learned the value of shaping projects at the earliest design stages through interaction with other members of a multidisciplinary project design team. He notes that projects quickly pick up momentum and therefore are difficult to change significantly once they have progressed beyond the earliest design stages. Aspects of a project that seem socially unsound to the anthropologist can be modified—perhaps the entire project idea even abandoned, as Greeley shows—at these stages. This is probably no longer possible by the "project paper" stage (to use AID language), yet this is often when the anthropologist is called in. The social analysis exercise may then become one of rationalizing and justifying a project design *ex post facto*—that or face the opposition and scorn of those with a personal stake in seeing the project go forward.

Anthropologists working for development agencies, including as members of multidisciplinary teams, may fall victim to their colleagues' stereotyped image of anthropology. As Rhoades points out, anthropology is regarded by economists and agronomists as a "soft" science, as an abstract, purist, academic, interesting-but-useless discipline that seeks only the quaint and exotic. Anthropologists are thought to use non-replicable methods to gather overly-detailed information that is ideographic and non-generalizable to the wider society. They are thought to be individualistic, negativistic "loners" who don't make good team members. Understanding and sympathy with the poor often puts anthropologists in the position of providing critical or negative-seeming information or recommendations to nonanthropologist colleagues. As Firth (quoted in Colson, 1985: 195) notes, ". . . by and large what we have is uncomfortable knowledge, the kind of knowledge that challenges established cliches and puts into question accepted solutions, and so those who champion them." Sacherer in this volume also discusses problems associated with producing negative and unpopular findings, including the resulting marginal role of the anthropologist.

As Rhoades notes, there is usually an element of truth in all stereotypes. Rather than bemoan the unfair image associated with anthropology, anthropologists should sharpen their focus on important contemporary problems and learn how to convey their findings succinctly and coherently to nonanthropologists.

For their part, anthropologists may view economists, agronomists, engineers, and the like as narrowly-focused technicians whose rigid professional mindsets and cultural distance from local populations prevent them from coping with human factors or seeing the larger picture, especially when dealing with cultures quite different from their own. I am doubtless overstating the case, but anthropologists often do feel somewhat alienated from their colleagues. Perhaps just as anthropologists are "marginal natives" in the field (Freilich, 1970), they are "marginal professionals" when they apply their skills outside of universities. [Hoben (1984: 11) observes that anthropologists occupy marginal positions "not only within the power structure of their nation but within their universities as well."] Yet, marginality may have its advantages. For example it may not be possible to be a fully-accepted team member and remain sensitive and sympathetic to the viewpoint and needs of the poor.

I might add that it is not only the poor that development professionals need to be sensitive to, but host country counterparts as well. The former are often in advisory roles *vis-a-vis* the latter, a situation with considerable potential for conflict and misunderstanding. Local counterparts can easily perceive the usually better-educated (and always better paid) foreigner as overstepping his advisory role and acting paternalistic, culturally insensitive, arrogant, pushy, and "neocolonial." In my experience, anthropologists tend to function relatively well in such advisory roles, not only because of their general sensitivities to cultural differences but because they have a sense of fallibility about their own technical knowledge and skills which leaves them open to other interpretations and other ways of doing things. This is in contrast to the technical advisors who, no matter how polite they are, believe there are only two possible approaches, the right way and the wrong way, and as highly-trained American professionals they must know the right way. Sacherer in this volume, illustrates the effective way an anthropologist can relate to a local official who has not cooperated with other foreign advisors.

Returning to some of the problems encountered by development anthropologists, Curry mentions some of the disadvantages of the long-term overseas assignment: the anthropologist may miss academic conferences and opportunities to present papers, thereby losing opportunities to gain or maintain valuable professional contacts. The anthropologist may become forgotten, at least by the academic-based anthropologist. He may feel alone, wanting in collegial support and recognition. On the other hand, as Curry himself notes, the development anthropologist gains important contacts in other fields, learns valuable organizational and other marketable skills, and acquires valuable cross-cultural experience which will serve him well in or outside of anthropology. I would add that anthropologists at risk of being forgotten by the profession should publish their research and other findings in the professional journals.

A final theme that arises in many of the chapters is the pioneer role of the development anthropologist. Several of the contributors found that they were the only, or the first-ever, anthropologist working in a particular agency, organization, or specific job. In several of the accounts to follow, we see the anthropologist carving out a new role and filling a new niche. In this context, Greeley, Sacherer, Green, Rhoades, and DiBella variously discuss the expectations of colleagues and co-workers, the need to build a more positive and accurate image of anthropology, and expansion of the anthropologist's role. Regarding the latter, it appears not uncommon for the anthropologist to go beyond his formal scope of work and on his own initiative broaden his areas of activity and responsibility—breaking new ground, as Rhoades calls it. It would appear that anthropologists have the kind of general resourcefulness and skills that defy easy categorization by development agencies but are nevertheless most useful in development work, perhaps especially in the field context. As long as anthropologists rely on their personal and professional resourcefulness and continue to break new ground, their continuing involvement in development work is probably assured, whatever development paradigm might be in vogue with the major donor agencies.

## References

Cernea, Michael M. "Sociological Knowledge for Development Projects," in Michael Cernea, ed., *Putting People First: Sociological Variables in Rural Development.* Published for the World Bank. New York: Oxford University Press, 1985, pp. 3–21.

Colson, Elizabeth. "Using Anthropology in a World on the Move." *Human Organization,* Vol. 44, No. 3, 1985, pp. 191–196.

Copson, Raymond W. and Theodor W. Galdi and Larry Nowels. *U.S. AID to Africa: The Record, the Rationales, and the Challenge.* Washington, D.C.: Congressional Research Service, The Library of Congress, January 7, 1986.

Freilich, Morris, ed., *Marginal Natives: Anthropologists at Work.* New York: Harper and Row, 1970.

Hoben, Allan. "The Role of the Anthropologist in Development Work: An Overview," in W. Partridge, ed., *Training Manual in Development Anthropology.* Washington, D.C.: American Anthropological Association, 1984, pp. 9–17.

Hoben, Allan. "Anthropologists and Development." *Annual Review of Anthropology,* Vol. 11, No. 34, 1982, pp. 9–75.

Hymes, Dell. "The Use of Anthropology: Critical, Political, Personal," in D. Hymes, ed., *Reinventing Anthropology.* New York: Vintage Books, 1974, pp. 3–82.

Partridge, William, ed., *Training Manual in Development Anthropology.* Washington, D.C.: AAA and SAA Special Pub. No. 17, 1984.

Partridge, William and Dennis Warren. "Development Anthropology and the Life Cycle of Development Projects," in W. Partridge, ed., *Training Manual in Development Anthropology.* Washington, D.C.: AAA and SAA Special Pub. No. 17, 1984.

Schleisier, K. "Action Anthropology and the Southern Cheyenne." *Current Anthropology,* Vol. 15, No. 3, 1974.

Spain, David. "Anthropologists and Development: Observations by an American in Nigeria," in P. Stevens, ed., *The Social Sciences and African Development Planning.* Waltham, Ma.: Crossroads Press, pp. 17–28, 1978.

Thompson, Laura. "An Appropriate Role for Postcolonial Applied Anthropologists." *Human Organization,* Vol. 35, 1976, pp. 1–7.

# 2

# The Strategy of Development
# and the Role of the Anthropologist

*Edward Robins*

The modernization of the Third World is the focus of much scientific interest at present insofar as it is a proving ground for innovative technology and fashionable theory. Especially for agricultural and social scientists, this period presents opportunities for realizing the state of their art. Through the programs of international assistance agencies such as the World Bank and USAID, billions of dollars have been released for this effort. The objectives of development in this current style are tied to improving the general welfare of people everywhere by: managing population growth; improving health and nutrition; expanding educational and employment opportunities; increasing agricultural production; developing private enterprise; and generally boosting economies. Whether or not the "gap" between the developed and developing nations is actually narrowed in the process, and it appears that it has not been, is not at issue. Development in the absolute sense of moving forward is the standard by which this process is being judged. The promotion of advanced technologies which is integral to the process has been accompanied by sweeping social change. The considerable disruption in the lives of people undergoing modernization is not unexpected; yet the direction of change is not to be left unattended. Donor agencies, increasingly discomforted by the negative impact of new technology upon the social, economic, and political systems of targeted and other populations, have re-examined their strategies; the social soundness of projects has become a fundamental criterion by which the adequacy of their design and evaluation is assessed.

There is an experimental quality to this process. Each new technology that is introduced faces a unique local history in which political, economic, and sociocultural factors condition this impact. Too often insufficient research accompanies implementation, and technology is not well enough fitted to the sociocultural pattern. The field of development is littered with failed programs designed in ignorance of the social and cultural realities of target groups. Bennett has estimated that more than one-half billion dollars has been wasted in poorly conceived African cattle projects for this reason (cited in Heinen 1980: 453).

The identification of sociocultural configurations is fundamental in project design. Too often in the past this element was missing in the design phase. Programming technology compatibly with social systems requires a new and unique skill, for the "relationships," "values," and other conceptualizations of social scientists are not as readily observed or measured as are field dimensions and crop yields. The social scientist in this circumstance strives to comprehend the abstract "realities" of social systems and the tangible material components of technological ones in terms of one another. Despite the imprecision which inheres in the effort to elucidate "impact," the insistence the social scientist places on soliciting farmer/rural/local input into the design and evaluation processes has been undeniably rewarding. Not only has our knowledge been increased through contact with other people and the expression of what they already know to be so, but the very participation of those people for whom projects are developed renders the community more receptive to interventions. The time constraint under which projects are designed makes this already challenging undertaking more difficult yet, for rarely is there enough time to know the sociocultural pattern well. Project impact, a chameleon-like concept with which anthropologists grapple, is particularly illusory. Often we simply do not know what the results of planned change will be. The uniqueness of each program reduces, in principle, the generalizability of the lessons its implementation reveals. The difficulty in fitting the plan to the place is considerable.

Developing the capacity of Third World nations to satisfy the needs of their people, as they the people perceive them, is the challenge which faces applied scientists. The critical issues in this effort are not technological but social. An accommodation of technology to the local milieu is called for, or equally, the modification of the social pattern in a "sound" manner to accommodate technology. In fact the social system and the technological system operate in terms of one another. It is something we must give recognition to in our designs for progress.

The current orientation in planned change succeeds those earlier efforts which were socially deficient. Social scientists, particularly rural sociologists and anthropologists, are more visible now at all stages of the project process—design, implementation, and evaluation. The social factors which condition the impact of development are subject to scrutiny by these team members who are charged with ridding projects of those elements held accountable for past failures.

The new approach to development undertaken in the middle to late 1970s by the World Bank, USAID, the United Nations organizations, and concurrently by the governments of recipient nations placed the needs of the poor as first among its goals. Saint and Coward (1977: 734) comment:

> While increasing agricultural production was the primary objective up to and including the era of the Green Revolution, there is now a growing concern toward broadening the base of participation in the production process and

creating equitable arrangements for distributing the benefits from these production increases.

This has been variously described as the "Process" approach (Mickelwait,
et al., 1979), the "Emerging Orientation" (Saint and Coward, 1977), the
"People-oriented" approach (USAID, 1981), and the "New Directions" (also
USAID). It derives from the 1973 United States Foreign Assistance Act,
which served notice that programs not aimed directly at improving the
lives of the poorest members of society would be viewed as incompatible
with the fundamental goals of development. Prior to 1973 these goals were
otherwise. During the period 1948–1973 less than $1 billion of $25 billion
in World Bank loans were devoted to subsistence agriculture (Mickelwait,
1979: 2). Instead the maximization of the rate of increase of the aggregate
agricultural output and income of Third World nations was promoted in
order to increase GNP (Mickelwait, 1979; UNRISD, 1979; United Nations
Document No. ST/ECA/139, 1970). Rapid economic growth was adopted
as the fundamental means by which developing nations would be brought
into the modern world. Advanced technologies were introduced into targeted
areas in ignorance of prevailing sociocultural systems. Innovations were
expected to diffuse throughout social systems following their introduction
among the "best bets," i.e. the wealthiest and most powerful members of
society. Communication was cited as the key variable in facilitating this
process. Where change did not occur as expected, lack of information and
communications barriers were cited as faults (Saint and Coward, 1977: 733).
     By objectifying human behavior this mechanistic approach was doomed
to failure. The inappropriateness of a "blueprint" for development was
revealed. Programs could not be imposed uniformly with success upon
culturally different groups. Both in the field and in the donor agency the
impact of these programs created hardship and discontent (cf. Mickelwait,
1979; UNRISD, 1979; Warren, 1981; Barlett, 1982). The position of the
poor and powerless in targeted areas remained unchanged or grew worse.
Advances in agricultural technology increased absolute and relative income
disparities among farmers; little improvement was observed in the productive
capacity and livelihood of the poor farmer. Those already relatively wealthy
and powerful usually benefited most from the new programs. Meanwhile,
in the lending agency, unrealistic schedules impaired programs from the
start. Social issues, often considered last in the design process, were first
to cause trouble during implementation (Cernea, 1982: 5).
     An analysis of the results of development programs during this period
reveals the very weaknesses which more recent programs have attempted
to overcome. Those who benefited most and least from development could
be forecast in advance by identifying the initial distribution of productive
assets. Large landholders, for example, could adopt new methods and
technologies more easily because of their greater wealth, greater access to
scarce resources, and stronger political position. For the majority of the
rural population the overall standard of living declined. Many small farmers
and landless laborers faced underemployment and unemployment as tra-

ditional labor arrangements broke down. Political marginality and polarized interests in the rural areas excluded the poor from the decision-making process (Barlett, 1982). Such change, disproportionately favoring the elite, was destructive of traditional systems of cooperation and livelihood. That innovators had more education, more resources, and more land, that is, that they constituted a rural elite intent upon maintaining wealth and power by "organizational and institutional arrangements," apparently went unrecognized at the time (Saint and Coward, 1977: 733).

The underestimation of the human component in the change process often led to project failure. Time constraints forced programs ahead despite the overextension of the operational capabilities both of the lending agency and the recipient government (Mickelwait, 1979: 6). "By allowing collusion between parasitic local elites and economic pressure groups in the United States," writes Heinen (1980: 453), agency administrators failed to reach the "grass roots" level. Unsuitable, inflexible, and unrealistic programs could not be sustained; the much needed change in approach was mandated by the New Directions legislation in 1973.

The schedules adopted initially by donors wrecked havoc upon the administration of programs; in the field, "trickle-down" simply did not happen. "Recent experiences in agricultural development," note Saint and Coward (1977), "have highlighted human factor constraints in technology application . . . ." These factors are organizational and institutional, such as local infrastructure (markets, credit, transportation, storage), and reflect the considerable difference between the test conditions under which technologies are developed and the real ones under which they are implemented. Technology, it had been argued, was suitable for farms of various kinds, although experience has since shown this not to be so (often the unavailability of technologies, itself a considerable problem, made their relevancy a nonissue). The trickle-down concept proved to be misleading as well, as success was measured by the extent of use rather than by the distribution of benefits (Saint and Coward, 1977: 734).

The underestimation of the significance of social factors was the inevitable result of viewing farmers individually and not as members of social systems. Local groups were regarded as adversaries rather than as some of the many interest groups which would gain or lose according to the objectives of the program. Development, if understood normatively, would reveal that the decision to improve the welfare of some groups would add to the burden of others (UNRISD, 1979). The inclusion of the rural poor in the planning and administration of development was philosophically and technically sound, but with no acceptable measure of success to guide their appraisal of programs, development officers could not gauge the impact of already extant beneficiaries in confounding this process.

Development Alternatives, a Washington, D.C. based firm often engaged by USAID, has argued that AID does not have the capacity to evaluate its own projects, either absolutely or relative to the level of funds expended, and thus is unable to reach empirical conclusions about which strategies work and which do not (Mickelwait, 1979: 226, 229). More recently AID has strongly emphasized social soundness analysis in response to such criticism. There is little doubt that AID currently is as preoccupied with social soundness as it once was solely with technology as it attempts to fit programs more precisely to the needs of targeted groups. Heinen's (1980: 453) claim that AID has planned "over the heads" of targeted populations is less true today than it once was; that certainly had been true for the period prior to social soundness. The lack of consensus about what constituted a well-designed aid program reflected very much the dissimilarity of social systems into which aid had been uniformly introduced. Inappropriate generalization has more recently given way to the promotion of the unique qualities of each technical-social interface (cf. Hirabayashi, et al., 1980). Micro-level research is recognized as essential, giving expression to local knowledge systems.

> Efforts to increase productivity will depend for the most part on the success with which agro-technologies and appropriate organizational and institutional arrangements can be incorporated into systems of traditional agriculture, especially in which small farmers predominate (Saint and Coward, 1977: 733).

The new orientation in development broadens the base of participation while explicitly calling for more equitable arrangements in the distribution of the benefits of increased production. This is in essence the intent of the New Directions legislation. Earlier, the productive capacity and livelihood of those least endowed with assets, status, and power had suffered as a result of economic growth (measured by increases in GNP). Social development clearly did not inevitably accompany such growth as had been anticipated (cf. Bodley, 1982 for a discussion of the ethnocentric implications of the theory of cultural evolution, the basis of this illusory expectation). A higher standard of living and improved health, education, and social services are not inherently part of the development process; they must be addressed explicitly to render their occurrence more likely. Resolution 2626 (XVV) of the U.N. General Assembly in 1979 thus proposed that the ultimate purpose of development was to increase opportunities for all people for a better life. It was concluded that access of the poor to the decision-making process and the economy had to be improved to accomplish this end.

By locating the goals of development in the community developers give recognition to the indigenous sociocultural pattern. Technology is properly seated in society where it reflects the social system of which it is an integral part. The selection of a technology to promote the economic welfare of a targeted community is made to accommodate prevailing social arrangements. Social organization, emphasize Saint and Coward (1977: 734), is an independent as well as a dependent variable; by simulating existing systems of agricultural production, for example, a better fit can be made between technology and society. Cernea (1982) also calls for the mobilization of local resources. In supporting the reasonableness of local agricultural systems developers do more than induce confidence and promote faith among villagers; they give recognition to the dynamic equilibrium between "human needs and abilities and nature's resources and restraints" which is reflected in traditional agricultural and social systems (Saint and Coward, 1977: 735). Targeted communities, to no one's surprise, are no less systematic than are our own. To give a more measured meaning to the system of local adaptation, and to encourage project designers to plan more for the local milieu, Saint and Coward (1977) describe a typology of farming systems developed for Nigeria. Three principal categories of variables are established: (1) general ecological systems (citing environmental differences); (2) agro-ecological systems (based on variations in crops and technologies); and (3) cultural-economic subsystems. Farm types are subsequently developed, reflecting more precisely local features and local variation.

Improved communication between agency scientists, administrators, and farmers (all farmers, not merely innovators) is the basis of the "Process" approach, Development Alternatives' version of the New Directions. Programs which are constructed of local input are more likely to be accepted by the local group (cf. Rogers and Shoemaker, 1971). Field-testing ideas prior to the introduction of interventions is a means of giving credibility to the concept of "fit" among significant variables. Testing technology on farmers' lands, and developing if need be the agricultural support system for advanced technologies, e.g. highly trained technicians, an effective delivery system of agricultural supplies, expanded credit and marketing services, further contributes to this accommodation (Mickelwait, 1979: 5, 145). Critical reappraisal of the program should always follow its unfolding as the reciprocal influence of technologies and social systems generate deviations from the original design.

The decision to include the poor both in the planning and the implementation of development reflects the predicament in which the Third World poor are found: relatively powerless within nations themselves relatively powerless. Non-industrial countries have little influence in the world power structure and less access to economic resources than some transnational corporations; yet their citizens are well aware of consumption patterns beyond their reach (UNRISD, 1979). Without the support of governments and assistance agencies, programs meant to increase the poor's access to wealth and power will fail to secure their objectives.

The role of the scientist in this process is fundamental. By elucidating technical and social variables scientists can, in the typologies they develop, call significant relationships to the attention of government and donor alike. "Agricultural development strategies are tailored to socio-natural situations like seeds to micro-environments," argue Saint and Coward (1977: 735, 736). They recommend typologies based upon factors of agricultural production—such as labor availability and soil fertility, technology, environmental resources and restraints, and the institutional context—including land tenure, marketing, and political organization. The authors conclude that researchers might do well to employ a "limiting factor" perspective, in which those factors most limiting agricultural performance are identified (for example, water, credit, or markets). The organizational safeguards farmers construct to reduce risk likewise should be elucidated, as the pragmatism which guides farming provides a clue to the nature of local responses to proposed interventions.

The results of research should be made available to governments, donors, voluntary organizations, universities, research institutes, and the media to guide their respective involvement in the development effort. Research which identifies the strengths and weaknesses of target groups and targeted agricultural systems gives credibility to development rhetoric. The welfare of the farm family must take precedence over the temptation to experiment with technology. If not, farmers will identify the risk of adoption as greater than the potential benefit to be derived from it and fail to respond favorably to programs.

The articulation of local agricultural and social systems occurs at the grassroots level. The type of research which is variously called "consultative," "active," or "participatory dialogical," promotes an insistence upon "acceptable" technology (cf. UNRISD, 1979; Hirabayashi, 1980). It derives its strength from the communication between program designers, implementers and clients. The promotion of this approach reduces the likelihood that projects will be imposed upon people.

Micro-level research, through which indigenous arrangements are revealed, gives meaning to local adaptation in historical, functional, and experimental terms (cf. Brokensha et al., 1980, for a thorough discussion of this, and especially Howe, Howe and Chambers in that volume). When development strategies are linked to sociocultural systems programs are better received and more successful. Rogers and Shoemaker (1971) document the research which supports the practice of soliciting and including local input in development programs. The reconciliation of differences is expedited as well when there is local input.

Anthropologists regularly report the perspective of the people among whom they work (the "emic" perspective). This helps to remind us that indigenous models may already include knowledge which scientists, traveling full circle, eventually "discover" (cf. Richards, 1983). In developing nations rural people do not conceive of technology separately from the social and political structures in which it is embedded. Moreover, their recognition of natural ecological relationships as reflected in multi-cropping practices places humans more completely in the natural world than does mono-cropping and its constellation of non-biological inputs (Howe and Chambers, 1980; Howe, 1980). Control of nature is a Western attitudinal complex, and may be quite objectionable elsewhere (especially on religious grounds). Our choice as scientists is whether or not to accept indigenous pragmatism for the experience and know-how it represents; we fail to do so at the risk of not learning what our ultimate clients have already discovered to be so.

As anthropologists have made an ideal of giving expression to indigenous knowledge systems, their potential value as consultants in the "new" development is considerable. Heinen (1980: 454) comments on the value of the expertise of anthropologists in particular geographical areas and of social configurations. Policymakers, he advises, may seek the knowledge anthropologists possess in order to achieve their goals. "I am quite willing to be regarded as 'no different than consultants,'" he states, "if the view the client population is articulating through my reports will be heeded by those in power" (ibid.). Similarly, Wolfe (1980: 455) contradicts the notion of traditional society as homogeneous, citing multicentric economies, social and cultural pluralism, and "qualitatively distinctive systems hierarchically arranged at different levels of integration." Policy-makers need this more "realistic" view, he proposes, which is a "fairly basic part of the anthropological perspective."

The inclusion of anthropologists on project teams currently is compatible with the rhetoric of donor agencies:

> At least one member of a design team should have sufficient technical background to judge the appropriateness of different technological packages, but the critical skills needed on a design team were found to be not so much technical in nature as those that contribute to a sensible project in a particular political, economic, and social milieu.
>
> In most design exercises, a core group consisting of a rural development specialist, an anthropologist or rural sociologist, an economist (usually an agricultural economist), and an agriculturalist proved to be most effective. (Mickelwait, et al, 1979: 142)

Anthropologists, as noted earlier, customarily give expression to local points of view; they are sensitive to the ethnocentric pitfalls of cross-cultural comparison; they are experienced in field research in pre-industrial society; they view culture holistically, and they recognize that farming and technology are but part of larger systems.

While elucidating the sociocultural component in development, anthropologists can hope to promote respect for indigenous knowledge systems. These are the very systems which reflect the genius of other peoples. Farmers can be shown to be pragmatists seeking reasonable solutions to the problems of farming. Technological innovations may or may not appeal to them; by identifying the factors of which the farmer's decision is made, the reasons for which an innovation is accepted or not are revealed. Farmers learn too from the anthropologist. The logic behind the intervention is communicated; farmers can better understand the choices facing them. There is an opinion in anthropology which holds that anthropologists can effectively mediate and facilitate change. Davis and Mathews (1980: 452) propose that anthropologists "inform the peoples they study of the consequences of policy decisions, providing them with tools for effective political participation. . . ." The alternative, they note, is to "stand by passively" as others make the decisions that affect peoples' lives (ibid).

Sensitizing local groups and the development cadre is well within the capacity of most anthropologists. As Brace (1982: 760) has remarked, the majority of anthropologists spend the majority of their time teaching.

Translating from the professional idiom to the lay context is a skill well-developed among them. The anthropologist communicates observed and talked about behavior; as an outsider, he/she may impose meaning upon behavior which is revelatory. Anthropologists may point out weaknesses for groups to overcome when government services must be pressured into providing needed services, or identify existing structures to facilitate the adoption of new technologies (cf. Litsinger, et al., 1981). Helping the poor to better understand their position in society can be yet another contribution the anthropologist makes.

A scientist capable of mediating dialogue and guarding against presumption in the cross-cultural context is particularly well suited for development work. Although time constraints are part of the reality of assistance and will continue to be so despite the admission that development is "too complex a problem to be solved in a few months" (Mickelwait et al., 1979: 6), the reluctance of the anthropologist to know too quickly "what is going on" is a valuable asset. Anthropologists, accustomed to plodding unhurriedly through sociocultural fields, transmit a valuable lesson to other scientists: failure is most likely a result of impaired social relations, and is most likely viewed that way locally. A patient observer who cultivates a social etiquette will be better received and more successful where this perception prevails.

Various terms are used to characterize the role of anthropologist as go-between: culture broker, culture mediator, or as Warren (1980: 366) prefers, "communications facilitator." It is *expected* that anthropologists will bring "insight" to the development process, even if no one is exactly sure which revelations they would welcome. The social process is confounding; the science which elucidates it is not exact. There is freedom in the method of anthropology which makes particularly prominent the responsibility each anthropologist bears for his/her actions. The challenge before the anthropologist is to be convincing in other people's terms. That is what is really being asked of this scientist. And that is good. For to do otherwise is to indulge in the esoterica of one's own discipline, to the eventual boredom and irrelevance of outsiders. When they turn you off, your contribution is minimized. Anthropologists have gotten a foot in the door, which is all that's needed for a start. Recommendations which work will furnish them a more complete entry.

Functional integration in the development effort is as real an aspect of the agency environment as is the interrelationship of crops and the physical properties of ecological zones. Scientists who view other disciplines and their practitioners disparagingly are not truly prepared to do this work, for their chauvinism impairs their perception. Cooperation on many levels is needed for development to stand the chance of success. The agency team must be a model to others.

A recent report from the International Rice Research Institute (1982) reaffirms the place of anthropologists on the development team. Rhoades, et al. (1981) describes the anthropologist as "mediator" at the International Potato Center in Lima. Bredahl-Petersen (1980: 451) writes of the anthropologist as a mediator-broker serving both the donor and the community.

The expression at USAID (1982: Handbook No. 3) of the role of the anthropologist is revealed through the Social Soundness Analysis. The SSA requires an appraisal of the:

1) sociocultural feasibility of the project, i.e., its compatibility with the sociocultural environment into which it is to be introduced;
2) the spread effect, or the diffusion of new practices from the target group to others; and
3) the social impact of the program, in which the distribution of benefits and burdens among different groups is estimated.

The social soundness analyst cites the relevance of local values, beliefs, and social structures to the technological package under consideration; promotes cultural integration by fitting innovations into existing social patterns; solicits the impressions villagers and others have of their own circumstances; and evaluates the impact of programs upon people and the ways they live.

When the conditions of the target community are identified, they represent the model into which new ideas are fit. Each instance of development gives meaning to a new pattern and illustrates repeatedly the need to abandon programs imposed uniformly upon different groups in different circumstances. With more than one-third of all World Bank loans going to agricultural and rural development projects in developing countries, the cost of failure is considerable. In human terms, the consequences of poorly designed programs can be tragic.

The rise in the social consciousness of donor agencies during the past ten years represents a growth which has benefited both the programs these agencies promote and the projected beneficiaries of them. Although there is now some indication that the program of development, in its preoccupation with assistance to and involvement of the poor majority, has inadvertently created yet other, greater problems (cf. Morss, 1984), particularly insofar as a capable, trained human resource cadre has not been formed in Africa, the glaring failure to give recognition and respect to indigenous knowledge, to say nothing of the carriers of it, has been addressed and more or less rectified. The mandatory analysis of social soundness at USAID, for example, has given anthropologists a greater role to play in the development arena, which is good both for the anthropology profession and the peoples with whom anthropologists habitually collaborate. If anthropologists can promote an integration among the various participants in development, as well as the perception of integration in socio-technological systems, they will render more mature the development effort. Those issues, those problems which we are yet to discover, or are in the process of discovering (cf. Morss, 1984), will be confronted by a development profession which now includes anthropologists among its ranks. To the mind of the anthropologist, this is as it should be. We now have the opportunity to convince others of our value and the value of our perspective to the effort in which we are all involved.

# References

Almy, Susan W. *The Anthropologist at the International Agricultural Research Center.* Los Banos, The Philippines: International Rice Research Institute, 1977.

Barlett, Peggy. *Agricultural Choice and Change.* New Brunswick, N.J.: Rutgers University Press, 1982.

Bodley, John H. *Victims of Progress.* Menlo Park: The Benjamin Cummings Publishing Company, 1982.

Brace, Loring. "Film Review." *American Anthropologist,* Vol. 84, No. 3, 1982, p. 760.

Bredahl-Petersen, F. E. "Comments." *Current Anthropology,* Vol. 21, No. 4, 1980, pp. 450–451.

Brokensha, David, D. M. Warren and Oswald Werner (eds.). *Indigenous Knowledge Systems and Development.* Washington, D.C.: University Press of America, 1980.

Cernea, Michael. Interview, World Bank Report, March-April, 1982, p. 5.

Cochrane, Glynn. "Policy Studies and Anthropology." *Current Anthropology,* Vol. 21, No. 4, 1980, pp. 445–458.

Davis, H. Shelton and Robert O. Mathews. "Comments," *Current Anthropology,* Vol. 21, No. 4, 1980, pp. 452–453.

Heinen, H. Dieter. "Comments," *Current Anthropology,* Vol. 21, No. 4, 1980, pp. 453–454.

Hirabayashi, Edward, D. M. Warren and Wilford Owen, Jr. "That Focus on the 'Other 40%': A Myth of Development," in David Brokensha, D. M. Warren and Oswald Werner, eds., *Indigenous Knowledge Systems and Development.* Washington, D.C.: University Press of America, 1980, pp. 353–362.

Howe, Michael. "The Uses of Indigenous Technical Knowledge in Development," in David Brokensha, et al., eds.,Indigenous Knowledge Systems and Development, Washington, D.C.: University Press of America, 1980, pp. 335–352.

Howe, Michael and Robert Chambers. "Indigenous Technical Knowledge: Analysis, Implications, and Issues," in David Brokensha, et al., ed., *Indigenous Knowledge Systems and Development.*Washington, D.C.: University Press of America, 1980, pp. 323–334.

International Rice Research Institute. *Report of an Exploratory Workshop on: The Role of Anthropologists and other Social Scientists in Interdisciplinary Teams Developing Improved Food Production Technology.* Los Banos, Laguna, The Philippines: IRRI, 1982.

Litsinger, J. A., G. E. Goodell, P. E. Kenmore, S. P. Bandong, C. G. dela Cruz and M. D. Lumaban. "Assessing Rice Insect Pest Management Technology and its Transfer to Small-scale Farmers: An Interdisciplinary Case Study in the Philippines, involving Feedback from Social Scientist, International Rice Research Institute, Los Banos, The Philippines." 1981.

Mickelwait, Donald R., Charles F. Sweet and Elliot R. Morss. *New Directions in Development: A Study of U.S. AID,* Boulder: Westview Press, 1979.

Morss, Elliot. "Institutional Destruction Resulting from Donor and Project Proliferation in Sub-Saharan African Countries." *World Development,* Vol. 12, No. 4, 1984, pp. 465–470.

Rhoades, Robert, Robert Booth and Roy Shaw. "The Involvement and Interaction of Anthropologists and Biological Scientists in the Development and Transfer of Post-harvest Technology at CIP, International Rice Research Institute, Los Banos, The Philippines," 1981.

Richards, Paul. "Farming Systems in West Africa." *Progress in Human Geography,* Vol. 7, No. 1, 1983, pp. 1–39.

Rogers, Everett M. and F. Floyd Shoemaker. *Communication of Innovations.* New York: The Free Press, 1971.

Saint, William S. and E. Walter Coward, Jr. "Agricultural and Behavioral Science: Emerging Orientations." *Science,* Vol. 197, 1977, pp. 733–737.

United Nations. *International Development Strategy.* United Nations Publication No. ST/ECA/139, New York, 1970.

UNRISD (United Nations Research Institute for Social Development). *An Approach to Development Research.* United Nations Publication, Geneva, 1979.

USAID. *Indonesia Agriculture Briefing Paper.* Office of Agricultural Development, Jakarta, 1981.

USAID. *Handbook #3,* United States Agency for International Development, Washington, D.C., 1982.

Warren, D. M. *The Role of the Anthropologist in Rural Development Projects in Ghana.* Anthropology of Rural Development Series, No. 2, Institute for the Study of Human Issues, Philadelphia, 1981.

Warren, D. M. "Ethnoscience in Rural Development," in David Brokensha, et al., eds., *Indigenous Knowledge Systems and Development.* Washington, D.C.: University Press of America, 1980, pp. 363–376.

Wolfe, Alvin W. "Comments." *Current Anthropology,* Vol. 21, No. 4, 1980, p. 455.

# 3

# Breaking New Ground: Agricultural Anthropology

*Robert E. Rhoades*

## ANTHROPOLOGY AND AGRICULTURE: THE HISTORICAL INTERFACE

Since founding of the discipline until the present, anthropologists have studied virtually every manifestation of agriculture ranging from archeological investigation of the origins of agriculture down to ethnographies of modern industrial farming (Flannery, 1965; Reed, 1977; Bennett, 1969, Barlett, 1980). This emphasis has not been misplaced. In terms of sheer numbers, most of humankind are still tillers of the soil or are directly engaged in other forms of food production such as herding or fishing. Today, as always, the fundamental business of nations—including most industrial ones—is agriculture. Basic food production remains the primary human activity and, with increasing population pressure against finite natural resources, people will continue to seek ways to improve and intensify that production (Rhoades and Rhoades, 1980).

How is it possible, then, that anthropology is simultaneously a discipline that has dealt so directly and intimately with the world's rural people while having virtually no direct involvement in, or impact on, planned agricultural change? The answer lies in part in the history of anthropology and its institutional connections.

## The Past: Lost Opportunities

Anthropology's rural bias and concern with contemporary Third World peoples are tied directly to the very foundations of the discipline. In the mid-nineteenth century when formal social science disciplines began to develop in Western universities, the desire of each new discipline was to mark off territory in the study of European institutions and the Great Civilizations. History thus became the study of Western man, sociology the study of Western institutions, and behavior and economics the study of European commercial and capitalist conditions.

What remained for anthropology, the youngest discipline? Anthropology has often been referred to as the "slum child of the sciences," accepting subjects rejected by the established social science disciplines (Beals, 1973). The focus thus became the mass of humanity colonized by Europe, called at that time "tribal," "uncivilized," "savage," "native," and "exotic." Living largely in the marginal areas of Africa, Asia, North America, and Latin America, these same peoples today are called in development language "clients" or "target populations" for agricultural development programs.

Anthropologists studied these populations, often composed of small groups or communities, in their physical and cultural entirety. Thus, early anthropologists were simultaneously sociologists, economists, historians, biologists, linguists, and technologists of colonized peoples. With total societies to consider, anthropologists attempted to duplicate in almost every aspect what specialized disciplines were doing for different segments of European culture. Anthropology's contemporary impatience with the application of European models of psychological or economic behavior to subsistence agriculture populations can be traced to early field experiences with human systems radically different than those of European origin (see Wolf, 1964 for one of the best histories of anthropology).

The discipline served as an important information link between the colonized, often tribal or peasant populations, and colonial or neo-colonial government (see Foster, 1969: 181–217 for an early history of applied anthropology).[1] This colonial role primarily centered on the description of traditional ways and impact of European contact. Public health, education, and community development loomed as important early applied fields for anthropology.

Except for a temporary involvement with the Soil Conservation Service of U.S. Department of Agriculture in the 1930s (Foster, 1969: 202), however, anthropologists rarely touched base with applied agricultural researchers.[2] A notable exception was sociologist Charles Loomis (1943), one of the founders of the Society for Applied Anthropology, who spent half a year at Tingo Maria, Peru, analyzing problems of establishing an agricultural extension service. Loomis also worked in Costa Rica in the late 1940s and early 1950s where he helped establish the social science department in Turrialba which ultimately evolved into the Institute Interamericano de Ciencias Agricolas (IICA) of today.[3] The Peruvian Vicos Project, although not exclusively agricultural, subsequently had an impact on planned agriculture and policy in Peru (Holmberg, et al., 1962, 1965).[4]

Perhaps the most perceptive early work illustrating the uses of anthropology for practical agriculture is Pierre De Schlippe's (1956) *Shifting Cultivation in Africa*. De Schlippe, a practicing agronomist, discovered in the course of his work in Africa the great benefit of anthropological methods and theory. In what may be the first major publication advocating agroanthropology he set out to undertake research on the "borderline of agronomy and anthropology." His concerns (1956: XVI), so well stated 30 years ago, still go largely unheeded:

> Neither the agricultural research station nor the field anthropologist alone can give us the necessary understanding of agricultural practice in the humid tropics. The crucial problem, perhaps not even of Africa alone but of humanity as a whole, lies in the contact zone between man and his environment, between inhabitant and habitat, and therefore between two fields of research which have not yet undergone the necessary co-ordination.

Although important, these early efforts led to no lasting contribution by anthropologists to agricultural programs or the formation of an applied subdiscipline dedicated to agricultural problems. Edward Montgomery and John W. Bennett (1979) place part of the blame on the academic anthropology establishment for turning its attention away from food and nutrition matters in the 1950s and 1960s. The 1940s had witnessed considerable anthropological involvement in food and nutrition studies in the United States. Active in these efforts were outstanding professionals such as Margaret Mead and Robert Redfield. Developments in the universities in the post-war period, however, set anthropology upon a "return voyage to tribal ethnology and theoretical interests" and away from applied anthropology.[5]

They explain the consequences:

> . . . professional rewards have been given mainly to those anthropologists who have excelled in the traditional fields centering on the study of tribal and peasant humanity. Indeed, few examples can be cited of individuals preeminent as specialists in applied anthropology and contemporary complex society who have been given entry to the inner circle of the profession. Further, in the United States this has meant that the American Anthropological Association has not featured applied work as a major subdivision of the general discipline, nor has it invested significantly in the publication of research with contemporary themes (Montgomery and Bennett, 1979: 127).

William Whyte (1984) further argues that in part anthropology's aloofness toward planned agriculture derived from the anthropological worldview in the 1950s and 1960s:

> I believe there was a tendency in those years for many social anthropologists to look upon culture as if it were cast in concrete rather than thinking of culture in terms of a framework developed by the people to handle the problem of living in their particular environment and therefore flexible to admit a modification when they could see that change would be advantageous. In that era, I was inclined to attribute the failure of plant and animal scientists to include anthropologists and sociologists in their programs to resistance by biological scientists who wanted to maintain their own monopoly in the field. Now, although I do not doubt that such resistance was important, it seems to me that the prevailing orientation of many anthropologists in that era was self-defeating, insofar as their gaining partnership in these programs.

Anthropology's institutional location in the university structure has also been detrimental to involvement in planned agriculture. In the United States, most land grant agricultural colleges do not have anthropology programs. Even if one exists, it is generally located in liberal arts, not in science colleges. This structural position left anthropology isolated from planned agriculture during the early years of the post-war expansion of United States involvement in agricultural programs both at home and overseas. Throughout this key post-war period, few anthropologists entered development. At most, ethnographers were known for helping expatriates adjust to "cultural shock" or to interpret the "silent language" and "hidden dimension" of foreigners' behavior but not for making a substantial contribution to planned change (Hall, 1961; 1966).

It is also logical that international technical agricultural program leaders of the early USDA and "Point Four" programs would turn to their closest social science colleagues, agricultural economists, for input on the human component of agricultural development. Agricultural economists, however, did not gain their ground simply because of an inherited inside track. Economics as a profession has a "client relationship with society" (Thurow, 1977: 80). Anthropologists, on the other hand, were known to be arrogantly aloof, refusing often on moralistic grounds to apply their expertise to practical agriculture despite the wealth of anthropological knowledge available on primitive and peasant agriculture. Anthropologist Robert Netting (1974) has further argued that agriculture was simply considered:

> too basic for the ambitious new science of man, and the suspicion lingers that it is intellectually "infra dig." The supposed simplicity, concreteness, and lack of system in most non-western farming techniques did not attract minds stimulated by the complex, abstract order of kinship terminology, descent groups or ritual patterns.

It might have been, however, that the complexity of tropical agriculture puzzled technically naive anthropologists. A few ethnobotanists, cultural ecologists, and archeologists conducted important studies in the 1950s and 1960s revealing the finely adapted nature of agricultural and horticultural societies to social and environmental conditions. Some, such as Conklin's (1954; 1957) detailed study of Hanunoo agriculture, and Geertz's (1963) *Agricultural Involution*, have been widely read and cited by agricultural scientists. Anthropology's fundamental concern with basic food production, even in the origins of agriculture, is evidenced in any modern anthropology textbook (Harris, 1971). Twenty (20) percent of the articles in *Plant Agriculture*, a collection of readings from *Scientific American* magazine articles 1950 to 1969, were written by anthropologists and archeologists. In fact, the rural element is so deeply ingrained in anthropology that the term "rural anthropology" would strike many people as humorously redundant while "urban" anthropology is a legitimate subfield. Missing, however, was anthropology's involvement in planned agricultural change.

## The Present: International Agricultural Research

The watershed period marking the significant inclusion of social science into international agricultural research must be traced to pioneering efforts in the early 1960s at the Philippines' International Rice Research Institute (IRRI). Vernon Ruttan (1982: 308–309), the first economist to work in the international center system, recorded his early experiences that are not unlike those of anthropologists now entering agricultural research:

> When I arrived at IRRI, I was shown to an office in the very attractive new institute complex. The office was conveniently located near the library. It had a brass plate in the door with the label *Agricultural Economics*. In the weeks that followed, however, neither the director nor the associate director of IRRI conveyed to me a very clear idea of why they needed an agricultural economist or what contribution they expected from the economics unit at IRRI.

Agricultural economics went on from that point to make its mark on the international research center developing both the "constraints research approach" and later promoting "Farming Systems Research." Today, all but one international center in the Consultative Group on International Agricultural Research (CGIAR) have economics programs. At CIMMYT, the international wheat and maize center headquartered in Mexico, economics is the third major research program along with technical research on the two crops.

Anthropology's chance did not come until more than a decade later, in the mid-1970s. It is doubtful at this time that an international agriculture research center would have hired an anthropologist with core funds. Few administrators in agricultural research management had a clear idea what anthropology was or how it was relevant to their technical programs. Those few who did were economists who were concerned, as some still are today, with holding the limited turf they had so arduously gained. Sharing ground with anthropologists was an uncertain and threatening thought. Anthropologists had a reputation as critics of the "Green Revolution" (Ryan, 1979: 120). It was feared that the entire house economics had built might come tumbling down through a negative reaction by management, generally made up of biological scientists who sometimes lumped both anthropologists and economists into the category "social scientists," considered more alike than different.

The Rockefeller Foundation finally paved the way for the inclusion of the "non-economic social science perspective" by establishing and funding in 1974 its "Social Science Research Fellowship in Agricultural and Rural Development." The purpose was *not* to permanently place social scientists in the international centers but to give recent North American Ph.D.s experience in agricultural development. Whether by accident or design, the majority (twenty-one of thirty-three) of Rockefeller post-doctorates assigned to posts between 1975 and 1984 have been anthropologists.

In reflecting on the early years when the Rockefeller program was just getting underway, Susan Almy—then with the Foundation—writes:

> The biggest objection against anthropologists was that they sat in a single village whereas the centers were mandated to create knowledge useful at an international level. The RF fellowship program was begun in 1974 but only opened up to non-economists in 1975. The emphasis on anthropologists was entirely due to the greater response by them to the opportunity. I was very careful to advertise and write all the major agricultural economics, economics, geography, rural sociology as well as anthropology departments and journals. Among the other disciplines, good students tended to want to stay home after the degree, whereas the tide had just turned in anthropology and many students wanted nonacademic experience (Susan Almy, 1984).

A parallel development to the Rockefeller Foundation efforts was the formation in late 1976 of an American-based group known as the Anthropological Study Group on Agrarian Systems (ASGAS) or, after the name of its bulletin, the *Culture and Agriculture* Group. This organization has been instrumental in giving visibility to agricultural research among anthropologists (Barlett, 1980: 546). A similar informal association of anthropologists formed in Lima, Peru, in 1979 but with a more international focus than the U.S.-based ASGAS group. These late 1970s developments testify to the resurgence of interest in agriculture and food among anthropologists, an interest—along with Farming Systems Research—which has gained considerable momentum in the 1980s.

## THE CASE OF THE INTERNATIONAL POTATO CENTER

Not surprisingly the International Potato Center (CIP) was the first to receive a Rockefeller Foundation social science research fellow and has subsequently gone on to utilize more anthropologists than any other world agricultural research organization. First, CIP is located in Peru where anthropology is as strong in rural development, if not stronger, than economics. Second, the economists on the CIP staff were not antagonistic to "non-economists"[6] and had formed strong personal and professional links with anthropologists. This, in part, may be due to the marked ecological and human landscape of the Central Andes that has allowed a fertile interchange between the two disciplines. Finally, CIP—a new research center in the early 1970s—was seeking creative approaches to development. While it may not have been initially clear how anthropologists would concretely contribute to CIP's goals, Director General Richard Sawyer viewed anthropology and sociology as new and potentially useful disciplines.

Since 1975, fourteen anthropologists and two sociologists have worked in some capacity or conducted research in direct association with CIP. The majority have come to the center with their own funding or held temporary appointments. Two, both Rockefeller researchers, have been hired on the permanent senior staff although not simultaneously. In 1984, two continuing positions open to anthropologists or sociologists were added to the department. The CIP experience thus offers a unique experiment to illustrate the potential strengths and weaknesses of anthropology in agricultural research.

## Introduction of Development Anthropology and Sociology

The future of any new discipline in an agricultural research center rests in part on its early experiences with individuals representing that discipline. CIP was fortunate in that its first "non-economists" were individuals who understood and related well to agricultural scientists.

Among these were Clyde Eastman, a rural sociologist from New Mexico State University. Not only did Eastman look, dress and talk like an "aggie" (tremendous symbolic assets in agricultural development), he set down some basic principles which CIP economists and anthropologists have followed ever since. The first was plain, straight language in presenting the social science point of view. Although the institutionally more powerful biological scientists are notorious for using jargon, they tend to be intolerant of social science jargon.

Eastman's second principle was to keep all written reports short and to the point. In his six months' sabbatical with the center he generated a series of brief papers with such eye-catching titles as "The Cold Hard Realities of Agricultural Development" and "Should Peru Promote Potato Production?" These were widely read and debated by biological scientists in the center, as it struggled to define its goals in the early years. Without a doubt, Eastman helped establish a favorable impression of "non-economists" in the minds of the administration. Such pioneering efforts should never be overlooked in the varied fates that sociology and anthropology have had in other international agricultural centers.[7]

Another development anthropologist-sociologist who established contact early in the life of the center and made a positive impression was William F. Whyte of Cornell University. Although not officially attached to the center he offered constructive ideas on institutional building and mechanisms of technology development and transfer. Later CIP called on his expertise as consultant in the analysis of potato seed systems in Colombia, a work which influenced future socioeconomic research on seed. His practice of "applied" instead of "academic" anthropology helped correct the false image that anthropologists are only seekers of information about the quaint and exotic. And, like Eastman, Whyte's reports were succinctly and nonjargonistically written (Whyte, 1977).

### Ecological Anthropology and Appropriate Methods

Following recommendations of a 1976 planning conference, the young and relatively inexperienced social science group began to acquire expertise by concentrating research on a specific Peruvian potato producing region (Mantaro Valley) where it developed methodologies and built closer links to biological research activities. This social science program was funded by IDRC-Canada and subsequently called "the Mantaro Valley Project" (Horton, 1984).

The leader of the Social Science Unit at this time was Douglas Horton, an economist, whose personal ties with anthropologists were perhaps stronger than with economists. This was due in part to the long standing involvement in Peru of Cornell University (from which Horton obtained his Ph.D.). When it came time to gain an initial overview of the selected region—the Mantaro Valley—and where CIP has its major Peruvian research station, it was only logical that Horton would turn to an individual and friend who knew the valley well. This was Enrique Mayer, a Peruvian anthropologist, born and reared in the Mantaro Valley and who, like Horton, formed part of the Cornell "Peruvianist" group that post-dated the often bitter feuds of the Vicos project.[8]

The task assigned Mayer in the "Mantaro Valley Project" was to conduct an initial anthropological overview of the valley, define its major zones of production, and delineate types of producers found in each zone. Given Mayer's long-term knowledge of the valley and rapid survey methods, the task was completed in two months on a small budget of under U.S. $2,000. The resulting publication with its land-use map has subsequently come to be a widely read anthropological study of an Andean region as well as an inspiration to social scientists in terms of what can be done so rapidly and expertly (Mayer, 1979).

Mayer utilized the theoretical perspective of ecological anthropology to define the major agroecological zones and land- use patterns within the Mantaro Valley. His use of aerial photos, government data, and ethnographic "ground truth" techniques are excellent examples of how anthropology can be a powerful discipline to help focus agricultural research projects. With this information in hand, the newly constituted CIP agroeconomic team composed of economists and agronomists could proceed with planning and executing on-farm trials using known technologies as well as technology being generated on the CIP experimental station (Horton, 1984).

In addition to practical utilization for planning on-farm trials, the Mayer effort also set the foundation for illustrating how informal survey methods of anthropologists could be used for rapidly and inexpensively gaining an overview of agricultural land-use and cropping patterns in a region. This work went on to form the basis of future CIP methodological studies on informal or rapid rural surveys appropriate for developing countries (see Rhoades, 1982a).

## Ethnobotanical Research

A major reason for CIP's existence is the collection and maintenance of a world germplasm pool of wild and cultivated native South American potatoes. This germplasm "bank" contains natural resistances that can be utilized by breeders in improving potato varieties for developing countries. The complex folk nomenclature of native potatoes used by Andean farmers has long fascinated both anthropological and biological scientists (La Barre, 1947; Hawkes, 1947). However, how or why this information might be useful to a technologically oriented center such as CIP was never made clear. Ethnobotanical studies conducted in 1977 and 1978 by anthropologists Stephen Brush and Heath Carney provided basic information on farmer selection of varieties useful to the center's efforts at collection and maintenance of a world germplasm pool for utilization in developing countries. Their research revealed that farmers use a four-level system of classification, integrating wild, semi-domesticated, and domesticated species. Instead of a chaotic and random system, as is often assumed by outsiders, the researcher's data revealed a system of farmer classification, selection and use of native varieties as logical as the modified Linnean system used by biological scientists (Brush, et al., 1981). The realization of a complex native folk taxonomy prompted biological scientists to pay closer attention to the native classification systems and nomenclature for cataloging germplasm collection.

Other ethnobotanical data were useful for design of on-farm experiments. For example, Steve Brush demonstrated that mixed plots planted in native varieties are valued for their home consumption and culinary qualities while improved varieties are intended for market or exchange and planted homogeneously. For on-farm research it is important to understand this simple difference in farmer strategies. Otherwise, comparisons of home consumption plots with recommended, commercially-oriented trial plots may not make sense within the farmer's dual strategies.

## Nutritional Anthropology and Consumption Research

CIP contracted an anthropology post-doctoral researcher to study potato consumption and nutrition. Susan Poats' research focused on the role of potatoes in the human diet and the actual and potential impact of potatoes on nutrition in developing countries (Poats, 1983). This research project has helped to better understand the preferences of consumers, the ultimate clients of the International Potato Center. It also brought a degree of cultural relativism to the center's general thinking by emphasizing the important role of consumer preferences for color, taste, shape, and cooking quality in the selection of varieties. This research also helped dispel several myths about potato consumption and provided policymakers with a more solid basis for appraising the value of the potato as a food crop in their countries.

Specifically, CIP breeders are now aware that considerably more variation in color, shape, and size of potatoes may be acceptable in developing countries than in Euro-American countries whose markets demand uniformity in tuber size and color. The study also emphasized the nutritional importance to developing country consumers of dry matter content, a preference now being taken into consideration in selection of germplasm materials.

## Comparative Anthropology Applied to Agricultural Research: Peruvian Farming Systems in Worldwide Perspective

Anthropology has also made a contribution to CIP's program with its comparative methodology. A major problem in international agricultural research is extrapolation; that is, are results in one region relevant to other similar regions in areas of the world? The International Potato Center has long justified its programs in terms of conducting research in different agroecological zones of Peru presumed to be representative of other areas of the world. CIP conducts research in four distinct Peruvian regions: La Molina and Cañete on the arid coast; Mantaro Valley, in the highlands; San Ramon, in the humid, high jungle; and Yurimaguas, in the low Amazon Basin. These zones offer excellent natural laboratories for biological and agronomic research on the potato under different conditions.

However, this research has been mainly conducted on experiment stations and related to variables specifically of interest to breeders, virologists, and agronomists (temperature, soils, and precipitation). Relevancy of on-station research for on-farm conditions and existing farming systems in surrounding communities was not clear.

The Social Science Department up to 1979 had concentrated its efforts only on CIP's highland research site, the Mantaro Valley (Horton, 1984). My first research assignment, therefore, was to describe, as Enrique Mayer had done in the Mantaro Valley, the farming systems in the communities surrounding CIP's experiment sites on the coast, high jungle, and low jungle.

Peru presents to the anthropologist a superb natural laboratory for studying distinct farming systems and how a crop like the potato fits, or might potentially fit, into these diverse farming systems. With the help of two Peruvian anthropology students, the farming systems of Cañete (arid coast), San Ramon (humid, hill zone) and Yurimaguas (the low jungle) were studied using informal survey methods (Recharte, 1981; Bidegaray, 1981). These sites were to be compared to the highlands to discover similarities and differences between CIP's Mantaro Valley efforts and research being conducted in the lowland zones. These data, in turn, were to be compared to other world zones of roughly similar ecological conditions. Thus the study involved Peru, as a specific case, and a global dimension for comparison.

Two complementary lines of investigation were: (1) a comparative study of potato farming in the four main regions where CIP is now conducting research (station and on-farm); and (2) a global description and comparison of potato agriculture in developing countries from the perspective of agrarian ecology.

This study corresponded to a time when the Social Science Department was beginning to piece together a coherent picture from fragmentary information obtained during various studies covering potato production in different world areas. Except for CIP's statistical *Potato Atlas* (Horton, 1978), no single publication was available to give an overview of potato agriculture in developing tropical and subtropical countries. Suitable maps showing where potatoes were grown and under what kinds of farming systems were unavailable. One of CIP's roles is to gather, analyze, and distribute this kind of information in a form useful to developing countries.

The organizing scheme for the comparative study was drawn from ecological anthropology. The principal hypothesis was that similar ecological conditions will give rise to similar potato production patterns and farmer strategies. Therefore, roughly similar technologies will be applicable in similar zones. In analogous areas (tropical mountains, arid zones, lowland tropics), constraints and potentials are hypothesized to be similar, implying that each region need not be approached as totally unique. If true, this hypothesis could be very important in transfer of CIP-related technology. For example, the arid coast of Peru supports a potato farming system roughly similar to irrigated, desert potato producing regions of North Africa, and the Great Indian Desert, especially the Punjab.

Arid land potato production tends to be irrigated, commercial, dependent on imported seed, a "winter" crop, and oriented toward marketing in urban centers. Due to environmental factors similar technical problems should arise from salinity in connection with irrigation water usage, for example. It also seems logical that a farmer's problems with diseases, insects and pests should correlate with agroecological zones. Similar patterns can be isolated in highland tropics, hilly tropics, and subtropics. However, all technology must ultimately be adapted to locations specific to social and economic conditions and fit the cropping system.

## A "Movement of Ideas"

Anthropology has long searched for and attempted to explain regularities and parallels cutting across societies. Interest at CIP was shown in the comparative work because it illustrated to biological scientists how the Peruvian zones related to worldwide agroecological conditions. It was recognized, especially by management, that experimentation with new agricultural technology is an expensive and time-consuming process for scientists and farmers alike. Although technology has to be adapted to local ecological and cultural conditions, it is cost effective to utilize agricultural experience and knowledge gained in other areas. This is the essence of the extrapolation of technological principles: movement of ideas from one area where it has been developed to one where there may be a need. Agricultural history has shown that the transfer of technology between drastically different economic or ecological systems has often resulted in limited success (temperate to tropical zones, flatlands to mountains, etc.). Thus, the comparative anthropological exercise of analyzing how potato production in similar demographic and ecological zones manifest similar technological needs is, as one biological science colleague put it, a "novel contribution to our way of thinking about agricultural technology generation and transfer." Although it was a relatively easy task to compare in general terms the ecology of

Peruvian research sites with other developing country areas, a far more difficult task centered on the comparison of potato production systems. Since potatoes are often produced in remote mountainous areas with diverse ecological characteristics, government statistics or reports rarely deal with potatoes, favoring instead commercial crops and grains. As a result, the International Potato Reference files were established in which relevant production and post-harvest data were organized.

This required a global effort in data accumulation including feedback from CIP's regional offices, personal interviews with national program workers, and library searches. This research has taken almost five years but has yielded in-depth information on eighty developing countries in the Americas, Africa, Asia, and the South Pacific. The files are now being analyzed, yielding information ranging from the history of the potato in each country to details of major potato diseases and pests. For the first time detailed maps of potato production in developing countries can be developed.

Over the long run, anthropology's search for parallels, principles, and cultural laws may be one of its most important contributions to technical agriculture (see also Doherty, 1979; Cancian, 1977). Increasingly, given limited resources, research administrators realize a shot-gun approach is not a viable option. Systematic social science information is needed so policymakers can develop relevant, timely, and workable programs for target populations. However, this will require research administrators to look at the social sciences—including anthropology—as legitimate research areas which can make useful contributions if provided adequate incentives and resources.

## ANTHROPOLOGISTS AS INTERDISCIPLINARY TEAM MEMBERS

Anthropologists have generally served in two roles assigned to them by funding agencies and agricultural development project directors. One role is to conduct a social feasibility study prior to implementation of a project and the other is to conduct an evaluation of the project after it is finished. Rarely are anthropologists incorporated into a project from beginning to end. Anthropologists, like economists, are typically thrust into the potentially unpopular role of deciding beforehand if a project is going to be worthwhile (a sensitive point to technologists promoting the project) or evaluating if it was a success or a failure (also a sensitive point if the project fails). Anthropologists assigned these roles are frequently caught between their own intellectual honesty and the strong pressures brought by what project directors and biological scientists want to hear.

Despite anthropology's relatively new and tenuous links with agricultural research and development, its skeptics have not been lacking (see review by Van Dusseldorp, 1977; Simpson, 1978; Ryan, 1979). A major report to the World Bank on farming systems research (Simmonds, 1984) concluded unequivocally that anthropology was not needed. "Anthropology" writes

Norman Simmonds "would be . . . merely an expensive way of avoiding a few not very costly mistakes by On-Farm Research/Farming Systems Perspective Teams."

Are the methods and theories of anthropologists appropriate to agricultural development or are they incompatible with the highly empirical, interdisciplinary and time-constrained environments of technical research centers? A point-by-point discussion of the major criticisms of anthropologists can help answer this question.

### Anthropologist as Lone Ranger

The most common criticism is that anthropologists are "individualists" or "loners" who disappear into villages isolating themselves from technical research efforts (Simmonds, 1984). It is true in the past among traditional ethnographers, the highest professional ranking went to those who "ritually" immersed themselves into "primitive" societies, enduring personal hardships away from their own cultures only to return to vividly describe their experiences (Chagnon, 1968). Anthropologists, therefore, became stereotyped in the minds of agricultural scientists as those who select villagers to live among who are not necessarily representatives of the larger body of regional or world farmers. Anthropological research was considered site-specific, collected outside the framework of the organization's technical goals and of limited relevance to centers with national or international mandates.

Even when anthropologists are integrated into agricultural research teams they are challenged by a special dilemma not faced by most agricultural scientists: how does one strike a balance between sustained, close field contact with the clientele of agricultural projects while meeting the special requirements and needs of agricultural bureaucracies and team efforts? That which is perceived as aloofness is frequently a misunderstanding about differences between field research and experiment station research. For example, stories are told in one international institute about their "strange anthropologist" who refused to ride in marked vehicles, a behavior interpreted as the anthropologist's "fear" of being identified with the institute. The same anthropologist argued that was not the motive, but rather to have closer contact with villagers cooperating in the institute's project. Institute chauffeurs apparently refused to give villagers a lift on orders from the motor pool administration. Most technical agricultural research organizations are set up to facilitate research on an experiment station or in laboratories. Anthropological research is conducted in the field where few of the logistical support services of agricultural R&D institutes apply.

One of anthropology's roles is to keep research close to the ground, relevant to local cultural and social conditions while incorporating farmer perceptions and knowledge into research design. If anthropologists must give up this intimate, participant-observation role, their contribution to food technology-oriented institutes would be highly restricted. Nevertheless, to be effective anthropology requires adaptation of anthropological methods to the agricultural research process. It may also require greater institutional security for anthropologists. The "visiting" anthropologist, facing stiff competition in the academic job offerings, often thinks of gathering data publishable in anthropological journals for better subsequent employment opportunities. Temporary institute economists have been known to commit similar sins: e.g., the econometric study no one understands except economists. Offering anthropologists some degree of continuity and a productive function in interdisciplinary team work, not just as a service science, can go a long way in eliminating the "Loner" syndrome.

### *"Tortoise" Anthropologist*

Anthropologists have also been criticized for taking an inordinate amount of time to conduct research and at least ten years to write it up (Rockefeller Foundation, 1978: 17). Agricultural scientists enjoy declaring their concern is "Hunger" (with a capital H) and they don't have time to wait for the long-winded anthropologist. One author explains: "There is a basic incompatibility between the stress on speed in developing appropriate technologies and the valuable methods which generally characterize anthropological research" (Baker, et al., 1983: 7). Also, since time is money, the addition of an anthropologist to a team is not worth the extra cost. Anthropologists should be brought in only if special problems arise (CGIAR, 1978; Byerlee, et al., 1980; Simmonds, 1984).

Two misconceptions are involved here—that anthropological methods are inherently more time-consuming than, for example, formal questionnaires or on-farm trials—that ethnographic research is more expensive than other types of agricultural research. Anthropologists are in fact considered cheaper than other kinds of scientists since all they often require are rubber boots, altimeter, paper, pencil and willingness to grub out information in the harsh realities of village life. They also carry a lower salary price tag than economists and biologists since most to date have held temporary appointments or post-doctoral fellowships. One international center recently had to weigh comparative costs of adding a soil scientist or an anthropologist to their farming systems team. Both disciplines were considered important. However, the soil scientist with lab would have annually cost over three times more than an anthropologist with one vehicle and two field assistants.

Anthropological research, like most research, can be slow or fast depending on the job and the researcher's abilities. However, most agricultural experimentation tends by necessity to be painfully slow. If personal shortcomings do not slow agricultural scientists, seasons, plants, and animals will. For example, conducting a simple, on-farm potato storage trial takes over a year, not including analysis and writing up data. Even then, few self-respecting technologists have faith in only one season. Up against on-farm research, anthropology studies are potentially lightning fast.

A logical research area for combining long-term field anthropology with technical agriculture is "on-farm research" (OFR) which aims to identify or generate technology for specific groups of farmers (see Tripp, 1984, for an excellent discussion of OFR and anthropology). As its name implies, it occurs on farms, not experiment stations, and follows a fairly standard set of procedures. Anthropology with its total immersion in farmers' lives through participant-observation can be readily blended with agronomic field techniques. Working with farmers in their fields and stores, recording opinions, analyzing how other factors impinge on the outcome of trials, comparing traditional with recommended techniques, reformulating hypotheses for future testing over the coming years are all traditional anthropological activities geared toward agricultural research (Tripp, 1984). Used this way, there is no inherent conflict between anthropological methods and agricultural development research.

To be effective, anthropological research, whether "long and clean" or "quick and dirty" must be geared to the demands of agricultural experimentation. Planting and harvest dates force decisions, and the anthropologist must be willing to deliver information that can be translated into concrete action at times when crucial decisions have to be made. Short-term objective of applied anthropological research is not always an academically excellent publication, but to be effective in the adaptive agricultural research process. Over the long run, however, agricultural anthropologists may contribute new theory and methods to traditional ethnography. On-farm trials, for example, have never been used as an ethnographic tool by academic anthropologists despite a great potential to enrich participant-observation and provide data about agricultural organization.

## The "Soft" Anthropologist

The existing "pecking order" from hard to soft scientists in international centers is often mentioned as a problem in integrating anthropology into the research process (IRRI, 1982). Economists have a similar problem. Collinson (1982) describes a frustrated attempt to integrate farm economics into the Kenyan Ministry of Agriculture:

> The specialist orientation of the technical scientists was perceived to be diluted and his professional peer group status threatened if he cooperated with economists. Similar penalties exist in working close to the farmer, where science is "less pure."

Economists, in turn, often do not wish to be associated with what they perceive to be the weaker social sciences, anthropology and sociology.

It is true that social anthropology is, relatively speaking, "soft" or "qualitative" in a milieu where hard, quantitative data are highly valued. Fortunately, the past few years has seen an enormous push in anthropology toward formal survey methods, statistics, and computers. In some U.S. universities, such as the University of Florida, economics programs are even turning to anthropology for advice and instruction on microcomputers. the stereotype of the anthropologist ignorant of random sampling, unaware of hypothesis testing, and frightened by modelling is rapidly fading into history.

One hopes, however, the pendulum does not swing too far away from what anthropologists do best. Anthropology represents the discipline with the comparative advantage to keep development close to the everyday realities of clients. Qualitative field research complements formal surveys and on-farm experiments by fleshing out statistical data and bringing forth valuable information on beliefs, opinions, viewpoints, tastes, social life . . . all those phenomena which have never been successfully reduced to numbers. Frequently, the anthropologist's weakness in statistics is compensated by excellent writing skills or other forms of communication. The traditional agronomist learns to handle quantification, the traditional anthropologist learns to view relationships and illicit meaning from context. Anthropology is only half-science, the other half belonging to the humanities (Wolf, 1964).

An additional question arises: how much sophisticated quantification is really needed in field research with small farmers especially when understaffed, low budget national programs are involved? High powered academic economics, anthropology, or agronomy are not always clearly relevant (Tripp, 1984). Random sampling, linear programming and factor analysis may be necessary in some cases, but they must in the end be combined with common sense and down-to-earth procedures. Otherwise, in our computer age, the danger is imminent that we grow further away from day-to-day realities faced by farm families.

## "Nostalgic" Anthropologist

Anthropologists are often accused of personally identifying more with "target populations" than with the agricultural research process (Simmonds, 1984). This gives the impression that anthropologists are more interested in defending traditional ways rather than "improving" food production or working on teams with biological scientists. Agricultural scientists sometimes claim they find anthropologists "preachy," frequently berating biologists for not taking into consideration farmer logic, traditional adaptations, or knowledge (Rhoades, Horton, and Booth, 1984). These accusations are carryovers from a period when anthropologists felt uneasy about applied work which had not become a fully accepted part of their professional value system. Unlike economics, anthropology did not yet have a "client" relationship with society.

Even today some anthropologists and other social scientists often see themselves as defenders of the dispossessed against technology-for-technology sake projects that benefit the rich at the expense of the poor. Moreover, some agricultural scientists find pure social science research not only useless but immoral. The director of an international agricultural center (Sawyer, 1984) observed:

> While anthropologists often viewed themselves as defenders of traditional agriculture against the negative effects of modernization, individuals working to improve food production saw the social scientist's relationship to rural populations as unbalanced. Anthropologists came, lived in villages for a year

or more, and went home to publish books and articles in their language read mainly by other anthropologists. While many an anthropologist rose to full professorship on data drawn from farm families, little or nothing remained behind to improve the lives of their "informants."

Using any social or biological science critically and positively inside a team setting without giving up what each discipline does best requires experience and vision. Anthropological research can help pinpoint traditional ways and technologies which are adaptive and for which no better alternatives are yet available. Anthropologists should engage in "constructive conflict" with biological scientists if a technical project is "off-base" in human terms. The important factor is whether anthropologists feel they are more than mere appendages to research teams. The role of agricultural institute administration is important in promoting interdisciplinary involvement. If anthropologists are assigned only the jobs of conducting a feasibility survey before a project or an evaluation after a project, it is logical that they easily end up as outside critics.

### "Fully Replaceable" Anthropologist

Among the first bewildering shocks many anthropologists receive when they begin working in agricultural research organizations is the bold but common declaration by established economists that they can "fully substitute" for anthropologists. This overconfidence led one prominent anthropologist to remark sarcastically but understandably: "It appears the 'Green Revolution' not only produced Miracle Rice but Miracle Economists as well." Economists, who are still anthropology's best defenders in the system, have struggled hard and admirably for their place in the sun. Whether or not they feel threatened, they realize that research administrators frequently consider all social scientists including economists, as birds of a feather. Everyone knows one rotten apple spoils the peck. Economists' challenge to anthropologists to come up with more than superficial "social" or "cultural" tidbits is well taken. At the same time, economists specializing in Third World agriculture have recognized the power of anthropology over conventional economics in dealing with many important themes in agricultural development (Collinson, 1981; Ruttan, 1982).

Anyone who stays around agricultural researchers any amount of time observes a pecking order from plant breeder to economist and now to the Johnny-come-lately anthropologist. The breeder claims a good variety will create its own suction force so why does he need an agronomist standing between him and the farmer. The agronomist argues that an "economically aware" agronomist can do farm budgeting so why does he need an economist. The economist, in turn, says he can make "social observations" so why anthropologists.

The major problem with the "anything you can do I can do better" argument is that it denies the importance of disciplinary expertise other than one's own and limits approaches in the solution of technological problems. Anthropologists can also do partial budget analysis, conduct on-farm experiments, and make crosses. There is no special magic in any one of these acts. But each of these techniques is merely the tip of the iceberg for economics, agronomy, and plant breeding as any good economist, agronomist, and plant breeder will tell you. The same is true of anthropology.

## Using Anthropology Effectively:
### Developing Post-Harvest Technology at CIP[9]

At CIP an attempt has been made to develop a different approach to interdisciplinary team research. CIP's source research is organized around research "thrusts" involving collection and maintenance of a world germplasm bank, breeding to control disease and pests, agronomy, seed production and distribution, and post-harvest technology. CIP has adopted the philosophy that interdisciplinary research teams should work on these problems not in a fragmented manner but in a coordinated and continuous way. One of these teams has been composed of anthropologists and post-harvest technologists.

Since the late 1960s, the Peruvian government and various development agencies operating in Peru have sought technical solutions to help control the flow of consumer potatoes into the Lima market. As a result, numerous consumer potato storage facilities have been built around the country, including five large storages with a combined total capacity of 20,000 metric tons.

The largest storage complex is near the mining town of La Oroya, more than 3,500 meters above sea level. These naturally-ventilated, forced-air stores were built to take advantage of the low temperatures and high humidities at high altitudes during the night (Fernandez, 1976). The stores are situated roughly halfway between the major potato-producing areas of the Department of Junin and the Lima market. On initial impression, the idea behind the stores makes good sense. Potatoes could be held at La Oroya with minimum losses until prices improved in July or August in the Lima market. Theoretically, everyone gained. Farmers could get higher prices than if forced to sell immediately at harvest in May. Consumers gained as well by having to pay lower prices during the "critical months" for potatoes.

Any traveler along Peru's central highway from Lima to Huancayo, the capital of Junin Department, can visit the impressive Oroya storage complex. However it, and the others in highland Peru built during the same period and later, today stand empty, just as they have virtually every day since they were built. These stores are existing monuments to mistargeted development projects, although according to storage specialists, they are technically sound and extremely well-designed. The failure came through not understanding the post-harvest system of potato agriculture as it functions in the central Andes. Such mistakes are not unique to Peru. Similar potato stores, technically sound but equally empty, can be found throughout the developing world. Against this background of twenty-five years of frustrating failure in attempting to improve existing post-harvest practices, anthropologists working with biological scientists have developed a new approach.

## The Case of the Rustic Potato Stores

To understand the contribution of anthropology to this interdisciplinary research, it is necessary to study carefully the interaction—often conflictive—that occurred between anthropologists and storage technologists. Initially, anthropologist Robert Werge set out in the Mantaro Valley to study post-harvest activities and problems facing highland potato farmers. The storage specialists at first restricted their activities to conducting research on the experiment station, also situated in the Mantaro Valley. From the beginning, however, a dialogue was maintained between team members.

Werge's ethnographic information from farmers and their practical situation soon called into question research decisions taken by post-harvest specialists on the experiment station where controlled conditions are possible.

## Storage Losses or No?

An intra-team debate surfaced over the concept of "storage losses," a central issue for post-harvest technologists. The potato, a vegetable tuber, is highly perishable. Post-harvest technologists were logically concerned with how to design a storage system to reduce pathological and physiological "losses,"major problems in Europe and the United States. Werge, on the basis of an informal two-month study, argued that Andean farmers did not necessarily perceive small or shriveled and spoiled potatoes as "losses" or "waste" because all potatoes were used in some form. Potatoes that could not be sold, used for seed, or immediately consumed at home were fed to animals (mainly pigs) or processed into dehydrated potatoes that could be stored for long periods. Farm women claimed that shriveled, partially spoiled potatoes tasted sweeter and were sometimes more desired (Werge, 1977b).

Also, an underlying assumption of earlier post-harvest technological research in the Andes was that traditional farmer storage practices were "backward," a primary cause of "losses." Outsiders entering an Andean house have the impression of total disorder. Across the main living area hangs a string of ears of corn; against the wall next to the bed are farm tools; and below the bed are piled small, shriveled potatoes. Guinea pigs scamper about the room, hiding behind the worn straw mat that holds the potatoes. It is easy to conclude, as does a recent FAO proposal calling for more storage research in the Andes, that farmers' storage practices are inadequate.

Virtually all technical potato storage programs developed earlier in the Andes emphasized the need for specialized structures as used in Europe or North America. Unlike in developed countries, however, potatoes in the Andes are rarely stored in separate, specialized buildings. In the early 1960s, an ethnographer (Stein, 1961) noted:

the main economic function of the house is storage of agricultural products and tools and it serves to shelter at least some of the animals as well. Its functions in sheltering people are almost secondary to the basic purposes.

The house offers security against theft and the darkened rooms hide one's wealth against the prying eyes of neighbors and employees of the agrarian bank.

Anthropologist Robert Werge (1980) later concludes:

Concentration on specialized constructions derives from use of a model based on the contemporary European and North American practice of keeping domestic and farm activities separate in specific houses, sheds or barns. Potato farmers in developed countries have highly sophisticated storage buildings with large scale capacities, often constructed with special financing.

This model is not appropriate to the Andes where farmers regard the storage of food, seed and tools as a domestic activity. The flexibility of space within the household residence and the security of the house are not compensated for by technical advantages which a specialized storage facility can provide.

According to Werge's study, however, farmers had "problems," but different ones than scientists had originally imagined. Farmers claimed the difficulty was not with their storage technology *per se* but with "new varieties" that produced long sprouts when stored under traditional methods. The long sprouts had to be pulled off before planting and this was considered by farmers to be a costly process in terms of time and labor. As a result of this anthropology-technical science dialogue, Werge and his colleagues concentrated on a new method of storing *improved* seed potatoes under farm conditions.[10]

Since 1972 CIP had been experimenting with a technique long known to farmers in some developing countries: natural diffused light reduces sprout elongation (Dinkel, 1963; Tupac Yupanqui, 1978). However, it was not known if the technique could be widely used in storing seed tubers under farm conditions. On the experiment station, research demonstrated clearly that indirect light reduced sprout elongation and improved overall seed quality under Andean conditions.

The design of experiment station stores, however, was from the technologists' point of view. Questions remained. Was the design relevant to farm conditions and was it acceptable to farmers? Answers could only be found through continued ethnographic research and on-farm trials with farmers acting as advisers. Werge had been doing research on the architecture and uses of farmhouses and buildings with an eye on how the diffused light principle might fit. A storage facility separate from the house did not seem realistic because of lack of security and convenience. Nor did it seem possible to introduce diffused light into dark rooms traditionally used as storage areas.

Diffused light also produces greening in potatoes, often rendering them undesirable as human food. Many small Andean farmers prefer to store all potatoes in the dark, even those to be used later for seed. This is a precaution in case of later food shortages or if they must market consumer potatoes to acquire extra income. With these socioeconomic considerations in mind, the team inspected farmhouses and talked over the problem with farmer cooperators.

Many Andean houses have a veranda or corridor with a roof that permits entrance of indirect light. The team decided to set up special seed trays as used on the experiment station in the houses of cooperating farmers. The trays, similar to open vegetable crates, were stacked in corridors of farm compounds with diffused light instead of direct sunlight.

These on-farm experiments gave similar scientific results as did those on the experiment station (Booth, et al., 1983). Upon seeing that diffused light storage reduces sprout elongation, farmers expressed interest but were then concerned about cost of seed trays. In response, the team built simple collapsible shelves from local timber and used them in a second series of on-farm trials. The results were again positive but this time farmers were able to relate more closely to the rustic design of the stores. Throughout this adaptive process, scientists were learning more and more about technical and socioeconomic aspects of storage as well as about the proposed new technology itself.

When Werge left CIP in 1979 no evidence was available that farmers would accept the technology. The validity of the team's adaptive research approach still depended on whether farmers were willing to use the diffused light principle at their own expense. The design and initial testing of an appropriate technology is the first crucial half of the process. The second stage began after the idea of rustic, diffused light stores was introduced through CIP training courses to potato workers in Asia, Africa, and Latin America.[11]

It was during this same year (1979) that I joined CIP as its second staff anthropologist. On a trip to the Philippines, I had the opportunity to apply anthropological analysis to the first case of transfer to farmers of the idea of replacing dark seed potato stores with diffused light stores similar to those developed in Peru (Rhoades et al., 1979). A storage specialist at CIP, Robert Booth, had worked closely with national potato program workers the previous year to determine if the diffused light rustic store idea being studied in Peru was relevant to the Philippines' main potato producing region in northern Luzon. As a result, the farmers in one Philippine community decided to put up a demonstration diffused-light seed store. This store was followed by five more demonstration stores built by the Philippine National Potato Program (Rhoades et al., 1979; 1982).

As Booth and I visited the area later it was clear some adoption of the technology had taken place since his first visit. To better understand farmer responses to the innovation, we developed a questionnaire to be applied by national potato program workers (Rhoades et al., 1979). In addition in-depth interviewing of key informants provided ethnographic data detailing how the technology diffused through his or her community. This information was positively received by CIP biological scientists and helped alter the previous image of social scientists as only bearers of bad news. Subsequently, comparative studies have been conducted in several countries where the diffused light storage technology has been introduced (Rhoades et al., 1983).

Change agents from several countries involved in storage research expected that farmers would copy the demonstration stores. They had difficulty believing adoption could occur through farmers' own ingenious methods of adapting an idea to their conditions. Anthropological follow-up in adoption areas, however, demonstrated clearly that "technology" as a unique physical "package" was not being accepted. The diffused light principle was being translated into an amazing array of farmer experimental and adopted versions of potato stores each with its own cultural flavor. After exposure to a demonstration model, farmers began to experiment on their own. For example, in Peru many farmers began by simply spreading a few potatoes under the courtyard veranda away from direct sunlight, an experiment that involved no physical alteration of a building. Other farmers, either as a first stage adoption or elaboration of the spreading trial, constructed a simple raised platform under the veranda, a modification that allowed for better ventilation. Other farmers built simple structures, but few of these were exact copies of demonstration stores. In a few cases, associations of farmers built stores up to 100 tons capacity, many times larger than the rustic demonstration models. However, while these new physical storage structures in Africa, Asia, and Latin America reflected the unique cultural architecture of the area, the basic structural design remained similar. By 1983 more than 3,000 cases of adoption were documented.

Ethnographic information on farmer creativity in experimentation, and adaptation of the diffused light storage principle has been collected through follow-up evaluations around the globe (Rhoades, et al., 1983; Rhoades, 1984). It led us to urge national programs to establish demonstration stores encouraging farmer experimentation and illustrating different ways that the principle might be adapted. In many cases farmers did not automatically understand the relevancy of the principle, especially if the national program had constructed a costly demonstration model. Since extension workers sometimes became frustrated when farmers did not precisely copy their design, the CIP team emphasized in training courses the anthropological concepts of cultural adaptation (Bennett, 1976) and indigenous experimentation (Johnson, 1972).

Through this monitoring process, the post-harvest team learned from farmers how to improve the technology and avoid production contexts which might be inappropriate. For example, in areas where farmers want to break dormancy rapidly to meet a planting date, the diffused light principle offers few advantages. Early emphasis of what to expect and what not to expect from a new technology and by defining under what agroecological conditions a technology is likely to work or to fail, anthropology streamlines the transfer process, saving valuable time and resources needed elsewhere for agricultural development.

## Potato Processing

An even more illustrative case of how anthropologists helped define and debate the directions of technology development deals with the processing component of CIP's post-harvest technology research. Throughout the central Andes, potatoes are dehydrated by traditional methods of solar drying so they may be stored for up to a year or longer (Werge, 1979). At the outset of the project, organizations furnishing funds and CIP processing specialists believed farmers needed a more efficient and rapid way to dehydrate potatoes. Roy Shaw, a processing specialist, in attempting to develop this more efficient method designed a simple "black box" expected to speed up the drying process. Later, Werge and Shaw took the black box directly to farm households for testing. They soon discovered that faster drying was not considered important by their informants. What farmers wanted, according to Werge, were more labor-efficient methods in cutting and peeling potatoes.

In the rugged terrain of the Andes, great distances between fields and an enormous range of farm and off-farm activities place intense pressure on family manpower (see also Brush, 1977). To farmers it did not matter if two weeks or two months were required to dry potatoes. The "black box" offered no advantage over traditional methods (Werge, 1979).

Shaw, in thinking back on the experience, noted:

> We were again designing postharvest technology from a distance. Since we were dealing with a dehydrated product, the problem seemed one of solar drying. We knew about peeling and cutting, but since those were labor-intensive they were thought of as desirable and not as problems. (Shaw, 1979)

Based on Werge's findings, Shaw reoriented his technical efforts toward developing simple peeling and cutting equipment as components of a total system of producing dehydrated potatoes. Included also were socioeconomic components: the equipment must be culturally acceptable and capable of being built by local craftsmen with local materials. These components can be clearly recognized as the product of "anthropological thinking."

After Werge left CIP the post-harvest team did not entirely abandon the concept of solar drying, but looked for a context where it might fit. Only five of fifty-two families Werge studied sold part of their produce. The biological scientists assumed that demand for dehydrated potatoes among migrants from the mountains now living in coastal cities might justify a shift in scale of production of dried potatoes, the traditional *papa seca*. If it was realistic to produce dehydrated potatoes on a scale larger than the family level (village level, cooperatives, or commercial enterprises), improved solar drying efficiency would be desirable as part of a complete process. Low cost *papa seca* and starch processing plants were then designed and built with local expertise and equipment. These plants were demonstrated to possible clients in 1979 and 1980 through field days.

In 1982, the biological scientists requested a follow-up study of the program to transfer information regarding design, construction and use of potato processing plants, presumed to have been built as a result of CIP's training activities with the Ministry of Agriculture. However, results of this evaluation were disappointing. A number of individuals had started construction of plants but due to low prices and limited demand for *papa seca* had dropped their plans. This unfortunate turn of events again placed the anthropologist in the role of "bearer of bad news," since hopes were high that the processing work would result in the same kind of success that the storage project was having. Due to heavy travel demands, the technologists on the team were unable to participate in the follow-up evaluation.

Within time, however, the major conclusions of the follow-up were accepted: demand for *papa seca* was limited and industrial or village level plants aimed at producing solely *papa seca* or potato starch were not economically viable under present price conditions. *Papa seca* is mainly consumed as an ingredient in a festival dish, *carapulcra*, only once or twice a year, almost exclusively along the coast. In the highlands, *papa seca* is produced by individual households and stored mainly for their own use. Fresh potatoes are too expensive to use for starch processing in Peru given other crops such as maize and cassava. Recommendations were made that new and creative ways of diversifying the *papa seca* plant and developing other dehydrated products that might be included in mixes or soups be sought following a serious market-demand study (Rhoades, 1982b).

The technologists felt that one potential solution to the high price of dehydrated potatoes was to develop a packaged ready-mix, nutritionally balanced, and at a reduced cost. Cheaper ingredients, such as rice and beans, helped lower cost of the potato-base mix. A potato based, ready-mix could be targeted as a weaning food for low income, nutritionally deficient groups in Lima. In light of this new direction, the social science team members (sociologist and anthropologist) conducted a feasibility study (Benavides and Rhoades, 1982). An important topic for investigation was to understand why previous attempts at formulated mixes targeted for the urban poor in Peru had failed.

Once again the post-harvest group soon found itself embroiled in an intra-team debate. The social scientists argued that according to their findings poor people of Lima's *pueblos jovenes* were already consuming the elements in the presumed packaged mix in culturally preferred forms, as dried or fresh products readily obtainable on the local market at an equal price suggested for the potato-based mix. Interest in "convenience foods" among the urban poor was yet to be empirically determined. Following a debate in which the evidence was weighed, the technologists decided from a product development point of view that the most viable option was to optimistically move ahead with the idea of a formulated mix aimed toward the urban poor. The exercise of pursuing an acceptable mix was seen as a way to learn more about consumer preferences for processed potato products and to seek ways to expand the demand for potatoes.

Despite periods of "constructive conflict," the CIP post-harvest team remains committed to the idea that technical and socioeconomic matters are equally important, even when no agreement on a project's direction can be developed (see Rhoades and Booth, 1983 for a discussion of interdisciplinary team research). The approach which Booth and I jointly formulated, called by us "Farmer-Back-to-Farmer," combines anthropological and applied technological thinking (Rhoades and Booth, 1982).

## Farmer-Back-to-Farmer: A Model for Generating Acceptable Agricultural Technology

The CIP post-harvest team readily admits that adaptive research potentially involves at least three distinct groups each with their own perception of reality: social scientists, technologists, and farmers or other clients. Each view of reality can be considered true in and of itself and is based on the group or individual's relationship to the situation at hand. Technologists are under strong pressure by donors, administrations, and colleagues to produce a better technology that works and is adopted by farmers or consumers. Social scientists are faced with a "marginal man" or cultural broker's role: articulating their understanding of the farmer's situation to colleagues from biological sciences. Then, to complete the triangle is the farmer, the one facing the problem but who does not receive a guaranteed monthly check to "solve farmers' problems." Farmers live in both a technical and a social world based on agriculture; researchers simply study the worlds but do not have to live by the consequences of farm decisions. And all this boils down to an undeniable fact: the researcher and farmer see the world differently.

Briefly, the basic philosophy upon which the farmer-back-to-farmer model rests is that successful adaptive interdisciplinary research must *begin* and *end* with the farmer, farm household, and community. It does not posit that decisions as to what are important problems can be formulated on an experimental station or with a planning committee removed from the rural context and out of touch with farm conditions. The model subsequently involves a series of targets or goals that are logically linked by a circular and potentially recycling pattern of four basic activities: diagnosis, identifying solutions, testing and adaptation, and farmer evaluation (Hildebrand, 1978; Harwood, 1979: 38–40). Research must come full circle from proper problem identification to farmer acceptance or rejection. Research, thus, is client- and problem-oriented. Research, extension, and transfer are seen as parallel and ongoing, not sequential, disjointed activities.

### Understanding

The first activity in the farmer-back-to-farmer model is an understanding and learning stage. It is similar to the diagnosis stage outlined in farming systems research, although relatively more emphasis is placed on what anthropologists call the "emic" perspective; that is, putting oneself as much as possible into the farmers' shoes to understand how they view the problem in both technical and sociocultural terms. Thus, this stage does not simply involve administering a questionnaire wherein scientists decide the relevant questions and farmers struggle to fill in the blanks. According to the farmer-back-to-farmer approach, informal surveys or formal questionnaires are not the only early diagnostic methodological tools. Other techniques include on-farm experiments, farmer field days, farmer advisory boards, participant-observation, scientists working hand-in-hand with farmers in their fields in exchange for information. Methods used will vary from circumstance to circumstance, depending on the special nature of transportation, time, size of region, scientists' knowledge of local conditions and populations.

The understanding stage should include farmers, social scientists, and biological scientists each using their own skills to interpret a problem area. The farmer-back-to-farmer approach does not encompass specific methods for determining a ranking of constraints or priorities for agricultural policy at local or national levels but illustrates guidelines for effective design, generation, and spread of appropriate technology. Building upon, rather than replacing, traditional practices is the route to successful problem-solving.

Farmers with their long-term practical experience involving their land, mix of crops, climate and local socioeconomic conditions assume—according to the model—the status of experts in their own right and are equal members of the problem-solving team. In this beginning stage, biological scientists will naturally focus largely on technical problems. Social scientists, bound by their own selective perception, will focus on another set of phenomena: ecology, marketing, price conditions, credit restraints, or their interpretation of what farmers believe. The challenge is to weld these different perceptions into a common framework for action.

## Seeking Solutions

Once the problem is generally identified and the team shares some common ground, the search for solutions is the next but perhaps more difficult stage. Despite a general assumption that a vast pool of technology is ready to be transferred to farmers, the process does not seem quite so simple. In the search for solutions, a constant on-the-spot exchange is necessary between farmers and those who test hypotheses about potential technologies of the research station. This interchange should continue throughout the selection stage. Compromises, changes, reversal of direction, or even termination of projects may be appropriate (but difficult) at this stage.

The purpose of linking on-station and farm-level team research is to arrive jointly at a definition of potential solutions, and a portion of the farmer's problem always remains undefined. Proposed solutions are rarely ready at this early stage since farm problems are immensely complex, interrelated, and constantly changing.

*Testing and Adapting Potential Solution*

Once a solution or set of solutions is defined, the team—including extension workers if possible—should proceed to a testing and adapting activity. The objective now is to fit, with the farmer acting as adviser, the technology to local conditions. Generally, testing and adaptation occurs first on the experiment station followed by on-farm trials. Nevertheless, in the farmer-back-to-farmer organization of research, even during the transfer stage, the flow of information is circular between the field and the experiment station. The technology should pass through an agronomic or technical test, an economic test and a sociocultural suitability test. The series of tests have illustrated the constant need to modify the testing methods and the technology itself. CIP's storage team, for example, began by building costly seed stores on the experiment station but data coming constantly from farmers oriented the team progressively toward less expensive designs. During this adaptive process we have found that not only does the technology change but modifications are made as well in the testing methods.

During on-farm testing, the potential solution or solutions should be compared to traditional methods. This can still be considered an understanding stage for there may be influencing factors in the farming system yet unrealized by scientists and farmers. The testing and adaptation stage may require several recyclings to arrive at a technology worthy of demonstration and independent evaluation by farmers. And in other cases it may be possible that the traditional method cannot be improved.

On-farm research is not of much value if farmers do not feel they are a part of the research process and cannot make straightforward suggestions on the technology undergoing testing. This is not an easy task in those parts of the world where farmers are outwardly submissive to urban-based research scientists. Building rapport is the best way to gain farmer cooperation and this requires that scientists spend more time in the field.

*Farmer Evaluation: The Crucial Stage*

In agricultural development, it is a sad fact that technologies are typically released and forgotten. Storages are built, irrigation canals constructed, livestock or crop varieties introduced, all of which are rarely seen again by the innovators who, by then, have terminated their contracts and gone on to other assignments. Follow-up is rare, perhaps because the innovators assume the job is accomplished, that it is the responsibility now of a national program, or fear that the real results won't be palatable. However, according to the farmer-back-to-farmer model, follow-up is the crucial final link. Data must be collected on the reception of the technology by farmers, the ultimate judges as to the appropriateness of a proposed technology.

Until this point, all scientific evaluations remain at the level of hypothesis. Unless the circle is completed, unless research results reach the farmer, prior efforts can be considered fruitless and research findings will be shelved to gather dust. And if the technology is rejected by farmers, the research process should be repeated to determine reasons and seek ways to overcome the problem. It may only be necessary to return to the adapting stage, or if the technology is totally rejected, then a new slice of the "farmer problem" needs to be taken.

The final stage involves the independent evaluation and use by farmers of the technology under their conditions, resources, and management. At this stage, scientists must not only determine acceptability but understand how farmers continue to adapt and modify the technology. Likewise, the impact of accepted technology must be monitored to make sure the technology is not detrimental to the well-being of farmers or the society at large.

Although the farmer-back-to-farmer model shares many common characteristics with other farming systems models, the stress is clearly anthropological, blended with the technologists' thinking. In particular, the emphasis on the farmer's point of view, informal survey techniques, and continuous adaptation and farmer experimentation fit well with anthropological approaches.

## THE ANTHROPOLOGICAL PERSPECTIVE: AN OVERVIEW

What in fact has been the unique contribution by anthropologists to CIP's research? As social scientists, anthropologists generally cannot point to a specific technology as might a breeder point to a new variety which yields "x" tons more than traditional varieties on an experiment station. The anthropologist focuses on the clients, the people, the users of a technology, not the technology *per se*. The contribution thus comes through people-focused research and a "way of thinking" that helps identify problems and solutions followed by monitoring adaptation and acceptance by local populations of appropriate solutions. To some degree the role of anthropologists is that of "cultural brokers" between farmers and technologists. This forces the anthropologist, voluntarily or involuntarily, into a difficult "watch dog" role. If a technologically-oriented program is off base in terms of the human component, the anthropologist's role is to explain why and help steer a new course. Steering a new course, however, is not always popular, especially when programs or projects have built a momentum of their own.

Economists in technical research programs have carved out a niche based on the question: "Is a new technology or practice potentially more profitable in cash terms than the farmer's present technology or practice?" This important question is obviously more central to the analysis of technological change in fully developed market economies than in semi-commercial, subsistence systems based partially on exchange and reciprocity. With notable exceptions, the agricultural economist's model for analyzing a farmer's behavior focuses on the business element of the farm enterprise, not the whole household in its ecological, physical, and sociocultural environment. Maximization of profits is thus seen as a primary human motivation.[12] The business paradigm is powerful and appealing to agricultural development specialists who themselves originate from developed, free-market economics where profit seeking is highly valued.

Economics, as broadly understood, obviously involves a great deal more than simply maximization theory (Collinson, 1982). In fact, economics and anthropology have played methodological and theoretical ping-pong over the years causing sharp distinctions between the disciplines to be blurred.[13] It might be argued that the rise of Farming Systems Research reflected the growing realization that agricultural economics needed reorientation when dealing with small, subsistence farmers in developing countries (Redclift, 1983). This has brought about a strong anthropological orientation of many farming systems agricultural economists (Norman, 1980; Hildebrand, 1978). For example, Dillon and Anderson (1984) have suggested social scientists address four important matters in Farming Systems Research:

1. farmers' social milieu, including customs;
2. institutional and policy setting, including land tenure, credit, and taxation;
3. economic development, including market trends and opportunity costs;
4. attitudes and personal constraints of farmers including beliefs toward change, leisure, education, different food.

The reader will note that agricultural economics in training and past research experience, especially in the United States, only has a clear comparative advantage over anthropology and rural sociology in one area, that of the economic environment. The rest, especially the first and last, clearly fall into the domain of the "other" social sciences.

Although anthropologists do not generally translate their data into dollar and cents calculations or cost-benefit ratios, they offer a human-centered perspective on farming, cost-effective methodologies, and theories that dynamically trace linkages between farm household or unit, environment, technology, crops and animals, and the larger socioeconomic milieu.[14] Anthropology thus broadens our understanding of agriculture in developing countries. CIP anthropologists, for example, stressed components that other social or biological scientists rarely consider: concepts of space, time, and farmstead architecture in the post-harvest research, dualism in farmer potato growing strategies in the ethnobotanical study, relation between agrarian ecology, cropping patterns, farm types in the Mantaro Valley project, culinary, shape, and color preferences of potato consumers in the nutrition study, and the cross-cultural comparison and technology extrapolation in the worldwide potato study.

Methodologies included participant-observation (crucial in the farmer-back-to-farmer model), informal surveys, techniques to understand and recognition of the importance of indigenous knowledge systems, use of aerial photos and land-use maps, controlled cross-cultural comparison, ethnographic eliciting techniques. And anthropologists brought the theoretical perspectives of functionalism, cultural ecology, substantivism, psychological and economic anthropology, and systems theory. Anthropologists at CIP have used these diverse techniques and theories to help focus on problem areas, encourage farmer involvement in design of technology, link experiment station and on-farm research, follow-up and help adapt new technology to real farm conditions.

In addition to their methods and theories for understanding and predicting human behavior, anthropologists share a general orientation which is valuable for agricultural research and is different than the orientations of sister social sciences (see Montgomery, 1977: 43):

1. Direct, sustained contact with the people studied in their everyday lives and on their terms, to understand how they perceive the world and their problems. This "participant-observation" gives rise to the notion of "cultural relativism" which simply means "a people must be understood within the context in which they live," not to be judged from another context. This obviously has implications for the transfer of agricultural technology from foreign countries or from experiment stations to farms.

2. Recognition that "real" and "ideal" cultural patterns exist; that is, what people say or believe may have little relationship to what they actually do. Anthropologists argue that much of human behavior is "unconscious." While using formal questionnaires, they believe that relying only on questionnaires for information about farming practices is risky. For example, the Karimojong of Uganda, a semi-nomadic pastoral people who also farm, declare that only men and boys herd cattle while women and girls work in agriculture. Close ethnographic study, however, revealed this was the ideal behavior, not *actual* behavior. Men accounted for 35 percent of the labor in planting sorghum, 50 percent of the labor in planting millet, one-third of the labor in weeding millet fields, and over 50 percent of the labor during harvest (Dyson-Hudson, 1972; see also Vierich, 1983).

3. Recognition that a great deal of human culture and behavior is expressed in non-verbal ways (gestures, postures, use of space, modes of dress, intricate dietary patterns). For example, in the rustic storage case discussed above the anthropologist stressed the importance of local farmstead architecture in the acceptance of technology. In another case, anthropologist Mary Douglas (1974) has argued that food not only serves a biological function but also has clear aesthetic functions involving color and form and is therefore similar to clothing and housing. This may explain in part the importance of color of potato varieties in consumer preferences in many developing countries. The common belief held by some agricultural scientists that poor people will eat anything (thus all that is needed is more food) may need revision in light of anthropological studies of food preferences, taboos, structured sequences of consumption, and variations in meal types. Despite prevailing common sense theories, food preferences and taste

patterns are indeed among the most difficult aspects of human behavior to study.
4. Perception that all manifestations of human behavior are interrelated parts of cultural systems. This viewing or sensitivity toward relationships is the holism of anthropology. Unfortunately, "holism" has been considered a bad word in the practical world which connotes "wispy, intellectualized, convoluted explanations that fit some caricatures of the humanities" (Cancian, 1977). Nevertheless, agricultural systems are in reality powerfully "holistic" and not simply made up of potatoes, soils, credit structures, etc. in isolation of each other.

Compartmentalized research in agriculture often leads to laboratory or experiment station scientists who have little knowledge about farming. A scientist may be an expert on a single disease but know little about how the disease makes or does not make a difference in the real life or practices of the farmer. While anthropology is no panacea for the distance problem between applied biological scientists and farmers, or consumers, it does offer a broader, down-to-earth analytical framework for integrating different points of view.
5. Other special orientations of anthropology as an agricultural science include:

• Attention to a people's past experiences in studying a problem.
• Recognition that in any human group, significant variations among groups and between individuals occur.
• Conviction that valid cross-cultural generalizations can be made, an important aspect if agriculture research findings are to be transferred between groups and nations.

Although many of the above orientations are shared with sociology, basic differences between anthropology and sociology still remain. A report of the Rockefeller Foundation (1978: 5) explains:

Sociology training programs usually have a domestic focus and tend to limit consideration of the implications of group differences within a country to a few inductive variables—class, race, and religion. They stress the use of survey data, with its greater scope for statistical proof and lesser capacity to capture unexpected events, whereas the anthropologists stress lengthy open-ended interviewing and direct observation. Special methodologies are developed for the study of group processes and of particular types of organizational structures; while anthropologists use such methods they seldom concentrate on their refinement for general application. Like the economists, the sociologists focus more on probabilistic theories for prediction of group behavior, while the anthropologists emphasize contextual explanations and predictions.

Rural sociology and other social sciences, especially human geography, have much to offer agricultural research. However, while anthropology has moved aggressively in recent years in expressing an interest in agriculture, rural sociology lost considerable ground in the 1960s and 1970s when the discipline faced a morale problem and theoretical crises from which it is only now recovering (Newby, 1982).

## The Anthropological Concept of Culture

Cross-cutting and underlying all of CIP's anthropological studies is the notion of "culture." A dynamic blueprint or design for living, culture is learned behavior handed down through generations so that each new cohort of babies in a society does not have to start again from scratch. To some degree, what agricultural scientists call tradition is the anthropologists's culture. Developed in the mid–19th century, culture became anthropology's key conceptual contribution to philosophical and social science thinking about man's behavior and his place in the universe (Tylor, 1864). Most anthropologists agree that human culture is an adaptive, integrated, learned and dynamic system (Radcliffe-Brown, 1952). Proponents of anthropology's ecological school approach an agricultural region or technological problem with three components in mind, often placing them within the cultural systems framework.

### Human Ecology[15]

At the base of all human cultures are the practices, tools, machinery, weapons, and other technologies that articulate social life with the material conditions of their habitat. Agriculture (agri-*culture*) represents a behavior-environment interaction which is distinct from hunting and gathering, shifting cultivation, and fishing. Technological practices and inventories ensure survival, not only in terms of energy procurement but for protection against weather, disease, and hostile neighboring populations. Thus, when anthropologists approach a community the first question they ask is: How do these people make a living? More specifically: What is the environment like, and what technology and social patterns have they developed to exploit that environment?

### Social Organization

The practical requirements of production and reproduction require development and maintenance of an orderly social life. Order in society requires proper functioning and execution of energy accumulating activities (including agriculture) needed for survival and the reproduction of the population vital for the continuation of that society. Therefore, the social life of the farming population reflects the agricultural system. This linkage is central to anthropological "holistic" thinking, and explains why technological development must also be thought of as a social process. Patterns of migration, for example, may be a powerful but silent determinant of village technology and productivity. Optimising production the way an agro-economic team would prefer can quickly become frustrated if target villages are dependent upon extensive labor migration of the young and able-bodied.

The anthropologist should be able to help put proposed technological change in context, thus casting a clearer light on potentialities.

*Ideology/World View*

Anthropologist Marvin Harris (1971: 146) has pointed out:

> while every social species (bees, ants, apes, birds, etc.) have ecological patterns and social structures, only human groups have ideologies. Ideology includes explicit and implicit knowledge, opinions, values, plans, and goals that people have about their ecological circumstance; their understanding of nature, technology, production, and reproduction; their reasons for living, working, and reproducing.

Looking at farming through the eyes of farmers, a major premise of modern farming systems research has always been a central concern of anthropology (Malinowski, 1935; Redfield, 1934). Ethnographers have shown that under certain conditions ideology can be as influential over agricultural change as climate or plant disease. The American ideal, for example, of the 160-acre family farm when applied to the drier American Great Plains in the late nineteenth century ultimately led to the Dust Bowl of the 1930s, an ecological disaster on a grand scale. In Kenya, consumers consistently reject white skinned potatoes in favor of red skinned ones. The differences in farming strategies of different ethnic groups occupying the same ecological niche testify to the role of ideology (Bennett, 1969; Cole and Wolf, 1974). In Sri Lanka, a belief in "evil eye" affected the design and in some cases adoption of a new storage system where the potato crop was visible (Rhoades, 1984).

Agricultural scientists often forget that "agriculture" is a human-centered, controlled and manipulated process. People are at the helm. Being people they are psychological and symbolic beings, not simply organisms responding to natural conditions or profit incentives. Anthropologists through their cross-cultural perspective should be able to alert agricultural researchers of the influences of ideology, including that of scientists. Generally, ideology reflects and helps facilitate local survival, and should not necessarily be thought of as a barrier to technology improvement. Yet beliefs and attitudes can be a source of great frustration and must be considered in research.

Anthropology's potential and unique role in agriculture involves more than that of a "cultural broker" between farmers and technologists, although this role should not be slighted. Behind anthropological research at CIP, is a long intellectual history, well-founded theory, and appropriate methods, all of which have been developed through research among tribal and peasant populations now called "small or resource poor farmers," the targets of agricultural development projects.

Some economists argue that anthropologists should be brought into projects only if "unusual" or "special" problems arise (CIMMYT Economics staff, 1980; Collinson, 1982; Simmonds, 1984). A Technical Advisory Committee (TAC) of the International Agricultural Research Centers in reviewing

Farming Systems Research at four centers concludes that "production economics is essential at all stages of farming systems" research while sociology and anthropology "should not be regarded as necessarily having an essential or permanent status." (CGIAR, 1978: 64) They may, however, have consultative roles. It may well be that the breadth and holism of anthropology potentially allows it to grasp more precisely than other disciplines the intricacies, interrelationships, and dynamics of local farming in developing countries. This perspective can be used in the identification and design of appropriate technologies and projects or to evaluate adoption and impact. Anthropology's problem is not the weakness of theory or methods but its voluntary or involuntary lack of contact and exposure to agricultural programs.

## THE FUTURE: WHERE TO FROM HERE?

Now that anthropology is beginning to have a voice, however minor, in agricultural research and development, it is crucial that positive steps are taken to ensure continued input of this perspective. Vernon Ruttan (1982: 42) argues that there would be a substantial payoff to increasing anthropology and sociology relative to economics at IRRI and ICRISAT.

> Anthropologists, in particular, have demonstrated a capacity to understand the dynamics of technology choice and impact at the household and village level that is highly complementary to both agronomic and economic research.

In this final section, I suggest some directions to channel anthropology toward a formal recognition of its agricultural orientation. First, the anthropological approach to agriculture needs a name, an identity. *Agricultural Anthropology* has been put forth as a possibility (Rhoades and Rhoades, 1980). This name is important not only to identify the anthropological specialization but to precisely communicate to our colleagues that our concern is agriculture. We *are* agricultural researchers. This name is not without precedence. Agricultural anthropologists approach agriculture through their specialized perspective just as agricultural economists approach agriculture through economics, agricultural engineers through engineering, and so on. Agricultural anthropology is roughly analogous to the European disciplines of agricultural geography (as recognized in Germany) or agricultural sociology (as recognized in the Netherlands).[16]

Agricultural anthropology is the comparative, holistic, and temporal study of the human element in agricultural activity, focusing on the interactions of ecology, technology, social structure, and ideology within local and broader farming environments, and with the practical goal of responsibly applying this knowledge to improve efficiency of food production. Agricultural anthropology views agriculture neither as a mere technical process nor even as techno-economic combination, but as a complex human creation and evolutionary process that includes equally important sociocultural and ideological components in interaction with one another and the natural environment. Agricultural anthropology is broader in scope than other agricultural disciplines which focus, and rightly so, on specialized and limited problems in agriculture (Rhoades and Rhoades, 1980).

Second, anthropology must continue to report on successful work, such as that at the International Potato Center or CIMMYT. More case studies are needed showing how and why anthropology has made a positive contribution to agricultural research and development projects. Without carefully documented cases, well-written, and directed toward our agricultural science colleagues, anthropology cannot claim the credibility it needs to achieve a permanent place in agricultural research. Even when anthropology functions as a critic of programs, it should be documented how anthropological input served to benefit the clients of agricultural research and hence the effectiveness of the research process. Anthropology should not be pushed for anthropology's sake, but because agricultural development and its clients can benefit from the anthropological perspective. Anthropologists must demonstrate why agricultural research and development needs anthropology. To accomplish this, continued and full-time involvement is needed. The use of internships, such as the Rockefeller Foundation postdoctoral program, is an appropriate and excellent immediate solution to the problem of exposure.

Institutions wishing to employ anthropologists and other social scientists in their programs might examine closer the case of the International Potato Center. Mentioned earlier in this chapter are some circumstantial and personality aspects that helped secure a role for anthropology at CIP. Anthropology, however, succeeded not simply because of "good people." The quality of anthropologists was a necessary but not sufficient cause of success. Other international centers had equally capable, if not superior, anthropologists. Additional factors underlying success are related to the CIP organization of research and leadership:

1. CIP is characterized by a built-in flexibility which allowed anthropologists to freely seek topics where their expertise might be utilized. Anthropologists were not brought in and mandated or assigned only the role, for example, of helping economists or agronomists to understand social factors surrounding their on-farm trials. Anthropologists at CIP can more or less define their own projects as long as they are relevant to the applied job at hand. In this regard, anthropology enjoys the kind of freedom that early economists in the CGIAR system experienced, an important factor in the later successes of economics (Ruttan, 1982: 309).

2. CIP is a problem-oriented international center more interested in applied results than with science *per se*. If it works, use it. Thus, anthropologists were given a chance as equal partners with economists and biological scientists in interdisciplinary team research. Also team research was clearly focused on a specific crop and subsystem within

potato agriculture. There was never the difficulty of the anthropologist wanting to "study everything in a few villages." Instead, research immediately centered on potato post-harvest technology (processing and storage), potato consumption, or varieties. Within these areas the anthropologist could, if desired, study "everything" as long as it related to potatoes, development, and improving technology.

3. CIP leadership also was aware of the richness of the social science disciplines other than economics. For this reason, CIP has the only Social Science Department (as opposed to economics) in the CGIAR system. Rural sociologist Dr. Gelia Castillo served on the CIP Board of Trustees since 1978 and when her board term ended she was its chairwoman.

These structural characteristics of organization combined with the personality and circumstantial events explain why anthropology at CIP has succeeded. The CIP case might provide insights for other agricultural organizations interested in incorporating the anthropological perspective into the design and generation of technology. If anthropology is viewed as a weaker sister in a service role to strictly economics programs, the chances of success are probably greatly reduced. Ruttan (1982: 309) in reflecting on the experiences of social sciences in agricultural research notes: "Where a social science staff has been cast in a purely service-oriented role, however, low staff morale and difficulty in retaining an effective social science capacity have tended to result."

Third, anthropology needs to shake stereotypes that follow the discipline. One major image problem, and not entirely unjustified, is that anthropologists concentrate on "traditional" aspects of farming to the neglect of the market or "modern" sector. The bias toward the noble savage living in permanent harmony with nature still affects the thinking of some anthropologists. Understandably, any new discipline in a multidisciplinary research institute will have an image problem. This is especially true of anthropology which means different things to different nationalities, if it means anything at all. Thus at CIP an Englishman asks, "What is a scientist who plays around with ancient bones in basement laboratories doing in agricultural research?" An American colleague asks, "What do monkey specialists have to do with an agricultural center?" Still other nationalities identify us with the study of remaining "exotic savages," who do not practice agriculture. Our thing should be headhunting, not agriculture. Even fellow social scientists hold stereotypic views of anthropologists. Unfortunately, all stereotypes carry some element of truth. Anthropologists have always had a flare for the popular so it is little wonder that outsiders think of us as students of the exotic, quaint, and outdated. The practical relevance is not always clear.

While anthropologists obviously need to sharpen their focus on agricultural problems, some criticisms against anthropology are less understandable. Anthropologists obviously commit sins, such as writing wordy reports and spending too much time in fieldwork. However, other agricultural scientists commit the same sins, albeit in different forms and less recognized. Any potato breeder will tell you it takes a minimum of ten years to breed a new variety. CIP's storage experiments have been going on for a decade (eight years of on-farm research in the same valley). Economists at the International Crops Research Institute for the Semi-Arid Tropics in India have been researching the same few villages for over a decade. Agricultural research under any disciplinary label is a time- consuming process. Anthropologists also do not have a copyright on lengthy reports. I learned this culling through over 400 technical documents on potato production, many of which contain thick reams of pages on agronomic or biological experiments that few people will ever read. It may be, however, that anthropologists and sociologists—in their minority roles—are more vulnerable to criticisms when they commit the common sins of agricultural science.

Fourth, anthropological methods are perceived as difficult to replicate and have not been clearly explained to our fellow scientists. It is often charged that the scientific method is not clearly followed, no set of working hypotheses can be noted. Research is site specific and descriptive. Since random sampling is sometimes not used, critics charge that valid generalizations cannot be drawn. Anthropologists' earlier tendency to play down quantification, statistical methods, and clearly articulated models continues to affect anthropology's credibility among agricultural scientists.

Anthropologists sometimes tend to view society as static and concentrate their research on small groups (villages, tribes) and ignore communities that are fully integrated into monetarized economics. Also anthropologists in the past have largely been concerned with reporting what exists or has existed, and have not developed models useful for predicting agricultural change. This, however, is not true of cultural ecological and economic anthropological studies of agriculture (Raintree, 1984). Methods used by anthropologists, nevertheless, need to be better explained and the obvious erroneous assumption that anthropologists do not use quantification should be corrected.[17]

Fifth, anthropologists need to create a formal framework, or at least incipient structures at several levels that will push the discipline forward. Anthropology needs to formally recognize its agricultural orientation. I suggest we need to operate on two fronts: (1) promotion of the field and continued demonstration of why agriculture needs anthropology; and (2) training anthropologists to qualify and compete as agricultural scientists.

An association or organization is needed that will function to promote the field and serve as organizational pivot for interested persons. One possible organization to spin this development is the U.S.-based Anthropological Study Group of Agrarian Systems (ASGAS). Its already excellent work might be further intensified, however, if ASGAS could broaden its membership to include more international members, especially from developing countries. In university training, agricultural anthropology needs its analogue to the now flourishing programs in medical and nutritional anthropology. Although over the long haul we may see some formal recognition of agricultural anthropology, this is unlikely to happen in the near future.

The most we can realistically hope for now are "bridger" programs between anthropology departments and agricultural schools. However, in the absence of established programs much can still be done to link agriculture and anthropology through degrees and coursework combinations. An agricultural degree (preferably a degree in a technical area) combined with a doctorate in anthropology would be highly applicable. Such dual professional status is extremely attractive to potential employers, especially those in agricultural development (see Rockefeller Foundation, 1978: 18–42 for more information on training of anthropologists for work in agriculture).

One positive fact is that agricultural organizations do not harbor the same elitist attitude toward degrees as do academic anthropology departments. Rather than being "name-school conscious" agricultural organizations tend to be more interested in an agricultural background (in the United States most likely obtained in a land-grant college or through practical experience) than a "prestigious" anthropology degree. In the United States, the best possibilities for studying agricultural anthropology are at the Universities of Arizona, Florida, or Kentucky. Regardless of university, the student will not necessarily benefit from a narrowly focused, traditional anthropology program. Although anthropology should not give up holism, shifts in study concentration may be appropriate. Instead of learning structural linguistics or the fossil record in detail, a student of agricultural anthropology could better meet his or her needs by comprehending the principles of agronomy or plant genetics. Clearly, agricultural anthropologists need to be capable of handling technical parts of agriculture.

At this early stage of anthropology's bid to become one of the agricultural sciences, no guarantees can be written for future employment. Presently, few anthropologists are employed or even specifically trained to work in agriculture-related jobs. Perhaps as many as a quarter million people work in agriculture for the USDA, USAID, international and national research centers, and FAO. The number of full-time anthropologists employed in agricultural jobs in all of these organizations could probably be counted on two hands.[18] For example, out of 736 senior scientists employed in 1983 in CGIAR, *three* are anthropologists. And CGIAR prides itself on the use of anthropologists and sociologists! This is, in my opinion, a professional tragedy. Still, given the present dismal employment opportunities with a "pure" anthropology degree, the backing of an agricultural degree will be useful on the job market.[19] What is certain is that many agricultural organizations are more receptive toward anthropologists than at any time since the 1930s.

Anthropologists who bemoan the increasing fragmentation of anthropology may find the proposal for another subdisciplinary specialization disconcerting. The university and "academically" oriented may feel that a call for the application of anthropology to planned agricultural change may violate the intellectual detachment needed for objective research. However, agricultural anthropology can be understood as both a research and an applied field, broad enough to accommodate all anthropologists who work on agricultural-related problems throughout the world. Pure research must be as central to agricultural anthropology as applied research. The methods should be flexible to match the complexity of the subject matter. And anthropologists need to fill gaps not covered by other disciplines, including economics. Anthropology's ability to deal in a solid way with the important technical, ecological, and socioeconomic aspects neglected by the other agricultural sciences will be our most valuable asset.

In conclusion, anthropology as a discipline has more than a century of direct experience in agriculture, and an intimate association with farmers in every corner of the globe. Work at the International Potato Center is an applied outgrowth of this history and empirically illustrates that anthropology can play an important role in agricultural research and development. It is now up to anthropologists to formally recognize their agricultural roots and aggressively but professionally become involved in agricultural research. Anthropologists only lack formal recognition of their long experience with farming peoples and the will to articulate their expertise to the non-anthropological world, especially to other agricultural scientists.

## Notes

1. In the United States, anthropology's main applied involvement was in the Bureau of Indian Affairs. The establishment of the Bureau of American Ethnology in 1879 gave anthropology a stronger legitimate applied role within the U.S. government but no projects were concerned with farm problems *per se*. Parallel to these developments, however, a subdiscipline of economics—farm management— was developing its own governmental bureaucracy in the United States which evolved into the Bureau of Agricultural Economics.

2. Burleigh Gardner, Solon Kimball, and John Province worked for the Soil Conservation Service. Carol Taylor, a rural sociologist, employed Horace Miner, Oscar Lewis, and Walter Goldschmidt (1947, 1978) to do community studies in several states for the Department of Agriculture (Werge, 1977: 6).

3. I am grateful to Jeffrey Jones for bringing this information to my attention.

4. For example, Mario Vasquez—a key figure in the Vicos project—served as Director General of Agrarian Reform and Rural Settlement from 1973-1976.

5. In commenting on an earlier version of this paper, economist Douglas Horton noted: "How many anthropologists wanted to participate in agricultural projects? I have always been struck by my anthropology colleagues' concern with academic independence, intellectual honesty and other pretensions of purity, always feeling apart from and superior to the technicians and agronomists. Was this the source of the isolation problem, or the result (sour grapes)? Of course, Bill Whyte, Holmberg, and Barnett, were early allies. And they have been accused by their more purist colleagues of "selling out."

6. I dislike using the term "non-economists." It is, however, a linguistic category widely used in agricultural research. Unfortunately, it masks over the economic (not necessarily neoclassical) orientation of many anthropologists and lumps together sociologists and anthropologists. In many respects, sociology and anthropology are more distinct than anthropology and economics or sociology and economics.

7. To my knowledge, six of the thirteen CGIAR international centers have utilized anthropologists. At least three have decided that anthropology was not

worth continuing on core funding. CIP and CIMMYT are the only centers to make a solid long-term commitment to anthropology.

8. William F. Whyte was adviser to both Horton and Mayer at Cornell.

9. This section is based in part on previously published materials by Rhoades et al. (1982), Rhoades and Booth (1982).

10. This information is based on personal communication from Dr. Werge. Interestingly, still today CIP economists and biological scientists each have their own version of the story. I expect this is inevitable in interdisciplinary research: each discipline interprets the problem in its own way and perhaps overstates or misstates the position of the other discipline. Professional "ethnocentrism" in agricultural development is still more powerful than we like to admit.

11. The special interest that Robert Werge had in training as a transfer mechanism cannot be underestimated. The post-harvest thrust has probably been the most aggressive in CIP in using training.

12. As noted by Bennett and Kanel (1981), farm management grew into the field of agriculture economics which, in light of developments of the American farming context, "became increasingly focused on the farm as a business enterprise operating in the larger milieu of a capitalist national economy. Since the farm economist is concerned with the enterprise, his data are devoted to minute specifications of income, costs, yields, taxes and depreciation."

13. This is especially true of British agricultural economics of the African farm management school. The way Collinson (1982) defines the role of the farming systems economist is very close to my definition of the anthropologist's role.

14. Redclift (n.d.: 31) has pointed out—I believe correctly so—that Farming Systems research as recently adopted by many international centers rests on principles long known by anthropologists. Anthropology therefore has much to offer this new holistic and exciting approach in terms of theory and methods.

15. This section is based in part on a general treatment by Harris (1971). Anthropological theory is discussed in basic terms for the convenience of non-anthropologists.

16. I am pleased to recently learn that in the Netherlands and Switzerland the term agroanthropologist is used.

17. This does not mean anthropologists should become enamored with empiricism for empiricism's sake. Agricultural reports already have enough statistics and numbers jerked out of their socioeconomic and time contexts to last for ages. A balanced approach is needed.

18. Van Dusseldorp (1977) estimates that out of every 1,000 permanent scientists in agricultural research centers only one is a sociologist or anthropologist.

19. At the University of Arizona, for example, two 1984 Ph.D. Anthropology graduates prepared themselves to work in food-related areas. One student received three job offers from international organizations while the other received a university-based research and teaching position. Cultural anthropology students who had no special training in agriculture did not fare so well.

# References

Almy, Susan W. "Anthropologists and Development Agencies." *American Anthropologist*, Vol. 79, 1977, pp. 280–292.

Almy, Susan W., personal communication, 1984.

Baker, D., E. Modiakgotta, D. Norman, J. Sierbert and M. Tjirongo. "Helping the Limited Resource Farmer Through the Farming Systems Approach to Research." *Culture and Agriculture*, Issue 19, Spring 1983, pp. 1-8.

Barlett, Peggy F. "Adaptive Strategies in Peasant Agricultural Production." *Annual Reviews of Anthropology*. Palo Alto, Calif.: Annual Reviews, Inc., 1980.

Beals, Alan. *Culture in Process.* New York: Holt, Rinehart, and Winston, 1973.

Benavides, M. and R. Rhoades. "Socioeconomic Conditions, Food Habits, and Formulated Food Programs in the *Pueblos Jovenes* of Lima, Peru. A Preliminary Study." (Unpublished) 1982.

Bennett, J. W. *Northern Plains: Adaptive Strategy on Agrarian Life."* Chicago: Aldine, 1969.

Bennett, J. W. "Anticipation, Adaptation, and the Concept of Culture in Anthropology." *Science*, Vol. 192, 1976, pp. 847-852.

Bennett J. and D. Kanel, "Agricultural Economics and Economic Anthropology: Confrontation and Accommodation." Preliminary undocumented draft prepared for oral presentation at Inaugural Conference of Society for Anthropological Economics, at Indiana University, April, 1981.

Bidegaray, P. "Agricultura en la Selva Peruana: El Caso de Yurimaguas." Lima: International Potato Center (manuscript) 1981.

Booth, R., R. Shaw, and A. Tupac-Yupanqui. "Use of Natural Diffused Light for the Storage of Seed Tubers," in W. J. Hooker, ed., *Research for the Potato in the Year 2000.* Lima: International Potato Center, 1983, pp. 65-66.

Brush, S. B., "The Myth of the Idle Peasant: Employment in a Subsistence Economy," in R. Halperin, J. Dow, eds., *Peasant Livelihood: Studies in Economic Anthropology and Cultural Ecology.* New York: St. Martins, 1977.

Brush, S., H. Carney, and Z. Huaman. "Dynamics of Andean Potato Agriculture." *Economic Botany*, Vol. 35, No. 1, 1981, pp. 70-88.

Byerlee, D., M. Collinson, R. Perrin, D. Winkelmann, S. Biggs, E. Moscardi, J. Martinez, L. Harrington, and A. Benjamin. "Planning Technologies Appropriate to Farmers—Concepts and Procedures." Mexico City: Centro Internacional de Mejoramiento de Maiz y Trigo, 1980.

Cancian, Frank. "Can Anthropology Help Agricultural Development?" *Culture and Agriculture*, No. 2, 1977, pp. 1-8.

CGIAR. "Farming Systems Research at the International Agricultural Research Centers." Rome: The Consultative Group on International Agricultural Research—Technical Advisory Committee, 1978.

Chagnon, N. *Yanomamo: The Fierce People.* New York: Holt, Rinehart and Winston, 1968.

CIMMYT Economics Staff, "Assessing Farmer Needs in Designing Agricultural Technology." IADS Occasional Paper, 1980.

Cole, John and Eric Wolf. *The Hidden Frontier: Ecology and Ethnicity in an Alpine Valley.* New York: Academic Press, 1974.

Collinson, M. P. "Farming Systems Research in Eastern Africa: The Experience of CIMMYT and Some National Agricultural Research Services, 1976-81." MSU International Development Paper No. 3. East Lansing, Michigan: Department of Agricultural Economics, Michigan State University, 1982.

Collinson, M. P. "A Low Cost Approach to Understanding Small Farmers." Agricultural Administration, Vol. 8, 1981.

Conklin, H. C. "An Ethnobotanical Approach to Shifting Agriculture." *Transactions of the New York Academy of Sciences*, Series 2, No. 17, 1954, pp. 133-142.

Conklin, H. C. "Hanunoo Agriculture in the Philippines." Forest Development Paper No. 12, Rome: FAO, 1957.

Consultative Group on International Agricultural Research (Technical Advisory Committee). *Report of the First TAC Quinquennial Review of the International Potato Center (CIP)*. Rome: TAC Secretariat, FAO, 1976.

Consultative Group on International Agricultural Research (Technical Advisory Committee). *Farming Systems Research at the International Agricultural Research Centers*. Rome: TAC Secretariat, FAO, 1978.

Consultative Group on International Agricultural Research. CGIAR Secretariat. Washington, D.C.: CGIAR Secretariat, 1980.

De Schilippe, Pierre. *Shifting Cultivation in Africa*. London: Routledge and Kegan Paul, 1956.

Dinkel, D. "Light-Induced Inhibition of Potato Tuber Sprouting." *Science*, Vol. 141, 1963, pp. 1047-8.

Dillon, J. L. and J. R. Anderson. "Concept and Practice of Farming Systems Research," in J. V. Martin, ed., *Proceedings of ACIAR Consultation on Agricultural Research in Eastern Africa*. Camberra: ACIAR. In press, 1984.

Doherty, V. S. "Human Nature and the Design of Agricultural Technology." Paper presented at Workshop on Socioeconomic Constraints to Development of Semi-Arid Tropical Agriculture." Hyderabad, India: ICRISAT. February 19-23, 1979.

Douglas, Mary. *Food as Art Form*. London: Studio International. 188, 969, 1974, pp. 83-88.

Dyson-Hudson, R. "Pastoralism: Self-image and Behavioral Reality," in W. Irons, and N. Dyson-Hudson, eds., *Perspectives on Nomadism*. Leiden, Netherlands: J. Brill, 1972, pp. 30-47.

Eastman, C. "Technological Change and Food Production: General Perspectives and the Specific Case of Potatoes." Social Science Department Special Publications. Lima: International Potato Center, 1977.

Fernandez, Angel. "Infraestructura para la Comercializacion del Producto Alimenticio Papa: Informe Preliminar." Lima: Editora Peruana, 1976.

Foster, G. *Applied Anthropology*. Boston: Little Brown and Company, 1969.

Flannery, K. V., "The Ecology of Food Production in Mesopotamia." *Science*, Vol. 147, 1965, pp. 1247-56.

Geertz, Clifford. *Agricultural Involution: The Process of Ecological Change in Indonesia*. Berkeley: University of California Press for the Association of Asian Studies, 1963.

Goldschmidt, Walter. *As you Sow*. New York: Harcourt Brace, 1947.

Goldschmidt, Walter. *As you Sow*. Three Studies in the Social Consequences of Agribusiness. Montclair, N.J.: Allanheld, Osmum, 1978.

Hall, Edward. *The Silent Language*. New York: Fawcett Publications, 1961.

Hall, Edward. *The Hidden Dimension*. Garden City, N.Y.: Doubleday, 1966.

Harris, Marvin. *Culture, Man, and Nature*. New York: Thomas Y. Crowell Company, 1971.

Harwood, Richard R. *Small Farm Development. Understanding and Improving Farming Systems in the Humid Tropics*. Boulder: Westview Press, 1979.

Hawkes, J. G. "On the Origin and Meaning of South American Indian Potato Names." *Journal of the Linnean Society* (Botany), Vol. 53, 1947, pp. 205-250.

Hildebrand, P. E. *Generating Technology for Traditional Farmers: A Multidisciplinary Methodology*. Asian Report No. 8, New Delhi: CIMMYT, 1978.

Holmberg, A., M. C. Vasquez, P. L. Doughty, J. O. Alers, H. F. Dobyns, and H. D. Lasswell. "The Vicos Case: Peasant Society in Transition." *The American Behavioral Scientist*, Vol. 8, No. 7 (special issue), 1965, pp. 3-33.

Holmberg A., H. Dobyns, C. Monge, M. C. Vasquez, and H. D. Lasswell. "Community and Regional Development: The Joint Cornell-Peru Experiment." *Human Organization*, Vol. 21, 1962, pp. 107–124.

Horton, D. *Potato Atlas*. Lima: International Potato Center, 1978.

Horton, D., *Social Scientists in Agricultural Research. The Mantaro Valley Project.* Ottawa: International Development Research Centre, 1984.

International Rice Research Institute, *Report of an Exploratory Workshop on: The Role of Anthropologists and Other Social Scientists in Interdisciplinary Teams Developing Improved Food Production Technology*. Los Banos, Laguna, The Philippines: IRRI, 1982.

Janik, J., R. Schery, F. Woods and V. Ruttan, eds. "Plant Agriculture." Readings from *Scientific American*. San Francisco: W. H. Freeman and Co., 1970.

Johnson, A. W. "Individuality and Experimentation in Traditional Agriculture." *Human Ecology*, Vol. 1, No. 2, 1972, pp. 43–47.

La Barre, W. "Potato Taxonomy Among the Aymara Indians of Bolivia." *Acta Americana*, Vol. 5, Nos. 1–2, 1947, pp. 83–103.

Loomis, Charles. "Applied Anthropology in Latin America." *Applied Anthropology*, Vol. 2, No. 2, 1943, pp. 33–35.

Mayer, Enrique. "Land-Use in the Andes: Ecology and Agriculture in the Mantaro Valley of Peru with Special Reference to Potatoes." Social Science Department Special Publication. Lima: International Potato Center, 1979.

Montgomery, E. and John W. Bennett. "Anthropological Studies of Food and Nutrition. The 1940s and the 1970s," in W. Goldschmidt, ed., *The Uses of Anthropology*. Washington, D.C.: American Anthropological Association, 1979.

Netting, Robert. "Agrarian Ecology." *Annual Review of Anthropology*, Vol. 3, 1974, pp. 21–56.

Newby, Howard. "Rural Sociology and its Relevance to the Agricultural Economist: A Review." *Journal of Agricultural Economics*, Vol. 33, No. 2, 1982, pp. 125–165.

Norman, D. W. "Farming System Approach: Relevancy for the Small Farmer." Rural Development Paper 5. East Lansing State University, Dept. of Agricultural Economics, 1980.

Poats, S. "Beyond the Farmer: Potato Consumption in the Tropics," in W. J. Hooker, ed., *Research for the Potato in the Year 2000*. Proceedings of the International Congress in Celebration of the Tenth Anniversary of the International Potato Center. Lima: International Potato Center, 1983, pp. 10–17.

Radcliffe-Brown, A. R. *Structure and Function in Primitive Society: Essays and Addresses*. London: Cohen and West, 1952.

Raintree, J. B. "Bioeconomic Considerations in the Design of Agroforestry Cropping Systems." *Plant Research and Agroforestry*. ICRAF Reprint 11. Nairobi: International Centre for Research on Agroforestry, 1984.

Recharte, Jorge. *Los Limites Socioecologicos del Crecimiento Agricola en la Ceja de Selva*. Pontificia Universidad Catolica del Peru. Thesis, 1981, pg. 208.

Redclift, Michael. "Production Programs for Small Farmers: Plan Puebla as Myth and Reality." *Economic Development and Cultural Change*, Vol. 31, No. 3, 1983, pp. 551–570.

Redfield, R. and W. Lloyd Warner. "Cultural Anthropology and Modern Agriculture in Farmers in a Changing World." *Yearbook of Agriculture 1940*. Washington, D.C.: U.S. Government Printing Office, 1940, pp. 983–993.

Reed, Charles A., ed. *Origins of Agriculture*. World Anthropology Series. Chicago: Aldine, 1977.

Rhoades, R. "The Art of the Informal Agricultural Survey." Social Science Training Document Series 1982-2. Lima: International Potato Center, 1982a.

Rhoades, R. "Follow-up of Transfer of CIP Processing Technology." (manuscript) 1982b.

Rhoades, R. "Changing a Post-harvest System: The Case of Diffused Light Stores in Sri Lanka." SSD Working Paper 1984-1. Lima: International Potato Center, 1984.

Rhoades, R. and R. Booth. "Farmer-Back-to-Farmer: A Model for Generating Acceptable Agricultural Technology." *Agricultural Administration*, Vol. 11, 1982, pp. 127-137.

Rhoades, R. and R. Booth, "Interdisciplinary Teams in Agriculture Research and Development." *Culture and Agriculture*, Issue 20, Summer 1983, pp. 1-7.

Rhoades, R. and V. Rhoades. "Agricultural Anthropology: A Call for the Establishment of a New Professional Speciality." *Practicing Anthropology*, Vol. 2, No. 4, 1980, pp. 10-12 and 28.

Rhoades, R., R. Booth, and M. Potts. "Farmer Acceptance of Improved Potato Storage Practices in Developing Countries." *Outlook on Agriculture*, Vol. 12, No. 1, 1983, pp. 12-16.

Rhoades, R., R. Booth, R. Shaw, and R. Werge. "Interdisciplinary Development and Transfer of Post-harvest Technology at the International Potato Center," in International Rice Research Institute's *Report of an Exploratory Workshop on: The Role of Anthropologists and Other Social Scientists in Interdisciplinary Teams Developing Improved Food Production Technology*. Los Banos, Laguna, The Philippines, 1982, pp. 1-8.

Rhoades, R., R. Booth, F. Rutab, O. Sano, and L. J. Harmsworth. "The Acceptance of Improved Potato Storage Practices by Philippine Farmers: A Preliminary Study." Mimeograph. Lima: The International Potato Center, 1979.

Rhoades, R., D. Horton, and R. Booth. "Anthropologist, Economist, and Biological Scientist: The Three Stooges or Three Musketeers of Farming Systems Research?" Paper presented in Symposium: Farming Systems Research: The Integration of Social and Biological Approaches for Agricultural Development. American Anthropological Association Annual Meetings, November 15-19, 1984, Denver.

Rockefeller Foundation, "Society, Culture, and Agriculture." Working Paper. Workshop on Training Programs Combining Anthropology and Sociology with the Agricultural Sciences. New York: Rockefeller Foundation, 1978.

Ruttan, Vernon. *Agricultural Research Policy*. Minneapolis: University of Minnesota Press, 1982.

Ryan, James G. "Comment: Technology for Semiarid Northeast Brazil." *Economics and the Design of Small Farmer Technology*. Ames: Iowa State University Press (First Edition), 1979, pp. 119-121.

Sawyer, Richard. "Forward," in R. Rhoades, *Breaking New Ground: Anthropologists in Agricultural Research*. Lima: International Potato Center, 1984.

Shaw, Roy. Personal communication, 1979.

Simmonds, N. W. "The State of the Art of Farming Systems Research." Report to the World Bank, Agricultural and Rural Development. Washington, D.C.: The World Bank, 1984.

Simpson, S. "Anthropologist and Economist: Partners in Regional Development." Paper presented at the Annual Meeting of the Society for Applied Anthropology as part of the Symposium, "Cultural Problems and Ethical Issues in Regional Development," 1978.

Stein, W. *Hualcani: Life in the Highlands of Peru.* Ithaca: Cornell University Press, 1961.

Thurow, Lester C. "Economics, 1977." *Daedalus.* Fall 1977, pp. 79–94.

Tripp, Robert. "Anthropology and On-Farm Research." Unpublished manuscript. Mexico City: Centro Internacional de Mejoramiento de Maiz y Trigo, 1984.

Tupac, Yupanqui, A. L. *Aspectos Fisiologicos del Almacenamiento de Tuberculos— Semilla de Papa: Influencia de la Temperatura y la Luz.* Tesis. Lima: Universidad Nacional Agraria, La Molina, 1978.

Tylor, Edward B. *Primitive Culture: Researches into the Development of Mythology, Philosophy, Religion, Language, Art and Custom.* London: J. Murray, 1871.

Van Dusseldorp, D. B. W. M. "Some Thoughts on the Role of Social Sciences in the Agricultural Research Centers in Developing Countries." *Netherland Journal of Agricultural Sciences,* Vol. 25, 1977, pp. 213–228.

Vierich, Helga "Accomodation or Participation? Communication Problems." in Peter Matlon, et al., eds., *Coming Full Circle.* Ottawa: International Development Research Centre, 1984.

Werge, R. "Anthropology and Agricultural Research: The Case of Potato Anthropology." Lima: International Potato Center, 1977a.

Werge, R. "Potato Storage Systems in the Mantaro Valley Region of Peru." Lima: International Potato Center, 1977b.

Werge, R. "Social Science Training for Regional Agricultural Development." Paper presented at the Meetings of the Society for Applied Anthropology, Merida, Mexico, April 2–9, 1978.

Werge, R. "Potato Processing in the Central Highlands of Peru." *Ecology of Food and Nutrition,* Vol. 7, 1979, pp. 229–234.

Werge, R. "Potatoes, Peasants and Development Projects: A Sociocultural Perspective from the Andes." (unpublished) 1980.

Whyte, W. F. "Seed Production Systems: Notes for a Columbia Project." (unpublished) 1977.

Whyte, W. F. Personal communication, 1984.

Wolf, Eric *Anthropology.* Englewood Cliffs: Prentice-Hall, 1964.

# 4

# Problems and Perspectives in Development Anthropology: The Short-Term Assignment

*Edward Robins*

In 1981 I spent six weeks in Southeast Asia on a preliminary investigation of the social impact of rice intensification in Indonesia. For five weeks I traveled in East and Central Java, Bali, and West Sumatra after having briefly visited the International Rice Research Institute in the Philippines. The objectives of this *tournée* were limited and clearly defined: I would stop at the offices of FAO, the Rockefeller Foundation, the Ford Foundation, USAID, universities, and research institutes; I would meet with sociologists and anthropologists, economists, agronomists, political scientists, demographers, and public health officers; I would visit villages, in the company of Indonesian anthropologists, and speak with farmers; I would identify the issues related to agricultural development and social change in Indonesia, and report on them to the International Development Programs Center at the University of Wisconsin–River Falls, and to USAID. The lessons of this experience constitute a base from which most of this chapter is drawn, and are applicable more generally to the short-term assignment in development anthropology. The experiences I describe will be familiar to others, for they inhere in cross-cultural encounters of brief duration.

The role of the anthropologist in development programs largely has been to elucidate local sociocultural dynamics in an effort to render technical assistance programs more compatible with the local milieu. Ordinarily the anthropologist who lives and works among villagers knows them and the substance of their lives better than do the other members of the development team. The anthropologist strives both to promote a fit between the technological and social systems, and to represent to each of the parties collaborating in the program the views of the others. By tying together thus the assistance agency, the local group, and the host country government, the anthropologist acts as a culture broker. Translating from the idiom of one group to another is a process encumbered by the usual differences in perspectives, interests, value systems, and so forth. The skillful manipulation of conflicting, or at minimum, different interests is difficult even under the best of circumstances, viz., wherein the anthropologist knows well the individuals and the agencies in question. The short-term assignment asks of the anthropologist this mediation, but does not afford him/her the time needed to make the role credible. Where the anthropologist has worked previously in a country the difficulty may be mitigated some; for the newly arrived anthropologist, the challenge to fulfill expectations in the absence of the chance to lay groundwork is presented full bloom.

The perspectives the different members of the donor assistance team bring to the task before them likewise reflects various interests and approaches, and likewise enlists the anthropologist as mediator. As there is little time available and much to do, the skill of the development anthropologist is measured in the quality of the communication which evolves among team members, target communities, and government. It is quite likely that the anthropologist will be the only team member who regularly asks how the villagers and host country officials view the issue at hand, and depending upon his/her diplomacy and the sensitivity of the other members of the team, he/she may be seen as an antagonist, a necessary evil, or a genuine asset. In whichever capacity, the work is soon to be done; the members of the team may never work again together (the reputations of each one, however, will long live on). Under such conditions, where time is limited and the task is formidable, the development anthropologist makes, or does not make, a contribution.

The fact-finding mission I undertook in Indonesia was an opportunity to become better acquainted with the development milieu by way of tapping the experiences of professionals working in it. The extent to which I was dependent upon their views was both a strength and a weakness of my approach. By choosing issues which they recognized as significant, I was quickly educated to much that was current in the development effort in Indonesia. This element of short-term work, these interviews with in-country professionals, are fundamental and often fruitful. There is, however, a hazard inherent in going to such sources: their interpretation of issues, and their interpretation of you, the interviewer/researcher, influences much of what you will be told. This is in no way a problem unique to short-term assignments. Rather in this situation the researcher lacks the time to develop the familiarity needed to easily distinguish fact from fancy, and so is particularly exposed to the intimacies of the "polite" respondent. In initial interviews this can be particularly troublesome; with time and increased contact, fictions are more readily detected. It is helpful if many interviews are undertaken in the first days. These serve to orient the visitor, to reveal particularly useful sources to whom one can return later with thorny issues, and to furnish basic data from which more meaningful questions can be asked in subsequent sessions. It might be added that no methodological manual, no amount of counsel is a substitute for the personal judgment the anthropologist must ultimately rely upon. The especially personal, interpretive method employed by anthropologists is at least as much art as science, and experience and good sense are the researcher's most trusted allies. Anthropologists put in long field tours early in their careers, and in so doing gain experience difficult to come by in the short-term. It is their good fortune to have this behind them when they venture into development.

The language in which the interview is conducted is yet another element in the data collection effort which is more problematical in the short-term assignment than in longer tours. The discussions I had at Indonesian universities and research institutes were conducted in English, not uncommonly spoken by the educated throughout the developing world. When in villages I was assisted by an Indonesian interpreter, more often than not an anthropologist himself. I relied upon his translations. In the preferred situation the researcher already speaks the indigenous language; there are many anthropologists who would fit the bill in Indonesia. Knowledge of the official language is not sufficient for the development professional, however, who specializes in a relatively large geographical area and needs to speak a *lingua franca*. In my current assignment in Rwanda, French is necessary. The French language capability will permit me to work in any of the many francophone countries in Africa, interviewing the educated, the successful, the well-placed (mostly English speakers, in fact!). It will not, however, permit me to speak with 95 percent of the Rwandans. I still work with an interpreter. If I spoke Kinyarwanda I could converse directly with farmers, in principle. Yet I would not be permitted on the farm in the absence of an "official" Rwandan, someone to stamp an approval on the encounter. There is no denying the fundamental value in speaking the local language, but in Rwanda at least it is illusory to believe that language is the sole barrier which keeps outsiders and Rwandans apart. The presence of a Rwandan from the ministry or regional government sanctions the exchange; whether peasants fear more the city official than they do the foreigner is something yet to be demonstrated in this country. Thus the interpreter is a double-edged sword. His/her presence may inhibit or otherwise disturb the farmer, but it is nonetheless essential. In the absence of sufficient time to build rapport with local leaders and rural dwellers, the anthropologist must depend upon the skills and insights of his/her assistants. This is more a difference of degree than kind when compared to longer field tours. The information gained in the interview is understood in the context of other interviews, and other information. One should "make sense" of the deluge of input. So much for the anthropologist who tries not to make assumptions, for our "sense" may not be their "sense." In the short-term we cannot afford the luxury of denying our own inclinations. We need to get the work done. Under the best of circumstances our efforts to understand one another may betray us. In the short-term assignment all input is valuable and one is encouraged to collect it in whatever language suits the occasion. If a professional, say another anthropologist, can be an advisor, so much the better.

I have found that the reaction elicited by a respondent's comment is something in which people often take great delight. Extreme points of view may be spoken more to shock than to inform. The vehement critic may be a malcontent, a maverick, or a voice speaking out against repression. One doesn't always know, and one doesn't always have the time to find out. When widespread, the critical perspective constitutes an essential description of the process the anthropologist is investigating. In general I have found criticisms of the status quo to be a valuable aid in identifying the shortcomings of programs and policies. Ordinarily there are features of programs which are unacceptable to some people; discovering what these are underscores the role of interest groups in social systems. Substantiating criticism is essential though. There are people in power who are likely to be antagonized by it.

The opposite experience in which support is advanced on behalf of a policy should not be dismissed for its banality. Current or official doctrine may be so revealed and this too is of value to the anthropologist.

The intimacy between the anthropologist and particular members of the community ordinarily permits the anthropologist to acquire the detailed and hidden pieces of which people's lives are made. A fundamental strength of the discipline derives from this arrangement. For me, familiarity helps to guide my field sense, my "intuition." Short-term assignments end before this sense can be sufficiently developed. The anthropologist works with pieces of the social system, and furnishes an analysis from a less than complete set of parts. Despite making a mockery of "holism," this endeavor is of value. A deadline is a solid motivater, and the task before the anthropologist is to make sense quickly and reliably. Although this entails cutting corners, it too is different from longer field tours in degree more than in kind. Just as in other field situations, conclusions which cannot be drawn from incomplete data should not be. Additional research should be called for, in this instance during project implementation, to fill gaps in our knowledge. I have done this regularly, for each design or evaluation asks more of the investigator than can be provided in four to six weeks.

Whether one chooses to restrict the focus of investigation, as I did after a time in Indonesia, or to investigate a number of topics, but each one in less detail, as I do in Rwanda, adaptation to the time constraint is essential. In Rwanda, where I will be working for three years, the sum total of my work on different projects will enable me to put together a more complete picture of Rwandan society despite the rush to quickly design a particular project or program.

The problems which arise as a result of travel are particularly severe in the short-term. Travel in developing countries is time-consuming, fatiguing, and threatening to the health and safety of the visitor/researcher. In the six weeks I spent in Southeast Asia, I visited more than two dozen cities, villages and towns, and fought the effects of fatigue, diet, and climate throughout. The importance of being in good physical condition before and during the field assignment should not be underestimated. Each of us reacts differently to changes in climate and diet, and the routines we idiosyncratically follow in the field, bizarre by some standards no doubt, ought to promote our own welfare under trying circumstances. The level of tolerance among expatriates in matters relating to health are, of necessity, quite liberal. Those habits which keep the fieldworker working are the ones to follow. Whether one eats only well-cooked food, avoids salads at all costs, and drinks nothing but bottled or filtered liquids, or "goes native" and eats and drinks with a local clientele, the condition of the fieldworker in the end is what matters. It should be kept in mind that there is not much time for experimentation in the short-term. An incapacitating illness in the first week might not be remedied before the assignment ends. If the work isn't completed, the reason why will not be well-received.

The danger of travel in the Third World is more problematical. There are numerous road hazards: pedestrians, livestock, poorly marked roads, roads in varying states of disrepair or disintegration, contemptuous weather (and few if any weather reports), and most frightening, incompetent drivers. The safest bet when on the road is to place oneself at the mercy of a reliable, safe driver. My experience with AID drivers has been good, mostly. As a new arrival in town, it is helpful to discuss in advance the groundrules with the driver: destination, approximate travel time, road conditions, availability of restaurants and toilets, and so forth. It is a mistake, while en route, not to tell the driver to slow down or not to pass on turns if these threaten the safety of the occupants of the vehicle. One shouldn't be inhibited in these matters. Consider the alternative.

One of the legacies of colonialism in developing countries is a resentment of expatriates, and particularly advisors, who in assuming the superior position of the counsellor, are reminders of the detested subjugation of the past. This problem was pronounced in Indonesia; a variation on the theme occurs in Rwanda. International technical assistance in the 1980s, in the minds of some, continues to promote the dependence of developing nations upon former colonialists. These nations are economically bound to donors. The large number of expatriate advisors in the ministries makes even the local administration of local affairs less real than apparent. In Indonesia there was considerable resentment of the advice proffered by advisors. "Indonesians listen politely, and then do what they want." I heard that refrain repeatedly. Inevitably the expatriates responded in kind and spoke of the unreliability, the incompetence, the insincerity of Indonesians. This is classic ethnocentrism, and its identification falls to the anthropologist. He/she must attempt to promote communication among the antagonists for pragmatic reasons. It is not merely that ethnocentrism is "wrong," but rather that particular differences of opinion must be resolved in particular ways to the benefit of goals held in common. The resentment I have observed in Rwanda stems more from the insensitivity of short-term advisors. They *tell* Rwandans what to do before they *ask* them about their activities and guidelines. More than once I have gone to the ministry after the departure of a technical team to discuss the relative merits of the points they had raised in meetings in their heavy-handed way, and to make amends. The anthropologist who can persuade other short-term advisors to learn the local lessons *before* making proposals of their own will do development a great service. But the approach must be made diplomatically, emphasizing the pragmatic. The anthropologist can too easily be dismissed as an advocate and not taken seriously. Once estranged from other advisors, the impact of the anthropologist's contribution is minimized.

A final issue relates broadly to the expectations that donor agencies and to a lesser extent host countries have of the recommendations presented by anthropologists. Forecasting the social impact of projects is risky business. Since the USAID New Directions legislation in 1974, anthropologists and sociologists increasingly have participated in project design and evaluation, assessing the social soundness of programs. Unrealistic expectations of what these analyses can accomplish can lead to disillusionment with the social soundness component, not to mention the individuals who formulate it. Knowing what *is* happening in the target community is no guarantee of knowing what *will* happen. That anthropologists should understand local sociocultural dynamics is a reasonable expectation; that they are capable as well of knowing in advance the consequences of planned change is another matter entirely. What the anthropologist has to offer is an assessment of the fit between the program and the people. It is within the mandate of the anthropologist to propose programmatic changes if need be. These are unquestionably aimed at promoting change in the community. But there is no equation that can tell us in advance what will happen once our program is implemented. Significant change often is unrepeatable and unpredictable (see Heinen, 1980). This issue is particularly pronounced in applied anthropology, yet is fundamental to the discipline as a whole.

Gould (1982: 12) has remarked that "sciences which deal with objects less complex and less historically bound than life," are monolithic, based on regularity, repetition, and predictability. Organisms, he says, are "directed and limited by their past. They must remain imperfect in their form and function, and to that extent unpredictable." Shweder (1980: 306) has argued that predicting behavior requires the researcher to engage in the "unparsimonious proliferation of context-dependent insights." This is not so much difficult as cumbersome. "One can predict anything," he states (1980: 307), "with enough prior information."

For anthropologists working in the short-term the critical question is: what is the trade-off between thoroughness and the time element? The shorter the assignment the bigger the guess? If one is into guessing, that may well be true. By calling for additional investigation however during the subsequent project phase, the anticipated consequences of planned change can be presented as possibilities, as hypotheses, and the dynamics of social systems respected. It is worthwhile emphasizing that anthropologists themselves adapt to the constraints of the development environment. Familiarity with other projects and programs, the considerable literature on development, and the perceptions of in-country professionals are all critical factors in making social assessments. It is the anthropologist more so than any of the other development professionals who possess the expertise to make reasonable projections about the consequences of induced change, and we must not be reluctant to meet that challenge.

There are a number of studies of Indonesian societies which have highlighted the unforeseen and often undesirable consequences of planned change (see for example: Birowo and Hansen, 1981; Prabowo and Sajogyo, 1981; White, 1978; Sinaga, et al., 1977). If we assume for the moment that the deterioration in the welfare of the rural poor in Indonesia under the impact of "progress" was unintentional (that it may not have been is truly a disturbing consideration), we can illustrate how the behavioral "uncertainty principle" can be invoked to "account for" unanticipated impact.

The condition of the rural poor in Indonesia has steadily deteriorated as a result of rice intensification, in sociopolitical and economic terms. The capitalization of agriculture has increased the gap between the elite minority and the poor majority, and given powerful political clout to the wealthy few. It is now unlikely that the status of the poor will much improve in the foreseeable future (see Utami and Ihalauw, 1978, for a discussion of the process by which capitalized agriculture has undermined the traditional cooperative base of the Javanese village). An awareness of the operation of this process in Indonesia permits us to anticipate its occurrence elsewhere. We can act before the fact by sensitizing the donor, the host country, and other members of the project team to impact of this kind. There are real questions at present about the philosophy of development advanced by donors, about the direction in which programs are moving, and whether the *adoption* of interventions by a select local element takes priority over the *equitable distribution* of benefits. This shift away from the bottom-up approach, away from addressing the needs of the poor directly, should not signal the abandonment of aid to the poor as a fundamental goal and component of social soundness. The anthropologist who is charged with assessing impact and who previews inequities cannot endorse policy detrimental to the welfare of the majority regardless of the philosophy which guides development programs at present.

The capital intensive approach to agriculture which has been employed in the rice intensification effort in Java has favored farmers who sell their standing crop to middlemen as a means of financing expensive inputs (the *tebasan* system). Village labor, consisting largely of landless peasants habitually engaged to harvest the crop, is displaced by this entreprenurial approach to agriculture. As the system of patronage and reciprocity which had prevailed in Indonesia no longer provides economic security for the poorest of the poor, small farmers and landless laborers lose traditional prerogatives and bargaining power. Their position erodes. They lose ground to the powerful and wealthy. Farmers who borrow to finance inputs sink further into debt, ultimately selling their farms. They are enlisted into the corps of the rural landless, powerless and dependent. This largely "unforeseen" consequence of rice intensification is the very phenomenon anthropologists seek to identify when previewing impact. It may not have been previewed in Indonesia, given the failure there to undertake social surveys in advance

of promoting interventions; it certainly would be considered a likely occurrence at present, however, what with the experience of failed projects
behind us.

This insidious process in Indonesia is most apparent in Java. In the
absence of strong extended family ties and other social arrangements to
bind villagers together in a network of reciprocal obligation and responsibility,
the poor majority in rural Java have suffered from the harsh reality of
capital intensive agriculture more so than, say, the Balinese. Unilineal descent
groups and other mutual-assistance associations have mediated change in
Bali, and it has been less disruptive there. In one Balinese village I witnessed
the rigorous efforts of a women's cooperative collecting and transporting
sand to a cement factory. Descending the bank of the river, a woman would
fill her basket, place it on her head, and climb to the road to unload it.
These women who had depended upon work at the harvest before rice
intensification reduced the need for their labor reapplied their cooperative
effort to a new activity and remained gainfully employed in the process.
Elsewhere in Bali I spoke with farmers and community leaders who had
devised a system of intra-village assistance, essentially a "teach and visit"
internal extension program, in which the more progressive farmers instructed
and counselled others. The imposition by the village council of a policy
defining agricultural procedure for rice intensification guided the development
of the village as a whole. Rice yields were reported to be as high as 14
tons per hectare for the period preceding my visit. The increased revenue
generated from the sale of rice had been applied to the improvement of
village roads, schools, and administration buildings.

Whether or not these instances of social change in Bali represent isolated
cases in the more characteristic pattern noted in Java, and there is some
indication that they do (see Poffenberger and Zurbuchen, 1980), for the
anthropologist the lesson remains: familiarity with the process of social
change can guide the forecast of impact despite the expectation of the
unexpected. The social surveys which were not undertaken in Indonesia
prior to rice intensification, and which would have identified the negative
impact of capitalized agriculture, are precisely what the anthropologist
promotes. These and the other tools of the anthropologist's trade do not
make mystics of analysts, but the reverse. If the conditions in Indonesia
caused by rice intensification persist unchanged, agricultural development
in general and all who are associated with it will have a bad name. The
expectation of vanquished poverty and hunger which the Green Revolution
falsely instilled is succeeded now by disillusionment with socially insensitive
high-tech programs. Anthropologists must be cognizant of the lessons of
failed projects, incorporating them into the design of new ones. Identifying
the consequences of applied change is an intriguing challenge for the social
sciences, but it must not mask the much more serious and fundamental
issue which is stated in human terms: the social impact of new technology
can be devastating. It is the human element with which the anthropologist
is preoccupied, and which he/she is responsible for elucidating in development.

As a member of the development team the anthropologist affects a compromise among conflicting parties, among conflicting interests. Insofar as detrimental policy is not endorsed, the anthropologist may exercise skill in bringing together individuals and groups who, by dint of cultural background, professional expertise, or self-interest are otherwise inclined to promote and defend their own ground. The role is unique but not unfamiliar to the anthropologist: the go-between, the interpreter, the translator. The fundamental need to plan change with the interests of the majority clearly in mind sets the challenge for anthropology. The social dynamics of development must be elucidated. There is no one, to my knowledge, who does not fail at times to misconstrue the unfolding of development, nor to be surprised by it. It is an undisciplined and rebellious process, and we attempt to catch hold of it in fits and starts. We work under a considerable time constraint. We are asked to see what has not yet occurred. For the anthropologist the expectations of others may be the most debilitating handicap of all. Yet who is more prepared to face this challenge? The anthropologist may spend a career, a lifetime, on the margin of culture. Having one's motives and perspectives poorly understood (to say nothing of the "theoretical bankruptcy" we are alleged to suffer from), or merely misjudged by members of one's own culture as well as others, is to be expected. Intimacy with one's place on the fringe is what the professional strives to attain. What I am primarily recommending is a mixture of good sense—anthropological and otherwise; tact in dealing with others; patience with the inevitable breakdowns with people, processes, and things; a goal-oriented spirit to overcome real or apparent conflicts of interest; and confidence that one can do a competent job given the framework within which one must operate and when the anthropologist may be in no position to alter the job.

## References

Birowo, Achmad T. and Gary E. Hansen. "Agricultural and Rural Development: An Overview," in Gary E. Hansen, ed., *Agricultural and Rural Development in Indonesia*. Boulder: Westview Press, 1981, pp. 1–27.

Gould, S. J.. "This View of Life." *Natural History*, Vol. 91, No. 9, 1982, p. 12.

Heinen, H. Dieter. "Comments." *Current Anthropology*, Vol. 21, No. 4, 1980, pp. 453–454.

Poffenberger, Marc and Mary S. Zurbuchen. "The Economics of Village Bali: Three Perspectives." *Economic Development and Cultural Change*, 1980, pp. 91–133.

Prabowo, Dibyo and Sajogyo. "Sidarjo, East Java and Subang, West Java," in Gary E. Hansen, ed., *Agricultural and Rural Development in Indonesia*. Boulder: Westview Press, 1981, pp. 68–78.

Shweder, Richard A.. "Rethinking Culture and Personality." *Ethos*, Vol. 4, 1980, pp. 255–310.

Sinaga, Rudolf, Abunawan Mintoro, Yusuf Saefudin, and Benjamin White. "Rural Institutions Serving Small Farmers and Laborers." *Rural Dynamic Series No. 1*, Agro-Economic Survey, Bogor, 1977.

Utami, Widya and John Ihalauw. "The Relation of Farm Size to Production, Land Tenure, Marketing, and Social Structure–Central Java." in *Changes in Rice Farming in Selected Areas of Asia*. Los Banos, The Philippines: International Rice Research Institute, 1978, pp. 129–140.

White, Benjamin. "Political Aspects of Poverty, Income Distribution, and Their Measurement: Some Examples from Rural Java." *Rural Dynamics Series No. 5*, Agro-Economic Survey, Bogor, 1978.

## Additional Sources

Astika, Ketut Sudana. "Social and Economic Effects of New Rice Technology: The Case of Abiansemel, Bali." *PRISMA, Indonesian Journal of Social and Economic Affairs*, No. 10, Jakarta, 1978, pp. 47–56.

Collier, William. "Agricultural Evolution in Java." Institute for Population Studies, Yogyakarta: Gadjah Mada University, 1976.

Deuster, Paul. "West Sumatra and South Sulawesi," in Gary E. Hansen, ed., *Agricultural and Rural Development in Indonesia*. Boulder: Westview Press, 1981, pp. 79–94.

Franke, Richard W.. "Miracle Seeds and Shattered Dreams in Java." *Natural History*, January 1974.

Geertz, Clifford. *Agricultural Involution*. Berkeley: University of California Press, 1963.

Hansen, Gary E. *Agricultural and Rural Development in Indonesia*. Boulder: Westview Press, 1981.

Ihalauw, John and Widya Utami. "Klaten, Central Java," in *Changes in Rice Farming in Selected Areas of Asia*. Los Banos, The Philippines: International Rice Research Institute, 1975, pp. 149–177.

Kahn, J. S.. "Tradition, Matriliny and Change Among the Minangkabau of Indonesia." *Bigdragen Tot Ne Taal-,Land-En Volkenkunde*, Vol. 132, 1976, pp. 64–95.

Naim, Mochtar, *Merantau: Minangkabau Voluntary Migration*. Singapore: University of Singapore, 1974.

Peacock, James. *Indonesia: An Anthropological Perspective*. Pacific Palisades: Goodyear Publishing Company, 1973.

White, Benjamin. "Population, Involution, and Employment in Rural Java," in Gary E. Hansen, ed., *Agricultural and Rural Development in Indonesia*. Boulder: Westview Press, 1981, pp. 130–146.

Widodo, Sri, Nasrullah, and Hidajat Nataatmadja. "Rice and Indonesian Agriculture," in *Farm-Level Constraints to High Rice Yields in Asia: 1974–1977*, Los Banos, The Philippines: International Rice Research Institute, 1979, pp. 85–96.

World Bank Survey. *Employment and Income Distribution in Indonesia*. Washington, D.C.: The World Bank, 1980

# 5

# A Short-Term Consultancy in Bangladesh

*Edward C. Green*

*January 18, 1985*

En route from Johannesburg to Athens on Olympic Airways. A rather funky flight, full of Greek merchants and their families who have migrated to South Africa and seem to now be visiting the old country. When the seat belt sign first went off, I was the first to jump out of my assigned seat and grab an empty row of three seats in order to stretch out horizontally. In fact I was the only passenger to do this. Another pushy American.

I don't know too much about the job in Bangladesh, but I feel moderately confident. Less than five years ago I was on my way to Sudan on my first international consulting assignment feeling totally inexperienced and inadequate for the job. Now, going over some of the briefing materials Washington sent me, I see mention of some of my own applied research in Swaziland.

Most important of all right now is that after my dinner of souvlaki and grape leaves, I can stretch my cramped body out on three whole seats. What luxury! Presumably Olympic Airlines hasn't figured out how to fill every seat by targeting odd segments of the population and offering irresistible deals, such as 60 percent off regular price for Macedonian shepherds who pay 30 days in advance.

A telex was waiting for me at the Jan Smuts Airport in Johannesburg informing me that the Athens-Dhaka flight turns out to be full, but they've put me on the waiting list. So much for my travel agent's assurances in Swaziland that nobody travels from Greece to Bangladesh at this time of year. The telex advises that I not despair, because I'm almost sure to be able to catch another flight from Athens that will get me to Dhaka after a day and a half detour to Jidda, Saudi Arabia. Let it happen.

This first appeared in *American Anthropologist*, Vol. 88, No. 1, March 1986.

*January 14*

En route from Athens to Dhaka on Bangladesh Airways. No trouble getting on the flight; in fact it's only half-full.

I spent most of today walking around the Flea Market and other parts of touristy Athens. Southern Europe is just beginning to emerge from the coldest winter in memory. Today it became warm enough to sit at a sidewalk cafe and pose as a world-weary international playboy.

A couple of uneventful hours went by during which I reviewed the nature of my assignment in Bangladesh. All I know is what was contained in a couple of telexes from AID/Bangladesh that were photocopied for me in Washington: a medical anthropologist is specifically requested (how often does that happen?) to evaluate beliefs, behavior, and attitudes relating to childhood diarrhea and use of oral rehydration salts (ORS). AID is planning to add ORS as a product line in the Bangladesh Social Marketing Project, which has been successfully marketing contraceptives for over a decade. The basic idea of social marketing is to use Madison Avenue marketing techniques to achieve socially desirable goals, such as reduced population growth or reduced infant mortality through adoption of ORS. Good thing I went to a social marketing conference in Washington last month. I'm up on the latest approaches.

*January 20*

No one to meet me at the airport, but at least they've put me up at a five-star hotel. It seems my assigned partner, a consultant from Washington, whom I haven't met, missed his connection. Anyway he's not here, and there are no messages.

I rested for an hour then took a taxi down to the AID office to learn more about my assignment from the population and health officer. I learned from him that I'm expected to assess the feasibility of social marketing ORS and to design some qualitative research to guide an ORS education and communication program. I know this is just the job for a medical anthropologist, but how did they know?

There's a curious poster on the AID office walls that advises: **If you catch fire, fall and roll!** Maybe this job is more dangerous than they're letting on.

Back in my luxury room just before dinner. The hotel was just opened a couple of years ago. It was built in the middle of one of the worst slums in Dhaka, a good part of which was bulldozed and concreted over to make room for the hotel. But some of the old shantytown remains. From my window on the fourth floor I have an excellent view of the hotel's 40 meter swimming pool, health club, snack bar, and outdoor bar. Blocked from the guests' view by a high wall (but visible to me on the fourth floor) are little shacks propped on stilts and poised precariously over mud flats. Each shack seems to have many residents. I wonder if such extremes of wealth and poverty are found so close together anywhere else.

Talk about nonobtrusive research methods—I can observe most aspects of life in this shantytown from my vantage point, including cooking, washing, and toilet behavior. An anthropologist who doesn't like to rough it could plant himself by this window with a pair of binoculars and within a few months have enough data for a thesis. And every so often he could break to watch one of the excellent video films offered on hotel TV.

## January 22

AID is considering importing a new brand of condom. I saw a guy at the office today blow one of these condoms up like a balloon and try to pop it with his fist. And I always thought those things were tested electronically.

## January 23

My partner and I went to several urban and rural pharmacies to see which brands of ORS were selling well. Pharmacies in Bangladesh are usually tiny and, in Dhaka at least, clustered together in certain areas. The pharmacists were amenable to being interviewed, so we additionally tried to find out what they know about ORS preparation and use, what advice if any they give on diet during cases of serious childhood diarrhea, and what their customers seemed to know about these things.

One interesting finding from the point of view of social marketing is that the more expensive and imported brands of ORS sold better in town, ostensibly because customers assumed these were superior to cheaper, locally made brands. This needs checking out. Maybe pharmacists realize higher profits on the more expensive brands, so they push them more.

## January 24

Since tomorrow is the Islamic Sabbath, Thursday nights around here are like Friday nights in the Christian world. There was a Thank-God-It's-Thursday bash at the American Club in Dhaka this evening, featuring a Texas barbeque and square dance. It was actually the first time the square dance band had performed together and they were delighted to learn that I play fiddle, after a fashion. The AID assistant population officer played a pretty mean back-up guitar, and we also had two banjo pickers, a mandolin player, and another fiddler (a sociologist).

As the evening progressed, there was a great deal of exaggerated redneckery, of letting it all hang out in the company of fellow Americans. I myself became a Good Ole Boy for the evening and reveled in it all. After all, anthropologists ought to have a culture too. My partner, a Sri Lankan with decades of Asian experience in family planning, somehow knows how to do Appalachian clogging. Unfortunately, he couldn't make it to the dance, so I never got to witness this.

## January 25

We were invited to dinner tonight at the home of a Bangladeshi filmmaker who does family planning ads for local TV and movies. Three beautiful Bengali actresses from Calcutta were there; they have roles in some ads currently being produced. It turned out to be quite a party: good scotch, good conversation, and excellent Bengali cuisine. I was the only non-native to the subcontinent.

One guy from the locally staffed Social Marketing Project confessed after a few scotches that he couldn't quite understand how an American was going to come and tell Bangladeshis about the intricacies of their own culture. "We're keeping an open mind," he assured me. "Maybe we aren't looking at our culture in enough depth."

Good God, how to respond to that? I tried to justify my role as best I could: somebody needs to pull things together, perhaps with an objectivity that a local person—even an anthropologist—might lack, and someone with in-depth experience in other cultures can discover patterns and connections that others might miss. . . . All this didn't sound too convincing, even to me. I concluded that maybe much of the value of someone like me is simply that I can talk to both poor villagers and to development planners and policymakers.

An anthropologist newly arrived in a country is in a rather untenable position, since he's supposed to be—or expected to quickly become—a country expert.

## January 26

I've been going around and getting briefings from all the various agencies that work in diarrheal disease control, especially those that promote ORS. I've been especially eager to talk to sociological-type researchers who have looked into behavior and attitudes relating to diarrhea and its treatment. It takes a certain amount of art and diplomacy to get researchers to share their hard-earned and still-unpublished research findings with short-term consultants who zip in and out of a country and who get a certain amount of credit for putting such research findings in their own consultant reports. Since I've been in the position of "local expert" in two other countries, I know what it's like to have one's brains picked by visiting consultants. When I'm in the role of picker, I try to be completely up-front with the pickee and I give credit where it's due in my consultant report.

With an annual income per capita of just over $100, Bangladesh is listed as the second poorest country in the world, after Chad. Life expectancy at birth is 48 years. Over 70 percent of the population is said to survive on less than 1,800 calories a day. A corollary to this is that most women are anemic even before they are pregnant, and babies from such mothers are born weak and undersized, especially when births aren't properly spaced. To make matters worse, the colostrum—the first breastmilk produced after childbirth and containing large amounts of protein and immunizing agents—

is typically discarded as impure or dirty milk. Traditional birth practices themselves leave much to be desired. Neonatal tetanus abounds.

Still, the average woman produces 6.2 kids during her childbearing years. Bangladesh has a population density of about 1,620 per square mile. It's said that the entire population of the world would have to live in the continental United States for the U.S. to have the same population density. India, which has its own population problem, has announced plans to build a fence along its border with Bangladesh to stem the tide of illegal immigrants entering India. Bangladesh, its pride wounded, has announced plans to build watchtowers at intervals along the same lengthy border to ensure Indians don't try to sneak into Bangladesh.

Development assistance groups working in Bangladesh seem to regard population control (no euphemisms here) as the number one development priority. Some people feel that draconian measures, such as those taken by China, may be necessary to decisively reduce population growth here. AID's Social Marketing Project is regarded as illustrative of the best approach a noncoercive or capitalist society can take, since it makes use of entrepreneurship and the profit motive to make contraceptive technology as widely available as possible.

## January 26

This afternoon, two colleagues and I went by cycle rickshaw through Dhaka's lethal traffic to the old section of town. Much of the urban Hindu population—consisting mostly of Untouchables—that remained after independence seems to live in this section. The streets are too narrow to permit passage of a rickshaw but not the throngs of people that seem to be pressing in all directions at once. There are rancid open sewers, stagnant now because of the dry season. Beggars of all ages, but mostly children, followed us and even tugged at our clothes. There's a Mother Theresa orphanage in the neighborhood, but some kids seem to be living in piles of rubble covered with cardboard, visible in tiny alleyways off the streets we walked along.

One little girl with large, soulful eyes followed me for the entire walk around Old Dhaka. Remembering how I was literally mobbed by dozens of beggar kids some years ago in Delhi, I waited until we had climbed back into rickshaws before slipping this girl a rather large bill. She stuffed it in her torn dress and proceeded to run alongside my rickshaw, which quickly picked up speed as we maneuvered into heavy traffic. I tried to shoo her away because she was now clinging to the back of the rickshaw and her legs were running faster than they could have on their own power. I was terrified she'd be run over when she finally had to let go. Just when I was trying to get my driver to pull over, her strength seemed to give out and she somehow stumbled back to the sidewalk unharmed. Her eyes were still on mine as she was swallowed up by the crowd.

*January 27*

I was lucky to be able to go on a field visit with a Bangladeshi anthropologist who is also looking into health beliefs and behavior. She received her degree from one of the top anthropology departments in the United States. We found we knew several people in common.

It took two hours to get to the villages in Tangail District where she's been working, so we had plenty of time to talk. Four of her research assistants were with us, and they proved good sources of information. I learned about *chira*, a rice-based home remedy for diarrhea, and about perceptions of intrinsic qualities attributed to foods and medicines. Many foods scientifically known to be nutritious, alkaline, and low-fat are in fact locally perceived as *nirog* (disease-free) and "cooling." Hats off to folk wisdom once again.

Before walking around the villages we decided to cook up some lunch from strictly *nirog* foods purchased at a local market. I insisted on paying since everyone was devoting so much time to my nonstop questions. The research assistants did the bargaining; they knew prices would go up several hundred percent at the very sight of me. We eventually feasted on fried fish, rice, salad, and four cooked and elaborately spiced vegetables. Seven people were fed with 70 taka (under $3) and there was food left over. The very meager continental breakfast at my hotel costs 100 taka.

After lunch we drove as far as the roads could take us, then walked the last stretch to reach one of the villages where my hosts have been doing research.

The villagers we met were used to being asked questions and so mine didn't seem to disturb them. There was some occupational specialty by village section. In one, for example, an extended family owned no land but managed to make a living by weaving cloth for the *lungi* skirt that men traditionally wear. They were proud of their craft, but complained that earnings were not keeping up with rising costs of all the things they are required to buy. Only the cash remittances of a brother now working in Libya seems to be keeping the family business from collapsing.

In another section of the same village, people made their living from farming and seemed slightly better off. We spoke with one man who was having an early dinner of rice garnished with a few peppers; he said he couldn't afford meat or other vegetables.

Unlike the areas of Latin America and Africa I'm familiar with, villages in Bangladesh may have been in the same spot for centuries or even millenia. It boggles my mind. There must be many ancestor spirits around.

By the end of a long afternoon I felt I had absorbed a bit of the ethos of village life in Bangladesh. People were undernourished but things didn't appear as bad as I had expected. The quality of rural life certainly seemed superior to life in the urban slums and shantytowns, and I was told most Bangladeshis realize this. Only the most dire circumstances—and then mostly among the landless—force people to take their chances in the slums.

One gets the feeling that if only fertility rates would drop quickly and decisively, life here could be pretty good.

My anthropologist colleague and I had plenty of time to talk shop during the long drive back. We covered such topics as whether there are incentives to write and publish among the non-academically employed and why anthropologists tend to be apolitical. She told me she didn't see many fellow anthropologists in her line of work. I told her neither did I.

*January 28*

The International Center for Diarrheal Disease Control, Bangladesh (ICDDR,B) operates a field cholera hospital and research station in Matlab, Comilla District. The best way to reach Matlab from Dhaka involves an hour-long speedboat trip down the Meghna River. ICDDR,B gets a lot of support from AID, so my partner and I, as AID consultants, were given a tour of the Matlab operation.

Life on the Meghna, a tributary of the Ganges, seems relatively unaltered by the passage of centuries. Fishermen in crude sailboats search up and down the river for places to drop their nets. Some travel as far as the Bay of Bengal, leaving their families for months at a time.

We visited a couple of riverine villages near the cholera hospital. Even though health and educational interventions are greater in Matlab than anywhere else in the country, the villages we saw seemed poorer than the ones I visited yesterday in Tangail District. And few if any of the kids appeared to be attending school. We were told school fees were high and anyway the kids were needed to help out at home.

A comment was overheard by an Indian woman in our group—apparently the villagers didn't think she understood Bangla. This woman drew the guy who had made the comment into a conversation. It seems he had developed suspicions about the oral cholera vaccine trials underway in Matlab. Since women but not men in the 5–20 age group are getting the vaccine, isn't this really a way to give birth control medicine to unsuspecting women? Our ICDDR,B guide explained to him that men in that age group couldn't be used for trials and followups because too many of them were absent for too long from the villages.

We got a tour of the cholera hospital, including a children's ward where dehydrated kids were being given ORS by their mothers. The children lay on army cots with a hole cut in the centers so that diarrhea can be caught by buckets placed strategically underneath. Having seen this kind of ward in African clinics, I was impressed by the absence of bad odors.

Not everyone in our group was favorably impressed. A tall, middle-aged German woman—silent until now—whispered to me, "We must see what they do with the dead bodies!" I didn't know how to respond to this. A few minutes later, having gained some information somewhere, she again leaned toward me and confided, "As I suspected! They allow the families to take the dead bodies home! This spreads cholera. We might as well cut off the money for the hospital and let them all die!"

On the boat trip back, a doctor in our group had to stop to deliver supplies to another children's cholera ward in a little out-station. There we saw a child so dehydrated that it refused to swallow any of the ORS its mother held to its lips. It was eerie: the mother was young and beautiful and seemingly resigned to losing her child. She seemed passive and fatalistic as we tried to show her gentle forcefeeding techniques. The mothers I know back in the United States would be hysterical and demanding to speak to the person in charge. Get the Surgeon General here at once.

### January 29

My hotel is becoming an armed fort. The Islamic Development Bank is gearing up for a big conference, and for the last couple of days, foreign ministers and other heavies from all over the Islamic world have been arriving. Security gets tighter every day. There's a metal detector and X-ray machine at the door that's become the hotel's sole point of entry, soldiers with machine guns are everywhere including at poolside, and personal bodyguards of sheiks are lurking menacingly in the upstairs corridors.

Anyone who has contemplated the view from my window knows how easy it would be for a have-not in the shantytown to lob a bomb over the hotel wall. I hope I get out of this consultancy alive.

### February 1

My return flight didn't work out quite as planned. I sat from 1:00 a.m. to 7:30 a.m. in the Bombay airport waiting for a Kenya Airways connection that should have left at 4:30 a.m. Now I'll miss my connection in Nairobi and have to spend two days either there or in Johannesburg before I can get a flight to Swaziland. With only the clothes I'm wearing.

Yesterday was tough. I got up at 5:45 a.m. to finish my sections of our report to AID. We had to give two debriefings for a total of three hours, one at AID and one late in the afternoon at the Social Marketing Project. Intensive proofing and editing of the 45-page report was squeezed in between our presentations, but I still didn't have a corrected draft in my hands when I was taken to the airport last night. I just hope they send me one eventually.

AID seemed impressed with our findings and recommendations, and the result is that they want my partner and me to return soon to actually conduct some anthropological and ORS market research.

I was taken from the final debriefing to the American Club restaurant, where the newly formed Bangladesh String Band made our second appearance, playing old-time music for the dinner crowd. After a two-hour performance, an AID car took me to the airport. Dhaka was starting to feel like home.

Now I'm in Nairobi trying to decide what to do about missing my connection. On the flight from Bombay I sat next to an old woman who has clearly never been on a plane before. From her dress and appearance, she might have been a tribal minority from the Chittagong Hill Tracts of Bangladesh or from the remote mountains of Burma. The multilingual stewardesses could find no language through which to communicate with this exotic woman. She refused all food and drink during the six-hour flight and she never went to the bathroom. She just sat rigidly forward in her unreclined seat the whole way. I got an expressionless look when I offered her a blanket from the overhead rack. God knows why she was going to Kenya. When the plane landed she turned to me and her face wrinkled into an astonishingly broad smile.

# 6

## Analyzing Irrigation's Impact in Northwest India: An Ethnographic Approach

*David J. Groenfeldt*

### Overview

This chapter deals with cultural aspects of irrigation development in two villages along the Haryana/Rajasthan border of India. My purpose is to outline an ethnographic approach by which anthropology can contribute both to the study of development and to the work of development. I call this approach "development ethnography" and situate it somewhere between traditional academic ethnography and agency sponsored socioeconomic impact studies. In fact, it can be said to subsume both, since it applies ethnographic methodology to particular concerns of socioeconomic development. The scope of development ethnography is best defined with reference to the diagram in Figure 6.3. The effects of a development project add an extra dimension to the ethnographic model. Not only is behavior—be it farming, marriage, or religious ritual—motivated by traditional values, but also by new factors introduced by development. By incorporating a development perspective into ethnographic research, this kind of study offers both a theoretical testing ground, and the potential for useful policy implications.

From December 1980 to April 1982 I conducted a controlled comparison of an irrigated and an unirrigated village as my dissertation fieldwork.[1] Both villages were within the command zone of the large-scale Bhakra Canal, built in the 1950s. Upon completing work in the irrigated village (and before starting work in the second village), the USAID mission in New Delhi expressed interest in my research, since irrigation development is one of their priorities.[2] Consequently, my wife and I signed a contract with AID to write two reports, my wife's dealing with the women and household economies (Stanbury, 1981), and my own describing irrigation's impact on the agricultural economy (Groenfeldt, 1981).

Irrigation development was, and is, a primary focus of AID's rural development program in India. Although AID did not have any projects in the district I was working in, it was involved in other parts of Rajasthan. The AID personnel I talked to were well versed on the economics and general statistics of irrigation, but they had no real "feel" for what was going on at the grassroots level. They wanted a case study that would help them to better interpret their numerical data.

This new role of report writing, and the responsibility of addressing the development issues which AID was interested in, forced me to view "my" village in a new light. It also gave me a new perspective on the uses of ethnography in understanding the development process. This chapter begins with an overview of my field research—what I was trying to do, where I was doing it, and the methods I was using. Next I discuss my conception of what an ethnography of development entails, and how it differs from both traditional ethnography and from purely socioeconomic studies of development impact. In the last section I present some of my research findings as evidence of the kind of information ethnography can provide; information which is useful not only to academicians, but to development agencies as well.

## Research Aims

The aim of my research was to measure the degree of cultural change brought about by large scale irrigation—the Bhakra Canal system in northwest India. In keeping with an earlier anthropological tradition, and in spite of advice from one of my advisors that, "Village studies became obsolete twenty years ago," I limited the scope of study to the village level. I chose two study villages located in the same region (see Figure 6.1); one village was mostly (82 percent) irrigated, the other was mostly (78 percent) unirrigated. These would form the basis for a controlled comparison modelled after the study done by Scarlett Epstein (1962; 1973) in South India. In both her study and mine, irrigation water had been available for roughly twenty-five years, which was long enough for the social system to have made its adjustments, but still within the memory of the elder residents.

One criticism of Epstein's study (Hunt and Hunt, 1976: 406–407) was the proximity of a large town within walking and cycling distance (4 to 6 miles) of her study villages. Epstein's most important finding was that drastic social change can occur in a village that has not been specifically targeted for economic development (irrigation). Residents of her unirrigated village found new employment opportunities in the nearby town, which stimulated a high level of urban influence. In the wet village, irrigation development allowed the residents to remain primarily agricultural and culturally traditional. Does irrigation development really promote "traditionalization" rather than "modernization?" It seemed to me that if the town had been far enough away to restrict access to the urban economy, Epstein's scenario might have been quite different.

## The Research Setting

In choosing my study villages, I was careful to stay away from towns, though it is difficult to know just how far from town it is necessary to go.

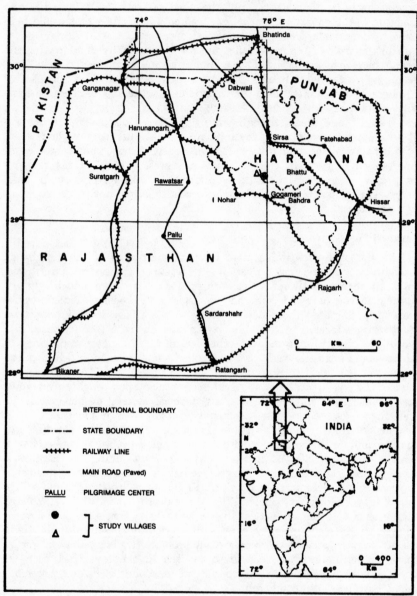

Figure 6.1  Location of the study area.

Fortunately, perhaps, other factors helped my decision. I was looking for a pair of villages as close together as possible in order to minimize environmental and cultural differences. The villages had to be about the same size with the same general caste structure, and one had to be unirrigated (dry) and the other irrigated (wet). I had already committed myself to working within or very close to the state of Haryana (for visa purposes), to the western portion of this state which is served by the Bhakra Canal (since this had been in operation for one generation), and to the southern portion of this command zone which was relatively arid (thus irrigation has been relatively more significant) and the population is culturally homogeneous.

At times I felt I was painting myself into a corner by trying to meet too many criteria, and was afraid I might have to either change the research focus or compromise on the criteria. In fact, I did relax my definition of what constituted irrigated versus unirrigated. The whole purpose of the Bhakra Canal Project had been to provide as many villages as possible with some water—enough to ensure against the devastation of drought but not enough to irrigate 100 percent of any village (Vander Velde, 1980: 311).

The villages I finally selected are located in an area known as the *Bagar*, literally "wasteland." Geographically, this is the northern fringe of the Thar Desert, an area where the introduction of irrigation waters was thoroughly appreciated; average annual rainfall is a highly variable 300 mm. Visually, the Bagri area fits the Western stereotype of Rajasthan. The landscape is dominated by scattered sand dunes, scraggly trees, and lots of camels, which are still the primary mode of plowing as well as transport. Daytime temperatures often approach 120 degrees in May and June, which is also the season for hot dry winds and dust storms. Ethically, the Bagris are predominantly Jats (an agricultural caste) originating from Rajasthan. Their speech is a dialect of Hindi comprising both Rajasthani, Punjabi, and Haryanui elements. Traditionally the Bagris relied on a mixed economy of pastoralism and farming. Villages were abandoned during prolonged droughts and reestablished during better times. The character of the region is nicely depicted in a local poem:[3]

> May my parents die for giving me birth in the Bagar
> Weeds infest the fields; thistles cause much pain;
> Even the water is brackish in the Bagar . . .
> The fields go up and down over high sand dunes;
> Black boys spend all day carrying camel loads;
> Their *dhotis* are tied above their knees,
> Their turbans are askew.
> They seldom have *chippatis* (bread) to eat,
> But drink sour *rabardi* (mixture of fermented buttermilk and millet flour).

And from a woman's song:

> I forbid you from ever going into the Bagar.
> Your hands are (smooth) like rubies;

They will become rough.
Your skin is golden; it will turn black.

The two study villages are located just 5 km. from each other on either side of the Rajasthan-Haryana border (see Figure 6.1). There is a primary school in both villages; both are connected to a market town 25 km. away by paved road and bus service. Only the irrigated village is electrified. Irrigation comes from the Bhakra Canal system which started operations in 1954. The "wet" village has 82 percent of its lands within the irrigation command zone. The "dry" village has 22 percent of its land—one large corner—within the command zone. Before irrigation, the wet village of Bagarpur (a pseudonym) consisted of only twenty-seven houses. Over half the land was owned by a single absentee landlord who was of the moneylending caste (*bania*), and had probably acquired the land through unpaid loans. An artifact of this period is the large number of elderly bachelors in Bagarpur, who were then too poor to attract wives. The fortune of the villagers changed after Independence (1947). The Surplus Land Act of 1952, and the simultaneous construction of the irrigation canal created a better life for the residents and also attracted thirteen immigrant families within a five year period. All were relatives of residents, or in the case of service castes, were invited to move in. Today Bagarpur has 101 households consisting of 70 percent agricultural castes (*Jat* and *Siami*), 19 percent untouchable (*Harijan*) castes (*Chamar, Dhanak,* and *Cheuda*) and 7 percent service castes (*Khati, Lohar, Nai* and *Brahmin*). The distribution of castes into neighborhood groups can be seen in the map of Bagarpur (Figure 6.2).[4] I have included this map to convey a sense of the spatial unity typical of Bagri villages. This is not necessarily matched by social unity, although members of the same clan (*gotra*) generally constitute a real social (not corporate) entity.

Irrigation has enabled Bagarpur farmers to intensify their agriculture. Increased yields of the traditional chickpeas and millet crops, as well as new crops such as cotton, wheat, and cowpeas (for fodder), provide enough food and cash to support a growing village population. Even more important than the quantity of production has been the security of production. In a dry year, irrigation provides the guarantee of subsistence; in a wet year, irrigation ensures a sizeable surplus. The combination of increased production and increased security has resulted in an almost total reliance on agriculture in Bagarpur. Only two men work in non-agricultural jobs outside the village, and some farm labor is imported. Of twenty agricultural servants (*siris*) working on annual contracts, half come from outside the village. Even though wage opportunities center around the harvest and planting seasons only, the resident landless are generally able to make ends meet without leaving the village.

The dry village, which I call Chhotapur, is located on the Rajasthan side of the border. Before irrigation it was slightly larger than Bagarpur, but is slightly smaller now, with ninety households. Chhotapur lands have never been locked up by absentee landlords, so the Surplus Land Act had no effect. With no land for sale and no opportunities for service castes

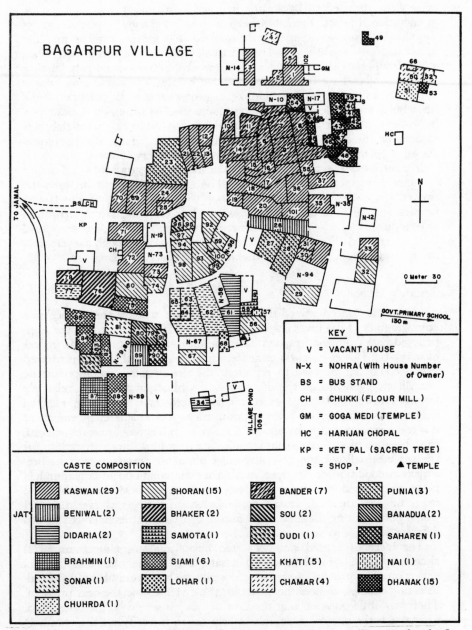

Figure 6.2  Map of Bagapur showing caste groups. The 12 gotra affiliations for the Jat caste are also indicated.

(who were attracted to Bagarpur's irrigated economy), there has been no in-migration. In fact, there has been a slow but steady migration out of the village. Some young men have married into sonless families in order to obtain new land (the usual postmarital residence pattern is patrilocal); a few families have purchased land elsewhere. Some functionally landless Harijan families have been forced to leave because of limited employment opportunities in the village. Unlike Bagarpur where 13 percent of the households are landless, there are no totally landless families in Chhotapur, but most of the Harijan families depend on wage labor as a supplementary income. Of the ninety households in Chhotapur, 62 percent are agricultural castes, 31 percent are Harijan, and 7 percent are service castes.

In contrast to the agricultural intensification of Bagarpur, the Chhotapur economy is marked by diversification. The economic contrast between the two villages is analogous to the contrast within Bagarpur, of the landed farmers and landless laborers. Just as the landless benefit from irrigation only indirectly (the so-called "trickle down" effect), so too, on a regional level, unirrigated villages benefit indirectly by irrigation through participation in the regional economy—the "trickle down" effect writ large.

## Research Methods

My initial conception of the research design was to prepare separate ethnographies of the two villages and then, in effect, to "subtract" the non-irrigated data from the irrigated data, the difference comprising the impact of irrigation. However, it was clear from Epstein's study that the unirrigated village could not be used to represent the pre-irrigated condition of the wet village. Even though the dry village of Chhotapur is located relatively far from town, the village economy is nonetheless tied to the regional irrigated economy. Many of the opportunities for outside employment, as bus conductors or truck drivers, or as agricultural laborers in nearby villages, exist because of the economic stimulus of irrigation. Since irrigation has affected both villages, the dry village of Chhotapur represents not the pre-irrigation condition of Bagarpur, but rather the condition of Bagarpur had irrigation entered the region but missed the village. My research could never uncover the *total* impact of irrigation on the wet village; instead I would be measuring the *differential* impact of irrigation development in two different kinds of village situations.

The methods I used can be sorted into three stages of research: (1) choosing the villages, (2) selecting a sample of households, and (3) data collection. The process of choosing the villages has already been discussed. Selecting a sample of households within these villages was the next problem. There was little question that the unit of analysis would be the household, since this is the primary economic unit in North India. While the economic household was not always coterminous with the architectural household (e.g., brothers who lived separately but farm communally), the concept of "household" was always valid, even though its definition had to be flexible to fit the situation.

*The Sample.* I needed a sample that was representative, large enough for some statistical manipulation, but small enough to be manageable. I settled on forty households in each village; this constituted a 40 percent sample for the irrigated village and a 44 percent sample in the slightly smaller dry village. The actual selection of households had to await the completion of a map and the census.

The map was my first field task which I began a few days after my arrival in Bagarpur (which I studied first). I wanted a map not only for drawing the sample, but for the varied spatial information and quick reference it could provide to names, village features, and activities. I made a good map, to scale, oriented north; the finished product can be seen in Figure 6.2. As it happened, the time I spent on the map was an effective means of introducing myself to the villagers (especially to the children . . .). Though there were a few skeptics ("Why are you making a map of our village— so America can drop a bomb?"), the majority of villagers was impressed with my hard work and seemed pleased that I could point out who lived in which house.

With the map and census completed and household numbers assigned, I took all the even numbers, which comprised a systematic sample of every other house (n=50) and then reduced the sample to forty by random numbers. This method ensured that all neighborhood groups, which are defined largely by caste and kinship, would be represented proportionally.

*Data Collection.* The data collection involved three more or less distinct techniques: (1) questionnaires, (2) field visits, and (3) participant-observation. In the eyes of the villagers, the formal questionnaires were most important, since I was obviously engaged in a concrete task. A long agricultural form covered household and hired labor, cropping patterns and practices, yields, and marketing. An equally long material culture form covered agricultural equipment, household possessions, architecture (including house and room plans) and interior decorations. These interviews were conducted with the aid of an interpreter in Bagarpur; by the time I got to Chhotapur I was able to speak Hindi well enough to do it alone.

In Bagarpur, I lived in a ramshackle little house (even by village standards) along with my wife, our interpreter, and our cook. My house is labelled "N-17" on the map (Figure 6.2), in the NE section of town. The label refers to *nohra*, which means an enclosure for animals. Before my arrival, this was the function of the house. In spite of its physical state, the location was a good one, since it bordered the Harijan quarter. While I was always treated as an honorary member of the Jat caste, since they were dominant in numbers and power, my physical proximity to the Harijan households was helpful in maintaining rapport and in generally observing a group who have learned over the years to be relatively reclusive.

## Material Culture

An unusual feature of my research strategy was an emphasis on material culture. Data on architectural features, agricultural tools, household possessions, and wall decorations was intended to provide a measure of changing cultural values. Unfortunately, material things themselves have little direct cultural meaning, but can be interpreted only in cultural context. What is the cultural significance of a bicycle? It depends what it's used for and who uses it. It might also be interesting to know who bought it and where. In the planning stages of research, I had hoped that some item or items of material culture could serve as indices for whole groups of changing cultural values; e.g., any household that owns a radio will be sure to have specific unique characteristics. While no single indices were found, sets of material variables did show significant patterns to which I ascribe cultural meaning. An inventory of modern possessions (e.g., radio, hangers, stainless steel utensils, etc.) showed significant similarities between the Chhotapur and Bagarpur samples. However, an inventory of wall and doorway decorations (a traditional practice) revealed a significant difference: Chhotapur houses are decorated in more traditional fashion. The material data are unambiguous, but does it really mean anything? My explanation (Groenfeldt, 1983) is that these two sets of variables, possessions and decorations, represent *modern* and *traditional* behavior respectively. The fact that there is a similarity in possessions, which are purchased by men, suggests that the men of both villages are equally "modern" whereas the women, who paint the decorations, are not. Based on their decorations, the women of Chhotapur are more traditional than the women of Bagarpur. There are more value-laden statements here than can be defended in this short chapter, but I offer this case as one example of the cultural potential of material data.

Whatever its utility in unravelling cultural values, material culture is probably most useful in the realm of data collection rather than data analysis. There are three inherent advantages to material culture as a method of data collection. First of all, material objects reflect real behavior as opposed to ideal behavior; the informant either owns a radio or he does not. Of course, his cousin may own one that he borrows, or he used to have one. But for the most part, I would claim that answers about material possessions are more reliable than answers about behavioral activities. Secondly, questions about common objects—plows, chairs, books—are innocuous and can easily lead to information about associated activities. For example, asking where a chair was purchased led to one informant talking about his previous career as a "doctor" (medic) in the town where he bought the chair. Thirdly, nearly every class of behavior has some material correlate(s). Most behavior can be studied more easily through non-material data; for example, to ascertain if a child goes to school it is easier to ask the parents directly rather than ask if there are any books, or a slate in the house. One important aspect of behavior which was certainly clarified by a material approach was the system of patron-client relations between artisans and farmers (the local variant of the *jajmani* system).[5] By inventoring the agricultural equipment of a household first and then asking about the source, I was able to collect data on which carpenters, blacksmiths, and leatherworkers performed services, and to what extent outside commercial competition is affecting farmers' demand for these services.

## Irrigation Development and Ethnography

When I first thought about fieldwork, I was not specifically interested in irrigation; my primary concern was to do a village ethnography in North India. Unfortunately, simple ethnography is no longer a ticket to a Ph.D.; while its educational value to the young anthropologist is undiminished, the marginal value of straight ethnography, at least in North India, is subject to the law of diminishing scientific returns. I needed a theoretical slant to my initial goal of straight ethnography. Since I was interested in the concept of cultural coherence (Linton, 1936: 353-358), I decided to look for a situation where a traditional village society was undergoing a discrete and significant change, a situation where the integration of the cultural system would be under stress. Large-scale canal irrigation seemed to provide all the required features—a drastic, rapid change in the economy whose effects could be traced through the sociocultural system.

At the time I began fieldwork, my conception of what I was doing was a study of how a specific change (irrigation) ripples through the cultural system. It was only after I began the actual fieldwork, and had occasion to talk to officials at AID, World Bank, and Ford Foundation, that I became interested in irrigation issues as a particular aspect of development anthropology. My self-image evolved from that of an academic anthropologist studying culture change to that of a development anthropologist studying irrigation.[6]

In the village of Bagarpur, irrigation water is the most significant manifestation of a more general development process, a process that is not easy to define. In some ways, the concept of development is analogous to the concept of culture, each entailing a complex set of values and beliefs. In the case of development, the values and beliefs originate from an outside agency such as the World Bank or the Indian Planning Commission, and are imposed on the region where development is to take place. Hoben (1982: 352) suggests that development, ". . . requires a far-reaching and fundamental transformation of society from 'traditional' forms which constrain economic growth to 'modern' forms which promote it and resemble our own."

Development *projects* are the concrete expressions of development values; Gittinger (1982: 3) describes projects as, "the cutting edge of development." To the extent that projects are planned by outsiders, the values of development are alien to, though not necessarily in conflict with, the traditional values of the people being developed. While I agree with the general sense of Hoben's statement about development, we cannot assume that any particular development project will necessarily require, "a far-reaching and fundamental transformation of society." On the one hand, the project may not be inimical to local values, and on the other hand, traditional cultural values may shape the project's impact.

In the environs of Bagarpur and Chhotapur, the Bhakra Canal Project has been "the cutting edge of development" since 1954. The irrigation water originates in the Himalayas and is stored behind two massive dams (Bhakra and Nangal) in the state of Himachel Pradesh. A vast network of canals carries the water into parts of Punjab, Haryana, and Rajasthan. The aim of this development project was economic—increased agricultural production and insurance against drought. As intended, the economic impact of the project has been substantial, but there have also been significant repercussions in social institutions and in cultural values; this is the "transformation of society" which Hoben refers to. For example, the *jajmani* system of economic and ritual obligations between castes is breaking down, and family composition is changing. At the same time, many pre-existing cultural values have persisted and find new forms of expression in the irrigated economy. Dowry payments, for example, have increased, and are often financed with subsidized bank loans intended for agriculture.

### A Model

The impact of culture on development is less obvious than the impact of development on culture, but its very subtlety should suggest its importance to an anthropological analysis of development. Predicting gross economic impacts of irrigation does not require much cultural training; this is really the function of an economist rather than an anthropologist. Our forte lies not in grand prediction but in detailed explanation, and a full explanation of irrigation's impact requires that we pay attention to both aspects of developmental impact. With apologies to Geertz,[7] I refer to these two aspects as *impacts of* and *impacts on* development.

This distinction can be seen graphically in Figure 6.3. In the first model, development affects behavior (a) which eventually affects cultural values (b). This is the impact *of* development, or the "social impact" of development: development is doing the impacting and society is absorbing those impacts and changing to fit the new situation. In the second model, the causal arrows are reversed, with cultural values influencing behavior (b) which then affects the course of development (a). This is culture's impact *on* development. An example would be subverting agricultural loans for dowry expenses. Both models are deterministic in the sense that behavior is determined—by development in model 1, and by cultural values in model 2, but in neither model do development and cultural values interact directly; one does not determine the other, but they are mutually influential.

The combination of *impacts of* and *impacts on* development constitute a framework for conducting development ethnography. Any aspect of culture which is somehow related to development, either in a passive sense (impacts of) or an active sense (impacts on), becomes a relevant topic of research. For example, an analysis of marriage ceremonies did not seem relevant to an understanding of irrigation development in Bagarpur. Specific customs which are associated with marriage, however, did offer potential insights into development. Dowries have increased, competing with productive capital; the ritual role of the *nai* (barber) continues to be important in marriage

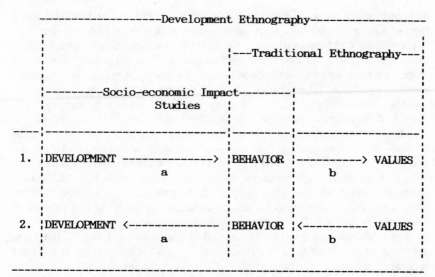

Figure 6.3  A model of development ethnography.

arrangements and may serve to prop up the larger system of jajmani relations; the goods given in dowry represent new prestige standards that are probably connected to irrigation; even the women's songs express ideal values which represent an emic view of development.

Development ethnography is broad and holistic. With a careful analysis, an infinite number of interactions could be drawn between irrigation development, cultural behavior, and cultural values. Clearly, certain interactions are more useful than others if our goal is to understand *development*. Most development is aimed at changing behavior—e.g., replacing subsistence farming with irrigated, relatively high technology, cash-based agriculture. Evaluating the impact of a project is the task of socioeconomic impact studies. The scope of such studies entails an analysis of *behavior* as both an impact of and an impact on project aims. Traditional ethnography is also concerned with behavior, but seeks to connect cultural behavior to underlying cultural values.

To understand how and why traditional cultural values are changing in Bagarpur, we cannot limit the analysis to the interaction of values and cultural behavior. Behavior is changing because of irrigation development, and cultural values must make some adjustments. On the other hand, to understand the effectiveness of irrigation development, we must go beyond the scope of socioeconomic impact studies and investigate the values which influence development.

AID's interests were behavioral, not ethnographic. Their assumption was that irrigation development has changed behavior, and my task was to report on the extent of the behavioral change, specifically economic and socioeconomic change. Their economic interests centered around the adoption of Green Revolution technologies by the Bagarpur farmers—fertilizer use, cropping patterns, marketing, etc. Their socioeconomic interests revolved around two issues: (1) water management, and (2) social equity. The water management issue was important, since the farmers' ability to organize themselves affects the operation of the irrigation system. The equity issue included both the distribution of irrigation water among farmers and the spread of irrigation benefits to the landless—the "trickle-down" effect.

These socioeconomic issues have little overlap with the cultural concerns of traditional ethnography. Both involve the same economic, and to some extent social, behaviors, but these behaviors are contextualized differently. The ethnographer links behavior to cultural values, while the AID officer relates behavior to the goals of the development project. Development ethnography incorporates both sets of concerns in studying the process of development impact in a culturally holistic framework.

If this sounds too good to be true, there is indeed a catch. What I am referring to as "development ethnography" is still ethnography. It calls for long-term fieldwork of the sort that a development agency is not likely to be willing to pay for. In my own case, AID did not pay for fieldwork, but merely for the time it took to write the report (five weeks). While there are probably some instances when development agencies will decide it is in their best interest to underwrite ethnographies, for the most part, paid development work will probably entail socioeconomic analysis *sans values*. Ethnography, even development ethnography, will continue to be an academic pursuit.

## Research Findings

When I signed the contract with AID after spending four months in Bagarpur, I felt I had a fairly good understanding of village life. In discussions with the AID program officer whose decision it was to hire me, we discussed what topics I should address. I was confident that as a holistic ethnographer, whatever information they wanted I would have already gathered. This was the case for data on agricultural practices and the economic data for landed and landless. However, when they asked me how the irrigation system was managed, I was at a loss. I knew that each farmer was allotted water on a weekly schedule, and I knew that the state was somehow in charge, but I did not know any of the details. Though I was studying irrigation's impact, I had not thought of the political ramifications of irrigation management.

Back in Bagarpur, I asked some questions and found out that all farmers (between 20 and 85) in one *chak* (the area served by one watercourse) comprised a loose political body which used to be presided over by an elected *morhab*. It was the morhab whose duty it was to allocate water rights. The reason I had not known about this as part of my general ethnographic research was that the morhab duties had been assumed by a state agency (HSMITC, Haryana State Minor Irrigation and Tubewell

Corporation) after 1976. Even so, the chak members continued to be responsible for cleaning and minor maintenance of the watercourse. Four of the six watercourses that service Bagarpur's fields extend into adjacent villages, thus comprising a unique (though loosely formed) intervillage political structure.

The basic data on agriculture was of background interest to my ethnographic aims. Some of the statistics were included in my census forms, providing a 100 percent sample for occupational categories, total land owned, land irrigated, etc. However, in India as elsewhere, things are not always as they first appear. Total land owned, for example, seems like a straightforward question, but there was a reluctance to reveal financial information, including land information. Families that owned land outside the village did not always feel compelled to tell me. The few largest landowners whose holdings exceeded the legal limit (34 acres per family of five) also saw no reason for full disclosure. My census data on landholdings are not completely accurate for these reasons, but for the 40 sample households, I eventually got reliable data just by asking a lot of interrelated questions—e.g., how many fields they had and what they planted, and their yields, etc. By the time I arrived at this stage of research, I had been living in the village long enough to earn the farmers' trust, and it would have become increasingly difficult for them to conceal such public information anyway.

One category of economic data that I never did succeed in gathering fully was information on outstanding loans. Ever since Malcolm Darling's 1925 book entitled, *The Punjab Peasant in Prosperity and Debt*, the issue of rural credit has been recognized as a key feature in the area's development. From a theoretical perspective, the issue of indebtedness is a fascinating one because it involves economic, social, and cultural values on both a local (village) as well as regional (state) level.

The collection of credit data provides a good example of the relevance of an ethnographic approach to the practical issues of development studies. The following quotation is from my AID report, introducing the topic of farmer indebtedness:

> Nearly every farmer in Bagarpur has a loan outstanding, taken either from a bania (moneylending caste) or a bank. However, questions regarding the existence of these loans, much less the details, met with resistance from both the borrowers and the lenders. The villagers consider their debts to be personal information which the questioner has no right to ask about and they have every reason to conceal. The landed are suspicious that some of their land may be taken away or that loan misuse will be brought to light, while the landless are always afraid of their creditors. The banias have a long tradition of secrecy regarding their financial dealings and the bank officials maintain a bureaucratic silence in order to conceal endemic bribery. During the course of research, however, enough facts emerged from the more candid informants to show the general patterns of indebtedness (Groenfeldt, 1981: 51–52).

The "candid informants" included one villager who held a post on the board of directors of the local land development bank. Through his assistance

I was able to collect lists of bank loans given to Bagarpur residents, though not always with the names of clients. Using these data, I found the average debt per household to be Rs.12,432 from bank sources alone, not counting debts to banias or to other villagers. I estimated the total average household debt at over Rs.14,000, and this in an economy where the typical farm wage is Rs.10 per day (about $1).

Over two-thirds of the total village debt had been borrowed during the previous 15 months, reflecting recent official government policies to promote agricultural credit. By offering low-interest loans, and by setting credit quotas for bank managers to meet, the government was trying to encourage productive investment. The Bagarpur data suggest that these policies had some positive effect. The number of tractors in the village increased from one to four during this period, and the number of tubewells increased from zero to three.[8] From the data I was able to collect, I estimated that roughly half of all loans were actually used for some economically productive purpose, although not necessarily the purpose for which they were given. The other half were used for consumptive behavior—e.g., marriage expenses, drinking, or gambling.

There is probably a correlation between loan misuse and bribes to bank officers. Although small bribes are often necessary even for legitimate loans, bank inspectors can sense their advantageous bargaining position when they know that agricultural loans will be used to meet social expenses. One ostensible tubewell loan in Bagarpur required a Rs.700 bribe to the LVO (Land Valuation Officer) who knew that the Rs.20,000 loan was actually being used for gambling and drinking; there was, in fact, no tubewell.

These are some of the economic aspects of credit behavior in Bagarpur. The availability of credit has been exploited both for productive purposes (as intended by the government) and for impractical consumption. Using the terminology of Figure 6.3, cultural values, in this case prestige values, have influenced economic behavior (Model 2b) which in turn has affected development (Model 2a).

In addition to prestige values, another important category of cultural values which affects credit behavior has to do with caste. The landless, nearly all of whom belong to untouchable (harijan) castes, cannot qualify for bank loans, except in Rs.500 allotments from the local cooperative society. Even the bania will not advance loans to the landless. The only collateral a landless worker can offer is his labor, and the only person to whom his labor has any value is the landed farmer. Large loans advanced to a landless worker take the form of an annual labor contract with a farmer. The worker receives an advance on his salary (at 24 percent interest), and agrees to work full-time for the farmer. Smaller loans can be repaid in the form of daily labor at any time during the season. A landless family's burden of debt is constrained by the landowner's unwillingness to lend much more than can be repaid through one year's labor. However, a longstanding relationship between a landless untouchable family and their landed high caste patron can result in an extension of credit. For example, one landless family that still owed Rs.1,800 on a Rs.3,000 loan taken two years earlier was successful in obtaining an additional Rs.5,000 from the same landowner to use for their daughter's marriage expenses.

The most significant difference between landless loans and landed loans is not the purpose for which they are spent, but the rate of interest at which they must be repaid. If a landowner wants Rs.4,000 for marriage expenses, he can easily take a dairy loan or a crop loan from the bank at 12 percent interest. For the landless who must borrow from the landowners, the rate is twice as high.

These are some of the social aspects of credit behavior in Bagarpur. The availability of low-interest credit has not benefited the poor. By limiting bank credit to the landless, but extending it to the landed, the traditional caste distinctions have actually been enhanced. In this case, cultural (caste) values have not affected the level of economic development, but rather the equity of that development.

I have discussed the role of prestige values and caste values as *impacts on* development, using credit behavior as an example. The traditional cultural values operating in Bagarpur have been seen to influence both the effectiveness of development and the equity of development. This process is portrayed in Figure 6.3, Model 2. There is another dimension of cultural values which serve to structure development, and that is the prestige values and the caste values held by the development agents themselves. I am referring to the bank managers who give the loans, the bank inspectors who take the bribes (as do some managers), and the officials of the Integrated Rural Development Programme (IRDP) who administer special credit schemes to the landless, and look the other way as these funds are appropriated by the landed farmers and unscrupulous bank officials.

The corruption which occurs where urban bank officers and civil servants interact with Bagarpur villagers is partly a symptom of the cultural gulf between educated petty officials and "ignorant" villagers. Civil servants who are themselves usually from village backgrounds, take great pains to present an identity as educated urbanites; they wear urban clothes, smoke cigarettes instead of *bidis*, and visit villages like Bagarpur as seldom as possible. For example, the Cooperative Society secretary, an employee of the Cooperative Bank, is officially posted in Bagarpur to administer loans and keep accounts. In fact, the secretary visits the village no more than twice a month, spending most of his time in town, presumably enjoying himself. Similar patterns of passive corruption can be found among agricultural extension workers hired to contact a list of farmers on a two-week schedule, informing them of the latest agricultural recommendations (the Training and Visitation system introduced by the World Bank). I never did meet the extension agent assigned to Bagarpur during my six months in the village. The unwillingness of development agents to visit the villages they are hired to develop is an expression of their prestige values interfering with the development process (Figure 6.3, Model 2).

The cultural values of caste also operate at this supra-village level, and influence the character of development in Bagarpur. The civil servants responsible for government development schemes are usually of the same caste as the Bagarpur landowners *Jat*, and share a similar caste prejudice against the Harijan (Untouchable) community. When officials from the IRDP office roared into Bagarpur late one evening to announce a loan subsidy scheme for the landless poor, the values of urban prestige and caste prejudice were very much in the air. They had only a few hours to spend in the village, they said, since they had to get back to town that evening. They were treated to typical hospitality (tea) at the sarpanch's (head of the village council) house. Meanwhile, anyone who wanted a loan was supposed to come and see them immediately. No messengers were sent to notify people, and even if they had been, Harijans are not going to visit the house of a wealthy landowner, especially at night. Not surprisingly, no Harijans came, nor would the IRDP officials go to the Harijan section of the village to recruit applicants; that would be demeaning to both urban prestige and their caste consciousness. They drove back to town, and left the paperwork with instructions for filling out the forms.

As a result of this visit, six Harijan men and one Jat man, all of whom were actually poor, received camel carts valued at Rs.3,500 each. They agreed to repay Rs.2,300 over a three-year period, at 4 percent interest. The intent was that the landless could go into the transport business with their carts, and earn some money. In the eyes of the villagers, the IRDP officials were "putting the cart before the camel," since only two of the recipients owned camels to pull the carts. The logical thing to do was to sell the cart to a landowner who could use it, and keep the cash. This was illegal, however, and involved a bribe to the bank manager who handled the loans for IRDP. The final result was that the Harijan recipient sold the cart to a landowner for Rs.500 below the market price, the bank manager took Rs.300 as a commission, and the intended recipient of a Rs.1,200 productive loan subsidy was left with Rs.400 which would probably go towards consumption. The landless recipients of Rs.400 considered themselves fortunate; the bank manager considered himself astute, and the landowners who purchased the carts considered their Rs.500 discount to be well deserved.

I have used the example of credit and loan schemes even though my topic is irrigation, because money has a way of highlighting cultural values. Credit which originates outside the village brings the villagers face-to-face with the human agents of the development process. The net effect of development is shaped not only by the cultural values of the villagers, but by the cultural values of those all too human agents. In Bagarpur's development, credit behavior presents the strongest case for the utility of studying culture's impact on development.

What effect has irrigation had on credit behavior? At the time I wrote the AID report, I had not yet worked in Chhotapur, so I could not directly compare the indebtedness of Bagarpur with an unirrigated situation. However, the villagers themselves offered some observations. One old widow told me that, "In the old days debt was due to crop failures; now debt is due to whiskey." This struck me at the time as the sort of statement one could expect from a grandmother who imagined that young people just aren't what they used to be. While living in Chhotapur several months later, however, I came to appreciate her perspective more. The average debt level in Chhotapur was well under Rs.1,000, or less than 10 percent of Bagarpur's indebtedness. Even those farmers in Chhotapur with irrigated land had no debts to speak of. One evening in the course of filling out the standard agricultural form with one of my sample farmers, I asked him if this was indeed the case, and if so why. He taught me a new word, *nesari* which means "loose living" having connotations of drinking, gambling, and prostitution, in approximately that order. The residents of Bagarpur, he told me, are *nesari*; they drink too much, gamble too much, and accumulate large debts as a result. In an area where a bottle of legal liquor costs the equivalent of two days wages (and illegal liquor is even more), there is a logical connection between drinking and debt.

The distinction between nesari behavior and traditional behavior is not the quality of the behavior but the quantity. In Chhotapur some men also drink (no women do in this area), but it has not become a serious economic liability to any family. Perhaps this is because of the total absence of gambling in Chhotapur, whereas it is common in Bagarpur. My friend—and this was confirmed by other informants—could not name a single irrigated village that was not considered nesari. Only dry villages, though not all of them, were deemed non-nesari (there is no specific term for its absence).

While these data are purely qualitative, there was general agreement from residents of both villages of a behavioral distinction. This also conforms to intuitive logic. Irrigated landowners have more money, and especially more ready cash; they can afford relatively extravagant pastimes. The losers in this are the small landowners and landless of Bagarpur who try to compete in prestige behavior. Drinking is certainly not an economically sound recreation for the poor. While the residents of Chhotapur can joke about the habits of their irrigated neighbors, the changing prestige values in the irrigated economy may serve to further differentiate the rich from the poor.

## Conclusion: The Uses of Culture in Development Studies

The mingling of cultural forces which influence credit behavior suggest that the process cannot be fully understood by examining only the external behaviors; the cultural reasons lie much deeper—in the realm of prestige values, caste stigmas, and in the cultural gulf separating village farmers from urban bank officers. Against the standards of development ethnography, the socioeconomic, behavioral analysis which AID wanted appears to be incomplete. Cultural values can have real effects on the way development unfolds.

What does development ethnography have to offer an agency like AID? It would be unreasonable to take the position that a detailed cultural analysis is necessary in every development study. I would suggest a specialized role for development ethnography, namely, in any situation that requires an answer to *why* as opposed to *what*. For an evaluation of a specific project's impact, restricting the study to socioeconomic variables is probably adequate: How many hours do women work? What is the wage scale in different seasons? What are the patterns of education or health care? What is the level of indebtedness among small farmers? To answer such questions, the cultural values which ethnographers study can be largely ignored, although the methods which ethnographers use (participant-observation) might be necessary. The utility of development ethnography lies beyond, and before, specific projects. Feasibility studies at the design stage of projects and evaluation studies of existing projects for the purpose of establishing policy would seem to be two situations justifying ethnographic analysis.

One of my favorite pastimes during fieldwork was to fantasize what I would have done differently had I been in charge of bringing irrigation to Bagarpur. I didn't have many ideas for improving the irrigation system; it seemed to function quite efficiently. The one big equity problem with irrigation is that it doesn't benefit the landless except indirectly. The Ford Foundation has experimented with a system of water coupons which both landed and landless receive and can sell (in two villages near Chandigarh); my wife had an idea for creating grazing strips along all the watercourses— the grass would be watered from natural seepage, and the Harijans would be given exclusive grazing rights. Both seemed to be good ideas if they had been imposed as initial conditions for building the watercourses.

The approach taken so far in assisting the Bagarpur landless is not directly linked to irrigation. The landless have been encouraged to pursue household enterprises—camel cart transport, dairy buffalo, sheep herding. These ideas are not bad in themselves, but they all require money. Since the landless have virtually no money, they require loans, and to make the loans attractive, they must be subsidized. Subsidized loans constitute a prized resource in a cash-poor rural economy, and the more prized the resource, the less likely the intended recipients will be the actual recipients. There is raw economic and political power involved here, but there is much more to it than merely this. The cultural values of the farmers interact with the values of the landless, and this dynamic interacts with the urban values of the development agents. The task of the development ethnographer is to evaluate and explain these interactions in terms of the development goals.

## Notes

1. Research funds were provided through the Berkeley Professional Studies Program in India, a USAID Title XII grant administered through the University of Arizona, a grant from the Graduate Student Development Fund (University of Arizona), and a National Resource Fellowship (South Asia) administered by the Department of Oriental Studies, University of Arizona.

2. I had prior contact with the AID mission, since I needed clearance from them to conduct Title XII-funded research. In the process of explaining what type of

study I intended to carry out, it became clear that the mission was interested in village-level data that could put some "flesh" on the masses of numerical data they usually deal with. They were especially interested in knowing how village women were being affected by irrigation. My wife, also an anthropology doctoral candidate, was with me in Bagarpur, and was able to oblige AID's interest in village women, while I could provide data on the irrigation system and the agricultural economy. In spite of the promise of so much useful data, however, the mission personnel did not recruit us to write reports. It took a bit of marketing on our part to convince them to go through the red tape and commit some of their surplus funds to our project.

3. The author wishes to thank Dr. A. S. Chharia of Haryana Agricultural University for preparing the translations.

4. There are 10 castes represented in Bagarpur. In the "Caste Composition" Key at the bottom of Figure 6.2., the first three rows represent *gotra* (clan) names, all belonging to the *Jat* caste; the bottom three rows represent the remaining nine castes.

5. The *jajmani* system as commonly described in the literature did not operate in Bagarpur. The local system of *barsodi* relations involving patron-client transactions for annual grain payments was limited to the artisan castes.

6. Surprisingly little has been published on the ethnography of irrigation development. There is a growing body of literature on the sociology of local water management (Coward, 1976, 1979; Chambers, 1977; Wade, 1979; Merrey, 1979) which focuses on the capacity of local political structures to deal with the responsibilities of irrigation management. These studies are oriented toward specific development issues. A much smaller, more academic literature on irrigation development concerns studies of indigenous systems which have been taken over and expanded by state or national governments (e.g., Lees, 1973; Bacdayan, 1974). As for ethnographic accounts of "true" irrigation development—the case of an irrigation system being introduced suddenly from the outside, except for Pasternak's (1972) study, Epstein's original research (1962) and her restudy (1973) appear to be unique.

7. This is an allusion to Geertz's (1973: 83–93) observation that symbols function as *models of* and *models for* social and psychological reality.

8. Whether tractors *should* be encouraged is another matter (see Binswanger, 1978; Roumasset and Thapa, 1983); tubewells are less controversial.

# References

Bacdayan, Albert S. "Securing Water for Drying Rice Terraces: Irrigation, Community Organization, and Expanding Social Relationships in a Western Bontoc Group, Philippines." *Ethnology*, Vol. 13, 1974, pp. 247–260.

Binswanger, Hans P. *The Economics of Tractors in South Asia*. New York: Agricultural Development Council, 1978.

Chambers, Robert. "Men and Water: The Organization and Operation of Irrigation," in B. H. Farmer, ed., *Green Revolution?: Technology and Change in Rice-Growing Areas of Tamil Nadu and Sri Lanka*. Boulder: Westview Press, 1977.

Coward, E. Walter. "Indigenous Organization, Bureaucracy and Development: The Case of Irrigation." *Journal of Development Studies*, Vol. 13, No. 1, 1976, pp. 92–105.

Coward, E. Walter. "Principles of Social Organization in an Indigenous Irrigation System." *Human Organization*, Vol. 38, 1979, pp. 28–36.

Epstein, T. Scarlett. *Economic Development and Social Change in South India.* Manchester: Manchester University Press, 1962.

Epstein, T. Scarlett. *South India: Yesterday, Today and Tomorrow.* New York: Holmes & Meier Publishers, Inc., 1973.

Geertz, Clifford. *The Interpretation of Cultures.* New York: Basic Books, 1973.

Gittinger, J. Price. *Economic Analysis of Agricultural Projects.* Baltimore: Johns Hopkins University Press, 1982.

Groenfeldt, David. "Farmers' Response to Irrigation Opportunities: The Status of the Green Revolution in a Haryana Village." *USAID/India Report.* New Delhi, 1981.

Groenfeldt, David. "Social Consequences of Irrigation in the Bagar Region, Northwest India." *South Asian Anthropologist,* Vol. 4, No. 2, 1983.

Hoben, Allan. "Anthropologists and Development." *Annual Review of Anthropology,* Vol. 11, 1982, pp. 349–375.

Hunt, Robert C. and Eva Hunt. "Canal Irrigation and Local Social Organization." *Current Anthropology,* Vol. 17, No. 3, 1976, pp. 389–411.

Lees, Susan. *Sociopolitical Aspects of Canal Irrigation in the Valley of Oaxaca.* University of Michigan Museum of Anthropology. Memoir 6, 1973.

Linton, Ralph. *The Study of Man.* New York: Appelton-Century, 1936.

Merrey, Douglas J. *Irrigation and Honor: Cultural Impediments to the Improvement of Local Level Water Management in Punjab, Pakistan.* Colorado State University, Water Management Technical Report No. 53, 1979.

Pasternack, Burton. "The Sociology of Irrigation: Two Taiwanese Villages," in W. E. Willmott, ed., *Economic Organization in Chinese Society.* Palo Alto: Stanford University Press, 1972.

Roumasset, James and Ganesh Thapa. "Explaining Tractorization in Nepal: An Alternative to the 'Consequences Approach'." *Journal of Development Economics,* Vol. 12, No. 3, 1983, pp. 377–396.

Stanbury, Pamela C. "Irrigation's Impact on the Socioeconomic Role of Women in a Haryana Village." *USAID/India Report,* New Delhi, 1981.

Vander Velde, Edward J. "Local Consequences of a Large-Scale Irrigation System in India," in E. W. Coward, ed., *Irrigation and Agricultural Development in Asia.* Ithaca: Cornell University Press, 1980.

Wade, Robert. "The Social Response to Irrigation: An Indian Case Study." *Journal of Development Studies,* Vol. 16, No. 1, 1979, pp. 3–26.

# 7

# Anthropology in the Context of a Water-Borne Disease Control Project

*Edward C. Green*

In March 1981, I was hired by the Academy for Educational Development to assist in the implementation of the AID-funded Rural Water-Borne Disease Control Project in Swaziland. The project called for a KAP (knowledge, attitudes, and practices) study relating to water and sanitation in Swaziland. The primary purpose of the study was to provide baseline data for the design of a national health education strategy aimed at reducing the incidence of water-borne diseases. Further anthropological contributions were called for in the Project Paper, such as identifying potential human resources for the delivery of health education, designating traditional opinion leaders and informal communications networks, identifying patterns of visual literacy and perception and discovering something about Swazi ethnomedical theory and practice.

One of the attractions of the job for me was that the project seemed to be designed with unusual sensitivity to the importance of sociocultural factors. Instead of limiting anthropological input to the latter stages of project design—which was often the case until the early 1980s—here was an AID project specifically calling for a medical anthropologist to spend two years conducting first-hand research and generally assisting in project implementation. The research findings were to guide not only the main project component, health education, but two other components as well, namely public health engineering and environmental sanitation.

I approached the task at hand with some trepidation upon my arrival in Swaziland. I had only started calling myself a development or medical anthropologist two years earlier when, as an NIMH postdoctoral fellow, I worked on a feasibility study for a WHO mental health project for Southern Africa. Prior to then I had been university-based and concerned with rather traditional academic pursuits. Since 1979, I had gained some experience in the areas of public health and population through short-term consultancies in Africa and Washington. When the Water-Borne Disease Control Project came along, it seemed to be just the kind of challenge and logical career step that I had been looking for. But I wondered if my experience and training were really adequate. I had only recently and very briefly had dealings with the likes of epidemiologists and public health engineers (Green, 1981) and I was new to the related fields of health education and development communications, both of which were central to the Water-Borne Disease Control Project.

Swaziland is a small, mountainous, landlocked kingdom surrounded on three sides by South Africa. I had read two of Hilda Kuper's books on Swaziland years before as a first-year graduate student, but I had heard little about the country since. I spent a few pre-departure days at the Library of Congress digging up anything I could find on Swaziland. It seemed that there had been no major published ethnographic work since Kuper's, and that was based primarily on fieldwork in the late 1930s.

I surmised that in spite of some modern political apparatus, Swaziland was still very much a traditional monarchy. The survival into the 1980s of a traditional African political system was credited to the charisma and political skills of King Sobhuza II, who was about to celebrate his sixtieth year on the throne. I made a note of Kuper's comment on page one of *An African Aristocracy* that King Sobhuza was well-read in anthropology and even subscribed to several anthropology journals.

Certain features of Swazi society seemed relevant to development projects of any sort. First, the rural population, comprising nearly 90 percent of the total population, lived in dispersed extended family homesteads rather than in villages. This might mean relatively weak organization at the community level and it would probably raise problems in community outreach and information dissemination. Secondly, Swazi society was highly stratified and both centralized and authoritarian in its decision-making. This would seem to inhibit health education approaches based on participatory planning, self-reliance, and local initiative. Thirdly, Swazis are patrilineal, patrilocal, and patriarchal. The resulting subordination of women would present special challenges to health-related projects, especially those focusing on water and sanitation since these matters are considered women's responsibilities.

The project's technical team consisted of five advisors: a health educator (who was also Chief of Party), a public health engineer, an environmental sanitarian, an epidemiologist and an anthropologist. The epidemiologist and I were to be essentially researchers; the other three were to work closely with Swazi counterparts in the promotion of measures intended to reduce the incidence of diseases related to inadequate water supplies and sanitation. A certain amount of direct counterpart training was also expected of the latter three. Central to all our efforts was the development of an effective, viable Health Education Unit (HEU) within the Ministry of Health. I should say a bit more about the HEU because this is the government office to which I was assigned.

Prior to our project, health education activities had been carried out by a few public health nurses in the Public Health Unit, under the supervision of an expatriate health educator provided by the World Health Organization.

In April 1981, a few weeks after my arrival in Swaziland, a new building was opened. It was to be the new headquarters for an autonomous Health Education Unit. The Swazi staff (all women) consisted of three health educators, one nutritionist, and a graphic artist. The expatriate staff (all men) consisted of the WHO supervisory health educator, our project health educator, and myself.

Foreign technical advisors usually advise and leave administration to host country officials. However, two of our project team members were supposed to fill supervisory administrative roles for the duration of our project. One of these, the health educator, was to become the head of the HEU, according to the terms of the Swaziland-USAID contract. However, it proved difficult for an outsider to move right into a position of supervising local staff, especially with the experienced WHO health educator still on staff. This led to ambiguities and conflicts in leadership of the Unit that had an overall negative effect on the project during the initial months.

My role as researcher/planner had far less potential for conflict. I was in the Ministry of Health to learn and only later to advise; I was therefore not in the awkward position of trying to teach Africans what to do in their own country. As an ethnomedical researcher, I naturally took an active interest in traditional beliefs and customs. This meant I spent a good deal of time asking questions, an activity that fortunately was interpreted by my Swazi colleagues as showing respect for their culture.

It is worth noting that the Ministry of Health had never before had an anthropologist or sociologist on staff. Even before I conducted my KAP survey, Ministry officials began to find unanticipated uses for their new resource. My first extra assignment was a "quick and dirty" survey to determine the social feasibility of placing drinking water tanks in areas at high risk for cholera that had inadequate water resources. It was important to know if people would actually use the tanks and avoid traditional sources of drinking water. After five days of fieldwork and an equal amount of time for tabulation, interpretation, and writing, I was able to submit a useful report to the Ministry within two weeks of the initial request.

However, the KAP study was my main contractual obligation. The project paper (the main planning document for the project) budgeted for a sample-survey design and methodology for the KAP study. Yet I had some doubts about the appropriateness of such an approach. In addition to the general problem of obtaining valid data through survey methods in rural Africa (cf., for example, Cohen, 1973), the information I was after related to sensitive areas such as toilet behavior, personal hygiene, and health beliefs. The impersonal, pre-coded questionnaire typical of survey research is notoriously deficient in eliciting information of this kind, even if it has value in measuring patterns that are reasonably well established.

After considerable discussion, review of previous surveys in Swaziland, and preliminary ethnographic fieldwork, I presented a modified research plan to the AID mission in Swaziland. I proposed that an informal study of health beliefs and behavior, focusing on traditional healers and their patients, be carried out before considering a sample survey. The study would hopefully provide a fund of qualitative data that would be valuable in the design and interpretation of surveys and it might well provide information that surveys could never discover. My plan was to rely on the traditional methods of key-informant interviewing and participant-observation, at least in the early stages of research.

I also proposed a study of health behavior, beliefs, and attitudes that would rely on Rural Health Motivators (RHMs) as informants. RHMs are individuals, usually women, who are chosen by their communities to receive about eight weeks of training in preventive health care at a regional clinic. After training, RHMs work among their neighbors, promoting homestead sanitation, the purification of drinking water, proper infant nutrition, and other practices related to disease prevention.

I felt that RHMs would make good culture brokers, since they are insiders in their communities yet they understand and promote public health goals. I expected that they would be likelier than their neighbors to give candid and truthful replies to sensitive and even embarrassing questions about what their neighbors thought and did. Furthermore, with a smaller sample of respondents than the KAP survey would require, we could use a flexible, open-ended interview schedule. My previous ethnographic research experience in Surinam had left me with an abiding preference for this type of interview instrument.

In both the ethnomedical and RHM studies I wanted to personally conduct interviews and make direct observations in order to have maximum quality control over the incoming data. I suppose my anthropological training and orientation would have made it difficult for me to sit in my office in the capital city, with no "feel" for Swazi culture, while hired interviewers did the actual fieldwork and then presented me with data that would have been difficult to interpret or evaluate. In any case, I felt strongly that the two proposed studies were at least a necessary adjunct to a sample survey; they might even eliminate the need for a survey and could thereby save the project considerable money.

The revised research proposal was written, submitted to AID and the Ministry, and accepted with minimal delay. Over the next six months I interviewed a non-random sample of forty-two RHMs in eight regional clinics. A Swazi woman who had spent her senior high school year in the United States assisted me as a translator in most interviews. She also helped me develop effective probing techniques which were used when RHMs gave stereotyped and self-serving answers such as, "The people around here boil their drinking water because we have been teaching them how important this is."

Since each RHM visited approximately forty homesteads, the interviews provided information based on nearly 1,680 homesteads, representing some 3 percent of the estimated 50,000 homesteads in Swaziland. It seemed possible to regard our RHM-visited homesteads as reasonably representative of Swaziland as a whole, since they were situated throughout the country's four major topographic zones. I felt quite good about the quality of information collected in this study. We found we even had quantifiable data on such things as the number of pit latrines built or under construction—information the RHMs had no trouble remembering since they were required to report monthly on latrine progress. On the whole, it seemed like not a bad piece of research for under $300, the only direct costs to the project being the translator's hourly wage. Of course a full accounting of costs would have to include my salary, vehicles and fuel provided by the Swazi government, and salaries of support staff. During the same period of time I conducted a number of in-depth interviews with traditional healers and I managed to observe some of their practices, both of which provided an excellent introduction to Swazi culture. I spent considerable time in rural homesteads and thereby got a feel for the culture as a whole. The healers themselves thought it perfectly natural that a white foreigner would be interested in their curing methods. Since I did not inquire about the one thing they were secretive about, actual formulas for preparing medicines, they seemed unthreatened by my presence and were quite free with information.

Within six months of my arrival I was able to provide general sociocultural information and specific health-related findings to guide other components of the project. But several questions arose in my mind. Was it enough to continue in this manner? How reliable were my research methods, and could they be replicated in a future evaluation of the project? A second, follow-up KAP survey was in fact called for in the contract as part of the project's summative evaluation during its last year of AID funding.

After some thought and discussion with colleagues, I began to reconsider the value of a KAP survey. I realized that a homestead survey yielding quantitative data would in fact be a useful baseline to establish for any future studies or evaluations. And if I decided to conduct the survey, the data and methodological experience from the two preliminary studies would certainly help develop a better survey instrument, serve as a validity check on the incoming survey data, and improve data interpretation. In short, I felt a lot better at this point about attempting a national survey. A KAP survey would also provide an opportunity to contribute to a more general project objective, namely institution-building, or strengthening local capacity to carry out various technical activities on a continuing basis. Specifically, it would involve the training and participation of various nationals, thereby strengthening social science research capabilities in the Swazi government and in collaborating institutions like the University of Swaziland.

Over the next month I worked on the recruitment of interviewers and on questionnaire construction. With help from the newly formed Social Science Research Unit of the University of Swaziland, I recruited eighteen student interviewers, three supervisor-interviewers, and one faculty assistant. I also hired ten interviewers who worked seasonally for the government's Central Statistics Office. While only a few of these were even high school graduates, all had some interviewing experience. Five drivers and two additional supervisors were hired, bringing the fieldwork team to thirty-nine, including myself.

Although based primarily on the needs of the project, questionnaire content and wording followed to some extent that of previous water and sanitation studies conducted in Africa and elsewhere, so that our results would be comparable to those of other surveys. Four successive drafts of the questionnaire were pretested by the three graduate assistants with forty-five rural respondents living outside the areas selected for the survey. The first three pretested versions were in English so that I could evaluate the responses and guide any revisions. The last version was in siSwati.

The final questionnaire included sixty-nine questions of which sixty-five were pre-coded and four were open-ended. Of the pre-coded questions, twenty-three allowed for write-in options. Interviewers were also free to write in answers that did not conform to the available categories for any of the questions. I knew these concessions to data validity would add considerable time and effort when it came to tabulating responses, but we could not be certain in advance about the range of responses of any of the questions.

Next we derived a stratified cluster sample based on data from the most recent census. In the first stage, a sample of eighty-nine census enumeration areas (EAs) representative of Swaziland as a whole were chosen with help from the Central Statistics Office. In the second sampling stage, specific homesteads were chosen from recently derived Central Statistics Office lists of homesteads covering the selected enumeration areas. Using a table of random numbers, five homesteads were chosen from each selected enumeration area, resulting in a sample of 455 homesteads that represented just under 1 percent of the estimated 50,000 homesteads in Swaziland. Given the cultural homogeneity of this area, the subject matter of the survey, and the results from the two earlier studies, this was an adequate sample size.

Because of the cohesive kin-group structure and relative lack of specialized roles in Swazi society, it seemed appropriate to regard the homestead (*umuti*) as the basic response unit for a survey of this sort (cf. Drake, 1973: 63–66). The head of homestead or other adult family member standing in for the head (frequently a woman) was considered a representative spokesperson. At the same time, it was desirable in some questions to ask what the individual thought or did. In this way, associations with predictor variables related to individual characteristics could later be analyzed.

I conducted some ten hours of training for the interviewers prior to beginning fieldwork. Since most of the interviewers were students, the fieldwork period was chosen to coincide with the University's three-week Christmas vacation. Local chiefs and their assistants had been notified of the survey by letters from their district commissioners and by public radio messages broadcast over a period of a couple weeks. As it turned out, chiefs were often absent from their areas during the early period of fieldwork because of their participation in the annual "first fruits" (*Incwala*) ceremonies. This meant that the usual visit to the local chief demanded by protocol could often be dispensed with, saving us considerable time.

Almost without exception, respondents and local authorities were totally cooperative. This was partly because Swaziland was then in the middle of its first outbreak of cholera and people were concerned with this little-understood disease. We introduced ourselves as government workers researching the causes of cholera—which was a truthful way of putting it—and so we were quite welcome. As a further inducement to cooperation, each respondent was offered a cholera information packet which included potentially life-saving oral rehydration salts.

The most time-consuming and therefore expensive aspect of the survey was locating the pre-selected homesteads. This often meant long drives or walks, and much asking of directions; and sometimes families had moved or no one was at home. Related to this problem was the fact that earlier census-takers often recorded only the "European" first name of the homestead head, whereas often the person was locatable only by his traditional given name.

Interviews usually took between thirty to forty-five minutes to complete, yet because of time spent locating homesteads, an average of only two and one-half interviews per day could be completed by an interviewer. In retrospect, and weighing the various costs incurred against the marginal benefits of using a probability sample, I would think twice before repeating our sampling procedure. It is true that we could calculate sampling error with a fair degree of presumed accuracy (7 to 8 percent in this case). However, sampling error is probably not as important as the inaccuracies that can be introduced during interviewing, translation, questionnaire construction, coding, tabulation, editing, or analysis. It may be that for a survey of this sort, designed to guide health policies and educational strategies, a systematic sample in the final sampling stage would be adequate. That would mean, for example, choosing every tenth or twentieth homestead in randomly pre-selected enumeration areas. Some of the time and money thereby saved could then go into efforts to reduce various types of response error.

Fieldwork was complicated by various logistical problems such as vehicles breaking down, and by supervisory problems over things like overtime pay. In fact, such problems made it difficult to carefully monitor incoming questionnaires and discuss interviewing experiences with fieldworkers on a daily basis. Were I to conduct another survey of this type, I would use fewer interviewers, supervise them more closely, and allow a greater amount of time for fieldwork.

Over the next few months, I spent part of my time interpreting the analyzed data and writing the survey report, and the remainder on new research projects. The survey report also presented information from the traditional healer and the Rural Health Motivator studies, which added considerable qualitative flesh to the quantitative bones of the sample survey. The combined report was printed and several hundred copies were distributed locally and to interested agencies abroad. I made several oral presentations to the Swazi government, AID, the Academy for Educational Development, and to other groups and agencies. I also revised and later published some of the KAP survey data in health-related journals (e.g., Green, 1985a, 1986).

I was mindful of the observation, attributed to Alexander Leighton, that "the administrator uses social sciences the way a drunk uses a lamp post: for support rather than illumination." Therefore I had no great expectations about the immediate impact of our study. However, several of the KAP report recommendations did contribute to changes in national health policies and procedures. For example, previous Ministry policy had been to promote only pit latrines made with concrete slabs. The survey showed that fully two-thirds of the latrine floors in our sample were made from wood or other locally available materials. Survey data further suggested that reliance on concrete slabs, which usually required the direct assistance of one of the twenty-odd health assistants available for the entire country, actually served as a constraint to latrine construction in rural areas. Indeed, latrines built from local materials were found to stand up well over time, contrary to a pervasive belief among government officials and foreign advisors that wooden latrines are quickly destroyed by termites.

By October 1982 the Ministry of Health was developing a newly designed radio campaign aimed at improving homestead sanitation. Departing from previous policy the Ministry encouraged people to build latrines from local materials if a health assistant were not available to help with the construction on a concrete slab. Technical details for the building of wooden and other local-material latrines were provided in the radio broadcasts.

Since the survey showed that 82.6 percent of respondents had a working radio in their homestead, I suggested in my report that the radio was an under-utilized medium for health education. Meanwhile, interest in radio was developing in other quarters. By early 1983, two development communications consultants from the Academy for Educational Development completed a series of in-country workshops during which seventeen radio programs were developed with the assistance of the Swaziland Broadcasting Service. The programs were intended to raise health awareness, present information, and promote behavioral change through use of true-to-life dramas about rural people and their problems. In addition to vernacular, believable dialogue, programs featured music, humor, and realistic sound effects in order to create a familiar rural setting in the listener's mind. Messages were often phrased in ways compatible with traditional beliefs, an approach that seems self-evident but which is often difficult to implement in developing countries.

We were under no illusion that we had found the great panacea in health education. It was recognized that maximum effect of radio campaigns could be achieved only with the reinforcement of printed materials and face-to-face contacts with extension workers and perhaps trained local leaders. Yet health campaigns using carefully designed radio dramas represented a new and promising approach for the Swazi government.

After pre-testing the programs on cassettes with representative rural listeners, the first of the radio dramas was aired in April, 1983. I later helped design and conduct evaluation research to monitor listeners' response to the campaigns, and to assess program impact. Approximately a year later the Academy for Educational Development signed a contract with AID to establish a development communications capability within Swaziland Broad-casting Services in order to disseminate a broad range of development topics by radio.

Another recommendation contained in the KAP report, based largely on information from the ethnomedical research, was that more could be done to present health messages in the familiar idiom of traditional beliefs. Even though Swazis may not understand biomedical germ theory, there are many traditional concepts of health and disease that can be built upon for purposes of influencing attitudes and behavior. For example, Swazis believe that unseen agents can cause disease. Some diseases are thought to be "in the air" (*tifo temoya*) and highly contagious; people are infected by "breathing" unseen agents into their bodies. Swazis believe in other environmental dangers as well: poisons and spells may make certain places unsafe, and some diseases may be contracted by simply walking past a location where traditional medicines have been mixed if the area has not subsequently been purified.

Practices relating to disease prevention were also found to be widespread. For example, certain medicines (*tinyamatane*) are routinely given to children through inhalation or traditional vaccination (*kugata*) in order to protect them from a variety of supernatural dangers, and entire homesteads are protected from sorcerers' attacks by driving ritually prepared pegs into the ground around the perimeter of the homestead.

I recommended in the KAP report that health education messages be designed to accommodate certain traditional health beliefs without com-promising public health objectives. For example, mothers might be more receptive to having their children vaccinated against childhood diseases if the practice were presented as a form of *tinyamatane* that protects against diseases that are locally acknowledged to be within the medical doctor's sphere of competence. I pointed out that to ignore traditional health beliefs is to avoid reality; to challenge or confront them directly is to create stress, confusion, and resentment among the people the Ministry is trying to influence.

During the ethnomedical study I had developed an appreciation not only for the important role and function of the traditional healer in Swazi society at all levels, but I had come to respect the sincerity and altruistic motives of many healers I came to know. In fact, I kept up my contact with herbalists, diviner-mediums and Christian faith healers throughout my stay in Swaziland, often coming to them for insights into Swazi beliefs and behavior. Yet my Ministry colleagues, both Swazi and expatriate, often appeared to have a strong negative bias against healers. A brief review of Ministry-traditional healer relations is in order.

Prior to 1983 the Swaziland government had a rather ambiguous policy toward traditional healers. There was an attempt in 1945–1946, during the colonial administration, to pass legislation that would provide for the registration and taxation of traditional healers and would attempt to control their activities. Prior to that time and dating back to 1894, all "witch-doctoring" was considered illegal in Swaziland. Thus the 1945–1946 proposed legislation would have amounted to official recognition of healers on the part of the government. However, due to vigorous opposition by the incumbent director of medical services (the top government physician), the legislation never went into effect.

King Sobhuza II had always maintained that there was much of value in traditional healing. He had recommended a scientific study of traditional healing should be undertaken before anyone attempted to restrict or alter practices and he believed that Swazis would ultimately benefit from a health service that combined the best aspects of both traditional and modern medicine. In 1954, the King issued an "order-in-council" by which much of the previously drafted legislation became law. Since that year, healers have been registered and taxed. However, the King's dream of a syncretistic health care system was no closer to realization in the early 1980s then it had been thirty years earlier.

In August, 1982 the Health Ministry requested through AID that a respected Swazi chemist engaged in research on traditional medicines and I collaborate in producing a report on indigenous healers. The objectives of the report were to: (1) designate the specific areas of possible cooperation between the modern and traditional health sectors; (2) evaluate the feasibility of a national association of traditional healers and make recommendations regarding the role of government in promoting, monitoring, and liaising with such an association; (3) assess the potential for paraprofessional training of healers; (4) summarize legislation, customary law and government policy regarding healers; and (5) assess manpower in the traditional health sector.

I was delighted with the request since it gave me a mandate to expand an area of research which I believed to be very promising. I felt that some sort of national survey of healers was needed since I was not sure how representative my previous findings were from the approximately twenty healers I had come to know. Furthermore, policy makers are always more impressed with quantifiable data. The MOH and AID agreed to support a survey of traditional healers.

Since no national lists of healers were available—at least complete, up-to-date lists—a strict probability sample was out of the question. It was also not certain what kind of cooperation we could expect from healers themselves, or whether permission to interview could be obtained from all local chiefs. It seemed best for two interviewers who had worked on the KAP survey and were now working under me in the Health Education Unit—to begin by interviewing healers in their own home areas, where they were known and where permission to interview would not present a problem. We later expanded our interview areas to include any areas where the interviewers had kinship or friendship connections, or where the Health Education Unit happened to be working on other surveys or evaluations. At the same time, we purposely sought a balance between the four topographic zones of Swaziland, between which social, economic, and other differences are known to occur.

Between August 1982 and February 1983, 142 healers were interviewed: thirty-five in the Highveld, thirty-six in the Middleveld, twenty-nine in the Lowveld, and forty-two in the Lubombo region. The usual procedure was for the interviewers to try to contact all types of healers (diviners, herbalists, faith healers) in a chosen area by means of referrals based on the social networks of healers themselves. If any systematic bias entered our sample, it might have been in the type of community chosen for interviewing. Yet Swaziland is a small, culturally homogeneous country and we found considerable similarity of knowledge, beliefs, and practices between healers in the four regions.

An open-ended questionnaire was used and, as with the RHM survey, a lot of rich detail and serendipitous information was obtained in this way. The interviewers obtained data on things like the recruitment and training of healers, the types of diseases most commonly treated and methods of treatment, the problems commonly referred to clinics or hospitals, the degree of mutual cooperation between healers, the potential for cooperation with doctors or nurses, and healer attitudes toward receiving training in aspects of modern medicine. I checked information the interviewers were obtaining with my own sources among healers and I sought greater detail on things like traditional categories of illness, theories of disease causation, and attitudes toward cooperation with MOH personnel. I also tried to observe patient-healer interaction, curing ceremonies, preparation of medicines, and other behavior.

We also attempted to estimate the number and type of healers in Swaziland by means of a census in selected areas. We chose four rural communities representing three of the four topographic regions, as well as four peri-urban communities, for a door-to-door census. We found healers in forty-eight residential units out of 598 surveyed, amounting to an 8 percent "coverage" of both rural homesteads or peri-urban households (we found rural/urban differences in "healer density" to be minimal). Assuming the surveyed areas to be representative of Swaziland, and having a fairly good idea of the mean number of residents in both rural and urban residential units, we were able to estimate a total of 1,292 healers in peri-urban areas and 4,150 healers in rural areas. This amounts to about one healer per 110 population, compared with a physician:population ratio of about 1:10,000 for Swaziland.

After analyzing and interpreting the survey and census data, my colleague Lydia Makhubu and I co-authored the report requested by the Ministry. Two hundred copies of the final report on traditional healers were printed in Swaziland and distributed to interested parties in and outside of government. A shortened version was presented at an international health conference in Washington, D.C. in June 1983 and later published (Green and Makhubu, 1984). As with the KAP report, I made several in-country public presentations of the findings from the healer study, including one before the Swaziland Dental and Medical Council and another with Dr. Makhubu at the University of Swaziland that was televised.

A primary recommendation of the report was that seminars for traditional healers be established in order to upgrade healers' skills and to provide a forum for the exchange of information. The first such regional seminar occurred in June 1983. A major objective of the seminars was to train healers in the use of oral rehydration therapy and to develop an integrated, inter-sectoral approach to preventing and treating diarrheal diseases. Other areas of potential cooperation were discussed at the seminars such as appropriate patient referrals, the promotion of childhood immunizations, and the development of a national traditional healers association.

Since the first seminar in 1983, others have been held in various parts of Swaziland. Some have been attended by well over 100 healers per session. The planning and conducting of these seminars is now entirely in the hands of local staff of the Health Education Unit, cooperating closely with the Public Health Unit. The seminars seem popular and there is preliminary evidence of behavioral and attitudinal change on the part of healers and even of Ministry personnel as a result of the seminars.

Information relating to diarrheal diseases provided by healers at seminars as well as the success of the healer survey led the Academy of Educational Development and the Ministry to ask me to consolidate my existing research findings and conduct any additional research—provided it was fairly quick—in order to provide an information base for a mass media campaign concerned specifically with diarrheal diseases and the promotion of ORT. The campaign was to be sponsored by the centrally-funded AID project then known as Mass Media and Health Practices (in its second, expanded phase the project has become the Health Communication for Child Survival project).

The Swaziland Ministry of Health requested, and AID granted, a six-month extension of my original, two-year contract. This enabled my two interviewer assistants and I to conduct some very focused key-informant interviews with healers and their patients relating to diarrheal diseases and their therapies as well as to understanding of dehydration and oral rehydration. We interviewed over a three-month period, after which I analyzed the data and wrote a report. Of course two years of intermittent field research among healers preceded this last series of interviews, so my report on beliefs and behavior relating to diarrhea was no quick and dirty survey. The report, which was later revised for publication (Green, 1985b), provided the basis for the design of a culturally-sensitive mass media program that relied in part on the active participation of seminar-trained traditional healers. The media program was later evaluated to have been especially effective (Sanghvi, 1985; Hornik and Sankar, 1985).

In retrospect the traditional healer research, which led directly to the development of government policy and to the establishment of healer seminars and a program of cooperation between indigenous and biomedically-trained health practitioners, has probably had more of an impact than the KAP survey called for in my original contract. Opportunities have a way of arising once an anthropologist is working overseas on project implementation.

In summarizing my experience on the Water-Borne Disease Control Project, I would say that anthropology has a great deal to contribute to health projects in developing countries. I found that time-honored, qualitative anthropological methods are essential in obtaining certain kinds of information and that such methods can supplement or be successfully combined with survey methods in order to enhance data validity. Of course data validity is more important than the reliability of research methods when dealing with rural African populations and when research data may quickly shape public policies. A statistically elaborate survey, if unguided by the traditional concerns and methods of anthropology, can produce misleading data which in turn can misdirect public policy. It can also hurt the reputation of anthropological/sociological research (little if any distinction is made in Africa between anthropology and sociology).

I feel my assignment in Swaziland was successful from a personal point of view. I gained valuable experience in several technical areas that were quite new for me—sanitation, epidemiology, health education, nonformal education, development communications, and public health engineering—and I learned much from working in a LDC government ministry. I also received two honorable mention Praxis Awards (1982 and 1983) from the Washington Association of Professional Anthropologists for the impact of my research on Swaziland government policy. This kind of recognition and collegial support is very reassuring for an anthropologist working abroad in development work, out of touch with academic anthropologists who, in spite of shrinking employment opportunities in universities, continue to define and dominate the discipline.

In addition, I was able to accumulate a wealth of publishable data from my various research activities. I felt consoled by the thought that if I ever returned to an academic position, I wouldn't have to spend the rest of my days dreaming up new ways to interpret old dissertation material.

Of course my job was not all research. I was often asked to brief visiting consultants and officials, help organize and participate in workshops and seminars, provide several types of training and orientation, help develop health plans and policies, and share in the bureaucratic-administrative workload that accompanies any such project—just to give a partial list. These activities enhanced my skills in several worthwhile areas.

I confess being bothered by the thought that as American technical advisors enhance their careers with each new overseas assignment, poverty continues to grow in Africa and other less developed areas, both in relative and absolute terms. There are those who charge that any form of development assistance, however charitable or humanitarian it might appear, serves primarily to preserve an existing economic world order in which the most developed countries exploit the poor countries with the help of elites from the poor countries. Instead of paternalistic, dependency-fostering assistance programs, it is argued, there should be a fundamental restructuring of power relationships at national and international levels, or at least a gradual empowerment of the poor through so-called participatory or bottom-up development planning (cf. for example Gran, 1983; Hayter, 1982).

I suspect that critics of "establishment-approach" aid are fundamentally correct. However in the short term—my lifetime for example—I'm not sure exactly how or even *if* power relationships can be fundamentally restructured. Yet even with all these uncertainties I feel anthropologists can and should participate in projects directly concerned with life-protecting and life-enhancing measures, while at the same time seeking ways to improve the condition of the poor in ways that are more structurally fundamental. For me, the Rural Water-Borne Disease Control Project has served as a vehicle for the realization of some personally held humanitarian aims, while at the same time providing opportunity for professional growth.

## References

Cohen, Ronald. "Warring Epistemologies: Quality and Quantity in African Research" in O'Barr, W., et al. (eds.) *Survey Research in Africa: Its Implications and Limitations.* Evanston: Northwestern Press, 1973, pp. 36–47.

Drake, Max. "Research Method of Culture-bound Technique? Pitfalls of Survey Research in Africa," in O'Barr, et al. (eds.) *Survey Research in Africa: Its Implications and Limitations.* Evanston: Northwestern Press, 1973, pp. 63–66.

Gran, Guy. *Development by People: Citizen Construction of a Just World.* New York: Praeger Publishers, 1983.

Green, Edward. "Beliefs and Practices Related to Water Usage in Swaziland." *International Journal of Water Resources Development,* Vol. 2, No. 3, 1986.

Green, Edward. "Factors Relating to the Presence and Use of Sanitary Facilities in Rural Swaziland." *Tropical and Geographical Medicine,* Vol. 37, No. 1, 1985a, pp. 81–85.

Green, Edward. "Traditional Healers, Mothers and Childhood Diarrheal Disease in Swaziland: The Interface of Anthropology and Health Education." *Social Science and Medicine,* Vol. 20, No. 3, pp. 277–285, 1985b.

Green, Edward. "Have Degree, Will Travel: An AID Consulting Job in Africa." *Human Organization,* Vol. 40, No. 1, 1981, pp. 92–94.

Green, Edward and Lydia Makhubu. "Traditional Healers in Swaziland: Toward Improved Cooperation Between the Traditional and Modern Health Sectors." *Social Science and Medicine,* Vol. 18, Sec. B, No. 12, 1984, pp. 1071–74.

Hayter, Teresa. *The Creation of World Poverty: An Alternative View to the Brandt Report.* London: Pluto Press Limited and Third World First, 1982.

Hornik, Robert, and Pamela Sankar. "A Preliminary Evaluation of the Swaziland MMHP." Philadelphia: Annenberg School of Communications, 1985.

Kuper, Hilda.*An African Aristocracy: Rank Among the Swazi.* London: Oxford University Press, 1947.

Sanghvi, Tina.*Notes From the Field: AID-Supported Oral Rehydration Therapies.* Creative Associates, Washington, D.C. and Office of Health, AID, Washington, D.C., December, 1985.

Swaziland National Archives. File 1469, Volume 1.

# 8

# Development and Dissertation: Field Research Opportunities on a Pastoral Development Project in Niger

*John J. Curry*

## Introduction

As a recent Ph.D., I share with many of my former classmates the feelings of relief, of satisfaction, and of anticipation which attend completion of the dissertation, the leaving of the graduate school environment, the assumption of the "first job" after graduation. Unlike nearly all of them, however, I chose as my "first job" a contract position as a social scientist on an agricultural development project in Africa.

This non-traditional (for an anthropologist) career choice was not the result of an academic "mid-life crisis." On the contrary, it was, I feel, a rather predictable outcome of my pre-doctoral training, and of my experiences as a contractor on a livestock project in the Republic of Niger during the course of my doctoral fieldwork. In lieu of financial support from more conventional funding sources for anthropological dissertation research (e.g. NSF, Wenner-Gren, Fulbright, SSRC), I conducted my research as a technical staff assistant for the Niger Range and Livestock Project (NRL), under a Personal Services Contract with USAID.[1] My NRL experiences had profound effects on my dissertation topic, on the data I collected to research that topic, and my career choice of what is euphemistically referred to these days as a "practicing" anthropologist.

It is my purpose in this chapter to discuss the effects of my NRL experience upon my dissertation research and my career, and to offer some general observations concerning the positive and negative aspects of utilizing an overseas development contract as a means for dissertation support. As a background to this discussion I shall describe my experiences in the field in Niger, both as an independent researcher and as a USAID contractor. This will include brief descriptions of the Republic of Niger, the area of

Niger which I chose as my research site—the Niger Range and Livestock Project—its purpose and organization, and my role on the project. I shall follow this description with a discussion of what I feel are the major outcomes of my experiences. These include: the changes in the circumstances under which research was conducted as a result of the contract; the changes in both content and focus of my dissertation topic as a result of my NRL experiences, and the contractor role as a socialization process for me. Finally, I shall note what I consider to be the advantages and disadvantages of such an experience for an anthropologist considering either an academic or a non-academic career.

## Fieldwork on a Shoestring

When I began my doctoral fieldwork in the Republic of Niger in West Africa in May 1980, I was realizing a goal I had set for myself nearly a decade previously. My first exposure to the agricultural systems of the West African Sahel came in the fall of 1973, as a graduate student at the University of Maryland. I took a course on the subject from an African geographer who taught a seminar on the effects of drought on traditional land-use systems that semester. From the humid vantage point of the Atlantic Seaboard, the fact that Sahelian farmers could coax even meager harvests of millet and sorghum from the landscape under such arid conditions appeared to me to be unbelievable. Upon completing the seminar paper I resolved to learn as much as I could about farming practices of the Mossi of Burkina Fasso—the topic of my paper—and other agriculturalists of the Sahel.

This new-found interest in a corner of the world heretofore unknown to me I pursued a year later when I wrote my M.A. thesis comparing the social organization and agricultural practices of three West African societies, using data drawn from secondary sources. This vicarious introduction to what had become for me a genuine fascination I found totally unsatisfactory. What I really wanted to do was to conduct field research in West Africa so I could observe Sahelian agriculture firsthand.

In my naivete, I resolved to return to graduate school to pursue this goal. My first choice was the anthropology program at the University of Massachusetts, since a member of that department, Dr. Ralph Faulkingham, had conducted research in a village in Niger during the drought. He indicated that he was preparing to return to Niger to do further research. I saw this as my best chance to work in the Sahel.

To prepare for my field experience, I supplemented the traditional fare of cultural anthropology offered in the department with coursework in community and population ecology, international agricultural development, human adaptability, and peasant economics. During this time Dr. Faulkingham wrote a grant proposal to a funding agency and attempted to secure a research authorization from the Niger government for a field project which included myself and two other graduate students.

By the time our research authorization arrived, our potential source of funding had collapsed. One of the graduate students on the team chose to return to historical demography and to the NSF grant he left behind. We survivors elected to pursue the traditional sources of funding for dissertation research. My colleague was successful in obtaining a Fulbright to conduct research in Lesotho; I, however, came up empty-handed. This included attempts to secure funding not only from granting agencies but also from overseas projects funded by development agencies such as CARE and USAID.

In my search for funding, I soon realized that without any African experience I was caught in a vicious cycle of "no field, no funding/no funding, no field." No fun! For me, further delays were intolerable. Since my whole reason for returning to graduate school was to do fieldwork in the Sahel, a U.S.-based dissertation topic was to me an unacceptable alternative. It was overseas now or quit: my honor and more importantly my self-esteem were at stake.

I concluded that I had no recourse but to take the permission and run. I junked my car, cashed in my tax return, borrowed the airfare from my parents, and proceeded with my plans to conduct anthropological research in Niger on a shoestring.

In order to accomplish my plan I chose to undertake a study of the relationship between household agricultural production and seasonal labor migration in the village where Faulkingham had conducted his research. Located in the southern part of the Tahoua *department* in central Niger, the village known by the pseudonym of "Tudu" (Faulkingham, 1970), offered two major advantages over other possible research sites. Faulkingham's previous research provided me baseline information against which I could compare my own findings. In addition, it was the village for which we had obtained the previous authorization.This, I subsequently found out, greatly facilitated my entry into the field, and even prevented me from being arrested by the authorities once there![2]

With prospectus presented and prelims passed in May of 1980, I boarded a bus near the anthropology department on campus, a bus bound for the New York Port Authority Terminal. From New York, I flew to Paris, then to Niamey, the capital of Niger, where I caught a *taxi de brousse* some 600 km. to the east, to Madaoua—the local administrative center—and the village. A colleague later remarked that in bidding me goodbye at the university that day, she felt as though she were seeing me off to summer camp, duffel bag and all! A rather inauspicious beginning for a dissertation research effort in Niger, and, as I was to discover later, an AID contract.

## The Republic of Niger

My new home became the Republic of Niger, a large, land-locked country in the interior of West Africa (Figure 8.1). It occupies about 1,267,000 km., and is, thus, about twice the size of the state of Texas. Administratively,

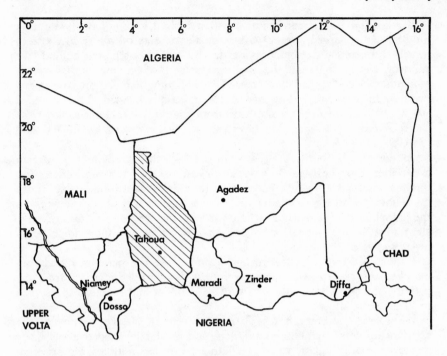

Figure 8.1   The Niger Republic and the Tahoua department.

Niger is divided into seven *departments*, which are divided into a total of thirty-five *arrondissements* in the sedentary areas, twenty-one administrative *postes* for the pastoral areas, and four *communes* for each of the four major cities (Curry, 1984: 104–106). The *department* of Tahoua (Figure 8.1), where the village is located, is about 106,000 km., or about 10 percent of the surface area of the country (Ministere du Plan, 1980: 59).

The population of Niger was estimated in 1977 to be about 5,098,427, of which only 11 percent live in urban areas. There are several ethnic groups. About half the population consists of Hausa-speaking farmers and traders, who are found in the greatest numbers in the Tahoua, Maradi and Zinder *departments*. Other important sedentary ethnic groups include the Djerma in the Niamey and Dosso areas, and the Kanuri in the Zinder and Diffa regions. The pastoral groups which derive their livelihood primarily from herding include the Twareg, various groups of Fulfulde speakers (commonly known by their Hausa name—the "Fulani"), and the Tubu in the eastern part of the country near Chad. The climate of Niger is semi-arid and is characterized by a single, short rainy season from October through May. While there is considerable local spatial and inter-annual variation in rainfall, the country can be divided into three broad climatic/ vegetational zones. In the extreme south of Niger is the Sudan savanna zone, a treed savanna which extends from the southern border to about

15 degrees north latitude. These areas receive on average between 600 to 800 mm. of rainfall per annum. Regions containing thorn steppe vegetational communities are often found between the 200 and 500 mm. isohyets, between 15 and 16 degrees north latitude. These are classified as sahelian. The subdesert, or saharan, communities occur north of 16 degrees. These receive less than 200 mm. of annual rainfall.

Despite considerable growth in the mining and industrial sectors during the early 1970s, the economy of Niger, like its population, remains predominantly rural. Agricultural and livestock production account for nearly half of the gross domestic product in 1977 (Ministere du Plan, 1980: 21). In addition the "traditional commercial sector," consisting of small-scale traders, makes up an additional 30 percent. The principal crops grown are the staple grains—millet and sorghum. While cattle are perhaps the most important type of livestock raised, particularly for export to neighboring countries, camels, sheep and goats are important sources of meat, dairy and other animal products for local populations, both sedentary and pastoral.

### Initial Fieldwork and the Pursuit of a Contract

I arrived in Niger tired, hot, and uncertain about the future. Among the first stops in Niamey were the U.S. embassy to register, and the *Institute Recherches en Sciences Humaines* (IRSH), the branch of the *Universite de Niamey* from which we had obtained permission originally. The director and the secretary of IRSH explained to me through the roar of the air conditioners that my permission, though granted, needed to be "actualized" by informing the Ministry of the Interior of my intentions, my research schedule, and my itinerary. The local authorities would then be notified by radio message of my impending arrival. This could, they told me, take some time.

With virtually no money in my pocket, I panicked at the thought of my money running out even before I arrived in the village. It did not take me very long before I realized that I was going to need some more reliable means of support than loans from my parents if I were to commence, let along continue, fieldwork. I drew upon the example of a colleague of mine who, a couple of years earlier, had packed up, gone to Bolivia, survived on a short-term consultancy or two from USAID, and ultimately obtained funding. I immediately began making the rounds at USAID where, I thought, lay my best chances for employment.

This initial job search within the American community in Niamey was useful in several ways. First, it introduced me to the structure of the embassy and of the USAID mission itself. I began learning a new vocabulary: charge d'affaires, mission director, ADO, vice consul. Learning this system is essential not only for obtaining employment opportunities, but also for facilitating such personal activities as visa renewal, etc. By contacting the various sections of the AID mission, I was able to find out about what were the then-current projects sponsored by AID, where they were operating in the country, and whether or not they might be in need of a social scientist.

A second useful aspect of the job search was the personal contacts I made as a result. These contacts provided me with useful information, established a base of support for my subsequently obtaining a contract, and helped alleviate my sense of isolation which at the time was rather severe. In general I found people at the embassy and the USAID mission to be sympathetic and helpful during the initial stages of my stay in Niger. The ambassador was very personable and provided me with general information on how to survive in Niamey. I was able to stretch my limited funds during my stay due to his advice. When I was having trouble extending my visa, the vice consul intervened and the whole matter was cleared up in an afternoon. AID program and project officers who couldn't help me at the time would give me leads to follow up. In fact, the recurring theme in my search for employment—short- or long-term—seemed to be, "Why don't you go over to the livestock project, they're always hiring anthropologists!"

Heeding this advice, I soon made my way to the offices of the Niger Range and Livestock Project (NRL), which, along with several other USAID projects, was located behind the Rivoli Hotel. There I met the project's USAID liaison officer. I explained who I was, my situation, and my willingness to accept employment, either short- or long-term, with an AID project. He was, as one might imagine, rather skeptical. He explained briefly the nature of the project and indicated that it might have need of a social scientist willing to study agriculturalists. He then gave me a copy of the project paper to read, said to look it over and see if I might be interested in perhaps working with them in future. He said we could discuss it further when I had finished reading the paper. As an ecologically-oriented research project in the pastoral areas of central Niger, NRL contained several social science positions and appeared to be just the thing I was looking for.

However, at our next meeting two weeks later the AID officer was noncommittal, even evasive, about my chances for working with the project. I came away rather disheartened from that meeting. By that time IRSH had "actualized" my authorization and I had secured an extended visa: I was ready to depart for the Madaoua area. I decided to cut my losses and go. I left with NRL directions on where to contact me should the need arise and boarded a *taxi de brousse* headed east. That, I thought, was that.

On my arrival at Madaoua I introduced myself to the assistant to the administrative head—the *sous-prefet*—and explained the nature of my stay. The next day I took a taxi to the village where I asked permission as Ralph's student to live and work there. The spokesman for the village headman (*mai gari*) said it would take several days to get a house ready, and that I should come back at the end of the week. Meanwhile I stayed at the house of a Peace Corps volunteer in Madaoua who loaned me some instruction books on the local dialect of Hausa to supplement my own text written in standard (Kano) Hausa.[3]

My first few months in the village were spent almost exclusively on learning enough Hausa to get along. Much of the initial "ethnographic data" I collected consisted of lexical items and phrases to help me survive.

Some of Ralph's old friends and key informants helped me, although I was to find out later that at first they were suspicious of my claim to be carrying on "Ralph's work" (ie., the village census) and *very* skeptical of my ability to learn the language!

One hot afternoon in June, about a month after I arrived in the village, I accompanied a Ministry of Agriculture enumerator to the next village to listen to him administer a questionnaire on household size and composition. We sat in the village headman's hut, he interviewing farmers, I attempting to follow the questions in my less-than-fluent Hausa. A large, white Chevy Suburban—which *only* the Americans drive in Niger—stopped at the entrance to the hut. The khaki-clad driver approached and said, to my surprise in English, "Are you John Curry? I've been looking all over for you. I have a letter from (the NRL liaison officer). I'm going up to Madaoua now, but will be back in two days to pick you up and take you to Niamey."

I quickly read the contents of the letter. In it, the NRL liaison officer said he wanted me to come to Niamey and meet with their senior consultant of socioeconomics to discuss the possibility of a full-time position on the project. I was rather unprepared for the possibility of full-time employment: I had all but given up hope. However, the possibility of escaping my then-current financial situation, in which I was barely able to afford compensation for informants, was irresistible.

"I'll be ready," was my immediate response.

Two days later the driver arrived at the appointed hour and we proceeded to Niamey. We arrived at the project headquarters just before quitting time. I was introduced to the rest of the project staff who was in town at the time. The senior consultant, for whose return to Niger the AID officer had delayed his decision on offering me the job, told me that the project would like to offer me a position to conduct socioeconomic research among Hausa farmers in the project area and its environs. Since I was already in a Hausa village learning the language and establishing rapport with farmers, the project felt that I was a likely candidate. Initially I was to conduct household budget studies in my home village, then proceed to a location in the southwest portion of the Abalak area in the Tahoua *department* to set up another study which would coordinate with the pastoral studies being undertaken near Abalak and Tchin Tabaraden.

I considered his offer for the blink of an eye and said, "Under the circumstances, I accept your offer." As is customary with development projects and the contracts they promise, my metamorphosis from lone-wolf anthropologist to AID contractor took a long time to materialize. Program officers in the AID mission serially discovered steps which had to be taken in order that the project be in a position to write up my contract. First there was the need to obtain a copy of my C.V. No problem, I always carried a dozen copies in my duffel bag. Then came the security clearance. Remembering every address and telephone number I ever had was quite a challenge. Once that wait was over, I then had to have the approval of my dissertation advisor. This required a cable to AID Washington and a telephone call to Massachusetts.

The hurdle which caused the longest delay involved a rather torturous journey through the labyrinth of the *nigerien* bureaucracy. In September when it looked as though everything was cleared for approval, someone remembered that I had originally obtained research authorization through IRSH. I would therefore need their permission to work on the project as well. This required the Livestock Service's requesting the Ministry of Rural Development, of which they were a branch, to request the Ministry of Higher Education, of which IRSH was a part, that I be "loaned" to them for the duration of my contract.

Meanwhile I had since returned to my home village to continue my own work. Weeks passed into months without any word on my contract. I completed a repeat census of the village as a follow-up to the baseline demographic work done by my advisor during the 1969–1973 drought. I had also begun a study of dry season gardening and labor migration in the village, thus adhering somewhat to my original dissertation topic.

By year's end my patience with the project's inactivity on my behalf had reached its end. Arriving at the project's field headquarters in the town of Maradi, I informed the project director, a *nigerien*, that I could no longer tolerate the delay in obtaining a contract, that I had run out of money (which was partially true) and would have to return to the U.S. soon (which was partially false) if something were not done immediately. If, within two weeks, the project failed to provide me with a contract, I would refuse any subsequent offers the project made. The director then assured me that there would be no problem, and he would attend to the matter of my being "borrowed" from IRSH personally. I was to return to the village and he would pick me up on the way to Niamey on the third of January. We would see the proper person on the following morning.

The whole affair took the project director about twenty minutes to conclude in the office of the secretary for the Minister of Higher Education. Two days later we received official copies of the letter authorizing my working for the livestock service. It took an AID contract officer a mere two weeks to type up a standard, five-page personal services contract, which I signed about six months after I received the initial offer. *Enfin!* I was now part of the Niger Range and Livestock Project.

## NRL and Pastoral Development in Niger

The development project for which I now worked was a collaborative research program between the Government of Niger's Livestock Service and USAID. The purpose of the project was to provide baseline research on the ecology of pastoral production in the central portion of Niger. This information was to be used to design a series of pilot interventions at the conclusion of the project, and to facilitate planning and implementation of a more comprehensive set of interventions in a subsequent project (NRL, 1976). These interventions would be designed to increase the economic and social well-being of the target pastoral populations while maintaining the capacity of the rangeland for sustained production in an ecologically sound manner.

The project design as a multidisciplinary research effort was the product of the then-current development philosophy for the country and for the pastoral regions in light of the experiences of the 1969-1973 drought. During this period of virtually no rainfall, the sedentary agricultural and mobile pastoral populations of Niger experienced severe damage to their local subsistence base, as harvests failed totally in some areas and large numbers of animals died. The famine, which occurred simultaneously with the drought, brought disease, misery and death (Curry, 1984: 13). Numerous causes for the tragedy were postulated, among them long-term climatic changes from air pollution, and environmental mismanagement by the local population (Watts, 1979: 3-7). Such critics of local production systems found particular fault with the region's pastoralists, whom they claimed contributed to the process of desertification through overgrazing sahelian rangelands.

Following the drought, the government, supported by revenues from newly-discovered uranium reserves and by international donor funding, embarked on an extensive program to promote the development of the country's human resources. It was believed that such a program would provide an efficacious and sustainable method of improving the population's ability to identify and to solve its own problems (Curry and Starr, 1983: 2). Schools, dispensaries, clinics, hospitals and roads were built, and large-scale efforts were made to organize the population into cooperatives and other institutions to promote grassroots participation in Niger's development.

The pastoral populations were largely unaffected in the initial stages of this development effort. This can be accounted for by the government's preference to begin work in the more densely populated southern agricultural regions and by the logistical and social difficulties of delivering social services to pastoralists.[4] Also the government lacked adequate knowledge of both pastoral lifeways—the economy, social organization and the production systems of herders—and of actual conditions in pastoral areas which would contribute to, or would deter, development efforts. In light of this knowledge gap, three donor-funded projects covering different geographical areas were initiated to research and define appropriate ways of proceeding with development in Niger's pastoral zone. One of these was NRL, which encompassed portions of the administrative *departments* of Tahoua, Agadez, Maradi, and Zinder (Curry and Starr, 1983: 3).

The sahelian areas of this region are inhabited by two principal pastoral groups. The Twareg, who represent the majority of the pastoral population of the NRL project zone, migrated to the area from North Africa in successive waves beginning around the eleventh century. Their language, Tamajeq, is a Berber tongue. Traditional Twareg society was highly stratified, characterized by a hierarchy of distinct social groups, composed of diverse ethnic elements.[5] Prior to colonial rule, the Twareg controlled much local agricultural and livestock production, and considerable long distance trade (Baier, 1980).

The Wo'daa'be are relatively recent arrivals to the area. Their migration into the region at the turn of the century from areas further to the south was facilitated by the French "pacification" of the Twareg, and the colonial administration's construction of public water points. The Wo'daa'be, in contrast to the Twareg, are a relatively unstratified society, where kinship provides the major bond linking different sectors of the population. The flexibility of their social organization permits the Wo'daa'be to lead a highly mobile lifestyle based on small economic units, while providing them with risk-minimization mechanisms through traditional forms of mutual aid (Curry and Starr, 1983: 8).[6]

## Project Organization

The multidisciplinary nature of NRL was reflected in the organization of project activities into several distinct though somewhat interrelated, components. These activities included: aerial censusing of livestock and construction of resource inventories for the project zone, vegetation mapping of selected areas, rangeland composition and productivity monitoring, water point utilization survey, range management experiments, veterinary assessment of pastoralists' herds, a livestock marketing study, an inquiry into the legal basis (both traditional and modern) for the formation of herders' associations, and intensive socioeconomic studies of sample pastoral, agropastoral and agricultural groups who live within the project zone.

Although some of these studies were conducted by short-term consultants (i.e., the aerial surveys, veterinary assessment, livestock marketing and legal studies), the bulk of the research was conducted by project staff, which included both expatriates and their *nigerien* counterparts. The project also sponsored about six members of the Livestock Service to pursue advanced degrees at U.S. universities in range management, animal science, and rural sociology.

The permanent project research staff was divided into two "teams"— one technical, the other socioeconomic. Each "team" was headed by a senior consultant who made several visits of varying length annually. These individuals were responsible for the overall design and execution of field research, for coordination of data analysis, and for dissemination of results. All staff members were however responsible to the *nigerien* project director for all administrative matters. This system provided overall guidance for research yet gave the permanent field staff considerable freedom in the design and supervision of their individual research programs. I feel that this flexibility aided me considerably in data collection for my dissertation, as I was to integrate personal research interests with project goals and requirements under this type of research regime.

Range management and animal production specialists comprised the permanent staff on the project's technical team. They conducted their research both in the field among pastoralists, and at two government ranches. They were assisted by five Peace Corps Volunteers, *nigerien* counterparts, and hired herders and interpreters. This team was responsible for resource inventory and mapping as "ground truthing" for the aerial survey, monitoring seasonal and inter-annual changes in range conditions at pasture exclosures through the project zone, and conducting range management and grazing experiments at the government ranches. One of the animal production specialists contributed an improved design for traditional wells which was tried on an experimental basis in the field. Another conducted an intensive study of traditional herd management and range utilization practices among a group of Wa'daa'be herders.

The socioeconomic "team" initiated both extensive and intensive field studies among pastoralists, and later agropastoralists and sedentary agriculturalists, in the project zone. While the extensive surveys such as water point utilization and the "economic subsector" surveys, covered most regions of the project zone, the intensive surveys of domestic economy were centered in the Abalak and Tchin Tabaraden areas in the southwest corner of the zone. This team, headed by the senior consultant for socioeconomics, consisted of technical staff assistants for Twareg and Wo'daa'be studies for communications, for agricultural economics, for human health; seven members of the Livestock Service who served as counterparts; a Wo'daa'be consultant and numerous enumerators.

Three social and economic anthropologists served on this team. One, the communications specialist, conducted a survey of water point utilization in the project zone. Another was the Wo'daa'be specialist. I was responsible for the study of Hausa agriculturalists who utilized the "transitional" zone at the southwest corner of the project zone.

Each anthropologist brought his or her own theoretical perspective to the project. The resulting diversity of opinion, which at times sparked lively debate among socioeconomic team members, had several positive outcomes. First, it gave the project a more robust anthropological approach to pastoral development than would have occurred had a single anthropologist been a member of the team. Second, the ensuing debates gave the project, at times, a lively intellectual atmosphere. Third, the opportunity to share ideas and "reading lists" on anthropological topics lessened the tendency for us anthropologists on the team to become theoretically "stale" during the course of fieldwork.[6]

## Fieldwork as a Member of NRL

The first several months of 1981 I spent with the project planning the data collection program for the agricultural studies. This data collection regime involved both formal and informal data collection methods. We conducted informal interviews in settlements where we had no previous information prior to formal censusing. In this manner we obtained information on the production system of the group, its history, and local perceptions of constraints to production. This informal baseline information would be supplemented periodically by discussions with key informants, a standard anthropological technique. For all the villages other than "Tudu," where accurate, long-term census information previously existed, we conducted a formal demographic census to determine household size, composition and resource endowment. In "Tudu," we administered this same census to our cooperator households which were drawn from the various *quartiers* of the village. From these censuses we drew our samples for the intensive household budget studies we conducted in two sedentary agricultural villages as part of the project's intensive socioeconomic monitoring study.

The primary data collection technique employed by the project for the domestic economy study was a variant of the "cost route survey" method (Eicher and Baker, 1982: 72). This involved a series of twice-weekly visits of sample households in which they were asked to recall the hours spent in various activities (both labor and leisure) by economically active persons in the domestic unit, and all economic transactions in the interval since the last interview. The multiple visit, or cost route, survey has been a favorite method of agricultural economists in West Africa since the early 1970s.[7] As an avid reader of David Norman's work among Hausa farmers in northern Nigeria, I was enthusiastic over the possibility of employing such a data collection method in my own research situation.

We began the formal collection of data in the village of "Tudu" in mid-May 1981. Prior to this I had selected my first group of enumerators, some of whom had worked on a similar study in the Zinder *department*. After an initial meeting to familiarize the village and the participating households, we conducted the household census and commenced interviews. We initiated a similar study in the village of Shadawanka, located in the project zone about 65 km. southeast of Abalak—at the end of June 1981. We continued until the end of October 1981. Attempts to initiate household labor and budget studies among groups of neighboring agropastoralists—one Ful'be-speaking, the other Tamasheq-speaking—failed. In the Twareg cases, this was due to difficulties in finding Tamasheq-speaking enumerators willing to live in the camps and establish rapport with the occupants, who in most cases belonged to a different social class. In the Ful'be case, the mobility of the group was our undoing: at the end of the 1981 rainy season, the entire group moved with their cattle to dry season pastures in northern Nigeria!

In addition to the multiple visit surveys, we collected supplementary data of various sorts. Field measurements allowed us to calculate yields of millet and sorghum. We weighed amounts of food and dairy products in traditional units of measure to use as conversion factors for the budget studies. We collected market price data on livestock and commodities essential to households on a (nearly) weekly basis at local markets for the duration of the survey. Thus we were able to monitor price fluctuations of the staple grains, millet and sorghum, and of various types of livestock and to compute the terms of trade for livestock (the major commodity for pastoralists) *vis a vis* grain (the major commodity for farmers).

The size of the quantitative data set collected by each portion of the domestic economy study proved to be one of the major problems which the project faced as it attempted to synthesize its findings at the conclusion of the project. Numerous person hours were spent coding, entering, and checking the data. Data were entered at a computer facility in Niamey, and another in the United States. For most of us on the socioeconomic team, computer literacy was initially a problem: we subsequently learned basic computer skills on the job. The data sets were so large that they required additional entry and clean-up work after the conclusion of the project.[8] Partial data sets were used by various members of the socioeconomic team to present preliminary results for the draft of the final report of the project, and for the design effort of the successor project, which effort began in January of 1983.

This design of the successor project, the Niger Integrated Livestock Production Project (NILPP), relied heavily upon qualitative data collected by the socioeconomic team as a result of each member's long-term familiarity with the project area and its inhabitants. I have elsewhere detailed the importance of this more "ethnographic" data for planning purposes (Curry 1986).

## NRL as Socialization Process

My experience with NRL gave me more than an opportunity to collect data for my dissertation. As a staff member of a joint Government of Niger/USAID project, I was responsible to both *nigerien* and USAID officials in a professional capacity. This required me to become familiar with the structure and protocol of both the host country and donor agency bureaucracies in order to be effective.

As a member of IRSH on "loan" to the *Service de l'Elevage*, I was in effect a government worker. This conferred upon me both a status and a set of responsibilities which I feel are quite different from that of a visiting scholar with host country academic affiliations. Although an expatriate (with the ambivalent status that implies) I was nevertheless an integral part of the *nigerien* bureaucracy, with ministers and project directors above me, livestock agents and counterparts beside me, and data enumerators and chauffeurs below me in the hierarchy.

An interesting confirmation of this integral status within the government bureaucracy occurred in the village of "Tudu" itself. During an absence from the village in September and October 1980 when I was attempting to secure my NRL contract, the village headman removed my belongings from my house to permit a school teacher and his family to live in the dwelling. He gave as his reasons for my displacement the fact that school teachers as *masu gomnati* (government people) had first priority on available housing in the village. With some embarrassment, he offered me a room in one of the "bachelor" huts in his own compound. At the conclusion of the school year in July 1981, I was given my choice of the school teachers' houses as a base from which I could conduct my study of the village for NRL.

This change in status required me to learn many new things in order to do my job. Ironically, one of these was French. While most expatriates arriving in Niger know French and use that as their initial field language, I, upon reaching the field, had concentrated upon learning Hausa in order to communicate with villagers as a "lone-wolf" anthropologist. As a government bureaucrat, I was required to at least follow formal and informal discussions in French. I therefore had to resurrect my very rusty high-school French with great difficulty in order to function.[9] With both French and Hausa I could adopt several field *personna*, one an "official" voice in French, another an "unofficial" (and often more precise) voice in Hausa. This, I feel, greatly facilitated my establishing rapport with enumerators and others during the course of fieldwork.

The other bureaucracy I was required to interact with was that of USAID as a personal services contractor. From this experience, which was in reality an extension of my job search, I became familiar not only with the structure, but also with the dynamics of an AID mission. As a member of the AID mission, albeit temporary, I also had the opportunity to meet and interact with permanent AID staff and short-term consultants and temporary duty (TDY) personnel. This experience afforded me the opportunity to meet people whom I had wanted to meet previously, to share ideas with, and to gain contacts and information which I consider to be valuable in future work in development.

At the conclusion of my contract with NRL in March 1983, I returned to the U.S. to spend an additional four months as a research associate at the University of Massachusetts to participate in the clean-up of the NRL data set. This additional support permitted me to clean enough of my data to analyze one of the villages in the study for my dissertation. My association with NRL had provided me with over two-and-one-half years of field support, the scale of which I could never have realized with a more conventional (academic) source of dissertation support.

In addition the NRL experience provided me with additional consultancy opportunities by which I was able to support myself during the year in which I wrote my dissertation. One involved collaboration with a colleague from the project to write a case study of the project for the Women in Development section of USAID (Curry and Starr, 1983). The other short-term consultancy allowed me to return to Niger in early 1984 to assist the Niger Integrated Livestock Production Project (NILPP) in designing their plan of work for that year. These opportunities became available to me only by virtue of my experiences with NRL and by the personal contacts I had made in the development community.

## NRL and the Changing Nature of the Dissertation Topic

The old saying, "The more things change, the more they remain the same," was certainly true of my dissertation topic in general, and the effect my NRL experience had on it.

As I stated earlier in this chapter, I went into the field with a dissertation prospectus based on a relatively simple-minded notion of direct cause/effect relationships between household agricultural production and dry season labor migration of farmers in the village of "Tudu." Most conventional analyses of labor migration posit "pull" factors such as urban-rural wage differentials (Todaro, 1977), or "bright lights" effects of modernization (Caldwell, 1969) as cause. I felt however that "push" factors such as shortfalls in household agricultural production may have equal or greater importance.

It was not long after I arrived in "Tudu" that I realized that no simple relationship existed between wet season production of millet and sorghum and dry season migration to Nigeria. In the intervening five years since Ralph's last visit and my arrival, farmers were cultivating dry season irrigated gardens of onions in ever-increasing numbers. They were selling the onions to buyers who appeared in large trucks from as far away as Abidjan on the coast. Irrigated onion gardening then, represented an alternative to dry season labor migration; an alternative made possible by another aspect of the regional economy—long-distance trade. My "lone wolf" research project now had become a study of migration versus onion gardening as an alternative to dry season occupational strategies. The manner in which individuals and households participated in the extra-local economy was becoming the central feature of my research.

My NRL experience further strengthened this research theme. It provided me with both the time and resources to collect the data necessary for such an investigation. Perhaps more importantly, it exposed me to aspects of the problem I never would have noticed had I been limited to a single village in the agricultural area near the border with Nigeria. By working in the "transitional" zone in a village with an important regional livestock market, I became aware of the importance of other forms of participation in the regional economy for household economic strategies. These included: livestock occupations such as intermediary or entrepreneur, various forms of petty commerce (used clothing, imported goods, prepared foods) and "traditional" occupations, such as butchery, praise-singing, and traditional medicine. The present village of Shadawanka was founded about forty years ago by Hausa to trade with pastoralists in the area: regional commerce can be said to have formed the *raison d'etre* for the village from its inception.

These and other results of my research for NRL forced me to rethink aspects of my dissertation topic. It was difficult for me in light of my experiences to consider "households" and "villages" in Niger (or anywhere else for that matter) as independent, somewhat static social units to be studied in isolation. Local production, particularly dryland agriculture, could no longer be regarded as the keystone of household survival strategies. In fact, certain aspects of the agricultural system became understandable only with reference to seasonal patterns of income-generating labor and the cash flow such labor provided households. This was especially true of the labor allocated by households to agricultural production: who was available, who did the work, what tasks were performed and when. My dissertation topic changed from a study of agricultural production and dry season migration to an investigation of the myriad of strategies, both local and regional, which households fashion in order to persist in that portion of the Sahel. This broadened perspective was, I feel, a direct outcome of my NRL experience.

## Conclusion

My association with NRL provided me with skills and experiences which have benefited me both in the academic and development environments. The "method and theory" I brought from graduate seminars to the field were sharpened and redefined by the "realities" of Sahelian everyday life. I acquired new skills, many of them administrative, and computer literacy as a member of the NRL team.

The NRL contract became my entree into a career path in international development. Through my NRL experience I learned the structure of several bureaucracies—State Department, USAID, and the Niger government—and how to function as a member of multiple hierarchies. I developed personal contacts with administrators, social scientists working for AID, and short-term consultants and contractors. These people, particularly the short-term consultants, not only became contacts for future job possibilities, but more importantly during my fieldwork, provided me an opportunity to discuss academic and development issues. This was a source of relief from the everyday routine and helped alleviate the feeling that I was becoming stale intellectually. Since NRL, I have had several positions and employment opportunities which were the direct result of my overseas experience, and the personal contacts I have made as a result of that experience.

The advantages to one's overseas career opportunities afforded by a USAID contract must be balanced by several potential disadvantages which might accrue to one's academic possibilities. Time and energy spent in international development work is often at the expense of academic career advancement. Meetings with government officials and USAID bureaucrats in foreign capitals often must substitute for on-campus committee meetings and journeys to professional meetings to present scientific papers. By being in the field, often weeks away from academic journals and newsletters, one is deprived of vital scientific and practical information necessary for keeping up in an academic sense. Deadlines for research grants—a vital category on the academic C.V.—come and go. Quarterly reports and summaries of research findings must be written in lieu of scientific papers and journal articles which carry greater academic prestige. Years spent overseas under contract rarely if ever count toward academic tenure, whether or not the individual is already on a university faculty, the exception being if one *publishes* research results in peer-review journals.

Even as a graduate student, overseas research carries a kind of academic "opportunity cost." While I was overseas, those fellow graduate students who pursued U.S.-based dissertation topics had the opportunity (which I denied myself) to write for grant monies, present papers at scientific meetings, remain in frequent contact with their committees, and look for academic employment while collecting and analyzing their data. As a result, these colleagues remained *au courant* with intellectual trends in both the discipline in general and our department in particular, in ways that we who were overseas, regardless of our funding source, could not. Thus, I was required upon my return to the university to catch up on the new intellectual trends in the department, since I was now considered by some members of my committee to have become theoretically "flabby" in my absence.

The multidisciplinary nature of the NRL project has exerted influence over my subsequent thinking and behavior as a social scientist. During the life of the project, I collaborated with scientists and technicians in range management, wildlife biology, animal production, veterinary medicine, and livestock economics. Despite (or perhaps because of) the fact that there were several anthropologists on the project, one was required to explain one's own anthropological approach to the problem at hand. Through these cross-disciplinary interactions, I learned much about the subject matters of other disciplines, and the way other scientists perceive and go about solving problems which we were confronting jointly. As a result of this need to communicate my own perspective to non-anthropologists, I even now am more comfortable discussing research problems in an interdisciplinary manner rather than from within an internal cross-paradigm framework.

As an opportunity to conduct doctoral dissertation research, my experience as a contractor on the Niger Range and Livestock Project had several advantages over other possible situations. I have indicated in this chapter the many ways in which NRL formed the environment in which I completed the field research, the analysis and the writing of the dissertation. In the field, I certainly commanded more resources—data enumerators and logistical support—than was the case as a "lone wolf" anthropologist doing fieldwork on one's own. The duration of the contract extended both my research authorization and my ability to remain in the field beyond the original one-year permission from IRSH. During this protracted field period, Ralph my advisor had the opportunity to visit me in the field, to witness for himself the changes which had occurred in "Tudu"—"his" village—since his last visit, and to interact with pastoral and agropastoral groups in the Shadawanka area, thus experiencing aspects of *nigerien* rural life hitherto unknown to him. His enhanced appreciation of my field situation greatly facilitated the preparation of the dissertation upon my return from the field. He subsequently became involved in the final stages of NRL and in the planning of the subsequent project, and obtained a grant from USAID for data clean-up and analysis of the NRL socioeconomic data set. This grant was one of my sources of support during the analysis and write-up stages of the dissertation.

I have noted in the preceding section how the NRL experience greatly expanded the scope of my dissertation research topic. The NRL project, as a research-oriented development effort, was perhaps somewhat atypical of development projects in the manner in which it emphasized basic research and relied upon both qualitative and quantitative data for planning purposes (Curry, 1986). However, overseas development projects are increasingly relying upon social scientists, particularly anthropologists, for expertise—a trend illustrated by the other contributions to this volume. As development projects employ more anthropologists, and administrators become more familiar with anthropological perspectives and issues, this could result in overseas development work becoming an even more favorable climate in which to undertake scientific, including dissertation, research.

Participation in international development by universities has received recent impetus from the establishment of Title XII projects in the field and international programs on campus. Increasingly, more anthropology departments offer courses and degree programs in "applied" and/or "development" anthropology. I believe this training of anthropologists to pursue non-academic careers serves to create a healthy linkage of the academy with development agencies.

In conjunction with this trend, I feel there must be a simultaneous awakening to the opportunities for scientific research which exist in development work. As more graduate students avail themselves of such opportunities, they will contribute more than just accumulated knowledge to the field of anthropology. They will help to eliminate from the discipline the implicit distinction between "applied" and "real" anthropology—an artificial distinction for a discipline whose goal is the understanding of the condition, at all times, in all its variety, of the human species.

## Notes

1. I conducted the majority of the field research referred to in this paper as a member of the Niger Range and Livestock Project, 683-0202, under USAID Contract No. 683-A-10003, and through research permission granted by the Institute Recherches en Sciences Humaines, Universite de Niamey. I gratefully acknowledge their support. All statements in this paper are the sole responsibility of the author.

2. About six months after I arrived in the village, the local youth group, the *Samariya*, held an evening fete on the grounds of the primary school. In attendance was the *sousprefet*. Seeing an unfamiliar face in the crowd, he summoned me to where he was sitting. I learned to my embarrassment that we had not met previously, and that I had gone through the initial formalities with his *adjoint*. He asked my business in the village, whether I had authorization to conduct research, and wouldn't I please produce it in his office at 8:30 the following morning. His stern demeanor changed abruptly when he saw the letter signed by the president himself! All of our subsequent meetings were very friendly.

3. The Hausa in the part of Tahoua where I lived spoke a variant of the Sokoto dialect of the Hausa language (*Sakwitanci*). Although mutually intelligible with the Kano dialect, Sokoto Hausa contains several phonetic and grammatical differences which can prove troublesome to the learner working from standard Hausa textbooks. I was often chided by the villagers for my clumsy attempts to speak what little Kano Hausa I knew. "That isn't Hausa, that's 'Kano-speak' (*Kananci*)," they would say. "The *real* Hausa goes like this . . . " I soon abandoned the Nigerian-oriented

texts I was using, in favor of the Peace Corps materials written for the local dialect. My ability to communicate with my neighbors increased dramatically.

4. National development efforts in the pastoral areas of central Niger prior to the inception of NRL were generally restricted to the drilling of wells, the inoculation of livestock against rinderpest, and, to a lesser extent, the establishment of "nomad schools" (*ecole nomade*) and dispensaries at government outposts.

5. The popular term for these people—"twareg"—was coined by the French. It most correctly refers to the noble class (*imajeghan*) in the social hierarchy of the numerous confederations which comprise the social organization of these pastoralists. These confederations are united by a common language, and by a complex series of economic and political ties developed through trading and warfare over the years. An individual will identify himself or herself by referring to either the confederation or social class to which he or she belongs. Thus, the more accurate term now currently being used by scholars would be "Kel-Tamasheq," 'Tamasheq speakers' (cf. Bernus, 1981).

6. (Curry and Star, 1983: 6–8). For definitive ethnographic treatment of Kel-Tamasheq societies in Niger, see Bernus (1981). The work of Dupire (1970, 1972) gives an excellent overview of Ful'be groups, including the Wo'daa'be. A history of the Wo'daa'be in Niger has been written by Maliki (1981).

7. For examples of the economic data generated by this method, see Norman, Pryor and Gibbs (1979). A good description of the methodology is given by Delgado in the volume edited by Shapiro (1979).

8. Data entry problems were legion. Coding of the data was done by enumerators in the field, and by project personnel in Tahoua and Niamey. Data were entered at computer facilities in Niamey, and in the U.S. Computer "crashes" in Niamey and irregular shipments of entered data to NRL from the U.S. caused considerable delay in completion of the data set. The inability of NRL to complete data entry and clean-up necessitated the project's contracting for this service at project's end. The work was also hampered by delays in the shipment of the data forms from Niger, and by the project's losing the original data sheets for the Twareg samples.

9. This resurrection of my "Victor Hugo" high school French in West Africa was tantamount to learning the language all over again. Consequently, my French is full of Africanisms, and my choice of tenses more closely resembles that of Hausa than it does the sequence of tenses learned in school. Several speakers of more standard French have noted the distinct West African flavor to my *parole*.

## References

Baier, Stephen. *An Economic History of Central Niger.* Oxford: University Press, 1980.

Bernus, Edmond. *Touaregs Nigeriens: Unite Culturelle et Diversite Regionale d'un Peuple Pasteur.* Paris: Memoires ORSTOM No. 94, 1981.

Caldwell, John C. *African Rural-Urban Migration. The Movement to Ghana's Towns.* New York: Columbia University Press, 1969.

Curry, John J., Jr. *Local Production, Regional Commerce, and Social Differentiation in a Hausa Village in Niger.* Ph.D. dissertation, Department of Anthropology, University of Massachusetts, 1984.

Curry, John J., Jr. "Anthropological Adaptations of Farming Systems Research to the Study of Pastoral Production Systems: The Case of the Niger Range and Livestock Project," in Jeffery Jones and Benjamin Wallace, eds., *Anthropological Contributions to Farming Systems Research.* Boulder: Westview Press, 1986.

Curry, John J., Jr. and M. Starr. "The Niger Range and Livestock Project: A Case Study of Women and Development." A case study prepared for the USAID-funded Women in Development Project at the Harvard Institute for International Development. Washington, D.C.: USAID, 1983.

Dupire, Marguerite. *Organisation Sociale des Peul*. Paris: Librairie Plon, 1970.

Dupire, Marguerite. *Les Facteurs Humains de L'Economie Pastorale*. Niamey: CNRSH, Etudes Nigeriennes No. 6, 1972.

Delgado, Christopher L. "An Investigation of the Lack of Mixed Farming in the West African Savannah: A Farming Systems Approach," in Kenneth H. Shapiro, ed., *Livestock Production and Marketing in the Entente States of West Africa: Summary Report*. Ann Arbor: Center for Research in Economic Development, 1979, pp. 70–145.

Eicher, Carl K. and D. C. Baker. "Research on Agricultural Development in Sub-Saharan Africa: A Critical Survey." Michigan State University International Development Paper No. 6. East Lansing: Department of Agricultural Economics, Michigan State University, 1982.

Faulkingham, Ralph H. *Political Support in a Hausa Village*. Ph.D. dissertation. Anthropology Department, Michigan State University, 1970.

Maliki, Angelo. "Historique du Wodaabe." Niamey: USAID Niger Range and Livestock Project Discussion Paper, 1981.

Ministere du Plan. "Plan Quinquennal de Developpement Economique et Social 1979–1983." Niamey: L'Imprimerie Nationale du Niger, 1980.

Norman, David W., I. H. Pryor, and C. J. N. Gibbs. "Technical Change and the Small Farmer in Hausaland, Northern Nigeria." African Rural Economy Paper No. 21. East Lansing: Department of Agricultural Economics, Michigan State University, 1979.

NRL. *Project Paper*. Niamey: USAID Niger Range and Livestock Project, 1976.

Shapiro, Kenneth H., ed. *Livestock Production and Marketing in the Entente States of West Africa: Summary Report*. Ann Arbor: Center for Research on Economic Development, University of Michigan, 1979.

Todaro, Michael. *Economic Development in the Third World*. London: Longman, 1977.

Watts, Michael J. *A Silent Revolution: The Nature of Famine and the Changing Character of Food Production in Nigerian Hausaland*. Ph.D. dissertation, Department of Geography, University of Michigan, 1979.

# 9

## U.S. Development Assistance to Morocco in Upgrading a Casablanca Squatter Community—As Seen Through the Lens of a Development Anthropologist

*John P. Mason*

### Introduction

This is a descriptive analysis of a shelter and community improvement program for low income residents of Casablanca's and, for that matter, Morocco's largest squatter community. While the program did not end up as it was intended to, it did have some positive, perhaps unexpected, results. This chapter will depict my roles, that of a development anthropologist in addition to a multiplex of other parts, in the cross-national context of development assistance. It will describe the place of a variety of United States and Moroccan officials, the people and community selected for upgrading, and the planning and evolution of the program itself. The lessons learned from this experience are presented so that they may help the development anthropologist, or those aspiring to that, become aware of the opportunities, pitfalls and dilemmas of the applied discipline.

It became clear to me early on in my more than four years of consulting on the squatter upgrading program, that Americans and Moroccans were often talking past each other, that certain unspoken political and cultural imperatives were responsible for many a crossed signal, and that very slow movement was attributable to different agendas and priorities (often hidden) held by the various parties. While I was able to perceive these differences, forces well beyond me precluded my effectively mediating them.

I would like to thank Eric Belsky, J. Robert Dumouchel, and Randall Trudelle for their helpful comments on an earlier draft. I am responsible for the chapter's content.

In my role as "development anthropologist" I will describe the intercultural context in which the program was initiated and evolved. In that role, I carried out field research in the squatter community for purposes of beneficiary analysis and social planning. However, much of my function in this U.S. government-supported shelter and community improvement program went far beyond anthropology, including the promotion, packaging, and managing of the technical assistance effort which was provided by my organization— a private, Washington, D.C.-based consulting and development group. As part of my work I was also constantly involved in negotiations, discussions, and planning sessions with U.S. and Moroccan government officials which led to management decisions which go beyond the purely anthropological prerogative.

Because of my level of involvement in the project, I do not profess to hold value-free perceptions of what happened or did not, in the name of "development." Nevertheless, I have seriously attempted here to peel away my own biases which evolved over several equally rewarding and frustrating years of working with Americans and Moroccans in trying to get this program implemented.

### The Moroccan Setting and U.S. Desire to "Show the Flag"

Morocco, with its geographic place at the entry to the Mediterranean and its important political position in the worlds of Arabdom, Africa, and Islam, is a key ally of the United States. It relies on military aid from the U.S. in fighting its war against the Polasario for a slice of the Sahara and is the recipient of considerable foreign development assistance. After Israel, Egypt, and Turkey, Morocco is the fourth largest recipient of aid in the Near East region, having in fiscal year 1985 received $33 million through the USAID. Such a level of development assistance, when coupled with credits for military armaments, represents a significant financial commitment to Morocco.

The official relationship between Morocco and the United States is mainly channeled through the position of King Hassan II, representative of the Alawite dynasty which has ruled since the eighteenth century. A testimony to the endurance of U.S.-Moroccan political relations is the persistence of the U.S.'s oldest active treaty, between itself and the Kingdom of Morocco, now over 200 years old. In fact, diplomatic relations with Rabat, the capital city, are so closely tied to the king that he fairly insists of the U.S. government that its ambassador be of a social level worthy of royalty.

In the context of selecting a politically visible development activity in Morocco's cities, the AID mission in Rabat and the AID Office of Housing in Washington had together been in search of a worthy urban project for several years. In 1978, the World Bank had funded a low-income community upgrading program in three Moroccan cities. AID saw this opening as an opportunity to enter onto the urban scene. Not unimportant in the rationale, as well, was the fact that several Moroccan urban centers were showing the signs of social and economic strain.

While Morocco's average annual population growth nationwide is just over 2.6 percent, not an excessive rate, its urban growth rate is over 4 percent—which is comparatively high (IBRD, 1984: 218–260). This figure becomes more significant when seen in the urban-national context: the urban population as a proportion of total population has reached 42 percent, which competes with some of the highest figures in the world. What is more problematic is that a growing portion of these urban dwellers is poor and in need of basic services. The cause of such continued rapid urban growth is complex, related to past and present government economic practices as well as deteriorating conditions in the rural areas.

One of the results of rapid urban growth in Morocco, as in many other developing countries, is the crowding of the *medinas*, or the original quarters or centers of now modern cities, and the growth of squatter communities (known as *bidonvilles* in French and better known in English as "slums," the latter of which is not used in development circles due to its derogatory sense). This has particularly been the case in Casablanca, which has 17 percent of the total national population within its regional perimeters, including large concentrations of squatter settlements. It was in that high density and high visibility context that Moroccan and American officials in the late 1970s decided to launch the squatter upgrading program.

### Finding the "Beneficiaries": Peeling Away the Layers of Government Bureaucracy

The AID mission in Morocco, which is part of the overall official U.S. presence but with its own office and administrative capability, perceived the need for non-subsidized and affordable solutions to urban squatting. Moroccan government officials seemed to be sympathetic to the concept, as evidenced by their agreement to a World Bank loan for squatter improvement projects in the capital city of Rabat and the regional cities, Kenitra and Meknes.

With its 20 million population and 1982 average GNP per capita income of $870, Morocco was ostensibly in reasonable economic shape, i.e., bankable. In fact, the World Bank characterized Morocco according to its "basic indicators" criteria as "lower middle-income"—by no means as badly off as most of the so-called low-income economies (IBRD, 1984).

Moroccan receptivity to external financial assistance to its urban squatter problem is perhaps best captured in the words of the Minister of Housing in a speech of February 1979 titled "Shantytowns: Fighting from Within to Prevent Population Displacement and Marginalization," which was his official presentation of a new shelter policy. The Minister stated that:

> The development of social programs away from the location of shantytowns does not solve the problem of their existence but, to the contrary, it promotes their proliferation. We therefore resolved to attempt another experiment that

would consist in fighting shantytowns from within shantytowns. (Government of Morocco, 1979).

The Minister meant, in short, that slums should no longer be cleared or leveled since that solution was socially disruptive but, more important, unaffordable. Earlier government shelter solutions to the squatter problem had in fact bypassed the very people they were directed at, since the replacement homes were for the most part unaffordable by the displaced squatter.

In response to these conditions, AID came to center stage: through its mission in Rabat and the Office of Housing in Washington. But the bureaucracy is more complicated than that, since the mission represents the Near East Bureau of AID in Washington, which in turn takes its lead from the State Department. The Office of Housing, too, has its representatives, in the form of regional offices, in this case, the RHUDO or Regional Housing & Urban Development Office in Tunis. That office oversees the technical and finance-management aspects of housing in AID's Morocco program.

The Office of Housing operates the Housing Guaranty Program. That program uses commercial bank loans for the explicit purpose of supporting developing country shelter programs for low-income people. In the case of Morocco a loan of $25 million for the squatter upgrading project was proposed to be made to the government with the Ministry of Finance serving as the guarantor. Under the guaranty program the U.S. government was to become the guarantor to the lending bank—in case of default. In some respects the Moroccans were treated by both the AID mission and RHUDO as if this loan had been a grant. While AID grants require much more bureaucratic control than loans, especially when the loan is backed by both the national treasuries of the U.S. and Morocco, the loan is a function of a "free market" where controls are typically less stringent than is the case with public monies.

In fact, it was difficult to qualify Morocco for the guaranteed loan, since Morocco's economic and financial situation had been deteriorating since 1977, as the result of a considerable decline in the world demand for key export products such as phosphates (U.S. Embassy-Rabat, 1979). Simultaneously, greatly increased government spending on development programs, consumer demand for imports, a poor harvest due to extended drought, rising energy costs and increased military expenditures all contributed to a large increase in the trade imbalance. The $25 million would provide needed hard currency to allow Morocco to continue paying its bills. The government was to be given a grace period, making it more plausible to repay the loan, in view of its balance of trade deficit. As time passed, the Ministry of Finance kept waiting for the interest rate to become more favorable. That rate did come down to about 11 percent during 1981, but the chance was missed as it shortly skyrocketed to 15 and 16 percent.

Of this $25 million total, beneficiaries were responsible for repaying approximately two-thirds of the amount, distributed over 11,000 families at

9 percent for fifteen years. The fact that a 9 percent rate of interest could be levied on beneficiaries in this Islamic country where "usury" is prohibited, represented no small level of negotiation by the agencies which were promoting development loans such as the housing guaranty.

Throughout the entire process in which officials of the American and Moroccan governments were developing the program and planning the project, beneficiaries were somehow never quite the focal point I had hoped they would be. That was understandable to a degree, given that considerable technical, financial and organizational details were necessary to launch the squatter upgrading program. I had tried to keep beneficiaries at the forefront of this program, not in any activist sense but conceptually, in terms of how the program would affect them, how they would participate and how their preferences would be accounted for in planning and implementing the project. (The success of my endeavor is considered later in the chapter.)

It is important to mention that the Moroccan squatters who were the object of the upgrading program were studied initially as part of the AID project planning process. In response to "New Directions" legislation of the 1973 U.S. Congress (also known as the Humphrey Bill)—in which the "poor majority" were designated as the principal object of American assistance—AID had been and continues to carry out social analyses of "targeted" beneficiaries in the countries where it assists. Thus were the residents of Casablanca's largest squatter community surveyed at the feasibility stage (Berger International, 1979a, 1979b). While this topic is raised later in the chapter, it is briefly noted that the socioeconomic survey referred to here was based on a very small sample and that its applicability to financial and physical planning projections was questionable. The result of the baseline socioeconomic data was that small lot and unit sizes were apparently not what were expected by beneficiaries, nor by government officials. As a consequence budgets had to be revised upwards to account for larger plot and house sizes and greatly increased displacements of residents.

### Ben M'Sik—Stepping Stone to a Better Life in Casablanca

The Ben M'Sik bidonville lies only 7 km. from the heart of downtown Casablanca. That city, with a population of close to four million, is Morocco's largest metropolis and also its financial and industrial center. The growth of Ben M'Sik as well as other squatter communities began after World War I, when peasants migrated to urban centers in search of work and basic life improvements and opportunities. As the traditional quarters became saturated, these new urban dwellers formed spontaneous communities. Equally, the French authorities who were occupying Morocco "helped" Ben M'Sik to grow during the 1930s through leveling other bidonvilles and forcing the residents into the bidonville of our concern. By the 1930s Ben M'Sik had become a magnet for the new migrants and by the end of that decade it had been permanently established more or less along its present boundaries. Having reached a size of 12,000 residents by World War II, less than a decade later it was over 50,000, due in part to a massive rural exodus caused by serious crop failures. By the late 1970s, Ben M'Sik had gradually increased to about 70,000 residents, consisting of over 11,000 households. Every housing unit is constructed with a wooden frame covered with flattened tin cans (thus the name "bidon" or tin can), tin sheeting, wood, cardboard, polyethylene sheets and whatever else is serviceable—generally to the exclusion of "permanent" materials.

The bidonville, situated on state land and privately held land, is divided by the highway linking Casablanca and Rabat. (Some say Ben M'Sik was split by the highway by *design*.) In order to hide the squalor of Ben M'Sik from the view of passersby, city officials erected several kilometers of high walls along the auto-route. Ben M'Sik is characterized by a very high density, approximately 1,000 persons per hectare (about 0.40 acres) in mostly single story structures, and services such as water, sewage disposal, electricity, and garbage disposal are very poor if non-existent. The picture one gets is of an over-populated, densely packed community of tin structures, with garbage scattered over the terrain, water lying in muddy streets and narrow alleys, and a pervasive smell of human and animal excrement (AID, 1979: 9). Yet, there is a palpable feeling of "community" in Ben M'Sik, street corner and other small business activities abound, and a strong sense of the residents' endurance to survive prevails. This bidonville has persevered for almost half a century, despite government administrative and economic forces working against its very existence. Lack of legal recognition of the right of the residents to remain there, minimal, unsafe levels of sanitation services, residents' inability to qualify for bank loans as a result of their lack of land tenure are examples of those negative forces.

The salient socioeconomic characteristics of bidonville residents (late 1970s) used in the project design are listed as follows:

- $110/month median household income (vs. $157 for Casablanca as a whole)
- 75 percent of households supported by male head, 16 percent by female head, 9 percent by sons/daughters
- 60 percent houses are more than 26 square meters, 40 percent less than 25 square meters, 14 percent less than 20 square meters
- $8/month estimated monthly payment for home improvement loan under proposed program. (AID, 1979: 28–30)

The surveys conducted by the Casablanca delegation of the Ministry of Housing and AID suggested that the Ben M'Sik residents were desirous of stabilizing their habitation, especially as some of them were members of families who had lived there since 1917 and because that was about the best opportunity they would ever get to eventually own their own plot and house in Casablanca.

## The Ben M'Sik Upgrading Project—
## ". . . with Every Good Intention"

As part of the agreement under which the Moroccan government would borrow the $25 million guaranteed loan, the Ministry of Housing had to demonstrate that it was capable of implementing the proposed project. The ministry responded by charging its Casablanca Regional Delegation with setting up an office to carry out what was named the Ben M'Sik Upgrading Project. The purpose of the project, as defined in AID's "Project Paper," (AID, 1979: 2–4) was to improve the overall community services and facilities for the 70,000 bidonville residents, including the improvement of 9,900 homes, construction of 1,200 expandable, core unit houses to help relieve some of the pressures of high population density, new water, roads and electricity systems, and several educational and health centers. A proposed industrial zone nearby was intended for small and medium size businesses in order to improve employment opportunities for bidonville residents. It would also result in the development of a social and economic program which would provide jobs, training, small business loans and requisite community facilities.

An important implication of the planning and implementation of Ben M'Sik was the capacity of the Ministry of Housing and its regional delegations to carry out this and similar squatter upgrading projects. The coordination of such a large and complex project was to be provided by a committee of participating ministries and local authorities and representatives, under the chairmanship of the Governor of Casablanca Region.

The project office was set up in late 1979 and was functioning actively when I first arrived there in spring of the following year. It was located in the center of Casablanca, near the Regional Delegation, but over 7 km. from the Ben M'Sik site. The office had three sections: technical, management and socioeconomic studies. Young Moroccans filled the positions of architects, planners, accountants, sociologists, and draftsmen among others. Several of them were so-called *civilistes*, or personnel who were required to perform government employment following completion of government-supported university studies. Such services are provided in lieu of military service.

Several things about the project office struck me upon my arrival in Morocco in the spring of 1980 to work out a technical assistance agreement with the AID mission in Rabat and the Casablanca Delegate from the Ministry of Housing and the project management staff. One was the distance of the project office from Ben M'Sik. Even if there was no appropriate place in the squatter community, an office could at least have been placed on the edge of the community. Granted, it was convenient having the office near the delegate, since he wanted to be close by to manage the project. In fact, the delegate had very limited time to manage, given the other numerous projects and programs of the Casablanca Delegation. The location of the office closer to the bidonville, on the other hand, would have facilitated planning of both the physical and, perhaps more importantly, the community development aspects of the project.

Another bothersome feature of the project office was the label of the section known as "socioeconomic studies." Although it may appear to be a minor detail, that name was inappropriate. Such studies are, of course, essential to the *planning* of any project, but not for the on-going development of the effort. "Community development" was more apt, but that was exactly what the project team was *not* doing and probably had no intention or desire of doing. I will explain this situation subsequently.

A third and related disturbing factor was the mindset of the architects who were responsible for directing the day-to-day project activities (the delegate was also an architect/planner but with a somewhat broader orientation in systems analysis). All of the architects had been trained in Paris, and had apparently absorbed the architect's ethos regarding "monuments." Without trying to sound too unfair, my impression was that these architects were not much different from many in the profession: they "needed" to design—if not erect—something worthy of their intellectual and esthetic capabilities. This is unfortunately not usually possible with low-income shelter solutions, or at least it is not perceived as offering great potential. But the subject is debatable, since designing a usable, affordable scheme for 70,000 squatters, using their input, must certainly be viewed as challenging. Yet, the tendency was for the technical section to over-design, producing structures and plans that were simply not affordable by the vast majority of the poor squatters in Ben M'Sik.

This may sound a bit too much like a bleeding-heart liberal view, outdoing the "New Directions" legislators and even the sticklers in AID who insist on totally cost-effective projects affordable to the "poorest of the poor." Yet, the principles of affordability, beneficiary participation, and replicability of a project are for the most part reasonable, both in terms of their tested use in creating successful projects, as well as, in my opinion, the good sociological and humanitarian sense which they make.

It is important to point out at this juncture that I—as anthropologist, Washington-based project manager—had been introduced to the program after many of the basic principles of the Ben M'Sik Upgrading Project had been formulated and made operational. In addition, I entered the picture at a point when most of the organizational factors were on line. To that extent, I was unable to have any impact on general project guidelines nor on the logistical organization of the project and the original workplan.

### So-Called "Participation" of Ben M'Sik Residents in the Project

One of the bothersome factors to me about the project was the definition by project staff of "participation." This definition was shared by the Casablanca Ministry of Housing Delegate and, it seemed, by the ministry itself. Participation meant the inclusion of survey results from research of socioeconomic characteristics of the Ben M'Sik population. Such information consisted of financial data relating to residents' ability to afford the project.

It also consisted of a minimal amount of data on preferences for house size, materials, kinds of services and facilities. Now the findings from the feasibility stage (Berger International, 1979a, 1979b) were quite adequate for the early planning phases, but the intention of including the residents' perceptions, preferences and sentiments about their willingness, much less ability, to pay for what they were getting was not fully met. Furthermore, Moroccan law itself stipulates such regulations as a minimum 60 square meter lot size, as well as a minimum standard of construction considered high (and thus expensive) by cost-conscious planners. These regulations had not been fully negotiated with government authorities before the project was actually underway, complicating the participation issue even further.

The reluctance on the part of the project staff to promote a participatory mode in working with the beneficiaries reflected the attitude, subtle as it was, of the delegate. He had had his own beginnings in the working class of that medieval, religious capital of Morocco, Fez, and though he seemed philosophically attuned to the need for residents' active participation, he was politically attuned to the folly of becoming a "cause célèbre." The delegate's position was a powerful one, at least within the Ministry of Housing—not so much vis-à-vis the Casablanca local authorities. He knew how to "play the game," which included, naturally, how to advance his own career. That, it became clear, did not include trumpeting the cause of the squatter residents.

It is useful to briefly contextualize the sociopolitical and cultural situation in which officials such as the delegate work. First, Morocco must be understood as a monarchy, with hierarchical authority descending in sharply pyramidal fashion from the king and based in part on the use of fear as a political weapon. Secondly, though on a very different level, language in this context becomes a critical factor. Starting with the king again, his complete mastery of French and standard and colloquial Arabic is significant. French is used with foreigners, mainly because it is the basis of the technical education of Moroccan counterparts. Arabic is sometimes used in the presence of foreigners to communicate something the foreigner is not intended to understand.

When I first arrived in Casablanca to meet the project team to work out the terms of the technical assistance agreement, several signals were communicated to me. One was, "Oh, isn't your brand of Arabic 'interesting'" (meaning, we're a bit surprised to find an American speaking "our" language). Granted, "Maghrebi" (Moroccan) Arabic is different from the dialects I learned, Egyptian and Libyan, yet the "eastern" dialect can be understood by the educated, since that is close to the Arabic they hear on radio and television. In fairness, the technical language many of the staff worked in was learned in France in French, making my use of even limited technical Arabic somewhat cumbersome. Eventually, many of the staff would speak with me in Arabic and we got along quite well, either in Arabic or French. This situation was due in part to class distinctions within Moroccan society, in which "well bred" people speak French. It also results from a sense of a French world view overlaying the Moroccan culture which is something more than just a veneer, yet stops short of a full-blown feeling of cultural inferiority.

A second experience—another metaphor which contained quite heavy symbolic overtones—concerned the "socioeconomic studies" section of the project. On first arriving at the project office, I inquired rather immediately about visiting the "bidonville." Any technical assistance agreement I would concur with—I said to myself (and wisely kept it there)—would have to account for squatter residents' inputs. By that I meant not necessarily more surveys, on which the team had placed great stress, but talking with residents and getting to know them personally and perhaps even helping them to "organize" for the project activity.

I requested that the head of the socioeconomic studies arrange for me to visit the bidonville. Although subsequently he and I became "friends," at that time he did not feel it was necessary for him to accompany me to Ben M'Sik. I persisted in my request and the head relented by arranging for his deputy to go with me. At the appointed time the deputy and a driver met me. The deputy, a university graduate in economics, was dressed as if we were going out for the evening, with the hemline of his expensive pants deftly touching ground level. Using a combination of French and Arabic, we wended our way to the bidonville, getting to know a little of each other en route. We got along fine, in fact. On arriving, I would say, for example, "Let's go over here and perhaps talk to so-and-so," to which he would respond, "Well, there's lots to see." He was right—there certainly was much to see in this vast sea of huts and humanity. But, I was most struck by the message in all of this: decent soul that he was, he simply did not want to get his pants dirty.

The above anecdote illustrates something I did not fully appreciate when I first arrived at the project: partly in deference to French (and general Western) dress codes, any Moroccan perceived to hold a "position" in Moroccan society wears a suit and tie. This prescription—a self-fulfilling prophecy which bears itself out in how one thinks others see him or her— often induces such persons as bidonville residents of "position" and ministry delegation drivers to follow the leader.

On the question of visits to Ben M'Sik, there was a pattern in the way visits would be made to Ben M'Sik, a pattern which was dictated not by the Casablanca delegation nor by the police authorities, but by an attitude and understanding which seemed to emanate from the kingship itself, both in its political and religious senses. It perhaps did not derive from the king himself, but from those surrounding him and their subordinates, the provincial governors.

The Moroccan reluctance to involve the "target" population (as development specialists label the beneficiary group) was based on a fear that this largest squatter population in Morocco could very well revolt and challenge the concept of kingship and the very position of the king. And perhaps there was some justification in this attitude, since it was known that certain political forces were at work in Ben M'Sik which had drawn a portion of the population to the opposition party. While political parties are legitimate and to a degree workable in Morocco, it was felt that associating the project too closely with the residents would lead to too much self-control and, following that, revolt.

The project's worst fears could not have matched what happened in Casablanca in the summer of 1981, namely a bloody riot in Casablanca over government-decreed price rises in basic food commodities. The "origins" of the riot, in which hundreds of people were reported by the western press as having been killed by government troops, had been pinpointed to Ben M'Sik and another squatter community known as Hay Hassani. Such a finding, at least as concerns Ben M'Sik, seems speculative, since most residents of the bidonville support the political party which backs the king, namely the Istiqlal (Independence) Party. Prior to the food riots, when the project was still on track, an elaborate socioeconomic plan was in the making.

### Preparation of a Socioeconomic Development Plan for Ben M'Sik and Finding Where the Power Rests

The socioeconomic development plan for Ben M'Sik included several different components. The major parts consisted of jobs, training, and micro-business upgrading. The Ben M'Sik residents would benefit from greater opportunities for finding and training for work and in improving their own very small businesses through loans and technical assistance. Tied to this was the development of an economic activity zone or industrial site which would generate jobs for residents as well as some space for bidonville small businesses, job training centers in a community facilities zone adjacent to the bidonville, an employment center, and a community and child care center.

This all sounded very good on paper, both in the Project Paper and the terms of reference designed cooperatively by an AID representative from the RHUDO office in Tunis and the ministry delegate in Casablanca. However, it was another thing to carry out the study upon which the socioeconomic plan was to be based.

On the study team organized by the consulting firm for which I worked were four Americans—myself as team leader, a small business upgrading specialist, a small loans specialist, and a training expert. In order to make our work relevant to the bidonville and to Morocco in general, I employed a Moroccan sociologist. I had agreed with the project team that we would jointly interview candidates for the sociologist position. When we came upon the obvious candidate, a sociologist who had done community level research and analysis, I asked some pointed questions about how he intended to approach the community and where he would start the process on entering the community, among other things. Questions about such topics were obviously sensitive, in addition to which my interviewing technique may have seemed too direct. Because of the tension in the meeting, I suggested that the sociologist and I adjourn to another room to discuss the position. Realizing that the project team wanted this sociologist on the study team, I wanted to discuss the exact terms of reference of the job with him in calm surroundings.

The point of this is twofold: (1) the Moroccan team wanted to have control of their American counterpart advisors, both from the technical and decision-making perspectives and, (2) there was a legitimate concern on the part of the team about the kind and extent of contact with the Ben M'Sik community.

The first element is important for understanding a basic tenet of the relationship between the Moroccans and their American advisors. This was the continuous sense of competition which I sensed the Moroccans—from ministry officials on down to certain members of the team—felt towards American officials and corporate officials of my firm. Such a sense of competition was not necessarily exhibited on the level of personal relationships, (I, myself had very positive, rewarding relationships with several members of the team), but seemed to be present in formal, official settings. This was certainly related to the Moroccan sense of "we know what we're doing, we've all been well trained, many of us in France, and we tolerate you because you're tied to this housing guaranty loan." Furthermore, another message which was unmistakable was a reflection of the French program of technical cooperation with Morocco. French *coopérants* working in Moroccan ministries were considered as employees of a particular ministry, taking their orders in like fashion. Project team members had similar expectations, though they implicitly knew that the relationship of AID technical assistance was premised on a totally different basis.

The second element, concern about contact with the community, seemed to originate in official doctrine about squatter communities if not the poor in general: an attitude that there is implicit in the condition of the poor a susceptibility to provocation by "radicals." Additionally, there is the potential problem of building up the expectations of the poor and then not making good on the promises.

To return to the study team which was to prepare the socioeconomic plan for the bidonville residents, there is one account which illustrates the Moroccan fear of contact between non-officials and the squatter residents. The consultant's team had been carrying out the requisite research, including what I had judged to be the critical role of the Moroccan sociologist in drawing in the residents to the program. To that extent, he was fulfilling the terms of reference of the study which requested the formation of local groups from Ben M'Sik to assist in determining the most appropriate use of human resources in the creation of jobs, arrangement of small business loans, and formation of training and other community services programs. In my estimation he did an excellent job of sensitizing the population and obtaining their participation.

At one point in the research, the Ministry of Housing Delegate, the project team leader, the Moroccan sociologist and I were requested to report to the "Pasha" or commissioner of the district inclusive of Ben M'Sik. It had been reported by one of the Pasha's local representatives, the "moqaddam," that the residents were being socially "aroused" by the research. What this meant was that resident interest in the project was being stirred, discussions with them perhaps giving the impression that an improvement program would be introduced and give them some stability in their lives.

The meeting was conducted in Arabic, since the Pasha and his assistants did not speak French very well (and which for *that* purpose my understanding of Arabic was deemed quite adequate, with an occasional translation to French for "purposes of clarification.") The message of the meeting was that the research group was welcome to work in the bidonville, but for the rest of the activity, the members would have to be accompanied by an official of the Pasha's office. This edict fit with the finding of an earlier researcher (Foster, 1974), who had found the authorities and residents equally suspicious of one another.

In that meeting I was struck with the hierarchy of authority, in which the delegate, who usually exuded a competence to lead his staff and deal with others in an authoritative manner, was considerably diminished in the political sense by the presence of the Pasha.

What became obvious to me following this meeting was that the Moroccan sociologist had succeeded in creating in the eyes of officials the perception that he was a revolutionary. He was, first, a Berber—a culturally "marginal" person. Linguistically, Berbers comprise over 50 percent of the population of Morocco, Berber women making up over 60 percent. But, politically, Arabs are dominant, epitomized in the descent of King Hassan from the Prophet of Islam, Mohammed. The sociologist was also an "intellectual," educated for several years in Paris, feared by some of the local officials as a radical, even "revolutionary" type.

The sociologist's weakness can be characterized in part as a resistance to authority. Following the completion of his fieldwork and at the formal end of his contract, he took it upon himself to visit the bidonville without mine or anyone else's knowledge or concurrence, apparently to add his personal touch to the research. Although it was never clear to me exactly what he was doing in those private visits, his presence in Ben M'Sik following the formal completion of the research was reported by some agent of the authorities to the police. The sociologist claimed to be employed by the "project"—but in fact his contract had terminated—and he was put in jail for the night.

The delegate vouched for the sociologist and he was released from jail, but with the warning that he not return to Ben M'Sik. In this sense, his actions reinforced the fears of the authorities, that all the squatter residents needed was a little outside stimulus to get them agitated. But the results of such "agitation" were never tangible, from what I observed. Meanwhile, the sociologist was sufficiently embarrassed that he did not look me up for a while.

These incidents over resident participation were the culmination of a long, gradual series of events. True, the delegate had sent several signals about the issue of sensitizing the Ben M'Sik residents. The irony is perhaps that the Moroccan sociologist who was recommended by the project team to provide the necessary sensitivity to the community development effort, in eliciting resident participation, was himself the very cause of the problem he was hired to solve. It could not have been forecast that he would end up in prison but, if nothing else, it was a graphic lesson of how *not* to go about doing community development work in Morocco.

### The Project Starts to "Go" and the King Says "Halt"

With the socioeconomic program planning activity completed, the implementation of that and the physical works could begin. After spending an embarrassingly long time searching for a French-speaking American architect-planner/upgrading specialist, my firm was finally able to place an experienced person in Casablanca. Suffice it to say that it took many months for the Moroccans to fit this resident advisor into their scheme, with no small degree of agonizing by him and cajoling by me. This was necessitated by the Moroccan perception of resident technical advisors along lines of the French cooperant—namely as an employee. The relationship between the resident advisor and the Moroccan project team finally did work, including that with the delegate himself, and the advisor was able to impart the critical principles of minimal design, affordability, and cost recovery in a manner that respected the professional integrity of the team.

Because of the importance of the community development activity for the project, I advocated with AID and the Moroccans the hiring of a good, grassroots-type community development advisor. It took over a year to obtain approval for the assignment of such an advisor, but finally Moroccans and Americans alike agreed on the position. I found such a person—again with good French (he was an American with French Canadian background)— and he was placed in the field. The advisor also worked out a good relationship with his Moroccan counterparts.

Meanwhile, the king had apparently tired of the walled-in ugliness of Ben M'Sik. The Minister of Interior came to fear the potential explosiveness of this massive squatter community, based in part on the food riots (described earlier) which took place in the summer of 1981 and in which Ben M'Sik residents were killed by riot control squads. As a result of these forces, including the king, the riots, and the Minister of Interior, as well as the apparent lack of progress of the project, the Upgrading Project was terminated. That is, the project as agreed to by AID and the Ministry of Housing was ended. Despite efforts to save the project, including a direct plea by the U.S. ambassador to the king himself. It did not die, however. While active AID involvement ended and the resident advisors were transferred along with the $25 million housing guaranty loan to a national level squatter upgrading effort, all was not lost.

I was informed that by mid-1984 a project which included new housing for the residents of Ben M'Sik as well as many of the facilities foreseen in the AID project plan was underway. Residents originally envisaged to benefit from the project were using their own funds to pay for the new houses. And while the physical planning standards were somewhat higher than those in the first plan, many of the original principles such as affordability, limited displacement, and cost recovery were applied by the same team for which technical assistance had been provided under AID. More than 10,000 residents had made their down-payments of approximately $2,000 each and were prepared to pay off loans of up to about $3,000 additional. By 1985, a total of almost 10,000 houses were in the works—just about the same number planned for in the original project document.

## Lessons Learned

Many "lessons learned" have derived from the experience described in this chapter. For purposes of clarity and brevity, I will classify them in three categories. These are (1) general, (2) project specific, and (3) anthropological.

The list of general lessons learned is headed by those lessons about people, systems, and cultures "talking past" one another. While the community upgrading effort pursued by the U.S. and Moroccan governments seemed to have been an earnest endeavor on the part of both parties, there were several unspoken directives, if not "hidden agendas," operating beneath the surface. Moroccans wanted "cheap" hard currency to help balance their trade deficit and fight their war against the Polasario. Americans wanted to lend commercial money and at the same time assist their Moroccan ally by means of a project such as Ben M'Sik. Although these motives were not inconsistent, there was much posturing on both sides over these motives, creating considerable confusion and delay. Such posturing occurred throughout the project development process and all along the administrative hierarchy of both governments.

While it may sound facile and gratuitous to suggest the role of anthropologist as "agenda clarifier" (see, e.g., WAPA, 1984) as the antidote to these kinds of problems, I believe there is some wisdom in the suggestion. It need not be just the anthropologist who performs this function—although understanding the cultural cues is sometimes critical to the activity—others could also provide that service. Clarifying agendas would have meant working with both Americans and Moroccans to get at least some of the basic mandates on the table. A proviso here, however, is that the parties often wanted to keep their agendas murky so as to maneuver their respective plans without too many objections from the other side. A second caveat is that one has to be at a fairly high level in the negotiation process to play the role of clarifier. In my particular case, while I was sometimes involved at such a level, I was a "consultant"—a somewhat ambiguous role without much power attached to it—and also I was not continuously present to play such a role. And the resident advisors representing my firm were invariably excluded from high level meetings and thus unable to feed back important information. Lastly, the process of negotiation may preclude such a clarifying role because that process, while it may muddle along without the clarifier, might not work at all with that person simply became it would serve to make the agendas too clear and thus objectionable to either or both parties.

Other general lessons learned concern the role of policy versus action. In the Moroccan case particularly, there were some explicitly stated policies about "fighting bidonvilles from within bidonvilles," meaning that the residents of such communities would be kept in place and play a participatory part in the upgrading process. Perhaps this was only a way of attracting more hard currency or, more generously, it may have meant to cure the problem of urban squatters. In any case, the requisite actions, both from the standpoint of AID policy and practical steps to complete the project, were often not followed either in fact or in spirit.

The "policy versus action" dichotomy was compounded by yet another general problem—namely the incompatibility of bureaucratic systems. Both the Moroccan government ministerial-authority system(s) and the American AID technical-administrative system are encumbered and, while I am unable here to recommend solutions for either system, both could have considerably streamlined their approval processes for this project. The bureaucratic constraints, however, are also as much a matter of what was discussed earlier, people "talking past one another," as they are of effective management organization.

For the Moroccan side of the bureaucratic picture, it was a question of a very top-down hierarchy, in parallel fashion, both in the Ministry of Housing and the Ministry of Interior (the latter being the "authorities"). This affected the ease with which decisions could be made, both in terms of who was responsible for a decision and the timing thereof. Long delays resulted from this. For the Americans, the problems derived from the AID bureaucracy described earlier in this chapter: a proliferation of offices and administrative steps and the geographical distance between AID offices. One of the major obstacles in the AID development process was the number of technical requirements imposed on the Moroccans in meeting the conditions of the loan. While I strongly support the spirit of AID policy (especially the legislation and policy which underlie the strategy for reaching the "poor majority"), there seem to be enough "conditions precedent" to effect the housing guaranty loan to boggle even a banker's mind.

Moving to the project level of lessons learned, there are several points to make about project efficiency. First is the complexity of the project, given its physical scale and socioeconomic scope. Encompassing over 11,000 houses, 70,000 residents, and an ambitious economic improvement program, the project was simply too ambitious. Conversely, the Moroccan staff designated to implement this project was too small and, through no fault of their own, lacking in experience.

A more reasonable approach would have been to begin much smaller. It would have been much more effective, at least on the level of shelter and infrastructure, to have selected a neighborhood and commenced planning and designing at that level. This approach would have made particularly good sense from the community development perspective. To have dealt with small sections of Ben M'Sik would have been managerially and sociologically more advisable than the global approach first used. It might also have allayed the fears of the authorities, given their mistrust over dealing with all 70,000 residents at once. As it turned out, the resident advisors did recommend a narrower approach, but by that time, the death knell had begun to sound on AID's version of the Ben M'Sik project.

Concerning the community development effort, it was in the stage of being closely hinged to the neighborhood physical upgrading strategy when the project as such was ended. Given the general Moroccan fear about participation of the urban poor and AID's reluctance to fully endorse "participatory" upgrading, such an approach had only limited prospects of succeeding, at least until it was too late. Moroccan and American officials alike simply did not fully comprehend what participation meant, and so they hesitated to accept on the basis of what they thought it meant. This was due at least in part to the fact that the principles had never been fully spelled out. Had that been the case, a fiasco such as occurred with the Moroccan sociologist need never have happened. In any event, by the time the U.S. community development specialist arrived, it was already too late. By then, AID's role in Ben M'Sik may have already been decided.

Similarly for the physical design and planning process, the cost effectiveness and affordability of the project turned out to be remarkably more achieveable when commenced at the more modest level of the neighborhood or communal section. Unfortunately, this strategy evolved a little too late to be used in the AID version of the project. It was used successfully, however, in the project that finally was implemented.

While many of the lessons described earlier certainly have implications for anthropology, they also apply to the broader development profession. The following considerations are more directly relevant to development anthropologists.

First is the question of timing the anthropologist's input. By the time I arrived, as mentioned earlier, the project design was more or less fixed in concrete. In hindsight, perhaps I could have made more of an impact on such strategies as the "starting small" one, but my visits to Casablanca did not necessarily coincide with critical moments in the planning process. So, between not being present on the ground floor and playing as much a managerial as anthropological role throughout the duration of the project, I was not always able to make the more singularly anthropological impact on that project I might have wished.

Another lesson learned concerns the need for down-to-earth, applicable information on beneficiaries. While a good piece of social research was done on the baseline socioeconomic conditions of Ben M'Sik as part of the feasibility stage, there were insufficient data on residents' preferences and ability as well as their willingness to pay for the proposed features of the project. Equally important, the baseline study failed to elicit attitudes and opinions about *how* residents would actually participate in the project. Hindsight permits me the luxury of stating the above—I only hope that for such projects in the future these omissions will be caught in time.

Related to the above and to the general theme of participation is the ethnocentrism brought to the project by some of the Americans involved. Whether presented in the form of cultural superiority—however benign—or worse yet of an ideology, it was bound to fail. What was needed was a dialogue with the Moroccan counterparts, supported by AID and the Moroccan Ministry of Housing, on the process of community organization. From time to time there were discussions about this, but usually after something had gone wrong and a Moroccan official would feel the necessity to dictate the "appropriate" form of participation. Of course, by then it was too late to have a dialogue.

Towards the end of the project, a workshop-seminar took place with recruits for social advisors' positions, in which an excellent dialogue took place. From this there was evidence of a change in attitude toward community organization. Local officials even seemed to have a change of heart and some of the recruits indicated they had successfully employed several of the community organization principles in the subsequent project.

Much of what has been discussed in both this lessons learned section as well as those on general and project specific topics, has touched on the need for intercultural communications and sensitivity training. I would heartily recommend cross-cultural sensitivity training sessions for professionals working on such a project as Ben M'Sik. This should take place at the outset and continue throughout a project, and in the case of the Morocco example, the training could have been jointly carried out by Moroccan and American anthropologists.

Finally, I must raise the factor of mixing "business" and anthropology. I, personally, feel quite comfortable with this mix, even though it often means making significant compromises in respect to my role as anthropologist. Anthropology in the context of international development work often translates as "quick and dirty" or expediency of one kind or another. This applies to all stages of project development, whether it is project research (feasibility or baseline studies), planning, budgeting, contract negotiation, management and, lastly, follow-up evaluation.

The compromises I have had to make over the years in my capacities as "development anthropologist," "director of research and evaluation," even a corporate "assistant vice president," have rarely involved me in ethical conflict. My different and cross-cutting roles have, nevertheless, entailed some very hard decisions and often required the foregoing the luxury of exploration and "thick description" which anthropologists are so used to and so cherish.

## Conclusion

While many anthropologists may be familiar with the dilemmas of the applied discipline, at least on the theoretical level, it has still seemed appropriate to point out the pitfalls and potential disappointments of "doing" development anthropology as I have attempted to do in this chapter.

When all is said and done, the need to provide constant feedback of knowledge and know-how from the "practicing" to the educational arena and vice versa, has become abundantly clear. In fact most anthropologists in the international development field are sympathetic to this need, as are some who are teaching development courses. That need is ever-growing, however, due in part to the increased role for anthropologists in development work. This means that more exchange will be required in years to come.

I trust that this chapter, using the concrete example of an anthropologist-cum consultant working on an AID program in Morocco, has helped to enlighten the discipline and thereby contributed to keeping the exchange process ever alive.

## References

Berger, Louis International. "Socio-Economic Survey of Ben M'Sik, Casablanca," prepared for USAID, April, 1979a.

Berger, Louis International. "Casablanca Slum Upgrading Program," prepared for USAID, June, 1979b.

Foster, Badi G. *The Moroccan Power Structure as Seen from Below: Political Participation in a Casablanca Shantytown (Ben M'Sik).* Ph.D. dissertation. Princeton: Princeton University, 1974.

Government of Morocco. "Shantytowns: Fighting from Within to Prevent Population Displacement and Marginalization." Ministry of Housing, 1979.

IBRD. *World Development Report, 1984.* International Bank for Reconstruction and Development/The World Bank, Oxford University Press, 1984.

Mason, John P. and Mona Serageldin. "An Operational Program for the Socio-Economic Development of Ben M'Sik, Casablanca, Morocco," for the Cooperative Housing Foundation, Washington, D.C., 1980.

U.S. Embassy (Rabat). "Foreign Economic Trends: for Morocco." March 1979.

U.S. Agency for International Development. *Project Paper (for) Ben M'Sik Shelter Upgrading.* (608-HG-001), 1979.

WAPA (Washington Association of Professional Anthropologists). Conference Handbook: Anthropology Career Conference '84. National 4-H Center, Bethesda, Md., October 20, 1984.

# 10

## Anthropology in Upland and Rainfed Development in the Philippines

*Sam Fujisaka*

Anthropologists working in development attempt to provide timely, problem-relevant information about project communities and people and adapted methods for gathering such data. Basic and applied research is conducted in order to improve the "fit" between technical innovations and local groups and circumstances. In working with upland farmers, rainfed agriculture, and forest resource users, information is needed about resources, resource access, management practices, technical knowledge and perceptions, social organization, agroecological and economic variables, and change processes over time. Social scientists contribute the "people" data; as other scientists work to develop the needed technologies.

Anthropologists can carry out field research, provide methodologies for use by project staff, offer research-based design or policy inputs, and participate in project implementation. Work can be traditional longer-term ethnographic research or more "rapid" research as required by projects as they move from appraisal to applied research and dissemination activities.

Agricultural development in the Philippines has resulted in intensification and improved production of lowland irrigated rice. More recently, rural development attention has turned to uses of public forest resources, upland rainfed agriculture, and to the farmers, migrant settlers and indigenous groups of such areas. The Bureau of Forest Development (Ministry of Natural Resources)—previously concerned largely with forest production and protection—recently instituted a national social forestry program to work towards upland development. The Ministry of Agriculture and Food has recently given more attention to upland rainfed agriculture. Universities, non-government agencies, and international research and funding agencies are also actively involved in these efforts.

This paper describes my work as an agricultural-ecological anthropologist, including: longer-term interdisciplinary research and the development of a social forestry project and more "rapid" research, research methods, and associated project work with a rainfed uplands farming systems development project. A discussion of issues follows.

My work in the Philippines was first funded by a Rockefeller Foundation postdoctoral grant for rural and agricultural development and later by the Ford Foundation. My base since 1982 has been the Program on Environmental Science and Management (PESAM or "the environmental science program") and the University of the Philippines at Los Banos. The environmental science program is an interdisciplinary group of scientists concerned with upland agroecosystems and upland development.

The uplands, legally areas of 18 percent or greater slope, are mostly public forest and include about 60 percent of the national land area. Deforestation and environmental degradation are serious problems. An estimated 70 percent of the tropical forest has been destroyed; and total Philippine tropical forest depletion within fourteen years at the present 7 percent annual deforestation rate has been predicted (ESCAP, 1982). Contributing factors are overcutting and wasteful practices by commercial loggers, illegal logging and log exports, lack of effective reforestation programs, fragility of the ecosystem, settlement and non-sustainable agricultural practices, and national forest resources policies. While data is poor and estimates vary, 7 million or more people (out of a national population of 50 million) now live in the uplands, compete for scarce resources, and have been described as the "poorest of the poor."

Philippine forests, resources, and peoples are primarily the responsibility of the forest bureau. Until the mid-1970s the forest bureau prohibited forest settlement. Settlers were incarcerated or fined and ejected from bureau lands. The policy was ineffective due to difficulties of implementation, increasing numbers of settlers, the large and often remote areas involved, and a general lack of public support. Since the late 1970s, the forest bureau, with assistance from universities and other agencies, has attempted to "work with" the uplanders to improve local systems of resource use and management. Projects assist settlers to adopt non-shifting, supposedly less environmentally damaging farming systems.

These efforts include what have been called "social forestry," "agroforestry," and "upland development." Initial work included communal tree farms, "improved" swidden management, resettlement, and land leases. In 1982 these were reorganized into an "Integrated Social Forestry Program" (ISFP): ". . . a national program to uplift the socioeconomic conditions of the *kaingineros* and other forest occupants and communities dependent on forest lands for their livelihood, and at the same time protect and improve the quality of the environment" (BFD, 1982). Participants are individually or communally granted twenty-five year renewable leases for parcels of land of up to 7 ha per individual claim. Continued residence and farming are allowed provided, among others, forest resources are not damaged. "Participatory approaches" have been sought (Aguilar, 1982; Bernales, Sagmit, and Bongalos, 1982; BFD, 1983; Cortes, 1982).

## Research and Upland Development in Calminoe

Since 1982 and as part of the environmental science program, I have headed an interdisciplinary research and development project at the upland community of Calminoe. Funding was provided by the Agricultural Development Council, Inc., and the Ford Foundation. The research team includes an anthropologist (myself), an economist, a botanist, a forest ecologist, and a tropical forester.

Calminoe is a pioneer community of shifting cultivators located between Mt. Banahao and southwestern Sierra Madre mountains near the Laguna-Quezon provincial border. Rainfall is high (5,500 mm., very short dry season); forest soils are largely acidic clays (pH 4.2 to 5.5). The site is at about 450 meters elevation and some 50 straight-line kilometers from the University of the Philippines at Los Banos. Access is via a rough, muddy track usually impassible to vehicles.

The area was primary Dipterocarp (tropical hardwood) forest until commercially logged from 1957 to 1980. Lands then became (*de facto*) available for settlement. Logging left a road to the area and to timber workers and families seeking land. More settlers, especially Seventh Day Adventists, followed from all over the country. The settlers, now numbering about 1,400, built homes of wood, experimented with crops and farming methods suited to local conditions, planted diverse home gardens, used shifting techniques for subsistence and commercial crops, have established perennials, and have been rapidly exploiting remaining forest resources. A government concern is that the land is part of the Caliraya watershed—which provides water for hydroelectric power and irrigation (and for the river featured in the movie "Apocalypse Now").

Research examined evolving interactions between man and forest-based agroecosystem in terms of: (1) the agroecosystem, (2) migration and settlement, (3) social organization and systems of cooperation and conflict, (4) evolving farming and forest resource use practices and related knowledge and perceptions, and (5) related national policy and institutional levels.

## The Luxury of Longer-Term Research Methods at Calminoe

Our longer-term university-based research combined several methodologies. Fieldwork included exploratory research, participant-observation, a formal sample survey-questionnaire, key informant interviews, informal structured interviews, photo-documentation, and different types of biophysical research on crops, soils, and fallow regeneration. Shorter and longer term methods, qualitative and quantitative methods, and social and biophysical sciences, all provided complimentary findings.

Exploratory research, a sort of "rapid rural appraisal"(RRA) (Carruthers and Chambers, 1981; Chambers, 1980; Collinson, 1981) consisted of informal open-ended discussions with community residents and area exploration. Some of the local problems and constraints were discovered. Research questions were made more specific:

1. What are the characteristics of the forest-based agroecosystem? What have been the human practices regarding the system and how has that system responded to human use practices? In what ways have these interactions been evolving and changing?
2. Especially for land and timber, what are the systems of resources access, use, and management? Land distribution, charcoal making, "carabao logging," and farming must be considered.
3. What were and are the patterns/dynamics of migration to the area; and what social organization developed considering the whole community; why have factions formed and what do they mean in terms of resources—including capital and labor—access and use?
4. What are the evolving farming practices—especially in terms of subsistence versus commercial cropping, the shift from annual food crops to intercropping of root crops and perennials, plot fallowing and regeneration, and soils management—and related perceptions, technical knowledge, and innovative behavior?
5. What is the situation regarding local, regional, and national jurisdiction over the area? What are the effects of national policies and institutional arrangements on local resource use?
6. Given both local circumstances and non-local institutional factors, what innovations could, if incorporated, lead to both improved welfare and agroecosystems sustainability?

Participant-observation involved living in-community (in our leaky wood-and-anahaw house) for periods from a few days to several weeks, participation in local events, and systematic observation and recording of conversations and events. A covered area at the front of our house allowed for conversations and gossip with passersby, which revealed undercurrents of feeling and behind-the-scenes manipulation. Participant-observation continued to indicate research directions, allowed for the establishment of rapport, gave depth and "reality" to data gathered through more extensive methods, and indicated processes developing over time.

Some of the initial research team members thought that survey instruments were inappropriate and that informants would be unresponsive, hostile, and suspicious. With the establishment of rapport, however, respondents were generally responsive and cooperative, with a few hesitant and others extremely informative. An interview questionnaire was developed, carefully translated (see Fujisaka and Duhaylungsod, 1983), pre-tested, and modified; houses were mapped and stratified by faction-based sub-areas; and 25 percent proportional samples were drawn from each division.

Project and interviews were explained; and consenting male or female household heads were interviewed. The interviews, in Tagalog, lasted about an hour. Responses were recorded; and follow-up prompts were allowed where appropriate and necessary. Questions were both pre-coded and open-ended. Coding, tabulation and statistical analysis followed. The sample survey provided representative data, indicated relationships and ranges of variation for some of the research variables, and is replicable.

More intensive and informal key-informant interviews were useful in exploring locally sensitive topics and significant events in the development of the community. Key informants included "important" local figures and those willing and able to share information. Iterative informal structured interviews were used to investigate farmer practices and related perceptions, categories, and technical knowledge.

Mapping, soil sampling and testing, measuring cut wood volumes, counting bags of charcoal produced, observing farming practices in farmers' fields, examining crops, observing soil erosion, taking plant samples to study plant succession and regeneration, farmer-managed field crop trials, and photo-documentation were other methods used.

## Some Research Findings

A comprehensive account of findings is presented elsewhere (Fujisaka and Capistrano, 1985). This section briefly discusses farming practices, related knowledge and perceptions, forest resources use, competing factions, institutional constraints, agroecosystem, and implications for upland development.

Farming practices were observed over time. Homelots contain a mixture of subsistence root crops and perennials and are used for farmer experiments. Forest slash-and-burn farmlots can produce a crop of rice or tomato followed by root crops, pineapple, other vegetables, bananas, citrus, other perennials, and fallows. Rice or tomato entails high costs, returns, and risks and requires new or long-fallowed lands and commercial inputs. Root cropping provides a safety-net, but may be somewhat nutrient depleting. Pineapple was productive without inputs, but generally has low returns. Choices depend upon specific land, labor, capital, and knowledge resources; and upon farmer assessments of associated risks. Land-use cycles are of several years with length of use and timing and duration of fallows dependent on micro-conditions, crops planted, and particular farmer circumstances. Fallow periods are generally being reduced due to greater land demands. Importantly, however, most farmers are also naturally shifting from production of cereals, vegetables, and root crops to establishment of perennial cash crops. The social forestry program—which considers pioneer shifting cultivation as wasteful and destructive—might best understand and then build upon such local agroforestry development.

Settlers arrived with substantial upland agricultural experience, sought information about the local agroecosystem, and experimented with crops and practices. Informal structured interviews elicited farmer knowledge and perceptions and results included the unexpected. Farmers said that lands were relatively poor when first cleared and burned, but were then significantly and continuously better after about two years of a light cropping-fallow combination. This was contrary to expectations (theirs and ours) that new forest plots are the richest and that production then drops off with use over a couple of planting seasons. We are now conducting nutrient cycling research to find the basis for the observation since results are directly relevant to testing of agroforestry innovations.

Settlers exploit different production alternatives and seek further diversification of income sources. Forest resources—including land, timber, slash, rattan—are exploited by residents and outsiders. Trees are cut to clear land and for timber. Some timber is used locally, but most is taken by carabao loggers—mostly outsiders with the necessary capital for chainsaws, trucks, carabao, labor, and bribes. Local residents receive a minor portion of the benefits from wage labor and some sub-contract logging. More recently settlers converted wood slash into charcoal using earthen pits; and benefits accrued more equitably to producers.

Long-term research revealed that resource competing factions had formed along religious, language, and place of origin divisions. Most settlers acquired lands from respective faction leaders. Factional organizations and leadership structures have formed, and each makes claims resulting in friction, implied threats, more polarization, and some overt conflict. Alliances are not fixed and factions do not neatly segment the population. Individuals and families have shifting and multiple situational loyalties. Problems for development are the free-for-all competition for resources and lack of cooperation among groups in resource management.

Long-term research also revealed important institutional constraints to any upland development. Local, provincial, and national level land and resource jurisdiction was confused. The nearby Laguna-Quezon provincial boundary location had not been settled and two different nearby municipalities claimed local jurisdiction. Each local faction allied with a different municipality. Nationally, the forest bureau and the Bureau of Lands (BL) did not know who had area jurisdiction. Some settlers hoped that the BL had jurisdiction since such lands could be made alienable and disposable—i.e., could be individually titled and sold. Confusion, claims, and counterclaims at the different levels added to local polarization.

Agroecosystems research indicated problems and encouragements for upland development: on the one hand, the secondary forest and patches of residual forest are being cut and converted for agricultural use. Use intensity is increasing; fallows are being delayed and/or reduced; and plantings, weedings, and burnings for some plots are increasing. Some conversion to grassland was observed. Low soil nutrient status is a major farmer problem, and logging, cultivation, and charcoal production mean significant net nutrient exports and changes in forest floristic composition. On the other hand, areas not so intensively used and allowed to fallow show relatively rapid regeneration and succession to secondary forest—due in part to the high rainfall and still adequate stocking of seed material. And, farmers are, as mentioned, shifting from annual to perennial crops. Research can monitor the race between possible resource degradation and farmer establishment of sustainable resource use patterns. Development efforts must try to favorably tip the dynamic balance.

## From Research to Upland Development

Our intention was that research would lead the design of development strategies. We joined forces with the Forest Bureau's Integrated Social Forestry Program in a joint effort that will (1) continue the search for appropriate technical innovations, and (2) address identified social and institutional constraints. Technical innovations will build upon farmer experimentation and their evolution towards perennial cash cropping. We introduced the A-frame for contour ditching and planting and provided seeds and seedlings requested by farmers for farmer managed trials, and an agroforestry nursery is being planned.

The social and institutional constraints, however, had to be addressed prior to technology development. Research-based project implementing guidelines outlined issues such as land jurisdiction and necessary negotiations, specified implications of different outcomes, discussed project eligibility criteria, and called for an immediate census and land survey. Working within the context of factions and conflicting claims was discussed. Landholding and resource use patterns were outlined, and ways to equitably respect existing systems were suggested. A system of conflict adjudication was detailed. A system of regulated carabao logging was recommended. Institutional-administrative arrangements were outlined. Finally, initial technical strategies for upland development were outlined.

We convened a meeting of concerned officials from the two provinces—governors, Bureau of Lands officers, forest bureau officers, military-police commanders—and the two nearby municipal mayors, the forest bureau's regional director, the director of the environmental science program, and local faction leaders. Issues were discussed and it was agreed that the location of the provincial boundary near Calminoe was unknown. However, provincial jurisdiction was irrelevant since the land falls under the jurisdiction of the forest bureau. The land, therefore, could not be made alienable and disposable; and local municipalities do not have authority over the area. The legitimate entity in the area was the joint forest bureau-environmental science project. Everyone agreed and pledged support.

While land jurisdiction was officially resolved, the issue was hotly contested locally by leaders in the "losing" position. We maintained neutrality and listened to the viewpoints of all concerned; and the situation is now hopefully being resolved to the satisfaction of the maximum number of residents. The census was carried out and farmer plots were mapped. Current problems involve outsiders entering the area and claiming lands in anticipation of the granting of land leases. Currently, the project has been slowed by political turmoil in the Philippines.

## More "Rapid" Anthropology and Farming Systems Development

The Ministry of Agriculture and Food (MAF) has started work with small farmers in upland rainfed areas via "farming systems" development projects. Projects are located where most lands are titled rather than public domain; and farmers may own land, be share tenants on other plots, and have (public) forest plots. Share tenancy arrangements vary widely for different types of lands and crops planted. Plots range from bunded rainfed paddy to shifting slash-and-burn forest parcels. Crops range from modern high-yielding rice varieties to upland polycultures of traditional rice varieties, corn, root crops, and perennials including cash crops such as coffee and cacao. Farmers may work as on- and off-farm wage laborers during parts of the year. These comparatively complex farming and livelihood strategies have not been well understood by the MAF in light of its work with irrigated lowland agriculture.

This section describes shorter-term work for the Farming Systems Development Project-Eastern Visayas (FSDP-EV). The project combines efforts of the regional MAF, the Visayas College of Agriculture (ViSCA), Cornell University, and the USAID. I took part in a mid-project evaluation (Sajise, Fujisaka, Baker, Hitchcock, and Bolo, 1985) and later returned to help improve methods for gathering data about project communities and farmers.

The project has worked in Samar and Leyte since 1982 to improve upland rainfed agriculture—mainly via selection, testing, and dissemination of component technologies that would ideally allow more cropping per year. Six field sites and offices were established and staffed with a site leader (usually trained in extension), an agronomist, an economist, a livestock specialist, a home technician, and support staff. Appraisal activities were carried out: "Sondeos" at some sites, "socioeconomic profiles" at others, and "benchmark surveys" at others. Trials were established on the fields of some ten to fourteen selected "cooperator farmers" at each site. Each site was to represent a different rainfed farming system in the region, and respective supposedly dominant cropping patterns were based upon abaca, coconut, rice, corn, and root crops. Various types of farming systems research, especially agronomic work on cropping pattern components, has been conducted by site staff and by ViSCA researchers.

In my opinion some project strengths have been:

1. The project combines government development efforts and academic research inputs with benefits gained by both institutions and by the project.
2. The project tries to improve small-farmer welfare by increasing overall productivity of the farming systems and has followed a research-based (FSR/E) approach in doing so.
3. Project human resources—planning and administrative staff, field team members, and ViSCA researchers—are good.
4. Conceptually, the project recognized the importance of initial diagnostic research, research preceding extension, farmer participation and working on farmers' fields. It also recognized that there are different types of rainfed farming systems in the Eastern Visayas.

There were also several interrelated project weaknesses:

1. Knowledge from and about farmers was insufficient in terms of ranges of practices, technical knowledge, and perceptions. Each site was characterized by major commodity crop and dominant cropping patterns. Farmers at each site were viewed as homogeneous.
2. Such assumptions made appraisal somewhat *ex post* and superfluous, and made establishment of recommendation domains problematical. Appraisal results were often long-delayed; and results were in forms that were not or could not be incorporated in project design.
3. The project worked with only ten to fourteen "primary cooperators" per site. How representative these farmers were or are is unknown.
4. Inadequate attention was paid to sustainability, possible negative longer-term agroecosystems effects of tested technical innovations, and systems change over time.
5. Little attention was paid to intra-community and intra-household dynamics and to important socio-institutional factors.

Overall, "single-shot" "rapid rural appraisal" (RRA) activities had been inadequate; and it was agreed that more effective appraisal of farmers and existing practices and improved field methods were needed. Field staff spent a lot of time in the project communities and could be trained to interact more with farmers; and project learning would not have to be limited to initial appraisal. The method should combine useful aspects of key informant interviews, survey methods, ethnographic techniques, and "rapid" approaches, and should address the problem identified by Chambers: "In rural development, a great deal of the information that is gathered is, in various combinations, irrelevant, late, wrong, and/or unusable anyway" (1980). My experience in Calminoe and other communities suggested the iterative process of informal and open-ended, but structured, interviewing.

## Iterative Informal Structured Interview

Informal interviewing is good for investigating focused problems and discovering new sets of data. Results complement more structured research—e.g., enterprise and risk budgeting, actual crop cuts and yield monitoring. The method sounds and is simple, but skills and practice are helpful. Interviewers must speak the informants' language, establish rapport, be technically well prepared while open to new knowledge, analyze replies and ask follow-up questions, recheck inconsistencies, and probe without leading. Results can go beyond "just talking to farmers" to re-definitions of project directions.

"Iterative" implies continued dialogue. Interview results are examined, internal inconsistencies and gaps are identified, and interviewers return to ask necessary follow-on questions. Knowledge is continually improved or revised; and a fixed "diagnosis" does not result.

"Informal" means no written questionnaire and open-ended questions. Interviewers start with guiding issues, curiosity, and analyze issues and responses as interviews develop. Topics are interactively explored until internally consistent pictures are pieced together or until the interviewer is confident that needed information can later be "distilled" from interview notes. The interview depends upon rapport and interviewer ability to listen, think, and respond with appropriate follow-on questions. "New" project-relevant information can be discovered and explored.

"Structured" implies that a minimum of specific topics are addressed. The interviewer may start with a list of general guide questions. Technical training of the interviewer is important since technically informed questions and comments allow the farmer to respond in corresponding greater depth. The method incorporates ethnographic techniques for eliciting farmer knowledge and perceptions—informant reasons behind practices—and informant terms and categories. Such interviews include various "Why do you?" "What do you call?" and "What is the difference between?" questions.

The method is an interview; and rules for formal interviews hold: the researcher explains the activity, asks permission, works to establish rapport, asks clear, delimited questions, probes without suggesting, repeats or explains as necessary, does not hurry the informant, asks appropriate, well sequenced questions, and takes notes. Such interviews may produce anything from very little to fascinating informant accounts—depending on interviewer, informant, and directions taken.

## A Training Course

A short course addressing aspects of FSR/EV (farming systems research/ Eastern Visayas) has been given each summer for project and other ministry personnel. Previous courses were at Cornell. The 1985 course was held at ViSCA and was to "increase and refine understanding of FSR/EV for selected MAF, ViSCA, and FSDP-EV staff." The major part of the course— "socioeconomic data collection"—offered the iterative informal structured interview and emphasized talking to and learning from farmers. Training included lecture, classroom exercises, practice in eliciting techniques, short field practicum, use of the method at the field sites, and discussion.

The training course was described elsewhere (Fujisaka, 1985). The field practicum and some results are discussed here. Interviews were conducted by pairs of trainees in three of the six project communities. Topics investigated were those of agreed upon relevance to the project:

1. land, labor, animal, and other resources; land access and tenure arrangements; and resource sharing arrangements
2. farmer soil/land-type terms, categories, and classifications; what each type is good for; which crops are suited to given lands or soils; and related knowledge
3. crops and varieties, cropping patterns, management practices and decisions, costs and returns, and farmer identified problems
4. reasons and knowledge underlying the practices; the answers to "why?" follow-up questions

5. fallow practices and knowledge; indicator species; fallow terms and categories.

The interviewers were also asked to note the following:

6. the "drift" of the interview; questions and sequences; discussions, and unresolved issues;
7. farmer problems observed or inferred from the interviews;
8. confirmations or contradictions of previously held ideas.

Interviewers were to do one to three interviews per day. It was stressed that one complete, detailed interview was better than more "by the recipe" sessions. Techniques were reviewed; we invaded farmers' homes and fields; interviews were carried out; and group review and discussion followed each day's work. Difficulties involved: (1) developing effective sequences of questions while listening and evaluating, (2) recognizing and addressing new information or possibly false preconceptions, and (3) listening to farmers without overly-hasty "translation" to English. Trainees wrote up their interviews. Data was tabulated, discussed, and informally analyzed upon return to ViSCA. We gathered the following results from Gandara, Samar.

## Resources and Income

The project had characterized Gandara farmers in terms of averages—numbers of farm plots, hectares of land, carabao, years of formal education, family members. A percentage were tenants; another proportion were landowners. Interviewers first said that people in a particular area had no upland plots. However, *all* respondents there had upland plots. In another case, it was hastily concluded that a respondent couple were landless laborers since they were working on someone else's land and said that they had no land in the area. After I supplied a couple of questions, we found that the informants had referred to immediately adjacent lands, and were actually share-tenanting a paddy, renting out a paddy in return for a loan, and had cultivated and fallowed upland plots.

Variability of resources and access was encountered. Families had combinations of rainfed paddy, small stream-fed paddies between upland and lowland areas, cultivated and fallowed upland plots—some with fruit trees, others covered with grasses—and coconut groves. Farmers had titled lands, lands without titles but having longstanding use-rights, and upland plots—possibly public forest lands. Families cultivated their own plots, share-tenanted or rented others, and tenanted or rented out one or more of their own plots. Initial characterization as "owners," "renters," or "share-croppers" was found to be inadequate. Some had access to little land; others had a great deal by local standards. Cropping and management varied according to land type and tenancy arrangement.

Credit or capital was scarce and expensive, and land sharing and credit arrangements were interrelated. In an arrangement called *bulig* or *tinuga*, the landowner provides land and money for seeds, half of the land preparation, and harvest labor. The tenant provides half of the land preparation and harvest labor and all of the weeding and postharvest labor. Income is shared equally. This arrangement is one of many. Others in Gandara include *prinda*, *plete*, *hopot*, *erensya*, *20 porsyento*, and *inupat*. When farmers discussed land tenancy, however, they usually first cited the system allowed and sanctioned by agrarian reform laws (and as usually appears in survey results). Similarly credit is "supposed to" cost a simple percentage of the loan but actually includes several local arrangements—borrowing P50 and paying back one sack of unhusked rice, borrowing P100 and paying back three sacks, and borrowing one sack and repaying two sacks.

Land access and distribution is a complex, thorny issue in such areas. Technical violation of agrarian reform laws combined with long-term traditional patron-client tenancy relationships complicate information gathering. National institutions can have overlapping or confused claims to public lands settled by farmers with long-recognized traditional use rights. Project staff discovered greater complexity concerning land resources, but found that they could acquire such sensitive information.

There was significant movement, some seasonal, of labor in and out of the community. Some families hired labor, others worked as hired labor. Some worked as rice harvesters in the irrigated lowlands and had to hire labor at other times. "Average number of carabao per family" could not reflect distribution. Some families had many; others none. Informants were quick to say they wanted carabao, partly we suspect because the project had distributed animals to cooperators. Established systems of carabao sharing among relatives and loosely allied families were discovered.

Income data were obtained in farmers' fields by discussing variable costs and piecing together returns. Discussion of a farmer's cacao enterprise, for example, covered problems such as pod-rot, source of plants, management practices including labor and use of fertilizers and insecticides, costs of inputs, followed by questions about number of trees, their ages, when and how much the trees produce, marketing, and market prices. Returns above variable costs were calculated later.

## Soil and Land Terms and Categories

Site staff said that farmers made few distinctions among soil and land types, and that farmer knowledge and behavior regarding soils and lands was "random." Waray-speaking Leyte farmers supposedly called all poor soils *pansil*; which the Cebuano-speaking Samar farmers called *umau.*Technicians said that farmers could distinguish red (*pulahon*) clay soils (*anapogon*), sandy soils (*basoon*), and "good" soils. Interviews using simple eliciting techniques demonstrated that farmers had a greater range of terms and corresponding practices (Table 10.1.).

Table 10.1. includes farmer term, translation, and connotation of soil and land types. Project staff had difficulties in *not* immediately translating and "lumping" farmer categories into English, their academic language.

TABLE 10.1   Gandara Farmer Terms for Soils and Lands

| Term | Translation | Connotation |
|------|-------------|-------------|
| galot-galoton | sticky-sticky | very sticky |
| mapilit-pilit | sticky-sticky | sticky |
| maitom-itom | black-black | very dark |
| matig-ana | hard | hard |
| mayomu | soft | soft |
| mapula-pula | red-red | clay red |
| bato bato | stone-stone | stoney |
| palanas | bald or bare | slippery |
| lulbaranin | faded | uneven |
| lugarugan | carabao wallow | wet lowland |
| pongango | corn cob | poor soil left behind |
| guitona-i | original | pure soil |
| bagnas | land after harvest of upland rice or corn | |
| bulas | field after camote is removed | |
| higad | slightly rolling | |
| tangid | steep | |
| danaya | undulating | |
| tugha | not yet planted to rice | |
| dagu | after planting rice | |
| danau | paddy rice plot | |

Practice was needed to consider terms in light of distinctions being made by informants. With less literal translations, more of the farmers' knowledge and perspectives emerged. While *lugarugan* "means" "carabao wallow" it refers to valuable moist, dark-gray, enriched soils. *Pongango* ("corn cob") refers to soils from which nutrients have been depleted although the land remains. *Lulbarinin* ("faded") refers to soils of uneven nutrient and moisture characteristics such that the crop is unevenly colored and sized depending upon location within the field.

Farmer terms and distinctions were also elicited in Leyte. Soils were: sandy (*basoon*); sandy and could not hold water (*mayiniton*); leached (*lubas*); poor (*umay*); sour or acid (*aslomon*); and clay (*hagkoton*). Land types included: *lamak* (flat lowland); *makilid* (sloping); *buntod* (hilltop); *patag* (lowland rice); *tabok, tambok,* or *tabunok* (rich, low-lying, with mixed vegetative cover, next to water); *tanhong* (shaded); *dagan* (washed down); and *ugmad* (newly opened). Farmers were discovered to make some cropping decisions based on their distinctions regarding soil color, texture, acidity, fertility, moisture, land slope, drainage, and shading. In place of preconceived "random" farming practices, technicians started to see more systematic, "logical" farmer land-use decisions.

## Cropping Patterns and Management Practices

The project had determined two or three existing farmer cropping patterns and a like number of patterns recommended for testing, evaluating, and dissemination at each site. Patterns were characterized in FSR fashion:

TABLE 10.2. Some Traditional Varieties Grown in Gandara

| Rice | Sweet Potato | Cassava | Taro |
|------|--------------|---------|------|
| pelet itom | kasapad | kalebre | kinosol |
| penalapay | ikeran | makan | pinalawan |
| kalimon | karenkit | pultan | |
| karawi | upop-ak | biyuda | |
| kalinayan | kahakop | | |
| imelda | tinampay | | |
| senorita | puyutini iyang | | |
| makarato | kasubri | | |
| bondok | kabot-ho | | |
| kumaggaykay | | | |
| peneli | | | |
| kenoto | | | |

for example, maize followed by maize or upland rice followed by fallow was to be modified by technical innovations to, for example, HYV rice followed by maize relayed with a grain legume. Interview and visits to different types of farm fields demonstrated that a variety of cultigens, including several minor crops and associated cropping patterns were important to the farmers. Tobacco, castor bean, cacao, coffee, eggplant and other vegetables, and specific traditional rice, corn, and other crop varieties were being grown by the farmers. The farmers were planting more traditional varieties (Table 10.2). than had been assumed; and had specific reasons for choices. Fallows were often for several years rather than seasonal; and respective patterns were really several-year rather than single-year cycles.

*Fallow Practices.* The project first paid little attention to fallows. The question, "What do farmers in your project area consider in abandoning or starting to plant a plot again?" had been posed to trainees. The reply was that farmers "just abandoned lands when production dropped" and that they referred only to "abandoned" or "empty" plots. Interviews showed that several so-called local terms (farmer terms in Waray) had been carelessly lumped and translated. The interviews revealed a range of ideas (Table 10.3).

*Superstitions.* Trainees recorded farmer practices or perceptions that they might otherwise dismiss as "superstition":

1. Cricket infestations can be reduced by placing nipa stalks around the paddy field.
2. Cricket infestations can be reduced by grinding a certain leaf and root, mixing with water, and spraying the field.
3. Worm infestations can be reduced by wrapping household garbage in a cloth, cutting the cloth into strips, and placing the strips around the field.
4. Sweet potato should not be planted at high tide or during a full moon.

TABLE 1Ø.3.  Some Fallow Terms in Gandara

| Term | Translation | Connotation |
|------|-------------|-------------|
| paukyon | stop | cease cultivation |
| pahuway | rest | let land rest to recover |
| diskanso | rest (from Spanish) | let land rest to recover |
| bakanti | empty (from Spanish) | vacant land, usually grass |
| guinbaya-an | abandoned | no cultivation, land may be depleted |
| pinahabog an banwa | let the grasses grow | allow land to regenerate natural vegetation |
| tugwayan | pasture | early grassland fallow |

TABLE 1Ø.4.  Some Gandara Farmers' Livestock Disease Terms

| Term | Translation | Disease |
|------|-------------|---------|
| pakdol | stumble | hoof-and-mouth |
| eget-eget | diarrhea | various |
| tukwaw | groggy, wobbly | avian disease |
| buti | small scabs | various |
| karog-on | falling hair | ? |
| kuto | lice | lice |
| hinga-hinga | labored breathing | respiratory |

5. Rat infestations can be reduced by placing bamboo stakes around the field.
6. Banana should not be planted by a standing person.

These practices were discussed in terms of farmer perspectives and possible scientific foundations. Since many thought farmers were guided largely by superstition, examples were given in which similar practices had been shown to have real, practical effects. Although we lacked a flashy local example, trainees agreed to record and examine superstitions.

Site personnel started to recognize the range and technical nature of farmer knowledge and distinctions. On their own initiative they collected what had been thought of as farmer misdiagnosis of livestock diseases (Table 10.4.).

*Whole-Farm Enterprise.* As interviewers discovered the systematic and complex nature of local farming strategies, they were better able to consider the whole-farm enterprise. This is illustrated by data from a four-hour interview with a non-cooperator farmer that included visits to his house, stream-fed paddy, and upland swidden plot:

1. His paddy was in an area between the lowland and upland areas and was formed after several cooperating farmers (*coporasyon*), mostly relatives, built a diversion ditch from stream to field. The land has

been cropped as paddy for four seasons and is still in the process of being leveled gradually due to limited carabao access.

2. Varieties planted are IR36 and IR42. Many Gandara farmers say these must be alternated (perhaps in response to blast?) for each to produce well.

3. Crickets are a problem for paddy rice. Crickets attack plants on the higher unsubmerged patches within the paddy. As confirmed by other interviews and observations, the crickets are, thus, a problem for farmers with paddy fields and limited traction access.

4. Soils and lands were assessed by color and vegetation with red and then yellow clays being poor and, at the other end of the continuum, dark loams being rich. Lands covered with *imperata* are the poorest; *talahib* covered land is better; and mixed shrubs and small trees the best of the fallowed lands.

5. On the multi-level, multi-sloped upland plot, the farmer cleared, burned, and planted UP-Ri5 and a native rice. Corn followed rice on less fertile portions; a second rice crop was planted on better areas. Cassava and camote followed rice or corn; and these were followed by a carefully spaced mixture of pineapple, sugar cane, different types of taro, banana, and papaya.

6. The informant was very specific in identifying different soils *within* the 1 ha plot, and in stating cropping sequences.

7. The farmer mulches, using crop residues, and stated clearly that the mulches protect the soils on the slopes from erosion.

8. The plot was opened section by section over several seasons such that at any one time the farmer would have a full assortment of crops corresponding in placement to the different and changing fertility of each sub-plot. The informant was very clear in describing the swidden plot as changing and developing over time from new plot to fallow.

9. The farmer experimented with different crops such as eggplant and peanut, tried to find solutions to problems affecting these crops, and adopted crops for which he successfully solved associated problems. Peanuts suffered from rats and empty pods, and were dropped. Eggplant was attacked by worms. The solution—chemical spraying—was effective but expensive and costs outweighed benefits. Spraying was dropped; but even counting losses due to worms, eggplant was still profitable enough to be adopted.

10. We asked about crop selection and timing after observing crops planted by others not following the timing followed by our informant. He explained the balance between farmer experience, uncertainty as to climatic conditions over the year, risk assessment, and possible profits of producing harvests out of season.

11. The farmer says that he places "priority" on his paddy field and leaves the upland plot relatively neglected during periods in which the paddy fields require a lot of labor.

## Informal Analysis of Identified Problems

Site staff were encouraged to do part of the analysis of identified farmer problems. For example, the cricket problem could be examined in the field using simple questions:

1. Could you describe the cricket problem?
2. Which crops and varieties are affected?
3. At which stage are the plants affected?
4. Have you observed if certain management practices affect the seriousness of infestation? Do you know why?
5. Do you know of and have you tried any ways of controlling the crickets? What was the result?

Answers suggested that crickets are a problem in portions of paddy fields not submerged due to incomplete leveling. This small observation can be checked, as can related issues of land preparation and traction access:

6. How do the crickets affect your different types of plots and different parts of single plots?
7. How do you prepare each plot?
8. Do you own a carabao? (If not) How do you obtain use of carabao for land preparation?

Further questions can follow in light of responses. Site staff can determine the extent of the problem, who are affected, local control methods and effectiveness, and possible ties between problem and management practices. Local solutions can be examined as possible best bets given local circumstances. Finally, needed back-up technical research could be called for. Such research could then build upon the knowledge already gained in the field and would be focused and directly project-relevant.

## Anthropology and Development: Some Issues

### Towards "Quick and Clean" Appraisal Methods

Social scientists have provided diagnostic information for development projects using various methods. "Rapid rural appraisal" (RRA) approaches are striving to economically provide good, timely data, and my use of the "iterative informal structured interview" seeks to contribute to the trend. Benefits and costs of different methods must be considered, however.

As an anthropologist, I appreciate longer-term field work. The Calminoe research enabled us to uncover local social dynamics and to observe processes and cycles unfolding over time. For example, we observed adoption of charcoal making and establishment of a local production-market system as national fuel prices escalated, and a later drop in local charcoal production as raw materials were depleted and prices to producers decreased when other upland areas increased production. Of course, most development projects do not have the luxury of longer-term research.

Projects have used standardized sample surveys; but these depend on adequate initial knowledge to formulate relevant questions, an instrument appropriate to local conditions, proper execution, and timely data analysis and feedback. The method has on occasion led to invasions of rural communities by armies of poorly trained researchers armed with thick questionnaires, queries of questionable appropriateness, and long delays in analysis and feedback. In the Philippines, such experiences have led to statements that the method was "not appropriate to the Philippine condition;" and, indeed, some of the initial Calminoe researchers were strongly opposed to the use of survey instruments. However, our sample survey provided needed quantitative data that characterized the whole community and allowed for statistical analysis.

The farming systems project encountered problems by assuming that initial "by the recipe" use of "rapid rural appraisal" methods would result in a final diagnostic characterization of farmers. Anthropologists and other social scientists need to continue to develop methods responsive to changing local circumstances and problems and to specific project needs and goals. Anthropology can best rely on its strengths to contribute methods—rapid or otherwise—that work to discover, elicit, describe, and analyze peoples' practices, perceptions, knowledge, and forms of organization.

## Anthropology and Interdisciplinary Development

Most research and development programs recognize a need to integrate biophysical and social scientific inputs. Effecting such integration, however, has been difficult. Disciplinary boundaries in the environmental program remain quite sharply drawn, and program members have referred to a "socioeconomic component" as a discrete, separate body of phenomena. Interdisciplinary integration has been achieved by projects or research that addressed specific problems in ways that required—in fact depended upon—different disciplinary inputs.

In the Philippines interpersonal relations are key; and interdisciplinary team members are effective to the degree that they get along with one another. The Forest Bureau organized an interdisciplinary, inter-agency working group in 1982 to provide inputs into its social forestry and upland development efforts. Members represent the bureau, different university programs, other government institutions, or non-government organizations, and the fields of forestry, tropical ecology, botany, law, education, community organization, economics, sociology, and anthropology. Working group activities included establishment of three social forestry pilot projects. Group effectiveness requires following Filipino culture and actions taken are based more on group discussions and non-confrontational consensus building than on disciplinary knowledge.

In reference to anthropology, incorporation in Philippine development has been limited by a tendency of some projects to call for agricultural extension rather than social science when problems concerning people are encountered, stereotypes about project peoples or the rural poor in general, standard operating procedures of development bureaucracies, and a non-developmental Boasian tradition in Philippine anthropology itself. Although an environmental science program colleague told me, "We don't need social scientists. We have the technologies. What we need are extension workers," all of the above counts are improving.

## Local Level Research vs. Project Models

Many anthropologists (e.g., Dove, 1981, 1983) find local level realities that are inconsistent with or contradictory to strategies or models of development agencies or projects. The Forest Bureau's social forestry program, for example, is trying to develop a participatory approach model characterized by community organization, addressing of felt needs, and "participation in the decision-making process." Assumptions include that upland development can be solved at the local level, that much of the problem of upland underdevelopment lies "in the heads" or cultures of the uplanders, and that there are workable technical innovations that should be adopted (Fujisaka, 1986).

## Social Organization and "Community Organization"

Many development projects in the Philippines first create formal local organizations for collective action and for supposedly furthering participants' awareness of their circumstances. Organization of participants contributed to the success of communal irrigation pilot projects of the National Irrigation Agency (Bagadion and Korten, 1980). Community organization efforts have also mobilized farmers to recognize and to confront the agencies or institutions "oppressing" them (Custodio, Lindo, and Santos, 1981). Social forestry projects—with much support from the development community—have assumed that community organization is a necessary first step.

Anthropologists point out that all communities are organized—i.e., have internal systems that regulate, structure, and constrain human relationships and behavior, and that introduced organization can mimic or conflict with existing channels. Local social organization in Calminoe cannot be ignored, and we are working within the existing systems because to introduce further organization would be counterproductive. The FSDP (Farming Systems Development Project/Eastern Visayas) organizations of "primary cooperators" are comprised of the locally more powerful and, to the degree that project benefits have accrued to these few, have exacerbated problems stemming from local inequality. Anthropologists need to continue their study of existing local social structure and must be able to indicate how such organization must be dealt with and can be utilized by particular development projects.

## "Felt Needs"

Most of the many discussions of social forestry in the Philippines stress the importance of addressing the felt needs of project participants (Aquino, 1982; Aguilar, 1982; Cagampang, 1982). The felt needs of the Calminoe settlers include chemical fertilizers for probably nonsustainable and ecosystemically damaging tomato production, free and open access to land and timber, chainsaws and carabao for (illegal) logging, granting of faction-exclusive resource rights, large quantities of coffee seedlings, and a better road to haul down logs and tomatoes and to bring up fertilizers and pesticides. While the project is engaged in various activities, it cannot aid in obtaining chainsaws, carabao, chemical fertilizers and new roads, and cannot encourage farming practices damaging to the agroecosystem or uncontrolled access to remaining forest resources.

## Participation in the Decision-making Process

Project strategies can unintentionally limit or preclude significant local decision-making by not offering meaningful alternatives. The Calminoe loggers want to continue logging; and farmers want to own their land. Decisions on these issues were made at the national level. Cooperators in the farming systems development project can only accept or reject introduced component technologies.

## Local, Supra-local, and National Policy

Social forestry sees upland development basically as taking place at the local level. For Calminoe, a number of non-local policy and institutional issues, especially concerning land jurisdiction, had to be addressed. Also, granting of land leases to settlers—especially when combined with technical assistance—may turn out to be counterproductive: in Calminoe and other social forestry projects outsiders have claimed the right to migrate to the sites, arguing that the policy intends to make land available to all interested Filipinos. The goal of working with extant uplanders while maintaining the resource base would be defeated by such in-migration. National policies, while general, need to reflect adequate local "reality." Anthropologists can assist by indicating vis-à-vis their project work some of the local effects of such policies.

## Implicit Assumption of Non-Rationality

References to unscientific practices, resistance to change, and farmer apathy are still heard. The assumption that obstacles to technology adoption are tradition, economic irrationality, laziness, or ignorance has sometimes led to more extension or community organization rather than continued technology development. Anthropologists have been asked to explain cultural peculiarities and to then find ways to convince people to adopt or participate.

Research over the past couple of decades shows that farmers are largely rational relative to resources, circumstances and associated constraints and risks. "They will adopt it if it works" is increasingly stated in the environmental science program. Wider acceptance of the idea would shift responsibility for local participation to a combination of social scientists investigating local practices and constraints, and natural scientists continuing development of locally appropriate and beneficial technical innovations. Calminoe farmers experiment, seek new knowledge, and innovate, and are evolving from shifting cultivation of annuals to permanent tree cropping. Calminoe and Eastern Visayan farmers readily adopt innovations if returns to labor, power, capital, and variable costs are perceived as reasonably positive.

### Intra-Community Diversity

Projects often implicitly assume intra-community homogeneity. The farming systems project communities were described in terms of modal patterns in order to construct recommendation domains. Farmers varied considerably, however, in resources, practices and strategies. Recognition of such diversity necessitates making technical innovations relevant to a wider range of people and circumstances. Projects can also face a dilemma of "good guys-bad guys." To avoid adding to faction-related problems in Calminoe, we have tried to work equally with both the more and the less accommodating persons and groups. An environmental science program team worked on a project in Mindanao in which residents are Roman Catholics, Yakans, and Tausug. The Tausug were said to be uncooperative and difficult. The team recommended working with the Tausug at some later time since they may eventually see benefits of the project and participate. Of course, they may also become further alienated.

Indeed most contemporary upland communities in the Philippines are not small, internally regulated face-to-face homogeneous societies. Communities like Calminoe and the one in Mindanao reflect combinations of religious, language-group, and socioeconomic diversity. The stronger, more powerful, and the better-off attempt to improve their positions at the expense of the weaker, less organized, and poorer. Project designs and technologies must consider equitibility among different strata and groups.

### The Technical Innovations

Local level research will naturally lead to a critical examination of the appropriateness of technologies (and policies) offered by development agencies. The Calminoe research led to some recommendations contradictory to social forestry policy, and differences may stem from our concern for farmer welfare while maintaining the agroecosystem against the bureau's continued somewhat primary concern for forest protection (despite current social forestry rhetoric).

Land rights and management were major concerns. Due to the impossibility of determining dates of arrival, land leases should be granted to all established farmer-settlers. This was contrary to a requirement that grantees must have arrived prior to December 31, 1981. Farmer land-use reflects the natural mosaic pattern of the landscape and resources. Rather than granting leases for single contiguous plots, rights over a settler's homelot and usually several small farm plots should be granted. Projects would prohibit shifting cultivation—i.e., shifting, burning, and managing several plots at different stages. A portion of the benefits of field rotations and fallows and of burning— pH increases, weed and pest control—would be lost. Given current technologies, farmers would have to intensify cropping, weeding, and pest control on their single lease holdings. These practices would mean greater investment, fewer returns, and possibly greater damage to the agroecosystem.

We suggested:

1. a modified version of the farmer system of plot shifting and fallowing, rather than forced non-shifting cultivation;
2. expanding upon farmer experimentation and the natural evolution towards permanent cash cropping, rather than pushing standard agroforestry technologies;
3. working carefully with all social segments—formally organized or not— rather than introducing community organization;
4. monitored use of plots inside the watershed rather than forcing resettlement;
5. carrying out census, land survey, and lease granting as soon as possible to preclude new clearing and settlement *in anticipation of* lease granting; and
6. monitored small-scale logging using "carabao" technologies in place of an outright logging ban.

Recommendations did not seek to restructure the social forestry program, but rather sought to make our particular joint project more appropriate to local circumstances while still meeting project goals. It is too early to tell whether the Forest Bureau has the flexibility to modify standard approaches.

### Different Models, Similar Communities

Obviously, different problems, e.g., health and roads, can be addressed by different agencies in the same or similar communities. More interesting are different development models applied to similar communities, conditions, and problems. Improving farmer or resource-user welfare is an expressed goal common to projects and agencies working towards upland and rainfed agricultural development. The environmental science program is primarily developing technologies that are sustainable in terms of the agroecosystem. Among others, the program works with soils and erosion control—strip cropping, contour planting, terracing, composting—and a range of crops and tree species suited to such measures. The social forestry program, concerned with forest protection, is developing community reforestation and agroforestry technologies, but pays less attention to food crop production. The farming systems project was trying to improve food and selected commodity crop production through cropping intensification and component improvements. I am working in an upland community similar to Calminoe with scientists from the International Rice Research Institute (IRRI). They are addressing problems of upland rainfed agricultural systems by developing improved rice-based cropping systems—improved rice varieties, management, and crop intensification.

The development projects, agencies, and models and the participating scientists stand to mutually benefit as they work to address such problems as "upland development" using the different approaches. Environmental science program scientists working on the mid-project review of the farming systems project probably injected a greater concern for agroecosystems sustainability. The same farming systems project owes much of its approach to farming systems work carried out at the University of the Philippines at Los Banos and IRRI. The social forestry program is, by design, gaining benefits from the inputs of its multi-agency, interdisciplinary working group. The environmental science program continually benefits from the involvement of its members in different projects. And, of course, I have learned "development anthropology" (as opposed to "anthropology") only by working with such projects, agencies and approaches.

## Anthropology and Development: The Philippines

In the Philippines, the work of anthropologists is being incorporated into rural and agricultural development projects, is aiding in understanding local project communities, and is contributing somewhat to the design of projects and technical innovations. Anthropologists traditionally have been trained as systematic participant-observers, spending time to understand local circumstances from the vantage points of peoples studied. Anthropologists in development need to continue the fieldwork tradition, modifying methods as possible and necessary. By working in local communities and on teams with bureaucrats, administrators, donor agency personnel, technicians, and other project researchers, anthropologists may be called upon to play middleman roles as the two interact. Problems investigated by development anthropologists often stem from constraints faced by local peoples and the possibility that introduced change might address such constraints. Rather than following "academic" interests, the anthropologist addresses project goals and problem-oriented plans of action. Again, effectiveness then depends on communicating research findings effectively and without disciplinary obfuscation. In spite of such roles and requirements, anthropology applied to development needs to be based on solid disciplinary foundations and fundamental concepts, theories, methods and analytical tools. Traditional anthropological methods were employed in Calminoe while modified methods based on the traditional were adapted for the farming systems project.

In the Philippines the idea that anthropology is purely an academic discipline persists. Starting with Frake and Conklin in the 1950s, anthropologists have produced many solid ethnographies and disciplinarily important cognitive or ethnoscientific studies. Much of the research was conducted in small indigenous or tribal communities, and anthropologists are still generally thought of as concerned with *only* the more pristine cultural minorities. Many anthropologists in Philippine universities contribute to the view by being quite "Boasian" in their focus on cultural differences, relativism, and traditional peoples. In view of the advantages of partial overlaps of culture and language and a relatively developed system of higher education, however, Filipino anthropologists and anthropology need to become more development oriented.

A local "development anthropology" would require comparative studies of project communities over time, refinement of community appraisal methods, a problem orientation allowing for incorporation of disciplines such as ecology, economics, agronomy, and forestry, and clarification of concepts and assumptions used in the process. Interdisciplinary problem focused work will have to deal with social and technological change in local communities that are part of the larger, complex society. Working linkages— such as those formed by the environmental science program—between development agencies and the university need to be established and nurtured. Whether the resulting development social scientists then maintain identities as "anthropologists" is immaterial.

By working on new approaches to solving important practical problems, the environmental science program, the Forest Bureau's social forestry projects, and various rainfed farming systems development projects are excellent first-generation, interdisciplinary, and multi-agency upland development efforts in which anthropologists and other social scientists can and should play an important part. The examination of issues raised in this chapter will hopefully contribute to the next phase.

## References

Aguilar, F. V. *Social Forestry for Upland Development: Lessons from Four Case Studies.* Quezon City: Institute of Philippine Culture, 1982.

Aquino, R. "Lessons from Experiences in Social Forestry: Findings from Nine Selected Case Studies." Paper, 11th Social Forestry Forum of the Bureau of Forest Development, Manila, 1982.

Bagadion, B. and F. Korten. "Developing Viable Irrigators' Associations: Lessons from Small Scale Irrigation in the Philippines." *Agricultural Administration*, Vol. 7, 1980, pp. 273-289.

Bernales, B., L. Sagmit, and F. Bongalos. *Social Forestry Projects in the Philippines: An Inventory and a Listing of Communal Forests and Pastures.* Manila: DLSU-IRC, 1982.

BFD (Bureau of Forest Development), Philippines. "Strategies for Implementation: Integrated Social Forestry Program." Manila: BFD-ISF, 1983.

Cagampang, F. V. "The Social Forestry Laboratory: Proposed Framework for Implementation." Paper. UPLB College of Forestry, Department of Social Forestry, Los Banos, 1982.

Capistrano, A. D. and S. Fujisaka. "Tenure, Technology, and Productivity of Agroforestry Schemes." Paper 84-06. Philippine Institute of Development Studies, 1984.

Carruthers, I. and R. Chambers. "Rapid Appraisal for Rural Development." *Agricultural Administration*, Vol. 8, 1981, pp. 407–422.

Chambers, R. "Rapid Rural Appraisal: Rationale and Repertoire." IDS Discussion Paper 155. Institute of Development Studies, Brighton, 1980.

Collinson, Michael. "A Low Cost Approach to Understanding Small Farmers." *Agricultural Administration*, Vol. 8, 1981, pp. 433–450.

Cortes, E. V. "Interim Guidelines in the Establishment and Implementation of Social Forestry Projects." Letter. Ministry of Natural Resources, BFD, Philippines, 1982.

Custodio, M., C. Lindo, and F. Santos. "Group Mass Base, Leadership, and Attitudinal Assessment." Unpublished. ACES, Manila, 1981.

Dove, M. "Theories of Swidden Agriculture and the Political Economy of Ignorance." *Agroforestry Systems*, Vol. 1, 1983, pp. 85–89.

Dove, M. "Swidden Systems and their Potential Role in Development: A Case Study for Kalimantan." *Prisma*, Vol. 21, 1981, pp. 81–100.

ESCAP. *Review and Appraisal of the Environmental Situation in the ESCAP Region.* United Nations Economic and Social Commission on Asia and the Pacific, Bangkok, 1982.

Fujisaka, J. S. "Philippine Social Forestry: The Participatory Approach Conceptual Model," in T. Osteria and J. Okamura, eds., *Participatory Approaches to Development: Experiences in the Philippines.* Manila: De La Salle University Research Center, 1986.

Fujisaka, J. S. "Iterative Informal Structured Interviewing: RRA Training and Experiences from the Farming Systems Development Project-Eastern Visayas." Unpublished, 1985.

Fujisaka, J. S. and A. D. N. Capistrano. "Pioneer Shifting Cultivation in Calminoe, Philippines: Sustainability or Degradation from Changing Human-Ecosystem Interactions?" Working Paper. Environment and Policy Institute, East-West Center, Honolulu, 1985.

Fujisaka, J. S. and N. Duhaylungsod. "Pagpanag-iya or Paginobrahanay? A Methodological Reminder for Philippine Social Scientists." *PSSC Social Science Information*, Vol. 10, No. 4, 1983, pp. 1–6 and 28.

Sajise, P., D. Baker, S. Fujisaka, I. Bolo, Baker, and D. Hitchcock. "Mid-Project Evaluation of the Farming Systems Development Project-Eastern Visayas." USAID-Ministry of Agriculture and Food, Manila, 1985.

# 11

## Experiences in a Private, International Development Agency

*Anthony J. DiBella*

### Introduction

Applying what we know about people to the solution of social problems has been a major focus of my life. Early in my career I had several opportunities to act out this aspiration when I was employed as a state social worker in Massachusetts, a psychiatric aide at a large mental hospital in Connecticut, and a community organizer in Appalachia. Such experiences were interspersed with social science training.

I do not know whether it was me or my environment, but my social science training always seemed to spawn certain firsts. I was the first B.A. sociology graduate at a small New England liberal arts college (Trinity) and the first recipient of an M.A. in applied anthropology from American University. I will soon be the recipient of an M.B.A. degree.

My first opportunity to apply my graduate training was in the amorphous field of consulting. For four years I was employed either as an independent consultant or with a consulting firm, always in the Washington, D.C. area. I must have worked on dozens of projects and proposals for various agencies, though my principal efforts were with the National Endowment for the Humanities and USAID.

For several years some friends encouraged me to seek employment with a private, voluntary agency (PVO). They convinced me that private, international development agencies were an appropriate setting for applied social science. After an extensive search for such an opportunity I was hired by Foster Parents Plan International. This chapter discusses the first major study in my new position and in the process provides some insight to the PVO experience.

I think it is unfortunate that the use of anthropology in a private, voluntary agency is not more widely recognized among the anthropology profession. It seems that when anthropologists talk about development anthropology or economic development, they always think or only think of the large bilateral and multilateral development organizations like USAID or the World Bank. The private, voluntary sector is a large one and should not go unrecognized. Furthermore, the small-scale nature of PVO activities brings them in direct contact with the people who are intended to benefit from their projects. It is because of this that anthropology in these settings is much more highly valued and relevant, for it is here that the application of anthropology can be recognized more easily. Large-scale development organizations that must design projects through multi-tiered bureaucracies or work closely with government ministries will always be far from the action in the field.

Established in 1937, Foster Parents Plan International (PLAN) supports social welfare and economic development projects in twenty-two countries. They include Haiti, El Salvador, Bolivia, Senegal, Burkina Faso, Sudan, Nepal, and Indonesia to name just a few. Funds are obtained from the support of "Foster Parents" through donor offices located in Australia, Belgium, Canada, Japan, the Netherlands, the United Kingdom, and the United States. These donor offices are responsible for all promotional and fund-raising efforts. In Fiscal Year 1985, 81.6 percent of all funds received by these offices were transferred to international headquarters which directs the implementation of all field projects.

Through the sponsorship of "Foster Children" Foster Parents Plan International provides a variety of program services to these foster children, their families and communities. Services vary widely from one field office to another but are generally focused in the sectors of health, education, community development, employment, financial assistance, and social services. The worldwide PLAN organization had an operating budget of more than $64 million in FY 1985, when it supported over 245,000 Foster Children worldwide.

On account of rapid growth in the organization during the last ten years, PLAN's senior management decided in 1979 to increase the size of the technical support staff at international headquarters. One area of concern was the establishment of an in-agency capacity to evaluate and research program effectiveness and impact. This concern was based on a variety of factors including the need to account more fully to the board of directors and sponsors about the impact of field programs. It was also recognized that research would be used for formative evaluation to re-direct program operations as needed. Finally, there was a need to provide a research capacity at international headquarters to work with program staff on a variety of tasks and policy issues.

While research studies had been conducted intermittently throughout PLAN's history, there had never been one staff person whose sole responsibility was the area of evaluation and research. My interest in relocating from Washington consulting was well-timed with PLAN's interest to establish a research function.

When I arrived at international headquarters in Warwick, Rhode Island in October, 1979 my inner sense of excitement and challenge was combined with some trepidations and uncertainties. One of my initial, major concerns was to understand the culture of the agency, how it shaped staff perspectives, and how it would serve as an environment within which the findings from evaluation studies would be utilized and/or interpreted and re-interpreted. Part of this assessment was to understand the sophistication of my audience towards research and their own values towards scientific inquiry. This was an assessment that had to be done at several levels in the organization from board of directors to senior management, other headquarters staff and field staff, to PLAN assisted families and communities in the field. Unfortunately, I did not have the luxury of taking as much time as needed to address and answer such questions before getting my feet wet.

It seemed to me that I could best legitimate the use of anthropology and, in fact, all applied social science by doing it and making it relevant to staff interests and concerns. Consequently, while obtaining an orientation to the agency's operating philosophy and field programs, I interviewed all program staff at international headquarters to identify those program policy issues and questions which remained unresolved and which research could seek to answer.

## The First Study

While a wide range of issues were identified through my interviews with staff, there was one that seemed to draw the most interest and attention. A new type of service delivery system had been operating at our field offices in the Philippines for several years. It was considered by many to be the best and one of the most innovative programs that PLAN operated in the field. Many PLAN field directors were interested in implementing a similar program model at their field offices. However, it was essential that the program be studied first before it was replicated elsewhere. The underlying concern was that we should try to learn from the experiences of the program in the Philippines so that we could determine its value and relevance to other field locations.

There are several aspects of this program which should be explained more carefully. During the last ten years PLAN has incorporated goal setting at three levels of program design. To be approved, each project proposal must contain specific objectives. Program staff have been interested in applying goal setting concepts to the development of client families and communities. The idea was to provide families with a framework within which PLAN's assistance could be directed.

When PLAN goes into a community, staff try to identify families which meet certain criteria. Family income must be below a certain level. The family must be motivated to participate in and implement projects. There must be at least one child in the family of school age who can become the "Foster Child." This is the individual officially sponsored by PLAN's "Foster Parents"—donors who make monthly contributions to fund the organization. While particular attention is paid to the progress of this child, the assistance provided through PLAN improves the conditions of the entire family.

The Family and Community Development Program (FCDP) in the Philippines was established to integrate various elements of goal setting for PLAN clients and communities. Families were required to identify their needs, priorities, and developmental objectives. This was intended to get families to participate directly in their own progress and to do so in a framework that provided direction and encouragement. Consequently, each family enrolled with Foster Parents Plan in the Philippines was required to have a Family Development Plan (FDP). This was a list of specific projects which each family wanted to implement. Once a year PLAN released funds that had accrued throughout the year in a Family Development Plan Fund, to achieve at least one of the family's project objectives. The program was structured and administered in the Philippines in rural locations throughout Luzon and the islands of Mindoro and Marinduque. At each location 250 families were serviced by a social worker and a case assistant. These 250 families all had FDPs and were also organized into a community association. The associations were run democratically and were required to have their own list of community objectives. When an association was ready to implement a project, it would receive PLAN funds that had accrued in a Community Development Fund. Since there was both a family and community development component to the program, it was named the Family and Community Development Program. Typical family projects include installing a new roof, raising chickens, and constructing a latrine. Community projects might include building a school, digging irrigation channels, and repairing the pump on a community well. Most projects were small-scale and their implementation required the direct participation of families.

The ultimate goal of the FCDP was the development of independent and self-sufficient families. To accomplish this and to diminish the possibility of creating any dependency, PLAN allowed families only a limited time within which to achieve their stated objectives. PLAN believed that the use of a specific timeframe of five years for family assistance would lessen client dependency, hasten family development, and provide an objective means for the termination of services. Along with the family and community development thrusts of the program, this use of five-year timeframes became the third most important policy element and dimension to the FCDP.

The field director in the Philippines documented the FCDP well so that it received much attention by staff at headquarters. Yet staff held a healthy skepticism about the impact of the program. It was also well known that our Philippines national staff were the best trained of any country where PLAN works. In the Philippines all social workers are college graduates; at African field offices social workers seldom have a high school education.

Our research goal was to study the FCDP program model and to compare its design with how it actually worked. The concern was to specify how the program functioned in the Philippines and why it worked the way it did. Besides trying to identify the characteristics of program impact and answering the question, "what?" I was also interested in the "how?" and "why?" Some of the questions I sought to answer included:

1. What impact occurred on PLAN affiliated individuals, families and communities when services were provided through the FCDP?
2. How and why did these impacts occur?
3. What factors were critical to the success and/or failure of the FCDP?
4. What FCDP policies should be changed to make the program more effective?

I first traveled to the Philippines in January 1980, to see the program in action and to prepare for the study. I also wanted to assess local resources that would help me collect and analyze field data. Before leaving on this trip, I drafted a research design based on experimental and quasi-experimental research methods. It did not take me long to realize that my preconceived notions would not work. The program setting had too many uncontrollable variables affecting the FCDP. Random assignment of families to the program was out of the question. Finally, program impact seemed slow to develop, so it might take two, three, or four years to observe changes in certain quantitative indicators, such as income or life expectancy.

After flying for nearly thirty hours, I arrived exhausted to meet the chaos of Asia. While my inner timeclock read midnight, it was noon in Manila, and 93 degrees with high humidity. Also this was my first personal exposure to either the Philippines or Southeast Asia, but I didn't let all this wear me away, at least not immediately. From the airport I went directly to the office where I got a briefing from Frank Campbell, PLAN's field director, about my schedule. A tour of the office followed. Finally, in the late afternoon I was escorted to the quiet confines of a Western type hotel room with all the comforts of a Holiday Inn and more.

That first week was devoted to learning about the FCDP from staff who accompanied me to the program locations. At the time of my visit, PLAN/Philippines operated in seventy-eight different rural locations. They had specific bounds and were serviced by different social workers, yet followed all the stated policies and procedures of FCDP. To me the locations provided a natural and representative framework within which a researcher could assess how the program functioned. I decided then to scrap my experimental design and focus my initial inquiry on a set of structured case studies.

I quickly realized that the only way to really learn what was happening in the FCDP program locations was to assemble a research team of Filipinos who could cut through the cultural barriers facing me. For example, although there are two major, national languages spoken in the Philippines—English and Tagalog—many families at the rural program sites could speak only local languages, such as Ilokano and Bicolano. I wanted to get data directly from the PLAN families and knew this could only be done if I depended on local researchers.

I spent a considerable amount of time meeting with research professors at several Philippine universities. To each of them I explained the FCDP program, PLAN, and my research objectives. It was a tedious process, but a necessary one. At the end of my three-week visit I had assembled a list of possible researchers who could help me coordinate the study, and I asked each of them to submit to me a statement of their qualifications and interests in the project.

After returning to PLAN headquarters in Rhode Island, I re-worked my research design and reviewed the qualifications and research proposals of the Philippine researchers as they came in. Considering my options, I decided to collaborate with Dr. Jules DeRaedt, a Belgian ex-missionary, now an anthropology professor at the University of Philippines in Baguio. To a certain extent my decision was based on logistics, since one of PLAN's regional offices was located in Baguio, a city whose favorable climate provided an ideal setting to base the research team.

While I was still at headquarters, Dr. DeRaedt recruited four fieldworkers. It turned out that they were all women with social science degrees who had studied under Dr. DeRaedt. Each fieldworker was given the responsibility to prepare case studies of two FCDP sites. In April 1980, I returned to the Philippines to train the fieldworkers and supervise them with Dr. DeRaedt's assistance.

My experience with the case study method is that it provides a significant amount of information which cannot easily be aggregated or else is too much a reflection of the fieldworkers' own biases. To avoid these difficulties, Dr. DeRaedt and I developed a specific case study outline for the fieldworkers to follow in their reports. To standardize the data collection process, three specific data forms were designed for the fieldworkers to use. All the case studies required the collection and analysis of four types of data including: (1) a review of secondary data available in the PLAN office; (2) completion of structured data worksheets for approximately twenty families in each location; (3) formal and informal interviews with social workers, PLAN and non-PLAN families, PLAN association officials and local leaders; and (4) participation-observation in the locations.

The fieldworkers spent eleven to fourteen days in each program location. During this time either Dr. DeRaedt or I visited them to supervise their work and to provide additional support and direction. After the collection of data in the field and the preparation of the case study reports, the research team met several times to discuss the findings and possible program recommendations.

I remained in the Philippines throughout the preparation of the first set of case studies. Following that, Dr. DeRaedt continued the supervision and coordination of the research team's activities. He also interviewed our field director and through his own observations wrote a report which supplemented the case study reports. All of these data were sent to the international headquarters in July 1980, where I analyzed them and wrote the final report.[1]

The release of our findings in September 1980 was quite opportune as a decision was then being made to decentralize the Philippines program from three regional offices to three totally independent field offices, each with their own field director. This increased staff flexibility to design and operate a program appropriate to local needs. It gave the field directors a free hand to implement our recommendations.

I discussed the research findings during my third trip to Manila in November 1980 during a meeting with all our Philippines field staff. That meeting proved to be a major event in disseminating the research findings. However, I also discussed the research at several meetings at headquarters and with the board of directors of PLAN International.

At these meetings additional research questions arose which suggested the necessity of an additional phase of field research. This resulted in my traveling in April 1981 to the Philippines for the fourth time. Dr. DeRaedt had organized another research team, one of whose members had worked with us during the previous year. While the methodology employed during the second research phase was almost identical to the fieldwork conducted in 1980, the on-site researchers had a slightly different focus. This was a result of the new research objectives and questions which had evolved from the first phase of our study. They were:

1. What happens to the PLAN association after a program location is phased out?
2. How would different staffing patterns affect program impact?
3. What are the specific types of skills and training needed for the staff working in the FCDP?
4. What are the best procedures for motivating clients?
5. How do FCDP programs change over time?

The design of this second phase of research provided a time dimension to our data collection. Comparisons could be made between the data collected in 1981 with those previously collected in 1980. We also wanted to compare data from program locations that had been phased out with those that were still operating.

Meanwhile, it had come to my attention that one of our former field staff in the Philippines had been transferred to Honduras and had designed a different type of program strategy based on his Philippines' experiences but adapted to the situation in Honduras. I saw this as an opportunity to add a cross-cultural perspective to this study. So in June 1981, while our fieldworkers in the Philippines were collecting data there, I traveled to Honduras for two weeks to investigate the design of the PLAN/Honduras program. I learned that initially the program started as a Family and Community Development Program (FCDP), similar to the one in the Philippines. However, it quickly evolved into a program where the focus was not on the objectives of an individual family but rather on groups of families.

After the data from the Philippines research had been analyzed, I prepared a second report which included those results as well as the findings from my trip to Honduras.[2] There was less emphasis this time around on making overall assessments of the program as this had been done in the previous report. Rather, issues of general concern to all field posts were addressed, especially with regard to the design and operation of family or group development type programs.

While this study on the FCDP in the Philippines and Honduras was my major responsibility for two years, it did not prevent me from making other contributions to the agency. As the only research specialist at PLAN headquarters, my advice was frequently solicited on such matters as baseline studies, project evaluations, social indicators, and project monitoring systems. These tasks resulted in field trips to Guatemala, Ecuador, Bolivia, and Indonesia.

## Cross-Cultural Policy Issues

Before describing some of the cross-cultural issues which emerged from our studies, I would like to make one general comment about difficulties in evaluating or researching programs cross-culturally. Aside from the traditional research problem of integrating quantitative and qualitative data, I have been faced with the problem of aggregating both quantitative and qualitative data from different cultural settings. To counter this problem, I have made efforts to structure the collection of qualitative data and to be more flexible in the collection of quantitative data. These are strategies which I employed in the FCDP research as well as other studies since.

One major program policy issue which was resolved from my research was the restriction of family assistance to a limited time period. This policy was referred to as the term of service concept. It was based upon the assumption that, by limiting the amount of time families would receive assistance, this would decrease their dependency on PLAN. The idea was also that, if families understood they only had a limited amount of assistance, they would make better use of their affiliation with PLAN while it lasted. The findings from our Philippine data indicated that clients did not make better use of PLAN assistance just because it was part of PLAN's procedures. While timeframes may assist PLAN administrators to plan budgets and levels of service, the validity of their use at the family level was highly questionable. There seem to be much better ways of motivating families to achieve development objectives.

Another issue which has been identified through these and other studies in which I have been engaged at PLAN is the appropriate cultural vehicle for providing development assistance. In the FCDP, PLAN provides financial support whose use is restricted to the achievement of pre-defined objectives. The group development approach is similar except that projects are identified by small groups of ten to twenty-five families. In both cases PLAN provides services that have a direct monetary value. These types of programs are regarded as improvements over programs in which cash assistance was provided directly to families without staff or program controls.

PLAN's international headquarters acts as an intermediary between the flow of resources from our Foster Parents (our sponsors who provide benefits) and our Foster Children, their families and communities (who receive benefits). Our field staff make choices regarding what mode or form these resources will take so that their use can be maximized among our program beneficiaries. I don't think that we are sufficiently aware of other research that has been done to assess the cultural appropriateness of one type of resource transfer as opposed to another.

Although large scale evaluation studies have been done in the United States during the last twenty years on alternative social service programs, their findings have limited applicability to our circumstances since PLAN operates in about fifty different cultural settings. It is difficult to set standardized and universal program policies because of this cultural variation, and it is for this reason that PLAN provides such a diversity of services in the field adapted to local needs.

## Utilization of Research Results

I have not discussed in detail the specific recommendations and findings from our studies in the Philippines and Honduras. Such a review would make this contribution quite lengthy and go beyond the general overview I have intended. However, I can say that the program findings and rec- ommendations which were generated from our studies have been directed towards resolving specific program difficulties which field staff themselves recognized and were unable to address. As a result, the research which we produced using anthropological techniques and addressing issues of an- thropological interest directly responded to problem areas which our field staff recognized. This resulted in a series of program revisions not only in the Philippines but at other field offices as well. Since the research on the FCDP in the Philippines, I have conducted several other studies. My last one was a feasibility study for opening a PLAN field office in Zimbabwe.

I have also had several opportunities to discuss with our international board of directors our entire research program. This has legitimated for them the depth of my commitment in achieving optimal program efficiency and impact. They have certainly been most helpful. Of great interest to me is that one of the board members is a Dutch anthropologist. The evaluation and research function at international headquarters presently has three complementary dimensions. The first major focus, which originally brought me to PLAN, is conducting independent research and evaluation. This includes studies of program policy areas such as education, health, and community development. We have also conducted impact studies of our programs in Burkina Faso and Bali. In this capacity, we act as the independent, hopefully objective researchers who can look at programs cross-culturally.

Our second focus is to provide support to the program department and our field staff in their own efforts to monitor project activities. This involves reviewing evaluation proposals and working with evaluation coordinators hired locally at our field offices. In this role, we act as in-house consultants on evaluation and as a resource which staff can draw upon as they review and redesign projects.

Finally, our contribution has expanded during the last two years so that we now serve the entire organization, not just program staff. Consultations and management studies generate information needed to assess strategic agency policies. This incudes consideration of agency expansion in new program and donor countries, analyses and projections of financial data, and assessments of administrative operations.

My experience at PLAN has been a positive one and has clearly indicated to me and to the many others who have supported our work that anthropology does have a constructive role in international development activities. This has enabled us to hire additional staff, for as the agency has continued to grow so has our evaluation/research responsibilities. Anthropologists have been included in a variety of contract research projects. Their contributions and successes have facilitated even further the legitimacy of an anthropological perspective. This development was no doubt aided by the fact that PLAN's projects are small-scale, close to the people, and shaped by the many cultural settings where we work. These characteristics are typical of the activities of other private, voluntary agencies in development. Administrators and applied researchers with anthropological skills would be wise to investigate these opportunities for social science application.

## Notes

1. DiBella, Anthony J. A *Study of PLAN's Family and Community Development Program in the Philippines: Summary Report on Initial Findings.* Foster Parents Plan International: East Greenwich, RI, 1980.

2. DiBella, Anthony J. *Further Studies of Family and Community Development Programming.* Foster Parents Plan International: East Greenwich, RI, 1981.

# 12

# Implications
# of Development Policies
# for Agriculture in Taiwan

*Ruth Ann Sando*

## Introduction

It was election time in K'ung Liao Village.[1] Months of planning, political maneuvering and controversy were almost at an end. Unlike previous elections, a winner had not been selected ahead of time and it was evident that the current headman might be replaced. During the course of campaigning, factions had developed and these reflected the controversy in the village over a nationally-funded community development project. The two opponents were the thirty year old incumbent who had been under thirty when selected for his first term, and a sixty-two year old former headman. On election day villagers gathered in southern Taiwan's intense heat to cast ballots at the community center. After the polling place closed, along with many villagers I sat and watched the ballots counted. At the last ballot, the vote stood at 163 to 241. The incumbent headman was re-elected.

I was living in the village conducting research for my dissertation on the effects of out-migration. It had turned out to be an excellent choice for a research site. Like many rural areas in Taiwan, K'ung Liao was rapidly losing population as villagers became migrants headed for urban jobs and residence. Village farmers were forced daily to deal with the consequences of depopulation. The reasons behind this depopulation were many and varied: low prices for crops, the need for increasing capitalization of farming, rapid industrialization and rural-urban income disparity. During the course of my research it became increasingly apparent that rural conditions were heavily dependent on national policies. The election of the headman in a village of fewer than 700 people mirrored this intrusion into local power

---

An earlier version of this article was presented at the annual meeting of the Society for Applied Anthropology, San Diego, March 17–19, 1983.

and autonomy. The inability of the village to prevent the election from going beyond the desired symbolic competition demonstrated the growing impact of national development policies.

Observing the antagonism between factions in the village during this election led me to explore my stereotype of the village as a fairly autonomous community. I found that the one continuous trend during Taiwan's long colonial history and modern post-colonial period has been nationally planned economic change financed by rural resources. Local history in Taiwan reveals that economic development policies under two different political systems had the same goal: to break down local autonomy. The election I witnessed was a small act in a longer-playing political drama that had been going on for many years. The objective of this chapter is to review this local history for clues to the impact on rural communities of national development policies promulgated under two forms of government. Because of its colonial background, the excellence of its historical documents, and its current role as a model of economic development, an examination of policy development in Taiwan from a rural perspective will shed important light on the extent and manner in which farmers participate in development.

## Agriculture in Colonial Taiwan

From 1683 to 1895 Taiwan was under the control of the Chinese government, administered as part of Fukien Province. It was populated by Malayo-Polynesian natives and Chinese immigrants. Control of the island was ceded to Japan as part of the settlement of the first Sino-Japanese war in 1895; for the next fifty years Taiwan remained a colony of Japan. For the people of Taiwan, the change to colonial status was most evident in the dynamic control exercised by the Japanese. While China had displayed little interest in the island, Japan planned an important role for it in building a Japanese empire. Initial resistance to Japanese rule by the Chinese living in Taiwan was overcome within the first decade; it took longer to overcome aboriginal resistance. During the period of pacification, Japan set up an administrative organization with long-range goals. Taiwan was to play a critical economic role as a major source of agricultural products flowing to Japan as well as a reliable market for industrial products leaving Japan. By utilizing Taiwan in this way, the food supply for Japan could become more secure and the balance of payments would be relieved by the new supplies, especially of the cash crop, sugar, produced within the empire (Puchala and Stavely, 1979: 118).

A brief description of major agricultural policies pursued in Taiwan during this period illustrates the route chosen by Japan for Taiwanese development. During the initial period, an inventory of all of Taiwan's potential resources was conducted. Japanese administrators began by surveying all agricultural and forest lands. Their surveys disclosed that approximately twice as much land was being cultivated as had been reported in the earlier Chinese records. The improvement in recordkeeping provided an increased tax base. Money and measures were also standardized, and the first population census was taken in 1905. Transportation projects were begun, including harbors, highways and railroad lines connecting major cities. Large-scale irrigation projects increased food production and the newly organized Farmers Association promoted new agricultural techniques.

One of the earliest colonial programs, undertaken in 1898 was the establishment of the *pao-chia* system. It became one of the most important means of controlling the population and making policies effective down to the lowest level. Under this program, each community was divided into units, *pao*, made up of several families, *chia*, bound together by collective responsibility for the actions of each member. The administrative functions of the *pao-chia* system included collecting taxes, transmitting regulations and information, making sanitary improvements, and administering agricultural improvement programs (see Chen, 1975: 391–416). The slogan of the Japanese administration was "an industrial Japan and an agricultural Taiwan." Agricultural production was stimulated through several means: increased irrigation, introduction of new seed varieties, and training programs for farmers. The increase in production was export-oriented, aimed at the growing needs of the Japanese empire. The two crops emphasized in the Farmers Association programs were rice and sugarcane, both of which benefited from improvements in irrigation. One irrigation project, the Chianan system, built in southern Taiwan, was one of the largest irrigation systems in Asia when completed. According to one geographer, after it was in operation the rice-growing area increased by 74 percent and the sugarcane area by 30 percent (Hsieh, 1964: 170). Irrigation systems also gave Japan more control over the Taiwanese farmer, since irrigation required that crops be coordinated and the government controlled access to water. This control meant that the Japanese administrators were able to manipulate the cropping patterns.

The government also reached individual farmers through the Farmers Association, which was organized around 1900. Membership was compulsory.

FAs eventually took charge of such important functions as the improvement and extension of seeds, the maintenance of a seed multiplication system, the prevention and control of animal and plant diseases, the training of agricultural technicians, the execution of agricultural surveys, the purchase of fertilizer, seeds, and equipment needed by members, and the management of warehouses. (Ho, 1978: 63).

The Farmers Association ran credit cooperatives which made money available to farmers, enabling them to adopt new technology. However, the work which contributed most to increasing production for export was the extension of agricultural information. New seed varieties were introduced and the police were called upon to ensure that the new seeds were planted.

The type of rice which came to dominate production in Taiwan was ponlai rice, which had a higher yield and was preferred by Japanese consumers. Although originally from China where it had been known since the first century A.D. (Chandler, 1979: 13), it was introduced in Taiwan as part of the rice improvement campaign by the Japanese who had grown it in northern Honshu (Myers and Ching, 1964: 556). Ponlai was first grown in Taiwan in the early 1920s and by 1935 was being raised on 305,000 hectares, more than any other variety (Grajdanzev, 1941: 54). The area devoted to native rice varieties quickly decreased.

> In 1903 there were supposedly 1,325 native varieties. In 1906 the government decided to allow the use of only 375 of them and the farmers of each village were further told to grow only three varieties which they could select from the 375. Meanwhile the government began producing and multiplying seeds of the three varieties, the work requiring four years to produce the seed needed by the farmers. After the seed was secured, the farmers were required to plant any one of the three varieties. No other varieties were allowed. The increase in yield reportedly due to replacement of inferior native with superior native varieties was 10 to 30 percent. (Chen, 1963: 287).

While the adoption of new varieties would seem to indicate that the Taiwanese farmer was ready to respond to any improvement in farming techniques, this was not the case. Taiwanese farmers had found ponlai rice costly to grow, requiring expensive commercial fertilizers. The motivation for these changes in the variety of seeds planted came from the colonial administration. Ponlai rice might never have become popular had its use not been backed by force.

> This exchange of low yielding native rice seeds for high yielding ones in the early decades of the 20th century was conducted under such police supervision. This may explain why the exchange was completed so quickly. Even after they were removed from formal extension work, police were occasionally called on to persuade reluctant farmers to adopt new farming techniques. (Ho, 1978: 63).

Although the production of rice increased greatly at a national level, this did not mean more food for farmers and their families. Between 1915 and 1926 the population of Taiwan grew by 15 percent while per capita rice consumption remained constant. At the same time, exports increased three-fold (Myers and Ching, 1964: 567). Later the situation for the Taiwanese consumer worsened. From 1925 until 1940 with population continuing to grow, per capita rice consumption decreased by nearly one-quarter (see Table 12.1.).

The extent to which the Taiwanese farmer had become tied to the Japanese market is illustrated by an examination of events in Japan. A decrease in Japanese rice production and an increase in domestic demand led to the *Komo Sodo* (rice riot) of 1918. In response, the government quickly took steps to import rice from its colonies, Korea and Taiwan, forcing Korean farmers to substitute sorghum, a low-quality grain, for rice in their own meals and forcing Taiwanese farmers to consume sweet potatoes rather than rice (Hayami and Ruttan, 1970: 570). At the same time, to

TABLE 12.1    Annual Consumption of Rice*

| Year | Total (m.t.) | Per Capita (kg.) | Population |
|------|------|------|------|
| 1925 | 631,343 | 158.15 | 3,992,000 |
| 1930 | 683,886 | 151.77 | 4,506,000 |
| 1935 | 576,004 | 111.95 | 5,144,000 |
| 1940 | 719,153 | 123.97 | 5,856,000 |

*Shen, 1971: 30.

ensure adequate rice for its future needs, Japan developed the *Sanmai Zoshoku Keikaku* (Rice Production Development Program), the methods of which have been covered above and which:

> . . . created the tremendous rice surplus that flooded the Japanese market: . . . net imports from Taiwan rose from 113 to 705 thousand metric tons . . . from 1915 to 1935. (Hayami and Ruttan, 1970: 571).

Unfortunately for the Japanese farmer, the program was so successful that it resulted in a flood of rice from the colonies and the depression of rice prices in Japan. Many Japanese farmers were forced out of agriculture. For Japan the long-range consequences of these polices shaped history:

> The so-called military reformists made this social uneasiness and disorder among farmers the spring-board for the invasion of Manchuria in 1931 and the other military adventures that followed . . . and (this) had not only economic but also vast social and political implications. (Hayami and Ruttan, 1970: 585).

There were also immediate ramifications for Taiwan: Japanese colonial administrators reacted by intensifying sugarcane production on the island (see Table 12.2.). How was this official change from an emphasis on rice to sugar production implemented? No new program was needed:

> Since the police penetrated to every village household through the *ho-ko (pao-chia)* system, it was relatively easy for them to insist on the adoption of new sugarcane or rice seeds and supervise their use. The early success of large sugar companies in increasing sugarcane cultivation in southern Taiwan was due to the assistance of local police, who compelled villagers to switch from existing food crops to cane. (Myers and Ching, 1964: 565).

Almost 95 percent of the sugar produced was exported. Individual farmers sold their crop to the large Japanese-owned mills where it was processed. The milling of cane was strictly controlled and farmers were required to

TABLE 12.2    Sugarcane 1902 - 1940*

| Period | Area (ha) | Cane Yield (kg.) | Cane Production | Sugar Production |
|---|---|---|---|---|
| 1902-10 | 30,823 | 31,134 | 959,653 | 82,236 |
| 1911-20 | 100,258 | 28,149 | 2,822,156 | 251,498 |
| 1921-30 | 115,757 | 43,836 | 5,074,342 | 498,353 |
| 1931-40 | 119,740 | 68,206 | 8,166,994 | 948,344 |

*JCRR, 1966: 47.

sell their sugar to assigned mills, creating competition between farmers but monopolies for the mills. (Grajdanzev, 1942: 62).

By the end of the Japanese colonial period Taiwan's agricultural production was responsive to the needs of the Japanese market. Cropping decisions, sales, acreage, seed varieties, use of fertilizers and equipment and other decisions for the individual farmer had been transformed into activities performed under direction. The *pao-chia* system and the work of the Farmers Association were primarily responsible for usurping autonomy from the farmer; however, the military and police force needed to ensure the success of these colonial programs reveals the asymmetrical power relations inherent in colonial administrations. The needs of Japan had immediate impact on the individual Taiwanese; the average farmer was growing food for export which he could not afford to eat himself. The trend toward manipulating agricultural production and resources was an important characteristic of Japan's colonial relationship with Taiwan. It is also characteristic of the entire development process.

## Agriculture in the Post-War Development Policy

After World War II, Japan lost Taiwan and its other colonies, and control over the island passed to the Nationalist government of China. Taiwan had suffered little damage during the war, and retained its strong economic base. Economic development in the post-war period has taken a new course: industrial development. In development jargon, Taiwan is now known as one of the "NICs" (Newly Industrialized Countries). How has this been achieved?

The economic base upon which the new government built was agriculture. An examination of the agricultural programs of the post-war period will demonstrate how the transition from an agricultural to an industrial economy was achieved. A number of important policies have been implemented in the last several decades which have greatly affected the lives and work of Taiwan's farmers. Among them are land reform, a rice-fertilizer exchange program, pricing policies, land consolidation, improvements in irrigation,

and land-use policies. A brief discussion of these policies will highlight the
impact of the recent development on rural areas.

The first important program carried out by the Nationalists was the
Land Reform Program, which took place in the midst of growing scarcity
of land. It abolished large estates, decreed the sale of land previously owned
by Japan or Japanese individuals, and the sale of lands owned jointly or
corporately by lineages and other groups. Under this program, many tenants
were able to buy their landlords' lands, and Taiwan became an island of
small family farms which it remains to this day. The Land Reform Program
also stimulated the movement of investment capital from agriculture to
industry. As one K'ung Liao villager explained,

> I inherited 2 hectares (4.8 acres) from my father. During the Land Reform
> Program it was all sold to tenants. For each hectare I received about $2,500.
> The government gave me corporate stocks but my wife sold them. After my
> land was sold I never bought any more land and never farmed again.

Land reform also decreased the average size of land holdings, increased
multi-cropping and intensified labor use.

It must be remembered that the main purpose of the Land Reform
Program was to abolish tenancy, and to do this, the position of the tenant
was strengthened at the expense of the landlord. A tenant's lease runs six
years and can be terminated before that time only if the tenant does not
pay rent for two years, dies without an heir, or gives up his right to the
land by moving out of the area or changing occupations (Mao, 1976: 178).
In addition, a landlord is not allowed to resume cultivation of leased land
if he cannot farm it himself, if his income is already sufficient for the
support of his family, or if the tenant's family will be left without a means
of support (Mao, 1976: 178). Because of these conditions, the tenant's family
will often continue to cultivate after the lease has expired. The tenant is
also favored financially. The highest rent which can be charged by a landlord
is 37.5 percent of the 1948 crop yield. Since yields have increased dramatically
since 1948, landlords are collecting much less than 37.5 percent of the
present crop yield. These disincentives discourage owners from leasing land
to tenants and farms remain very small in size (see also Gallen, 1966; Kuo,
1975; Pasternak, 1968, 1972; and Tsai, 1967).

Another important post-war program was the Rice-Fertilizer Exchange
Program, implemented in 1948. This program established barter ratios
between rice and fertilizer with farmers paying in rice for fertilizers. The
amount of rice necessary to obtain a kilogram of chemical fertilizer was
sufficiently high to constitute a hidden tax on agriculture. Taiwanese farmers
had become increasingly dependent on chemical fertilizers since the Japanese
period when officials promoted the adoption of new rice varieties requiring
large amounts of fertilizers. Under the Rice-Fertilizer Exchange Program a
government monopoly was established in fertilizer distribution which stimulated the establishment of a domestic fertilizer industry. The influence of
the program was substantial. Nearly 35 percent of the rice going through

the market came under this program (Lee, 1975: 141). The program ended in 1972 after twenty-four years.

Control of the rice price was achieved not only through the Rice-Fertilizer Exchange Program but also by requiring that land taxes, rent payments on land leased under the Land Reform Program, and payments for land purchased under the Land Reform Program be paid in rice rather than cash. The rice collected was: (1) rationed to the armed forces; (2) rationed to government employees and employees of public educational institutions; (3) exported; and (4) sold on the open market to stabilize the rice price (Shen, 1971: 334) (see also Hsu, 1972; Lee, 1975; Lee, 1971; Sasamoto, 1968; and Wu, 1970).

Several other agricultural products are affected by government pricing policies. Sugarcane, a major crop in Taiwan, is grown either on the government owned Taiwan Sugar Corporation plantations or by individual farmers under contract to the Taiwan Sugar Corporation. The price of pork, also one of the island's main agricultural products, is stabilized through the control of supply. Slaughterhouses are managed by public institutions, including the Farmers Association, which influence supply and demand.

The Land Consolidation Program, begun in 1959, was another important program. It was implemented in K'ung Liao in 1971. The objectives of the program were to: (1) improve irrigation, drainage and transportation; (2) reduce the number of paths and boundaries; and (3) improve conditions for farm mechanization (Tainan County Government, 1966: 7, 8). The program was financed by the farmers who were charged .14 hectare for each hectare they owned, plus an equivalent amount in cash. Those who were unable to pay were given three-year, interest-free loans from The Land Bank. Farmers were able to purchase from the government those lands obtained as payment for consolidation or resulting from more efficient organization of owners' plots. The Land Consolidation Program was aimed at relieving the problems of farmers with a number of small, widely-scattered fields and paving the way for the use of machinery on these small plots. Both factors would aid farmer efficiency and increase agricultural production (see Chang, 1981; Hung and Vander Meer, 1981; Huang, 1977; and Vander Meer, 1976).

Another policy for discussion is the improvement of the water supply for farmers. The Chia-nan Irrigation System was completed in 1930 and in the 1960s a number of necessary improvements were begun. One of these was the construction of the Tseng Wen Reservoir, completed in 1974. This reservoir greatly increased the supply of irrigated water and resulted in an alteration of the crop cycle. Previously only one rice crop could be grown in three years. After 1974, the cycle was modified to include a second rice crop. This modified crop cycle, which every farmer followed, was composed of one sugarcane crop, two rice crops, and two mixed crops over a three-year period.

Many K'ung Liao farmers believe that the completion of the Tseng Wen Reservoir in 1974 created more work for them but not more income. The period of growth for the sugarcane is shorter and the second rice crop has been added, but due to out-migration, fewer people are available to work which has driven up the cost of labor. Thus, although the production of rice has increased, the burden on the farmers has also become heavier. One villager discussed his experience with the new cropping schedule:

> Before the improvement in irrigation I could harvest about 226,797 lb. of sugarcane per hectare. Also there was more leisure time. Now the schedule is very tight and because the cane is not given a year and a half in the ground as it was previously, the harvest is down to about 151,196–181,435 lb. per hectare. The addition of one more rice crop is not profitable enough to compensate for the loss of about 45,352 lb. of sugarcane. Plus I must employ workers for the rice crop and now wages are high and labor is hard to find. It would be better to have the sugarcane which has a high export price and can be interplanted with mixed crops.

Legal restrictions on the ownership and use of farmland are additional rural policies which have far-reaching effects on rural life and work. For example, non-farmers cannot buy farmland.

> Any sale of owner-cultivated land must be approved by the government and the purchaser must show that he is a bonafide farmer. (Mao, 1976: 179)

Those who inherit farmland must also begin to farm it themselves or sell it. The buyer of farmland must live within 10 km. of the land. The purpose of these regulations is to discourage the establishment of absentee land-ownership and the alienation of agricultural land to other uses. Another measure which has had important consequences for farmers is the taxation of fallow land. Farmland which is unplanted is taxed at triple the rate of planted fields. Such fallow fields can be detected easily since fertilizers are purchased through the Farmers Association. At one point, a growing number of farmers in and near K'ung Liao became interested in converting their farmland into large fish ponds which are not labor intensive and can be quite profitable. However such conversions were ruled illegal and the fallow tax was applied.

These agricultural policies, while essential to development in Taiwan do not stand alone. The position of agriculture and of farmers in Taiwan today cannot be understood without reference to conditions in industry. Therefore, I will briefly summarize important policies related to industry.

Since the 1950s industrial development and foreign trade expansion have been encouraged through a variety of measures. Foreign investors have been given special privileges and protection. Tax incentives include five-year income tax holidays for new businesses and four-year income tax holidays for expanding businesses; tax-free export sales; business income tax ceilings; and special exemptions on duty on imported machinery and equipment (Lu, 1977: 14). The government has also made available low-interest loans, and since 1965 has created three tax- and duty-free export-processing zones.

Businesses in the export-processing zones are given additional tax incentives such as exemptions from business and commodity taxes and exemption from import duties on machinery, equipment, raw materials and semi-finished products (Lu, 1977: 13). Forty industrial parks have also been established (Tsui, 1977: 7) Taiwan's major industries include electronics, chemicals, textiles and machinery. Many of the world's industrial giants can be found in Taiwan, such as RCA, ITT, Hitachi, Mitsubishi, Gulf Oil, Phillips, Union Carbide, Asahi Chemical, Ford, Singer and Canon. No doubt another attraction for these industries has been that ". . . for more than twenty years, there have been no riots, no strikes and no serious labor-management strife in Taiwan" (Lu, 1977: 13). The high industrial growth rate owes much to these policies.

> Although the government in Taiwan has declared that agriculture and industry will be equally developed, agricultural development has always received less attention. (Tsai, 1978: 30)

The policies outlined above show a clear industrial bias. Since the 1970s when it became evident that there was a rapidly-growing gap between rural and urban incomes, steps have been taken to put some money back into rural areas. Encouragement of rural industrialization was one means (see Ho, 1979: 77–96). Companies were given financial subsidies to move out into rural areas with the dual purpose of reducing rural-urban income disparity and stemming the heavy flow of rural out-migration by improving rural living conditions and curbing underemployment. Another step taken was community development projects which subsidized the construction of community centers, road improvement, renovation of kitchen and bathroom facilities, and installation of road lights.

It was money from just such a project which fueled the antagonism in the election for the headman of K'ung Liao mentioned earlier. As such, it is worthwhile to explore the impact of the project more closely. The heavy flow of migrants out of rural areas alarmed planners providing urban services. They reasoned the villagers are more likely to stay where they are if their environment is improved; the urban view of the countryside being that it is dirty, unhygienic, backward and unpleasant. As a result, money was made available to improve the homes and communities of villagers all over the country. All a village need do was to tap into these financial sources. The availability of money from outside was probably a major motivation for the selection of the current young headman in his first term. An older, poorly educated, Taiwanese-speaking villager would not have been able to hold his own with township and county-level officials, so a younger, Mandarin-speaking villager who was a former teacher was chosen. His selection represented an active recognition of the widening influence of the government and the decreasing importance of village boundaries.

As a strategy to tap into government funding for villagers, the choice of the young headman was a great success. In 1975 the model village program[2] began with the paving of the main village road. A brick wall at the edge of courtyards fronting on the road went up the same year. Also in 1975 the Farmers Association oversaw the improvement of kitchen and bathroom facilities. Many people put in flush toilets and new bathtubs, had their kitchens tiled, and replaced their wood-burning stoves with gas-fueled ones. In 1976, twenty-seven public toilets were built, 150 tree pots and 200 trees purchased for roadside beautification, three pigpens built, and three old ones rebuilt. Eleven trash cans were placed in public areas. Another addition was street lights, the absence of which in some areas became an issue in the election. Also as part of the community improvement project, forty families received from NT800 to NT2,000 ($22.37 to $55.63) to make home improvements. Three of the very poorest families were able to rebuild their houses and for a while received a monthly subsidy of NT600 ($16.68). The support for rebuilding houses ran from NT38,000 to NT48,000 ($1,057 to $1,335). To qualify for this assistance poor villagers had to meet the requirements of having more than four children under the age of sixteen and no more than .5 hectare of owned land. There is now no one eligible for this program. An additional project was the construction of a community center.

This program was designed so that these improvements would be funded by money from both the national government and the villagers themselves. Each person, young or old, was assessed NT300 ($8.34). Landowners were to contribute NT3,000 ($83.44) per hectare owned. K'ung Liao village was to supply NT300,000 ($8,344) and the national government would match it with NT600,000 ($16,689). Therefore the villagers could receive all of these improvements and pay only one-third the cost.

Through contributions and borrowing, a fund of NT590,000 ($16,412) was collected. After the program was completed there was still NT500,000 ($13,908) left unspent. By giving an official about NT100,000 ($2,782) to keep their "good relationship," the village headman was able to get most of the program for free. Feeling that he had helped the village to get all these improvements for virtually nothing, the headman was particularly incensed by his opposition's talk that he had made a profit.

In the 1978 election, the village headman campaigned on his ability to improve the village, particularly through obtaining outside money. The opponent campaigned on his own honesty and the headman's suspiciously sudden improvement in economic status. Whether or not the headman had diverted some of the public money became a frequent topic of the late-night, outdoor gossip groups. The headman's supporters in these groups, upon hearing such criticism, would promptly disparage his opponent's ability to keep the money flowing in if, as they pointed out, he couldn't even speak Mandarin to the local officials. Judging from the final vote the issues were never resolved and the polarization of the village did not end with the election.

The other major effort to reduce rural-urban income disparity, rural industrialization, also had some unforeseen consequences in villages like K'ung Liao. As mentioned, one important goal of rural industrialization was the reduction of rural underemployment.

To remedy the shortcoming of unbalanced growth, more economic activities should be encouraged and more job opportunities provided in less developed regions to reduce the out-migration of population. . . . A number of industrial estates have therefore been developed in designated places in less developed regions. (Chang and Chen, 1978: 76, 77)

However, while the rural industrialization and community improvement programs were being implemented, the rural labor shortage was becoming increasingly severe. Out-migration was not a result of underemployment or unpaved roads, but a response to the worsening state of agriculture.

## Conclusion

The changes in K'ung Liao and other small farming communities during the Japanese period show evidence of specialization, simplification, and increasing economic dependency. Agriculture was reorganized along lines of importance to Japan. By providing irrigation with increased output of a few select crops the major goal, agriculture became more specialized. After gaining control of the water, and thus the ability to manipulate the cropping system, the Japanese, and later the Nationalists, could force the farmers' labor in directions which the administrators deemed desirable.

Through the pao-chia system, families within the pao were made collectively responsible for the actions of all members. If one family did not follow regulations, all were punished. This type of organization greatly increased the ability of administrators to carry out their policies. Administrators were responding to needs from Japan, which could be quickly passed down to Taiwanese farm families. The forced adoption of new rice and sugarcane varieties resulted in much higher levels of production, although most of each harvest was exported, leaving K'ung Liao farmers themselves with increasingly inadequate diets. Farmers were not able to operate on the basis of their own interests, but in the interest of the Japanese colonial empire.

Under the Japanese colonial administration, economic development focused on increasing agricultural production in order to feed Japanese consumers. As time went on, Taiwanese farmers, who were growing more than ever, could not afford to feed themselves adequately. Many K'ung Liao farmers' recollections of hunger during this period substantiate the historical data available. It is somewhat ironic that a development model which emphasizes farming should do so little for farmers.

What does a comparison of pre- and post-war economic development in Taiwan show us? In spite of the political, economic and historical differences between the two, there are important, underlying similarities. First, communication takes place in a hierarchical mode with information flowing from top to bottom. Those needs which are acted on are those of the nation, the colonialists, or the urbanites. Decisions are made at high levels, for the benefit of these segments of society and information then flows out regarding new programs and policies. Farmers, residents of rural areas, or colonists are the recipients of such information rather than participants in decision-making. It is my impression that the hierarchical flow of information moving from top to bottom constitutes one of the greatest problems for planners. In many cases they have no idea of the problems of farmers or small communities and no access to such information. The recent decision to promote rural industrialization as an answer to rural underemployment is a good example. This underemployment was identified as a problem through the empirical evidence of heavy rural-to-urban migration. In fact, local information proved that such migration arose from migrants' perception that agriculture was no longer an economically viable occupation. Underemployment in rural areas not only did not exist, but there was a severe labor shortage exacerbating farmers' problems and driving more of them out.

Another similarity in these two examples of development is the issue of political power. The imposition of agricultural policies under a colonial government in some cases became a show of power, as with the use of police force to make farmers plant new rice varieties. The declining ability of local areas to control their own resources and activities is characteristic of both models of development. Previous to becoming a colony, local areas in Taiwan were fairly autonomous. Within these local areas marriage partners were found, goods were traded, labor moved, defense was organized, and social services were performed (Sando, 1981: 1979). Colonial programs served to break down local barriers, particularly for economic exchange. At the end of the colonial period, the rice grown by a K'ung Liao farmer could become dinner for a family in Tokyo, a solider in the Philippines, or a Japanese administrator in Manchuria. The farmer himself could not afford to eat it, nor could his neighbors.

Are K'ung Liao farmers any more autonomous today? They grow mushrooms exported to the United States, rice and sugarcane sold anywhere in Taiwan, and meat and vegetables for any consumer interested. The true test of autonomy is whether they can meet their own needs. This they are still unable to do. In fact, a steady, heavy flow of migrants to urban areas demonstrates that the only viable solution seen for local problems is to leave local areas. Farming has become increasingly specialized and dependent on political decisions. Since these decisions often do not serve the best interests of rural areas, agriculture is in decline.

An examination of the agricultural and industrial policies in the postcolonial period in Taiwan also reveals hidden conflicts in economic goals. Economic planning has promoted economic development through industrialization and increased agricultural productivity. Agriculture has been drained to finance industrial development and continues to compete for land and labor with industry.

The goal of continued rapid economic growth and manufacturing expansion may be in conflict with the goal of preserving farm land, the various goals of environment protection, and the goal of balanced regional growth. In Taiwan . . . cities are built upon prime agricultural land; future urban and

industrial growth, as has past growth, will compete directly with agriculture
for the best rice lands. (Fuchs and Street, 1980: 320)

The competition between industry and agriculture is not evenly balanced
since most of the agricultural policies are disincentives while many industrial
policies represent subsidies.

This conflict between agriculture and industry for economic resources
is built into the current emphasis on industrialization as the route to
economic development. As Reynolds notes:

> The development literature now contains a dozen or so models of early
> economic development. These invariably contain an agricultural sector; but
> the internal structure of agriculture remains shadowy. . . . This doubtless
> stems from the fact that industrialization tends to be regarded as the focal
> point of economic development, with agriculture playing the role of a resource
> reservoir. (Reynolds, 1975: 1).

What is the role of agriculture in Taiwan? For some, the only role is
historical. Fei and Ranis believe that agriculture ". . . played its crucial
historical role to the hilt . . . without its central contribution the rest of
the success story would not have been possible" (1975: 362). The "success
story" they refer to is development through industrial growth. It is only
recently apparent, however, that the flow of resources from the agricultural
to the industrial sector cannot be sustained indefinitely and will lead to
agricultural decline. While Fei and Ranis approve of Taiwan becoming an
importer of food, others view with alarm the emphasis on industrialization
accompanied by growing food imports. Japan has already begun to examine
the problem of food self-sufficiency (see Ogura, 1976: 419–477). Undoubtedly
other nations are beginning to realize the political problems inherent in
the balance of power between food-surplus and food-importing nations.

As anthropologists, our focus is on communities and small groups. Our
most appropriate role is examining the fit between development policies
and local needs. Ideally, a discussion of local needs would precede policy
formulation. Anthropological analysis is appropriate for such local information
gathering. Moreover, the problems and implications of development are so
vast, reaching from the individual to the international level, that analysis
which is capable of moving between such widely disparate levels is essential.
Because economic development is a process which permeates society, the
work done by anthropologists may serve to tie together diverse levels of
analysis and become a valuable tool in examining the success or failure of
development policies.

## Notes

1. A pseudonym for a village in Tainan County in southern Taiwan.
2. The information about this program is from the Township Public Office.

# References

Chandler, Robert. *Rice in the Tropics.* Boulder: Westview Press, 1979.

Chang, T. S. and Chen Sun. "Land Use Planning in Taiwan, R.O.C." Sino-American Workshop on Land Use Planning. Taipei, January 4–12, 1978.

Chang, Wei-I. "A New Milestone for Farm Land Consolidation in Taiwan, R.O.C." Paper presented at the Annual Meeting of the International Geographical Union, Commission on Rural Development, Fresno, Ca., April 21–25, 1981.

Chen, Cheng-siang. *Taiwan: An Economic and Social Geography, Vol. 1.* Fu-min Institute of Economic Development. Taipei: Ching-hwa Press, 1963.

Chen, Ching-chih. "The Japanese Adaptation of the Pao-chia System in Taiwan 1895–1945." *Journal of Asian Studies,* Vol. 34, No. 2, 1975, pp. 391–416.

Fei, John, and G. Ranis. "Agriculture in Two Types of Open Economies," in Lloyd Reynolds, ed., *Agriculture in Development Theory.* New Haven: Yale University Press, 1975.

Fuchs, R. and J. Street. "Land Constraints and Development Planning in Taiwan." *The Journal of Developing Areas,* Vol. 14, No. 3, 1980, pp. 313–326.

Gallen, Bernard. *Hsin Hsing, Taiwan: A Chinese Village in Change.* Berkeley: University of California Press, 1966.

Grajdanzev, Andrew. *The Economic Development of Formosa.* Shanghai: Kelly and Walsh, 1941.

Grajdanzev, Andrew. *Formosa Today.* New York: Institute of Pacific Relations, 1942.

Hayami, Yujiro, and Vernon Ruttan. "Korean Rice, Taiwan Rice and Japanese Agricultural Stagnation: An Economic Consequence of Colonialism." *Journal of Economics,* Vol. 84, 1970, pp. 562–589.

Ho, Samuel P. S. *Economic Development of Taiwan 1860–1970.* New Haven: Yale University Press, 1978.

Ho, Samuel P. S. "Decentralized Industrialization and Rural Development: Evidence from Taiwan." *Economic Development and Cultural Change,* Vol. 28, No. 1, 1979, pp. 77–96.

Hsieh, Chiao-min. *Taiwan—Ilha Formosa.* Washington: Butterworths, 1964.

Hsu, Robert. "The Demand for Fertilizer in a Developing Country: The Case of Taiwan 1959–1966." *Economic Development and Cultural Change,* Vol. 20, No. 2, 1972, pp. 299–309.

Huang, Shu-min. *Agricultural Degradation: Changing Community Systems in Rural Taiwan.* Ph.D. dissertation. Michigan State University, 1977.

Hung, Mu-shan and Paul Vander Meer. "The Pros and Cons of Complete Compaction of Scattered Farm Plots at the Time of Land Consolidation in Taiwan." Paper presented at the annual meeting of the International Geographical Union, Commission on Rural Development. Fresno, Ca., April 23–25, 1981.

Joint Commission on Rural Reconstruction (JCRR). "Taiwan Agricultural Statistics 1901–1965." JCRR Economic Digest, Series No. 18, 1966, Taipei.

Kuo, Wan-yong. "Effects of Land Reform, Agricultural Pricing Policy and Economic Growth on Multiple Crop Diversification in Taiwan." *The Philippine Economic Journal,* Vol. 14, No. 27, 1975, pp. 149–174.

Lee, Shun-cheng. *A Case Study of Production Efficiency of Rice Growing With Special Reference to the Fertilizer-Rice Barter System in Taiwan 1950–1972.* M.A. Thesis. Faculty of Economics, Thammasat University, Bangkok, 1975.

Lee, T. H. "Government Interference in the Rice Market in Taiwan. Viewpoints on Rice Policy in Asia." Los Banos, The Philippines: International Rice Research Institute, 1971.

Lu, Lawrence. "Foreign Investment Perspectives in Taiwan, R.O.C." *Chung Kuo Chi Shang Yeh Yin Hang (International Commercial Bank of China) Economic Review,* Vol. 177, 1977, pp. 11–17.

Mao, Yu-kang. "Population and the Land System in Taiwan." Conference on Population and Economic Development in Taiwan. Institute of Economics, Academia Sinica, December 22, 1975 to January 2, 1976.

Myers, Ramon, and Adrienne Ching. "Agricultural Development in Taiwan Under Japanese Colonial Rule." *Journal of Asian Studies,* Vol. 23, No. 4, 1964, pp. 555–570.

Ogura, Takekazu. "Implications of Japan's Declining Food Self-Sufficiency Ratio." *The Developing Economies,* Vol. 14, No. 4, 1976, pp. 419–447.

Pasternak, Burton. "Some Social Consequences of Land Reform in a Taiwanese Village." *The Eastern Anthropologist,* Vol. 21, No. 2, 1968, pp. 135–149.

Pasternak, Burton. *Kinship and Community in Two Chinese Villages.* Stanford: Stanford University Press, 1972.

Puchala, Donald, and Jane Staveley. "The Political Economy of Taiwanese Agriculture," in Hopkins, et al., eds., *Food, Politics and Agricultural Development."* Boulder: Westview Press, 1979.

Reynolds, Lloyd. "Agriculture in Development Theory: An Overview," in L. Reynolds, ed., *Agriculture in Development Theory.* New Haven: Yale University Press, 1975.

Sando, Ruth Ann. *The Meaning of Development for Rural Areas: Depopulation in a Taiwanese Farming Community.* Ph.D. Dissertation. The University of Hawaii, 1981.

Sando, Ruth Ann. "Agricultural Out-migration and Rural Policy in Taiwan." Paper presented to the annual meeting of the Society for Applied Anthropology. San Diego, Ca., March 17–19, 1983.

Sando, Ruth Ann. "Doing the Work of Two Generations: The Impact of Out-migration on the Elderly in Rural Taiwan." *Journal of Cross-Cultural Gerontology,* Vol. 1, 1986, pp. 163–175.

Sasamoto, Takeharu. "A Salient Feature of Capital Accumulation in Taiwan." *The Developing Economies,* Vol. 6, No. 1, 1968, pp. 27–39.

Shen, T. *Agricultural Development on Taiwan Since World War II.* Taipei: Meiya Publications, 1971.

Tainan County Government, Republic of China. *Notes on Tainan County FarmLand Consolidation.* Taiwan (in Chinese), 1966.

Tsai, Hong-chin. *The Socio-economic Effects of Taiwan's Land Reform.* Taipei: Chia Hsin Shui Ni Publishing Co. (in Chinese), 1967.

Tsai, Hong-chin. "Development Policy and Internal Migration in Taiwan." *Journal of Population Studies,* National Taiwan University, Population Studies Center, Vol. 2, 1978, pp. 27–57.

Tsui, T. K. "Investment in Taiwan." *Chung Kuo Chi Shang Yeh Yin Hang (International Commercial Bank of China) Economic Review,* Vol. 177, 1977, pp. 11–17.

Vander Meer, Paul. "Land Fragmentation Through Land Consolidation: Chulin Village, Taiwan." *Proceedings of the Association of American Geographers,* Vol. 8, 1976.

Wu, Hweo-ran. "Economic Effects of Rice Control Policy in Post-war Taiwan." *The Developing Economies* Vol. 8, No. 1, 1970, pp. 52–78.

# 13

## The Locals Fight Back
## When Times Are Tough:
## The Ethnography of Health Care
## in Peru

*Kjell Enge and Polly Harrison*

### Introduction

Anthropologists suffer a very special disciplinary torment: the stress between pride in their special grasp of human complexity, and the drive to explain it with the simplest possible models. Two current models of bureaucracy—one which is basically a "dependency" model and another which Cohen (1980) has termed an "apologist" perspective—may have two effects that are not useful. One is that in seeking a single locus of responsibility or explanation, they may obscure the existence of several loci; this limits opportunities both for learning and for constructive adaptations. The other is that they diminish the potential power of the anthropologist's roles as analyst, pragmatist and, ultimately, theorist.

Carol Smith (1985) addresses these same limitations in the context of her analysis of the expansion of capitalism in Guatemala. She comments that anthropologists have increasingly flagellated themselves and their colleagues for ignoring larger processes affecting the small communities they study; they have increasingly seized upon global, highly economistic explanations for events and relations in peasant or urban marginal communities and have dealt with culture as a process *sui generis*, rather than attempting to deal with the relations among economy, social relations, and culture. The result is "a new kind of global functionalism" which sets aside complexity, contradiction, human creativity, and just plain cussedness. This excessive globalism tends to attribute potency and causality only to external forces, so that peasants, the masses, the poor, only respond to a world made largely by such significant, essentially outside others as regional elites, members of state bureaucracies, or international capitalists. The assumption is that local communities must either adapt, in a way that is often interpreted as some kind of social pathology, or become extinct; the off-chance that there might be some iterative connection between local and global forces is rarely explored.

Smith advances the concept that local-level processes can, in fact, help to shape regional and national structures in certain types of social formation. She asks:

> How does one examine and analyze a dialectical process that involves the articulation of different layers in a multilayered system? An obvious first step is to develop models of those structures that mediate between the local community and the world system. These structures include such things as regional class systems, state and political institutions, and specific forms of production and exchange that link the economies of small communities to the world system. (Smith, 1985)

The interesting focus then becomes the history and condition of middle-level institutions, regional and/or national, and how they relate and come to matter in the interplay of local and global forces.

Smith assumes as her primary task "to introduce Guatemalan peasants as active agents of the historical development of Guatemala." The present case is that of Peru; it treats the interplay among the national public health bureaucracy, local-level structures, and different strata of health adaptation and even power in a bureaucratic hierarchy which would seem, on its face, to be little congenial to either.

Britan and Cohen (1980) note the practical and disciplinary urgency for anthropologists as they turn from the study of local cultures to that of large-scale states, to consider new sets of institutions, using new perspectives, new concepts, and new assumptions about those variables and sectors of society that can offer the most important insights. Their choice is what they consider "one of the most central, ubiquitous, and powerful elements of complex society: bureaucracy."

> Bureaucracies are as old as the state itself, and their development has a central place in this evolution, providing a formal structure to administer complex tasks of production, distribution, and governance. Bureaucracies are a crucial link between changing local institutions and the modernizing nations of which they are a part. For complex societies they are a major means through which hierarchical relationships of power and authority are erected and maintained. (Britan and Cohen, 1980)

Anthropologists bring to the study of bureaucracy an approach that is especially theirs: a combination of its comparative and universalistic focus and its unique dependence on ethnographic methods of data collection. The present account, together with its accompanying analysis, attempts to go beyond traditional ethnographic description—of what people do, the functions they perform, the ways they think about how things are and ought to be, the setting in which all this happens—to broaden social, economic, cultural, and political contexts and the relationships among the structures in which those people live and work. Once the basic structure, or interrelated structures, are identified and defined, a "vertical slice" (Nader, 1980) can be taken and specific behaviors scrutinized ethnographically at all the interesting structural levels. A "horizontal" or cross-cultural perspective can then be applied to each level in a number of cases. Since bureaucracy is not a constant, but a variable social reality, bureaucratic forms, despite (apparent) structural similarity, may vary; their range of that variation is both practically and theoretically informative. Thus, those economic and bureaucratic factors which give to public health ministries throughout the developing world, an appearance of frustrating sameness, can still mask a surprising internal variability. The compelling finding in the Peruvian case is precisely that internal variability. The same bureaucratic structure, in this case the Ministry of Health, has engendered a substantial amount of local-level differentiation, which reflects more than just location in different ecological niches.

The findings and insights we refer to in this chapter are the results of the work done by four anthropologists, an economist and a physician. With one exception, the team members had either worked together before or knew others who had firsthand knowledge of workstyles and personalities. All the team members had extensive experience in Latin America, and three had previously worked in Peru; the physician had spend years in Bolivia and spoke fluent Quechua.

Consultant teams are most often put together by firms that hold Indefinite Quantity Contracts (IQCs) with AID. The dynamic that goes into the actual selection of personnel is highly fortuitous and can result in teams with a wide range of personalities and experience; our case was no exception. The resultant interaction over six months not just between team members, but also with the varied characters in the Ministry of Health and the international donor community, would in itself be the subject of another lengthy chapter. Our purpose here, however, is to examine local and national-level interaction within the health bureaucracy and the implications for policy options.

We think that as anthropologists, we were in a unique position to observe the dynamics of interaction between the different bureaucratic levels. Personnel at all levels were willing and at times eager to express their opinions as well as give us lengthy accounts of longstanding disputes, institutional histories and their own views about what should be done.

The descriptions of events and experiences presented here is a selective condensation of numerous events that took place between January and June of 1984. We worked in all of the major Peruvian ecological zones ranging from the shores of Lake Titicaca, the Amazon Basin to the arid desert coast of the North.

Our investigation consisted of an evaluation of primary health care delivery by voluntary health promoters in rural and peri-urban areas of Peru, which was done from January through June 1984 (Enge, 1984). Our sample covered eight of seventeen health regions located in representative geographical zones: desert coast, high Andes, and tropical lowlands. In the course of our study we interacted with health care personnel at all levels from the central ministry in Lima to remote health posts. We were able to identify positions of power, observe the process of decision-making, and document the resultant allocating of resources within the system.

The Peruvian Ministry of Health is responsible for providing services to approximately 66 percent of the 18 million population in an area twice the size of France. The structure of the ministry is the classical pyramidal form ubiquitous in the developing world; in Peru five levels can be clearly identified.

The top includes the central ministry in Lima and specialized centers and research institutes. The central level is concerned with program development, management, coordination, evaluation, and an array of support activities for the lower levels.

Next are seventeen regional offices responsible for the overall management and planning of specific geographical areas. Each regional office has a director and a large support staff. The regional office is often, but not always, located in the regional hospital.

The regions are, in turn, subdivided into one to four hospital areas which are the providers of institutionalized health care, direct administrators and supervisors of the two lowest levels, and the source of supplies and equipment for all other health care facilities within a defined area.

Large health centers staffed with MD's, dentists, nurses and auxiliaries constitute the third level. Usually located in urban and semi-rural areas, the health centers are intended to provide curative services to the surrounding population and act as the direct supervisory and supply link with the Health Posts. The center is, in theory, the lowest rung on the health-delivery pyramid where professional medical care is available. Often, however, inadequate physical plants, poor staffing, non-functional or non-existent equipment, and paucity of medicines and supplies have paralyzed many centers.

The Health Post is the smallest fixed-facility providing only out-patient and preventive services to semi-rural and rural populations in towns of 500 to 2,000 inhabitants. The post is simply equipped and staffed by an auxiliary nurse or health technician with about one year of medical training who performs basic curative procedures, attends emergencies, and provides health and family planning education.

Before looking at specific events and places, a consideration of resource distribution within the pyramid is crucial for understanding the nature of individual and group behavior. At all levels in the health system, and certainly at the lowest levels, health workers constantly complain about low salaries, a chronic lack of medicines and supplies, and that the higher level officials have no interest or concern for their plight. Area and regional level officials complain about need for larger budgets and more timely delivery of money and materials; directors and staff feel that too much is spent at the central level, and that they, the actual providers of health care, cannot function.

Financial and material deficiencies appear to have two causes: First, the administrative and management systems do not deliver resources where and when they are needed. Second, a chronic lack of financial resources limits the Ministry of Health's ability to support existing health infrastructure with resulting low productivity and cost-effectiveness.

The ministry's budget has increased drastically since 1980, but the purchasing power of the Peruvian Sol has decreased even more rapidly. The result is a net decrease in resources while the target population has increased by more than 10 percent. Furthermore, the ministry's infrastructure has grown, with many foreign donors supporting initial development costs, but insisting that the ministry bear most of the recurrent costs. This combined with the decreasing purchasing power of the budget is an underlying reason for the chronic logistics and management support problems for the health systems, especially at the area level and below.

To further complicate the picture, the ministry has since 1980 shifted financial resources away from supplies and services toward the payment of salaries. We have estimated that the average health worker has available today less than 50 percent of the material resources in 1980. In 1984, the proportion spent on salaries was in the 80 to 85 percent range; today it may be even more. Financial personnel at the regional and area levels feel this may be a conservative estimate.

Of the entire health budget, about 80 percent is spent at the central level, and then the remaining 20 percent is allocated to the regions where again 8 percent is consumed leaving 20 percent for the area level where the pattern is repeated with the net result of virtually no supplies and medicines reaching Health Centers and Posts; health workers receive their meager salaries, are the victims of skyrocketing inflation, and work in empty facilities with minuscule patient coverage.

The consequence of this expenditure pattern will be that the current chronic shortages will become worse. The productivity of the health system, both in terms of the quality and quantity of services, will almost certainly decrease from its current low level.

In view of the hierarchical structure and decreasing financial resources, the actors within the system are using their power to preserve their most important concern, their salaries. Since the system is a highly centralized pyramid, it is not surprising to see the increasing percentage for salaries with most going to the central level, the locus of maximum power.

What happens at the lower levels of the system? What have been some responses made by individuals and groups to cope with a steadily deteriorating situation? We found that the reactions and consequent behaviors varied from area to area and that the lower level workers were not necessarily destined to be passive victims of decisions made at higher levels of power. We have documented cases where local health workers have exerted pressure on the bureaucracy to achieve results where the outcome has been the maintenance of existing services or even improved health care for rural residents. Three cases will be described: a strike by voluntary health promoters, strong independent action and innovative programs by a local hospital director, and the co-optation of ministry trained health promoters by a private voluntary organization. These cases show that instead of a total paralysis and collapse of the health delivery system, local initiative can have effects felt all the way to the top of the bureaucratic pyramid.

## Puno Promoter Strike

Since the middle 1950s the Ministry of Health and other organizations have trained approximately 5,000 voluntary health promoters. These volunteers are supposed to deliver preventive, promotional, emergency and limited curative care for common illnesses, and distribute some basic drugs and family planning supplies. They refer cases to higher levels of the system as necessary and are the theoretical point of entry into the formal health care system. The promoter stands at the frontier between the public health system and the community.

In order to function well, health promoters must have adequate supervision, periodic refresher courses, and resupply of basic medicines and equipment. All promoters are volunteers who come from and reside in the communities they serve. Because of the deteriorating economic situation the ministry has not kept in contact with the promoters, and, as a result, many have abandoned their health activities; nationwide over 50 percent have quit.

In the southern department of Puno the outcome has been different. As conditions started to deteriorate the promoters instead of quitting organized a union and elected strong outspoken leaders. As conditions continued to deteriorate and, for all practical purposes, the ministry had abandoned the promoters, the union leaders decided to call a strike and issued a series of demands to the ministry. They called for a small salary to be paid by the government, increased availability of medicines and supplies, and provision of refresher courses.

The strike received a lot of attention in the press and the news quickly spread nationwide. Pressure began to mount for the ministry to respond. After all, the promoter program had been publicized as the best means to make health care available to the entire population by the year 2000, and now there was a strike; it could spread to other parts of the country.

The Minister of Health travelled to Puno and addressed the assembled promoters. He promised salaries and supplies. Apparently his promises were enough, and the promoters went back to work. The strike took place in early 1983 but by the middle of the next year no salaries were forthcoming. Increased supplies and medicines were made available and the ministry permitted the promoters to purchase medicines in local pharmacies and charge a small mark-up thus enabling them to keep revolving drug funds.

Most important of all, this local action shook the ministry to its very top and forced a response. It let the union know that local organizations have some power, and there was hope for the future. Still one of the most sensitive issues was a salary, and this demand had not been met; there was talk of a new strike, but to our best knowledge it has not occurred.

## Hospital Amazonico

The Hospital Amazonico, located just outside the city of Puccallpa in the Amazon lowlands, was a regional center for primary and outpatient health care. Beginning in 1980, the hospital has gradually been incorporated into the Ministry of Health, and by January of 1984, it was under complete ministry administrative and budgetary control. The recent history of the hospital and the nature of its services and leadership is an important example of local initiative. Prior to 1980 the hospital was a center of operations for a multitude of foreign controlled and financed health care projects. By the end of the decade antagonism had built up between the foreign donors and Peruvian personnel. The Peruvians resented foreign control and began to exert their own ideas and initiatives. The eventual outcome was that most of the foreigners withdrew, leaving the hospital essentially Peruvianized.

After the "crisis" the hospital director continued the training of voluntary promoters and the administration of sixteen health posts located along the Ucayali River and its tributaries. By the middle of 1984 the hospital had sixty-three promoters who were regularly supervised, supplied, and given refresher courses; something nonexistent in most other ministry hospital areas.

The Hospital Amazonico promoters were trained primarily to do prevention and community development work. Desertion was not a problem, and when one promoter decided to stop working, it, in fact, gave an opportunity to someone else. Another unusual feature of the Amazonico program was that the better performing promoters had an opportunity to receive further training and move up in the health delivery system. This was probably one of the major reasons for low desertion rates.

The training program also emphasized the use of herbs in addition to and sometimes instead of modern medicines for the treatment of parasites and diarrhea. Promoters were also trained to teach mothers to make homemade oral rehydration salts.

In another function, the hospital has formed dairy cooperatives and has given assistance for the successful marketing of dairy products. In 1984, a total of nineteen cooperatives had been established. One of the most successful coops had seventy-two head of cattle, producing 30 to 40 liters of milk per day. Part of the production was given to mothers and young children and the rest sold locally. The coops also marketed meat. The commercial activities made the coops self-sufficient, with funds for capital investment to expand production.

After the hospital came under ministry administration the budget began to shrink, with less liberty to shift line items according to need. The additional paperwork became a burden for an understaffed accounting department.

Financial constraints were not the only nor the major problems facing the hospital. In 1983 a major crisis began to develop which threatened the very existence of the rural outreach programs. A group of physicians and the director of the Puccallpa hospital area wanted to take over the Hospital Amazonico and make it into a treatment facility for long-term chronically ill patients. The modern operating rooms would be used for trauma patients and other emergency procedures.

Local politicians were enlisted by the Pucallpa physicians to help in the takeover of the Amazonico and make it into a profit-making, in-patient facility. The Amazonico director enlisted the help of national-level APRA *diputadas* who were able to outmaneuver the physicians, and public health was the victor. The Amazonico was in no way going to be associated with the hospital area but with the health region with its administrative center in Huanuco. The hospital would continue as the regional primary health care training and supervisory center and work to expand services and coverage.

Shrinking budget allocations, however, would continue to be a problem. But the director, rather than curtail activities, had been soliciting funds from other sources such as the Interamerican Development Bank, USAID, and the World Bank. As of the middle of 1984 he had met with some success and continued to be optimistic about future operations.

The dynamic leadership of the hospital had a strong motivational effect on the rest of the personnel. Educators and public health nurses were working to improve the promoter training and refresher curricula as part of ongoing and future training programs. Training manuals and equipment were constantly being revised and adapted for the next training courses.

Again local initiative, this time a ministry hospital, was able to organize and operate a functioning promoter and health post system which in other areas was disintegrating because of budget restrictions. A strong and cunning hospital director was able to ward off a takeover attempt and gain support from higher ministry levels by means of political intermediaries. Had he not gone to such lengths, the successful promoter program would have disappeared and the health posts would have deteriorated in both coverage and medical efficacy.

## Centro de Investigacion
## y Promocion del Campesimato (CIPCA)

Health Region I consisted of the northern departments of Piura and Tumbes with regional offices located in a large hospital on the edge of the city of Piura. Piura's health promoter program, like all other health programs, had been affected not only by budget restrictions but by heavy rains and flooding which destroyed countless dwellings, Health Posts and roads in the area in 1983.

Since 1980, promoter training programs financed by AID has trained 160 promoters. More programs had been planned for 1983, but due to the 1983 state of emergency, only a small percentage of the planned courses were actually held. No one at the regional office knew exactly how many promoters were actually functioning. The regional executive staff were not committed to public health and were frequently absent for long periods of time in Lima.

The original promoter courses in 1980 were forty-five days which were shortened to thirty. Up until the latest course in September and October 1983, a local private voluntary organization called CIPCA (Centro de Investigacion y Promocion del Campesimato), run by Jesuit priests, had collaborated in the design and implementation of promoter training programs with the Ministry of Health.

CIPCA has been involved with promoter development in a large dispersed rural community called San Juan Catacaos, just south of the city of Piura. When the program began in Catacaos in 1980, only ten active promoters were identified in the area, although many more had been trained previously by other organizations. By 1984, there were forty-two promoters in Catacaos. Thirty of these have been part of CIPCA's tightly-run program of continuing education and supervision.

CIPCA has been arranging "retraining days" for the promoters since 1981. To train promoters in the Catacaos area, CIPCA gave two or three retraining sessions of five days each in 1981 to the ten old promoters. These courses were followed by forty-five day course for ten new promoters each in 1981 and 1982. CIPCA maintained monthly meetings for the promoters at its headquarters in Catacaos which was separate from the ministry's health center in the same community.

The CIPCA dispensary was about 1 km. from the government facility where there appeared to be little interest in the promoters; although the Health Center had a Land Rover, it was apparently not used for supervision. At the CIPCA dispensary, however, the promoters had a continuing education meeting on the last Monday of every month and were given a stipend to cover expenses when they came in for these meetings.

The dispensary also had a large number of medicines for distribution to promoters, and CIPCA provided manuals for their thirty promoters. The promoters were obliged to keep track of all births and deaths in their communities. Most recently they had also been used in programs to control malaria, which in 1983 had a major resurgence in the Piura area.

The contract between CIPCA and the Ministry of Health which gave CIPCA the authority to work with promoters was due to expire at the end of 1984. When we worked in the area in early 1984, most health professionals we interviewed believed that the health promoters would not keep working for long after CIPCA stopped giving support and supervision. We do not know what has eventually happened but have no reason to be optimistic.

The CIPCA case demonstrates that a non-governmental private voluntary organization can be superimposed on parts of a paralyzed ministry health delivery system. Although CIPCA's efforts were limited to one community, knowledge of their activities had spread well beyond San Juan Catacaos. One of the keys to CIPCA's success was the strong leadership of four Jesuit priests, two Spaniards, one French and the other North American. Those individuals worked well beyond normal hours, personally knew local leaders and residents, and went to great lengths to motivate the promoters. Ministry personnel, on the other hand, were rarely seen outside the walls of their fixed facilities.

## Conclusions

The case studies show that innovation can occur at the lowest level of the health bureaucracy, as in the case of the Puiro promoter union, and produce a response and some changes from the highest level. We would not be surprised to find similar cases in Peru or other Third World countries.

The Hospital Amazonico is a case where middle-level institutions and personnel were in competition in the class struggle between hospital-based treatment orientations and public health. Again it was dynamic leadership and individual action which prompted responses from both the health bureaucracy and politicians.

In Piura we had a case where an outside organization in effect replaced government control and took over the administration of health promoters. We do not know of any similar cases in Peru or elsewhere but do not have any reason to believe that CIPCA is unique.

All three cases show that the local effects of a bureaucracy and its policies are by no means uniform in a country like Peru. We feel that to speak in general terms about bureaucracies without detailed examinations of local articulation is a form of simplistic reductionism. Our case studies also indicate that there is a dynamic interaction between the center, the middle and the very bottom, and the outcome of particular events is a function of recent history, structural relations and individual initiative and action.

Anthropologists who work in Third World health care are in an advantageous position to describe and analyze what, in fact, is taking place. Our contacts range from the top to the bottom, and our ethnographic methods reveal, in great detail, how local responses occur. In this study we employed a series of methodologies giving us access to personnel at all levels. Our Ministry of Health informal interviews covered high level policy makers, department heads, directors of Health Regions, hospital directors, local physicians, graduate nurses, auxiliaries, voluntary health promoters, and community residents. Although our stated purpose was to evaluate primary health care provided by health promoters, many interviews (there were almost 100) covered a range of subjects. Possibly this was a case where being the outsider with a legitimate purpose, doing a ministry contract evaluation, motivated people to speak their mind on whatever they felt important in the health delivery labyrinth; candid information came from the most unlikely sources, and we were, in fact, studying up and down at the same time. To observe a promoter lance an infected gum one day then talk to the general director of health services the next was not an unusual sequence of events.

Local residents were especially open and eager to talk to us and frequently asked that we visit their communities to see, firsthand, what the health conditions are "really" like. No doubt this was, to some extent, motivated by their perception that we personally could do something to improve the supply of medicine and related needs. We had to be very careful and make it perfectly clear we were doing a study that would lead us to make recommendations, but that we did not have any power, whatsoever, to act on those recommendations. Although the people we talked to said they understood our limitations, we think that in many places we were the only contacts they have had for a long time with Lima and the ministry. The result was an outpouring of information, opinions and emotion about current conditions and what should be done. One man involved in local politics near Puno said that unless the government started providing some tangible programs with benefits for rural residents, the whole region would rebel and begin to actively support anti-government groups such as the Shining Path guerrillas.

We feel that studies such as this one can also be used to plan new health interventions that involve the restructuring of bureaucratic relationships. Presently there is a movement to decentralize, meaning that projects would bypass central levels and provide funding and technical assistance to middle and lower levels. Decentralization is currently very popular with developers and policy-makers in international agencies. This is most probably the result of a not altogether too soon recognition that large centralized bureaucracies tend to absorb undue percentages of limited financial resources with little ever reaching the periphery. As more projects attempt to bypass the center, obstacles will no doubt be encountered and the competitive interaction will most probably intensify.

The key to understanding the interactive process is the identification and documentation of actions made by specific key personnel much like those in the cases presented above. Anthropologists are uniquely qualified to do this. In Peru there are many who must be observing the detailed effects of such new policies as they are being implemented by Alan Garcia's young administration. We look forward to seeing their analyses of bureaucratic change as the various actors move to enhance their positions and protect their spheres of influence. Only through detailed case studies involving key actors at various points in the bureaucratic hierarchy will we be able to understand the complexities of interactions between the center and the periphery. It is quite apparent, however, that a paradigm using vertical dominance cannot account for the wide variety of behavior we encountered in the Peruvian health delivery system.

### References

Banfield, Edward C. "Corruption as a Feature of Governmental Organization." Journal of Law and Economics, Vol. 18, 1975, pp. 587-605.

Britan, Gerald M. and Ronald Cohen, eds. Hierarchy and Society: Anthropological
    Perspectives on Bureaucracy. Philadelphia: Institute for the Study of Human
    Issues, 1980.
Cohen, Ronald. "The Blessed Job in Nigeria," in G. M. Britan and R. Cohen, eds.
    Hierarchy and Society: Anthropological Perspectives on Bureaucracy, Philadelphia:
    Institute for the Study of Human Issues, 1980.
Enge, K., P. Harrison, P. Cross, J. Davidson, and R. LeBow. "Evaluation of Health
    Promoter Programs, Ministry of Health, Lima: USAID, June 1984.
Nader, Laura. "The Vertical Slice: Hierarchies and Children," in Hierarchy and
    Society: Anthropological Perspectives on Bureaucracy. G. M. Britan and R. Cohen,
    eds. Philadelphia: Institute for the Study of Human Issues, 1980.
Smith, Carol A. "Local History in Global Context: Social and Economic Transitions
    in Western Guatemala," in B. R. DeWalt and P.J. Pelto, eds., Micro and Macro
    Levels of Analysis in Anthropology: Issues in Theory and Research, Boulder: Westview
    Press, 1985.

# 14

## Social Analysis in AID:
## Lessons from Africa

### Edward H. Greeley

### Overview

This chapter describes some of the experiences of an anthropologist working as a social analyst in USAID. The purpose is to illustrate some of the ways in which a behavioral science perspective can contribute to development work within a government bureaucracy. The paper takes as a starting point the need for anthropologists to understand and work constructively with the institutionally-shaped interests of development agency staff in order to ensure that the anthropological perspective effectively influences outcomes (Hoben, 1984: 14). It also emphasizes the need for anthropologists to be practical in solving development problems, and in so doing to seek new methodologies which can be incorporated in the tool kits of development practitioners (Cernea, 1985: 13).

The experiences described occurred during the five years I worked as the regional social analyst for AID in East and Southern Africa in the late 1970s and early 1980s, a time of significant change in the way AID did its development business. I was recruited during a period when key AID policymakers were implementing a "new direction" in development strategy which placed greater emphasis on understanding and working with the rural poor, and therefore called for the kind of skills and perspective commonly associated with anthropology. Social analysis was seen as having strong potential for improving the design and delivery of foreign assistance under the "basic human needs," "poverty alleviation," "bottom-up" approach which had been legally mandated by the U.S. Congress in 1973.

An important part of my job, the first of its kind in East and Southern Africa, was to deal with these high expectations as I gradually fleshed out an appropriate role for the regional social analyst. At the time social analysis was poorly understood in AID. Many of the AID staff who were aware of it tended to think of it as a kind of "shoehorn," helping to fit people to predefined projects performed by a relative outsider. Over time and with experience, this perception changed to one in which social analysis was more broadly accepted as a useful part of project work in the various stages of design.

## The Job: Social Analyst in a Regional AID Office

The academic-anthropologist consultant tends to focus on the people in the area concerned and tries to determine how proposed project interventions are likely to affect them. The USAID employee tends to focus on the project and asks the anthropologists how to make it succeed (Hoben, 1984: 13).

I was first hired by AID's Regional Office in Nairobi as part of a project design team to prepare the social soundness analysis for a seed multiplication project in Rwanda. At the time I was living in Nairobi and completing my Ph.D. in anthropology based on fieldwork carried out in Kenya. My previous work experience in Africa had included serving as Peace Corps Volunteer in Eastern Region, Nigeria in the mid-1960s and teaching in Kampala, Uganda.

Following the brief two-week consultancy to Rwanda, and another in Kenya, I was recruited full-time by AID in early 1977 to work as the regional social analyst in REDSO/ESA (the Regional Economic Development Services Office for East and Southern Africa). The position of social analyst was established by AID to help implement Congressional legislation which had called for a change in AID development policy—to work more closely with and direct more assistance toward the rural poor majority. My primary responsibility in the field was improving the fit of a proposed project within its social and institutional context. An additional—and crucial—aspect of the job, however, was to develop a methodology for conducting social soundness analysis of AID projects for use throughout the region.

At that time the main function of the regional office (there was a second one covering West and Central Africa in Abidijan, Ivory Coast) was to support the development work of the various country offices of the region by providing technical assistance on an as-needed basis. The specialized services REDSO offered included assistance in legal and procurement matters, project design and evaluation, as well as economic, technical and financial analysis for project and country program development. Our office supplied assistance to AID posts in eighteen countries from Sudan, Djibouti and Ethiopia in the North to Botswana, Lesotho and Swaziland in the South. The staff numbered some thirty professionals, most of whom spent about 30 to 50 percent of their time traveling outside Nairobi and Kenya on AID assignment. Trips usually lasted two to three weeks.

As the social analyst in the office I became involved in all phases of the development process from the preparation of country-wide analyses of development constraints, with recommendations to address those constraints, to the identification and preparation of specific development project designs, project implementation and monitoring, and project evaluation. My primary duties were to help ensure that AID-funded resources maximized the beneficial development impact on rural poor families, identify and help avoid harmful project-induced impact, and maximize local participation in the development process. Secondary duties included recruiting, managing and evaluating social scientists under contract to AID and assisting other REDSO staff by providing advice on the social aspect of any work they were performing. The workload revolved around requests for assistance by AID posts in the region, resulting in travel to the country, involvement with a multidisciplinary team, rapid research and analysis of the problem at hand, and write-up of certain sections of a project paper or other report.

In the five years I worked in REDSO, I traveled about 35 percent of the time and made at least one trip to fifteen different countries. The following illustrates typical assignments and includes brief comments summarizing the nature of my contribution to the process.

## Project Design

*Malawi.* In Malawi, I served as one of a two-member team preparing the project identification documentation (PID) for the Malawi Self Help Water Project and subsequently returned as the social analyst to complete the final design of the project in the form of a project paper (PP). As was usually the case when working on a PID design team, I offered to write the early sections of the document—the overview, the problem statement, and the outline of the proposed solution provided by the project. Typically the design officer in charge welcomed the assistance, and it provided me the means to define the problem and proposed solution from an anthropological perspective from the outset.

The water program in Malawi was working well but the Malawi Government wanted to expand it. The program design was a too-rare example of a "bottom up" community-based approach to building and maintaining sustainable, simple, appropriate rural infrastructure. Construction of gravity feed water systems, for example, required teams of several thousand villagers to dig trenches and lay pipe from mountain water sources 40 km. away to individual villages. Maintenance of systems included careful specification of roles and procedures, including, for example, designating the leader responsible for buying and keeping the spare washer for the community water faucet (to be "stored" on a nail on the door of the leader's house).

We designed the project taking into account the success of the on-going program. Our assistance aimed to help the Malawi Government scale up and expand its capacity to help communities complete more water schemes with our funds without overwhelming the on-going program. We did add two relatively new components: namely, research to explore in this "best case" context the relationship between access to water and improved health, and closer linkages between the water supply program and the Malawi Ministry of Health (including involvement of Peace Corps Volunteers). My main role, in retrospect, was emphasizing the potential of the existing program, increasing U.S. funding for it, and ensuring that we meddled as little as possible with its very effective "bottom up" community-based organization and operation.

*Burundi.* Again, in Burundi, I served on both the PID and PP teams for a rural road project based on labor intensive construction. Having previously served as social analyst on the same kind of rural road construction program in Kenya, I saw my role as helping to replicate some of the successful aspects of the program, while ensuring that the design reflected the particularities of the situation in rural East Burundi. Early in the design, I focused on the institutional aspects of the project, emphasizing the potentially helpful role of the strong local diocese of the Catholic Church in organizing and supporting local labor (paid for through cash wages and "food for work"). Such involvement was especially important for achieving the equity objectives of the project as serious ethnic conflict threatened possible inequitable labor recruitment practices. (Religious differences were fortunately not a factor in this situation.)

*Uganda.* For Uganda, I participated in project identification in the period just following Amin's overthrow by Tanzanian forces (summer 1979). The United States, like other donors, wanted to help Uganda in a timely and significant way, without funding a project which could not be implemented given the disruption in the country. I worked with other REDSO staff on the problem from afar, carrying out our planning in the REDSO office in Nairobi. In this case I drew from my previous residence in and experience with Uganda, and reports prepared by the few appraisal teams which had recently visited Uganda. I argued strongly that we should concentrate our assistance on helping to rehabilitate the small-farmer sector. After a decade of economic decline, Ugandan farmers needed hoes and other simple farm implements. In addition, I argued with others that our assistance should include helping to build Uganda capacity to manufacture such implements, through support to local industry.

Following lengthy deliberations, the hoe project was selected from among several alternatives, including assistance to the national airport, rehabilitation of Makerere University and importation of prefabricated hoe blades from outside East Africa. A REDSO team designed a program to import steel for hoe manufacture in Jinja (a factory town along the headwaters of the Nile). To ensure widespread distribution of hoes and hopefully rejuvenate these local organizations (as well as spur production), the approach included links to local institutions such as agricultural cooperatives and church groups.

Among numerous other project design efforts were the following:

- analysis of the rural poor of Zambia from the perspective of how AID can best support effective development activities in the agricultural sector;
- assistance, together with two other team members (an engineer and a design officer) in the preparation of a project identification document for a labor intensive roads and trails construction project in Lesotho;

• analysis of the social factors involved in design of a rural training project for school leavers in Rwanda, with emphasis on testing the validity of key assumptions of the project, including demand for the training, adequacy of the rural schools as institutions, and placement of school graduates.

The major task expected of me in all the design exercises was preparation of a report addressing the social soundness of the proposed activities. This report was included as part of the formal documentation of the project. For each of my assignments, however, I considered my most significant contribution to come prior to the writing of the report—when I was working closely with other members of the multidisciplinary team and participating in decisions about problem definition, the conceptualization of the project, and the allocation of resources to achieve project goals. And in each case (as with the Malawi water project mentioned above), I concentrated on the early process of problem definition (defining the problem in "people terms") and project conceptualization (how to solve this "problem").

## Where the Shoe Didn't Fit

Although less common, I was also involved in several design activities in which my principal contribution was to try to stop the project, rather than improve it. This task was especially challenging, as social analysis was relatively new to many AID officers, and it required careful application to establish its legitimacy and effectiveness.

In rural Djibouti, for example, a horticultural production project was identified for funding which promised to have enormous implementation problems. An agricultural economist and I visited the proposed project site, and came to the conclusion that we should not design the project. We knew this view would be met with disappointment in the Djibouti AID office, as no other promising project ideas had been proposed. In addition, a project once identified and "in the works" in AID is often likened to a railroad engine on the track; it is extremely difficult to stop.

In this case, we resorted to an historical analysis of previous efforts to make our point. Our review of past efforts showed a path of by and large unmitigated failures from those of missionaries in the late nineteenth century to the present. The list of past failures and other evidence proved cogent enough to support the recommendations not to go forward with the project, despite vigorous objections from a U.S. diplomatic officer in Djibouti.

A second project design to which I gave a negative vote of confidence was a proposed project under review in the late 1970s to train national civil service employees in Ethiopia. My position was that the project inappropriately directed resources to build up government capacity at a time when the government was acting irresponsibly, and that we should focus our resources more directly on the severe needs of the rural population. Ultimately, this project (and others in Ethiopia) failed to be approved for funding due to U.S. domestic legal complications. In the early phases of this design, however, my findings and position against the project were held against contrary views of other members of the design team and some staff in the AID mission. Two documents were very useful in carrying out my analysis: a profile on Ethiopia's agrarian reform recently prepared by an anthropologist for AID which reviewed the implications of the Ethiopian revolution for AID programming, and the AID guidelines for social analysis. Without doubt, the existence of prior documentation helped. While disagreeing with my analysis, those involved could at least see the consistency of my position with previous interpretations of the situation in Ethiopia.

## Program Analysis and Planning, and Evaluations

A major task for REDSO/ESA professional staff was analysis for and preparation of the overall country program which provides the framework for project identification and design. In Rwanda, I worked with a general economist and an agricultural economist to design a development assistance program which was characterized as one of the first in the region that took a "doom and gloom" view of population pressures pushing against fragile and scarce agricultural resources. This approach set the stage for a program emphasis on population growth which I thought was strongly needed.

On several other occasions, I traveled with one of the early AID teams to do the initial analytical work for what became a significant build-up in AID funded programs. An important first task on such relatively short trips included helping to focus the program on fundamental and socially sound topics. Another was to build up the capacity of the AID mission to do social analysis. This included linking AID staff with local social scientists competent in development work, and stocking the AID office library with relevant social analysis materials (in part to establish that much previous relevant work had been done and that new studies should be based on existing literature). Being on the early appraisal missions to a country provided a good opportunity to influence the course of overall country planning, such as with Rwanda and Uganda as mentioned above. In some instances, of course, I was less successful than others. In Burundi, for example, in the light of Burundi's volatile ethnic rivalry, I argued for a program focus on rural women and children and a relatively small-scale effort overall. This proposal was not heeded by mission leadership, who were planning a more ambitious program.

Program evaluations was another area where social analysts contributed to REDSO/ESA work. Two evaluations I worked on offered strong contrasts regarding the role of social analysis. In one, an evaluation of a regional planning project in Arusha, Tanzania, (where I was a team leader) I strongly supported the quality of the technical assistance component of the project. The expatriate team of eight, assisted by their knowledge of Kiswahili and previous East African experience, quickly established productive relationships with their host country counterparts. Not surprisingly, this team experience significantly improved the speed and effectiveness of implementation of the project, but was unfortunately undervalued by AID supervisory staff concerned with some other less favorable aspects of project implementation.

Their skill at project start-up stood in contrast to the relatively slow start-up of a team of scientists drawn from a U.S. university to implement an agricultural research project in rural Lesotho. There I worked with the evaluation and research project implementation teams and found myself in the unusual position of concluding that despite recruitment of a competent social analyst as a member of the research team, team dynamics and the lack of country and local language expertise by the social analyst had contributed to very slow implementation of the project.

A second contrast between the two projects was the degree of flexibility built into the design of the Tanzania project compared to the Lesotho project. This flexibility had led to an on-going dispute between the designers and implementors of the Tanzania project and AID staff for supervising implementation because the project was seen as too flexible and not conforming to a number of AID regulations and procedures. Fortunately, the eventual outside evaluation of the Tanzania project focused positively on the project's accomplishments (particularly as advisors had helped to build local institutional capacity) rather than on the perceived violations of AID procedures which had earlier captured the attention of AID staff.

## Lessons Learned

A number of lessons I learned in the early period of my work in REDSO can be applied to any large-scale multidisciplinary activity.

1. *Be familiar with agency guidelines, documentation, and terminology.* The more effectively the social analyst can communicate ideas and views in simple terms and in the framework of agency issues and concerns, the more likely the ideas will be incorporated in the project design.

2. *Start early in the project design process.* Early involvement improves the chances of socially sound project design by enabling the analyst to help identify problem areas and structure solutions to them. It also allows for early identification and possible rejection of proposed activities which threaten to have a significantly harmful impact on a segment of the beneficiary population. At this stage, it is possible to stop a project before it builds up so much momentum it can't be knocked off the track. One of the most important functions of the social analyst is to ensure that the project as conceived is socially sound, and if he or she is certain that it is not, to communicate the reasons for such a determination to the head of the design team as soon as possible. Late involvement may result in an over-emphasis on justification of the project (in social terms) during the time when the project design team becomes preoccupied with the "packaging" of the final document to be sent to AID offices in Washington for review and approval.

3. *Be constructive.* Very often in project analysis and design there are general ideas about what problems and solutions merit attention; but specific,

locally appropriate and practical ways to structure project interventions are lacking. In such a situation the team member who proposes a constructive approach will often see that approach adopted. The suggestion to organize a community group discussion to ascertain local perceptions of community needs, for example, or the initiation of a specific line of questioning of local officials during a brief reconnaissance of an area are examples of how early initiatives can help structure local participation in project design. Being able to offer positive, workable alternatives to counter less desirable proposals is one of the best means for avoiding impasses and project elements which are socially unsound. A constructive image can be useful when the social analyst must try to stop a socially "harmful" activity or project. Typically, the analyst having a reputation for being constructive will be more able to mobilize support in a veto situation than an analyst having a reputation of being consistently negative.

4. *Face data constraints early and pragmatically.* It is the rare project in East and Southern Africa in which a social analyst can be fully confident of the existing data base. However, collecting current project-related data is expensive and time-consuming. One must take a flexible and pragmatic approach in assessing the need for data collection. This requires judging the existing data against the accuracy level required. Such judgments should take into account project time and other resource constraints, local conditions, and assignment objectives. In these contexts, the social analyst must evaluate the cost benefits of our traditional small-scale, holistic, participant-observation methods of data collection. There are clear trade-offs.

On the one hand, in-depth community studies are extremely effective as means to understanding the dynamics of innovation and the processes of social change. On the other hand, such methods entail costs. They require time to accomplish. If existing studies are dated, they may foster misleading impressions of stasis in a rapidly changing society. More importantly, information may be out of date. Finally, such studies generally contain information that is too specialized or incomplete to be of development use.

Another data collection issue is determining the most judicious "mix" of information-gathering methods. The elaborate, single-round rural household survey is often not the most effective in terms of cost, time and relevance to project needs. This is particularly true when surveys are designed under time pressures and without an adequate review of secondary sources and sufficient field testing.

An approach that is under-utilized is the review of published and unpublished resources on the area under investigation. A "desk" review can be done well in advance of project design work and it places no burden on the host government or local area. Particularly when mixed with intensive local discussions and key informant interviews, the library approach can be very useful and time saving.

Another alternative data collection strategy is a small-scale pilot study. Planning an initial pilot phase to gain experience and local involvement in a set of proposed project activities is an excellent means by which to deal with information gaps. It also maximizes the participation of local people in project design because it is small-scale and flexible, and therefore accessible to interested parties in the community. Such "pilots," of course, do postpone the time when an agency can allocate a large bulk of money to address a particular problem. One means of shortening the time required between trials and full-blown resource commitment is to examine and replicate separately successful small-scale projects.

The identification and study of a successful development project in the target area offers an excellent means to make informed judgments about future interventions. In East and Southern Africa, for example, information useful to the design and implementation of "bottom-up" poverty-oriented projects by AID can be gathered in interviews with missionaries and other persons involved in small projects sponsored by private and voluntary organizations.

5. *Be a team member.* In the course of project development there inevitably comes a time when there is a breakdown in communication—misunderstanding as to allocation of responsibility, strong differences of opinion and judgment, time pressures, and thwarted expectations. In any organization, things go better when individuals make an effort to be flexible, positive, realistic in expectations, sensitive to others' special interests, and measured in the assertion of their own points of view.

The anthropologist's orientation as educator is useful in project development work. Very often, the face-to-face sensitization of other members of a multidisciplinary team to be more attuned to some of the social issues involved in a development activity is far more likely to result in a "socially sound" project than the filing of an independently written social soundness report. Simply filing the report, however accurate, may increase the risk of its being relegated to the annex section of the project document and, hence, overlooked.

6. *Maintain a balanced perspective.* In the AID Africa Bureau in Washington there has been neither the time nor the anthropological talent to provide regular peer support and "backstopping" for the work social analysts do in the field—let alone provide additional perspectives on a problem prior to the time of decision-making. This lack of "critical mass" for professional support to systematically back up or challenge the judgments of social analysts working on design teams means that the analyst carries the special responsibility of rendering balanced judgments which consider the widest range of perspectives and possibilities available.

Using the AID Social Analysis Guidelines helps to ensure that the analyst considers the factors critical to social soundness and project success. Over time, I developed my own set of categories for carrying out the project analysis based on existing guidance and field experience. This guidance was subsequently adapted for AID use and incorporated in the revised official guidelines in Handbook 3. They are included in Annex I of this chapter.

## Conclusion: Retrospect and Prospect

A very important aspect of AID and other large bureaucracies dealing with change is that they are in constant flux. Overall objectives undergo periodic revision and change, specific strategies fall in and out of favor, and staff requirements respond to the changes in a typically cyclical way. (The following discussion is summarized from R. Copson, et al., 1986.) In the early period of AID's assistance to Africa, from 1951 to 1972, U.S. assistance could be characterized as a "bottleneck" strategy.Under this approach, scarce U.S. development assistance targeted on efforts to remove specific impediments to economic growth. Technical and capital aid were directed at physical and human infrastructure development, including agriculture and education, but also included larger-scale capital investments in transportation, such as for roads and dams.

Under the "basic needs," "bottoms-up" strategy mandated by Congress in 1973, the emphasis switched to a small farmer strategy, with a concomitant need for social analysis, and anthropologists to assist in directing resources to the rural poor. Now, in the 1980s, the "New Directions" emphasis of the 1970s is giving way to a more "top-down" assistance aimed at building up a recipient country's economic infrastructure, fostering macroeconomic policies, and otherwise promoting the rapid accumulation of capital that can be plowed back into the economy. Needless to say, under this "accelerated development" approach, direct assistance to the rural poor gives way to more indirect approaches, such as supporting policy reforms which ease the governmental burden on peasant farmers and other producers and release their productive energies. The role of the social analyst therefore receives less attention, and the scope for the contributions of anthropologists to AID business changes. From a theoretical perspective, the role of social analyst is still key, but the domain of inquiry and responsibilities are broader, and more diffuse. For example, the need to understand the linkages between the small farmer family and the economic and institutional framework in which it operates is crucial to the success of a more indirect "top-down" strategy.

When compared to the type of specific, project-related development tasks described above, however, it is likely that few anthropologists will have the opportunity for the same kind of institutionalized systematic role that many were recruited to play in the "New Directions" period in AID.

## References

Cernea, Michael M. "Sociological Knowledge in the Development Approach," in Michael Cernea, ed., *Putting People First: Sociological Variables in Rural Development*. Published for the World Bank, Washington, D.C. New York: Oxford University Press, p. 14, 1985.

Hoben, Allan. "The Role of the Anthropologist in Development Work: An Overview," in W. Partridge, ed., *Training Manual in Development Anthropology*. Washington, D.C.: American Anthropological Association, 1984, pp. 9–17.

R. Copson, T. Galdi, and L. Nowels. "U.S. AID to Africa: The Record, the Rationales, and the Challenge." Prepared for the Committee on Foreign Affairs, Subcommittee on Africa, January 1986, pages vii to xiii.

## Annex I

### Guidance for the Project Identification Document

*Factors Affecting Project Selection and Further Development*

   *a. Social Considerations.* Consideration of social factors, including the definition and examination of project participants and intended beneficiaries, is expected to begin in the earliest stages of project identification. It should continue throughout project development so that relevant knowledge about beneficiary populations can be applied on an integrated basis to the merging project design, and so that future implementation and feasibility problems can be minimized. PID issues may or may not require specialized analytic skills, depending on the scope of the project and the extent to which project elements have been developed at the time the PID is submitted. (See Appendix 2C for further detail.) Considerable discretion may be used in determining the level of effort appropriate to a particular PID, but the following areas of concern should be briefly addressed:

   1. *Socio-Cultural Context:* Briefly describe the socio-cultural context of the project area, giving particular attention to social, economic and political factors that demonstrate a need for the project, or which will affect project activities.

   2. *Beneficiaries:* Briefly identify the location, size and relevant socio-economic characteristics of the group(s) the project will benefit (both directly and indirectly) as well as group(s) that may be adversely affected. Special efforts should be taken to specify how women will be affected. For indirect beneficiaries, explain how benefits are expected to reach them, and identify recipient country or Borrower/Grantee policies and practices that will facilitate or impede this process.

   3. *Participation:* Variations in access to productive resources, employment, basic services and information influence the capacity and willingness of men and women to take part in projects. The PID should indicate briefly how the proposed project will promote participation of beneficiaries during project design, implementation and evaluation. Also indicate what social, economic and political factors are expected to facilitate or constrain participation with regard to project activities and objectives, including those that are gender related.

   4. *Socio-Cultural Feasibility:* Given what is known about planned project activities and the socio-economic characteristics of planned participants, briefly identify feasibility issues to be addressed during project development.

   5. *Impact:* AID's primary objective is to help people in development countries meet their basic human needs through equitable, sustainable

growth. PID's should show how projects will contribute to this objective, giving particular attention to the differential impact the proposed project on various local groups or socio-economic strata. Special attention should be given to the differential impact of the project on men and women. Indicate whether activities initiated by a project can be sustained by recipient country or Borrower/Grantee organizations and participants after external assistance is completed, and whether project activities can be spread and/ or replicated.

Source: A.I.D. Handbook 3, 1982, pp. 2-2+3.

# 15

## Project Development in Kenya

### Edward H. Greeley

*Sociologists have to face the nuts and bolts of development activities, to roll up their sleeves and deal with the mundane, pragmatic questions of translating plans into realities in a sociologically sound manner. They need to link data generation, action-oriented research, social analysis, design for social action, and evaluation into a continuum, and thus stretch sociology's contributions far beyond simple pronouncements (Cernea, 1985: 10).*

### Overview

The purpose of the paper is to describe the contribution an anthropologist with extensive in-country experience and a willingness to roll up his sleeves can make to the work of a field mission of USAID. Specifically, the paper describes the role of a project development officer in Kenya in a time of transition in the overall policies of how AID approached social and economic development in Sub-saharan Africa. A major theme of the paper is the continuing importance of the kinds of contributions detailed country knowledge and an anthropological perspective can bring to the ongoing work of an AID field office, particularly, contributions which are replicable and useful in the manner called for in Cernea's statement, above.

A major question it raises, however, is whether AID's evolving policies and approaches adequately take into account a people perspective, and whether they can effectively, and fairly, address the development problems of Kenya and Sub-saharan Africa in the 1980s. At this point, it is too early to tell. What is clear, however, is that the willingness to try new approaches, especially attention to economic-policy reforms and agricultural development, is shared by most African governments and major donors.[1] What remains to be seen is whether the swing to a more direct promotion of economic growth will result in improving or diminishing the living conditions of Africa's rural and urban poor population.

The experience I describe covers three years, from 1981 to 1984. This was a time of evolution in assistance policies and strategies of most major organizations including AID and the World Bank. Particularly in Sub-saharan

Africa, there was growing concern amongst donors even before the drought and ensuing famine of 1984–1985 that the economic and policy framework for most African countries was not conducive to economic growth, and that African countries (in many cases with donor encouragement and support) were following the wrong strategies to promote development.[2] Government policies were hindering small-holder production by supporting food prices that were too low, and restrictions on marketing and other economic activities were further reducing farmer incentives. Donors and host government agencies were far too involved in the intricacies of designing and managing donor-supported development projects, many of which should have been left to the efforts of nongovernmental organizations and private enterprise. Too often, host government-supported projects proved not to be sustainable when donor funding was over, particularly given the generally unfavorable economic and social policy framework in which projects were expected to operate.

As will be described below, the transition involved a searching for better ways of supporting the development process. The revised policy included a de-emphasis on the need to identify and provide assistance directly to the rural poor and increased emphasis on the potential of the (free) marketplace to spur social and economic development. The emerging strategy was less "bottom-up" and people-oriented in nature, and more heavily concentrated on accelerating economic growth. The focus was on reducing the government's role in the direct support of development activities, and improving the environment for private sector activity in support of activities that would have a less direct impact ("trickle-down") on the rural poor than the previous so-called "bottom-up" approach. The operational image of the new "pro-growth" strategy was an "unleashing" of the productive energies and resources of private institutions and small farmers, rather than delivering assistance to directly meet the basic needs of the rural population.

AID's new policy and strategies evolved within the existing, legal framework of the basic human needs, poverty-focused legislation Congress had mandated in the early 1970s. It reflected an improved understanding, particularly in Sub-saharan Africa, of the magnitude of the problems facing the central governments of most developing countries, including economic policies which unfairly and inefficiently favored urban over rural interests, and supported donor practices leading to project proliferation and a lack of sustainability of development projects. On the U.S. domestic side, it also strongly reflected the philosophical views of the new Republican administration.

There were four cornerstones to the revised AID strategy: policy dialogue, private sector involvement, institutional development, and transfer of technology. The latter two fell clearly within the purview of the topics social analysts were expected to understand. The first two, however, did not seem to many in AID to fall within the domain of expertise of the social analyst. For many in AID, the idea and function of social analysis was confused with an unrealistic, idealistic, and nonsustainable social welfarism. Terms such as beneficiary analysis, direct assistance to the poorest of the poor, and rural participation were often negatively associated with what was considered to be the outmoded the basic human needs development strategy. The concepts and terminology of basic human needs approach were closely associated with social analysis and seemed unsupportive of the revised guidance.

## The Role: A Project Officer
## in the Kenya AID Mission

My experience in the Kenya mission, however, ran contrary to this perception. I found that an extensive knowledge of Kenyan society and training in anthropology (and social analysis, as practiced in AID) proved to be very useful to both the mission, and to AID in general in implementing the new policy directions. When it came to identifying and designing self-sustaining projects that were based on the self-interest and incentives of rural people and local organizations, my knowledge of local conditions and anthropological perspective were very useful. My previous AID assignment (1976-1981) as Regional Social Analyst in the East and Southern Africa Regional Office—based in Kenya—provided a highly relevant experience base. Semantics and perceptions notwithstanding, I found it easy to work along side other mission staff on the wide range of problems involved in development assistance, including proliferation of projects, lack of sustainability of project activities, and insufficient motivation for participation by intended beneficiaries of projects.

I served in several different capacities in the AID project office in the Kenya mission. Responsibilities included managing AID-funded projects (typically being implemented by a team of experts on contract, or an organization), designing and helping to implement development projects, and in the second and third years respectively, serving as deputy chief and chief of the project office. The office was one of six units in the mission. Staff in the office usually included three locally hired Kenya professionals, three AID career officers, and secretarial support. The mission had about thirty American staff and roughly the same number of Kenyan staff. As project officer I was responsible for a range of activities related to the design and implementation of development projects, and as such, was considered a "nuts and bolts" professional essential to the basic work of a field post, which was bringing about development through the funding of projects. My major work included the following assignments.

### Project Design

A main responsibility as project design officer was taking charge of the design of a project from start to finish. The process included organizing support for a wide range of contributions from different specialists, such as a lawyer, commodity procurement specialist, contract officer, economist, engineer, and technician. Substantial committee work was necessary to secure review and approval of the project documentation in its various stages. With multi-million dollar project designs, the design officer often personally carried the project document to the AID office in Washington for review and approval.

Design of the *Private Sector Family Planning Project* was one such task assigned to me. It was an appropriate assignment, as I had done my Ph.D. dissertation on indigenous and contemporary fertility regulation in the Kenya highlands, and thus had a good understanding of the problem. In the project, we were particularly concerned with several issues: the very high population growth rate in Kenya (at that point over 4 percent, the highest country rate in the world), the need to be efficient in selecting service delivery points which would meet the meagre existing demand, the high cost of establishing sustainable family planning service delivery points, the need to support a newly created national family planning council (perceived as an institutional rival by some officers in the Ministry of Health), and the need to find new models for non-governmental family planning service delivery which would be replicable, sustainable and compatible with fairly strict government health guidelines.

The basic project plan was to fund a team of U.S. and Kenya experts to identify and design subprojects to help start or improve family planning service delivery in existing "private sector" clinics run by manufacturers, tea and coffee plantation owners, church and cooperative organizations and women's associations. A guiding principle of the design was to show that such services were valuable to client workers or parishioners and to the organizations involved. Success was achieved when a sponsoring organization—having started up with project-funded assistance for training, construction, and purchase of supplies—was willing and able to sustain service delivery on its own.

An innovative aspect of this project was its nongovernmental orientation. This approach was highly favored by AID policymakers although at that time there was the widespread assumption that the only really effective "private sector" projects were driven directly by a profit motive, and operated within the cash economy of the country. While this project certainly did take into account the obvious interest of private firms in the possible economic benefits of increased family planning for their employees (through less time lost in maternity leave, for example), it was designed to tap a much broader array of motivation, including concern about excessively high population growth, and interest in the welfare of women and children. On the Kenya side, the nongovernmental orientation was acceptable to senior policymakers, but proved highly controversial to some administrators in the Ministry of Health who wanted strong Ministry control over implementation of the project. The project gained approval only after overcoming controversy within the Kenya government, but it has since gained a highly favorable reputation among Kenyan leadership and observers outside Kenya. The concept of the project has recently been replicated on a large ($40 million) worldwide scale by AID's central population office.

My anthropological knowledge of the country, its institutions, and the "family planning sector" from the family to the national level obviously contributed to the project design. As in all project design efforts, however, the final product was the outcome of a multidisciplinary team of professionals representing a number of points of view. My role in developing and negotiating the rationale and approach for the emphasis on the private sector drew on my understanding of Kenyan society and on an anthropological perspective. As an anthropologist, I have been trained to understand the values and motivations of men and women and families in various occupational roles, of local organizations and enterprises, and governmental entities within a holistic context. Using that knowledge, I was able to increase the likelihood of participation in project activities. This was accomplished by shaping the design to maximize the incentives for participation by those involved— including users of contraceptives, families in certain occupational categories, providers of contraceptive and health services, and governmental overseers of the project. In addition, a close relationship with Kenyan colleagues enabled me to ensure a high degree of host country involvement in the conceptualization and design of the project—an involvement which significantly improved the quality of the design and proved crucial in the lobbying necessary to gain Kenya government approval of the project.

## Critique of Project Design

Because of my professional background and position in the AID mission, I reviewed most project designs in some stage of their preparation. Participating in such reviews provided the opportunity to offer suggestions as to how the mission could constructively resolve project design problems. It also offered the opportunity to help respond to the increasingly stronger signals we were perceiving from AID headquarters in Washington to implement the new policy guidance, with its strong emphasis on policy dialogue and private sector activities. (Implementing the other two main policy directives, institutional development and technology transfer, was of less concern to the Kenya mission as these were already familiar themes. They were also areas in which the value of social analysis was clearly recognized.)

The reviews provided a useful forum for introducing alternative ideas derived from the anthropological perspective of how AID Kenya could constructively explore the potential of the revised guidelines. For example, a major design was planned for rural enterprise development, with a strong emphasis on building an outreach capacity in Kenya banks with rural offices to make loans to farmers for agricultural and rural development investments. Following precedent in rural Kenya, the loan program was organized for relatively large-scale farmers, with little being risked on the small farmer (90 percent of Kenya's population). In this case, being in the mission and sitting in on the design strategy meetings as a "regular" made a difference. I proposed a "bottom end" of the project, which would include a separate $6 million component that focused on the small farmer and included very small loans and business advisory assistance for individuals and income-generating local groups. The component was offered in the context of how to ensure that this private sector project was "socially sound," and it was accepted as such. I was assigned to work with the responsible project officer to help develop a scope of work for its design.

An important and innovative aspect of this component was its flexible design. The mission had long experience with the small enterprise subsector, and I and a colleague were in the process of carrying out an evaluation of some of the small enterprise development projects we had previously funded and were about to complete. Among these was an operations research project designed to test methodologies for development of such rural enterprise development projects. Experience in evaluation of this and other projects, as well as our general familiarity with the subsector, enabled us to develop a flexible design which provided for a core group of U.S. and Kenyan small business experts whose task was to identify and fund a series of subprojects throughout the life of the project. Subprojects were to be selected according to criteria we initially established that would later be refined by the core team during project implementation. Such a design assured an incremental learning process by the core project implementors, and was innovative in AID terms because the subprojects were not all identified and funded at the time of formal project approval, as was the usual practice.

## Project Implementation

One of my most satisfying tasks was serving as project designer and manager of several different kinds of research activities. These included operations research on development of nongovernmental institutions for health and family planning service delivery, small scale enterprise development, community water supply, rural roads construction and maintenance, the woman's role in on-farm storage, development of English instructional curriculum for radio in primary schools, and development of charcoal cookstoves. Most of these activities were project components or separately-funded projects and involved periodic interaction with a range of subject experts based in the field or visiting Kenya in the capacity of consultant advisors. These activities provided me with the opportunity to work on other priorities, i.e., adapting technologies for use in Kenya settings, and strengthening institutional frameworks to support technology transfer.

Another highly satisfying task as design officer (and part-time social analyst), was identifying and helping to recruit qualified and competent Kenyan professional behavioral scientists for work on project designs and implementation. (I use the broader term "behavioral scientist" in order to include the broad range of professionals who can carry out the social analysis function.) This role was particularly important in the design of the Private Sector Family Planning Project. It was important in other activities as well, such as arranging the successful meeting between a Kenyan regional planner colleague (who had spent years developing an improved cookstove and was seeking a consulting job in order to market it) and the project manager responsible for a Renewable Energy Project seeking a cookstove advisor.

During project design, an important task was to provide for appropriate behavioral science involvement in project implementation; for example, establishing a position for an anthropologist on the long-term technical assistance team of a farming systems research team. My field experience as well as mission experience in this function was favorable and indicative of the extent to which behavioral science expertise was contributing to project implementation during the period when meeting basic human needs was a high priority in the Agency. Table 15.1 depicts the roles that behavioral scientists have played in implementation of AID-funded projects in Kenya. The situation in Kenya was unusual; for purposes of generalization it should not be considered the norm, but rather the "best case." Kenya is a country where there are an unusually large number of social analysts locally available for design and implementation assistance (e.g., at the university and connected with other international and bilateral organizations). AID's regional office (REDSO/ESA) has employed two social analysts since the late 1970s (both with considerable experience in Kenya); and the Kenya AID mission had included professionals with anthropological training on its staff.

Table 15.1 also presents "best case" data from another perspective. The projects included are only those that have been identified by the AID Kenya mission (and in two cases by Washington AID offices which have responsibility for managing some research projects) as being especially noteworthy. They are identified in an annual exercise undertaken when AID headquarters in Washington compiles a list of successful projects worldwide to show Congress as part of an annual formal presentation. The list of all Kenya projects is a much larger one (there were over forty projects on the books in 1984). The extent of behavioral science involvement in the entire list is far less than among those "successful" ones, which suggests that there may be some positive relationship between more successful projects and those with relatively greater behavioral science involvement.

## Program Planning:
### The Kenya Social and Institutional Profile

Although not in the job description, one of the major activities I undertook in the mission directly utilized my country experience and anthropological knowledge. On my initiative, but with approval of the mission director, I worked closely with another anthropologist experienced with AID and working in a consultant capacity to design and complete a "Social and Institutional Profile" of Kenya. Our profile was the first of a program of such "SIPs" conceived by behavioral scientists in the policy arm of AID. The concept of the profile was based on the assumption that sound program and project identification was the best way to ensure good design and effective implementation, and that social analysts have one of the best vantage points from which to identify a problem and its most effective solution.

Table 15.1  Behavioral Scientists in Selected A.I.D.-Funded Projects in Kenya

| Selected Projects 1/ | Design Input by Behavioral Scientists | Behavioral Scientists on Project Implementation Team 2/ | Sex | Ratio, Behavioral Scientists to Total Team |
|---|---|---|---|---|
| 1983: | | | | |
| Radio Language Arts | Medium | Socio-linguist, Ph.D. | M | 1/4 |
| Sheep and Goats Research | High | Anthropologist, Ph.D | M | 1/4 |
| Rural Private Enterprise | High | Social Work, Ph.D. Pol. Science, M.A. Social Work, M.A. | M F F 3/ | 3/4 |
| 1984: | | | | |
| Egerton College | Medium | None | | |
| Population Studies Research Institute | Medium | Demographer, Ph.D. Demographer, Ph.D. | M M | 2/3 |
| Renewable Energy Development, Cook-stove Component | High | Regional Planner, Ph.D. | M 3/ | 1/3 |
| Rural Planning | High | Pol. Scientist, Ph.D. Rural Sociologist, Pn.D Demographer, M.A. Planner, Ph.D. | F M M M | 4/5 |
| 1985: | | | | |
| Kenya Gov't Policy Dialogue | Low | None | | |
| Private Sector Family Planning | High | Sociologist, Ph.D. Anthropologist, M.A. | M F 3/ | 2/3 |
| On Farm Grain Storage | High | Anthropologist, Ph.D. | F | 1/4 |

1  Selected for list of successful projects submitted annually by A.I.D. to Congress.
2  Including discipline and degree.
3  Kenya citizen.

To get approval to do the SIP, I first had to generate an interested constituency from an initially skeptical mission staff. Research and write-up took a year and included arranging for seven different contributors to prepare sector papers, and synthesis of the final document carried out by a skilled social analyst contractor with extensive knowledge of Kenya and experience with AID. Fortunately, the mission director supported the effort throughout, so that the project was completed despite the fact that it was perceived by some as a deviation from my normal responsibilities.

The final document, a book-length analysis of Kenya's society and economy, focused on the processes of development within the major sectors, institutions, and population groups. It was designed to provide information in a format directly useful to development practitioners to assist them in carrying out more informed program planning, project identification, and project design at the country and sector-specific levels.

As a document, the Kenya SIP was considered a success. It was well put together, offered useful insight for development professionals working in Kenya, and was valuable to staff in other AID missions who subsequently prepared SIPs. As a contribution to program planning and project identification, it had more modest impact. Its ideas and text were useful in preparing the countrywide strategy statement required of AID missions on a periodic basis (the "Country Development Strategy Statement"), in particular in discussion of agriculture and in the emphasis given to generation of off-farm employment. Initial hopes to the contrary, it was used relatively little as a source in the policy dialogue that the AID mission was initiating with the Kenya government. Although conceived as a complement to the World Bank Memoranda and other numerous economic studies of Kenya, it never generated the kind of interest and distribution that some such reports receive.

In retrospect, it proved an extremely valuable exercise for a few AID professionals, particularly in helping articulate ideas and concepts related to the strategies being developed under the new administration in Washington. It effectively profiled the nature and role of Kenya's private sector (broadly defined as nongovernmental, as opposed to simple "for profit" in orientation), and described the dynamics of its institutional development (institutions being in part categorized by how and what kind of rewards they are organized to seek). It highlighted trends in important development processes which did not tend to receive mission attention because they were not prominent in core AID sectors, yet which offered interesting possibilities because of their impact on development changes in several sectors. Among such processes having cross-sectoral impact were: agroforestry (in agriculture, environment, fuel supply and income generation) and breast feeding (in health, nutrition, and fertility regulation).

## Lessons Learned

My experience in Kenya gave me a good opportunity to explore some of the ways in which a social analyst with good knowledge of the country and region, as well as AID, could contribute in a practical and systematic way to the work of an AID mission. I have described some of the processes of mission work in the paragraphs above. Of special interest to me was being able to assist in the implementation of AID's evolving policy directions, such as by identifying and supporting nongovernmental and private enterprise development activities. Among the lessons I learned from this effort were the following.

*Focus, in Project Development, on the Incentives of Individuals, Groups, and Institutions.* Understanding incentives, incentive structures, and the constraints to pursuing incentives is basic to program planning and project design. Positive incentives are typically the source for successful participation of the rural population, an objective central to the thinking of implementors of the basic human needs strategy. Thus, a good understanding of incentives and incentive structures helps to predict and improve the scope for participation in a project.

A recent World Bank study lends support to the need to focus on understanding relevant incentives as the key to designing successful projects. In the 68 projects studied, evaluators found problems with participant incentives in 37 percent of them (Kottak in Cernea, 1985: 350). This focus is especially appropriate in designing the new generation of projects which include a strong social dimension, such as "social marketing" in the case of family planning methods and "social mobilization" in the case of planning for mass immunization programs, or "community mobilization" in the case of forestry or anti-desertification projects.

*Explore Nongovernmental Ways for Promoting Development.* Very often governments are over-committed to development activities, and have neither the staff nor financial resources to implement and sustain development activities. On the other hand, governments tend to be very slow in relinquishing their responsibilites and spheres of influence. In the delivery of social services in Kenya, for example, nongovernmental options were consistently found to be overlooked in comparison with government programs. The Kenya government's own resistance to change, and to relinquishing involvement and control over donor-provided resources, was an important aspect of the problem.

We found in Kenya innovative means for self-sustainable family planning service delivery in church-based health care systems, and among a wide range of factories, plantations, and other private enterprise organizations. Involvement of nongovernmental institutions in promoting income generation and enterprise development offered great potential. With changes in restrictive governmental policies in the health and water sectors (e.g. in allowing cost recovery for service), much could be accomplished concerning provision of health care and potable water supplies.

*Be realistic in what can be accomplished from efforts originating from a distinctly anthropological perspective.* Despite my own very positive experiences in a field mission as a direct-hire AID employee, caveats are in order. Such a favorable perspective can be misinterpreted. A lesson I frequently relearn is the limited extent to which AID as a government agency is able and willing to profit from the perspective of an anthropologist with extensive local knowledge of a country. As one of a number of relevant sources of knowledge, the social analytical perspective is relatively costly yet its benefits are not easily measured. In many cases, anthropological knowledge and views are not sought, and local level knowledge and experience are under-utilized in the design of development projects. In large part this lack of use is an outcome of the serious budget and staff constraints placed on the Agency in recent years. These constraints are very significant, have impact on virtually all phases of operations, and are likely to increase. Lack of such input, however, is also due to changing priorities and fashions among development agencies. Despite the need for the kind of advice provided by social analysts with extensive country knowledge, the concepts and terminology of social analysis developed in the late 1970s in AID are currently fading from the development vocabulary, and they are not likely to reappear in the same form.

## Conclusion

In some respects however, recognition of the importance of social factors to success in development has not declined. A new terminology is emerging which includes such concepts as "social marketing" and "social mobilization," "small farmer incentives" and "unleashing the productive resources of the rural resident," all clearly focusing on the "people perspective." In time, perhaps the label "rural investment advisor" will come to mean social analyst. Evaluation results have consistently pointed to the importance of social factors in development work. Kottak, for example, in the paper referred to above has found in his study of 68 evaluations that:

> attention to social issues, which presumably enhances sociocultural fit and results in a better social strategy for economic development, pays off in concrete economic terms: the average economic rates of return for projects that were socioculturally compatible and were based on an adequate understanding and analysis of social conditions were more than twice as high as those for socially incompatible and poorly designed projects (Kottak in Cernea, 1985: 328).

My experience in the Kenya mission strongly reinforced my view of the high potential for social analysis in AID design, broad planning, and implementation. There continued to be a significant fit between what social and institutional analysts can contribute to development planning, and what the requirements were for effective and equitable implementation under the new policies and emphases ushered in by a new Administration and by increased knowledge of what are appropriate responsibilities of various actors in the development business. This conclusion is perhaps obvious, given the need for the kind of information, perspectives and skills that trained social analysts can provide in cross-cultural situations.

The extent to which this perspective is perceived as *essential* to AID's work, with its current emphasis on policies and strategies that accelerate economic growth, will be revealed only through time. I think, however, that the basic issue is the ability of social analysts to contribute clearly, tangibly and efficiently to solving the problems of development. I believe that development professionals in AID, at least in the areas of Africa where I have worked, see social analysis as appropriate. For some, it is seen as a relative luxury, as not important enough to warrant the effort and expense for its effective inclusion. To others, social analytical input can help guide AID work in the search for better approaches and can increase the quality of project investments, but it is not seen as crucial. In a period of declining resources, what is thought to be non-essential must be sacrificed, and hence social analysis may be sacrificed. To the extent that it come forward with better ways for doing development, it will remain relevant.

## Notes

1. As exemplified in the recently completed United Nations Programme of Action for African Economic Recovery and Development 1986–1990.
2. World Bank Accelerating Development in Africa paper.
3. See the Social Soundness Analysis, Appendix E of the Kenya Private Sector Family Planning Project Paper, September 1983.

## References

Cernea, Michael M., ed. *Putting People First: Sociological Variables in Rural Development.* Published for the World Bank, Washington, D.C. New York: Oxford University Press, 1985.
Cernea, Michael M. "Sociological Knowledge for Development Projects," in Michael M. Cernea, ed., *Putting People First: Sociological Variables in Rural Development,* pp. 3–21, 1985.
Cernea, Michael M. "When People Don't Come First," in Michael M. Cernea, ed., *Putting People First: Sociological Variables in Rural Development,* pp. 325–356.
Fleuret, Patrick, and Edward Greeley. "The Kenya Social and Institutional Profile." Unpublished Manuscript. USAID/Kenya, Program Office, 1982.
USAID, "Kenya Private Sector Family Planning (615–0223) Project Paper." 1983.
USAID, "World Bank Accelerated Growth in Africa: An Agenda for Action." Washington, D.C., 1981.
United Nations General Assembly. "Consideration of the Critical Economic Situation in Africa to Focus, in a Comprehensive and Integrated Manner, on the Rehabilitation and Medium-term and Long-term Development Problems and Challenges Facing African Countries with a View to Promoting and Adopting Action-Oriented and Concerted Measures." a/s–13/AC.1/L.3, May 31, 1986.

# 16

## Applied Anthropology and the Development Bureaucracy: Lessons from Nepal

*Janice Sacherer*

### Introduction

This chapter is based on three years' experience working with a multidisciplinary rural development project in Nepal and represents a great deal of personal suffering and pain. In retrospect, much of this was inevitable given that I was working in one of the three poorest districts of one of the world's ten poorest countries for a project with some major deficiencies in the project design (Sacherer, 1981: 1–2, 9–19). Much of it, however, was self-inflicted due to my own carelessness and naivete. Although I already had two successful academic research projects behind me, I was woefully unprepared for the realities of development anthropology in the Third World. I write this in the hope then, that it might spare other prospective applied anthropologists some of the delusions and mistakes I suffered, and also in the hope that it might contribute to changes in the way that we train development anthropologists.

It was certainly my own experience that development anthropology is a quantum leap beyond the demands of academic research in terms of theoretical complexity, methodological difficulty, physical hardship, and personal frustration. In addition, it tends to foster philosophic questions and doubts not encountered in academic research, ranging from the value of development to the nature and future of the human race as well as raising questions about one's own personal worth and sanity. This complex experience could well be described in a book with separate chapters covering such topics as changed methods of field research (the anthropologist as reluctant statistician and participant-employer), the anthropologist and the diplomatic bureaucracy (dilemmas of peaceful development and when to alienate everybody by taking a personal moral stand), the difficulties of fieldwork as a way of life (how many times can one live alone in an obscure village, learn yet one more foreign language, and suffer through amoebic dysentery in the name of science), the anthropologist as cultural interpreter and marginal everything (suffering personal criticism from left, right, and center of the Western development bureaucracy, multiple layers of indigenous elites, Western technical workers in the field, academic anthropologists, and from the occasional passing tourist who thinks the present situation is so picturesque and quaint that it ought not to be changed at all).

From these many possible topics, I have chosen to write about the problems of my interactions with the technicians and development bureaucrats of my own particular aid organization since I feel this was the area of my graduate training which was the weakest, it was one of the two areas which caused me the greatest amount of personal grief, and it was the area in which I most justly deserved some of the abundant personal criticism I received. It is also the area which seems to me to be most open to constructive change.

I know from many anecdote filled conversations with other applied anthropologists that my experiences and problems were not unique. However, with the exception of Wax (1971: 59–174), the field of applied work has yet to furnish the same genre of lengthy and detailed personal field accounts which began appearing in the academic literature some 20 years ago (Berreman, 1962; Freilich, 1970; Golde, 1970; Jongmans and Gutkind, 1967; Middleton, 1970; Powdermaker, 1966; Spindler, 1970). For this reason, I have chosen to cross-reference my experiences whenever possible, with the observations of others, but especially the review article by Hoben, "Anthropologists and Development," which appeared in the *Annual Review of Anthropology* in 1982.

I will begin by describing the major problems I encountered in the course of working with my particular aid organization and then proceed to examine the various criticisms which were leveled at me by co-workers of the same organization. I will analyze the validity of these critiques as objectively as possible, and I will examine some of the contributions I ultimately made to my particular project and its targeted poor. Finally, I will conclude with some purely personal and therefore subjective observations of a philosophic nature.

Needless to say, none of the opinions expressed in this chapter necessarily reflect the views or policies of my employing organization, the Swiss Association for Technical Assistance (SATA); all of them remain my responsibility alone. I have always appreciated SATA's open-mindedness in hiring me as a foreigner in their midst, particularly as I was the first though happily not the last, applied anthropologist they ever employed in Nepal. I have continued to believe as I did then, that SATA's general philosophy of integrated rural development and actual field methods were the most effective and culturally sensitive of any of the development organizations working in Nepal. Indeed, it was precisely because of my high opinion of their organization that I found our many adversarial encounters so personally painful. It was also for this reason that I was exceptionally satisfied to discover during a revisit to the project area five years later that many of my controversial recommendations had been implemented. In fact, none of the present day project technicians I spoke with could even remember when these policies had ever been in doubt!

## Problems of Development Bureaucracies: The Anthropologist's Point of View

### Applied Anthropology as Crisis Management

Ideally from the anthropologist's perspective, any rural development project should be preceded by an in-depth anthropological survey of the needs and problems of the targeted peoples of the region, with practical programs planned accordingly. However, applied anthropologists are often hired only after deep conflicts and difficulties have surfaced and the project's basic structure has crystallized. This is a problem which seems to have plagued applied anthropology in general (Hoben, 1982: 359; Foster, 1982: 193-194) and has been mentioned by others as a specific problem in Nepal (Justice, 1977). There are several consequences to late involvement, each creating a particular difficulty to be overcome by the anthropologist, not the least of which is trying to provide solutions to structural problems without changing the structure.

In my case, SATA had decided to hire an anthropologist only after its Integrated Hill Development Project (IHDP) was four years into its first five year plan and having a number of difficulties. This IHDP project was a multi-sector rural development scheme (forestry, horticulture and agronomy, education, health and nutrition, women's work, and cottage industry), in combination with a labor-intensive road building project employing up to 8,000 manual laborers who worked for minimal wages and free food.

From my perspective, both then and now, one of the primary reasons for the difficulties many of the individual sectors were facing, was a policy pursued at the beginning of the project which called for maximum action after minimum planning (Sacherer, 1981: 3). While I can appreciate the IHDP planners' desire not to waste valuable time in endless theoretical discussions, I feel that a great deal of time was lost in the end because the only preliminary social science research commissioned in the target area was a hurried walk-through by an economist (Schmid, 1971) which seemed to be a statistical justification for the plans already made. This brief and inadequate survey was obviously not a valid reflection on the work of the individual surveyor who had already distinguished himself with a uniquely detailed and useful work on the cultural ecology of Nepal (Schmid, 1970). While I have never had the opportunity to speak with him on the topic, I can only presume that he found the whole situation extremely frustrating. The problems of being a short-term consultant have been discussed before in the anthropological literature, sometimes with humor (Green, 1981), sometimes with gravity (Cheesman, 1982), and sometimes with evident anger (Evleens, 1982), but never with any particular solution.

While interviewing for the Nepal job, I was told that I would be working in a food surplus area which was one of the more hopeful regions of the whole district and that the chief ethnic group was the Tamang, a Tibeto-Burman tribal group quite similar to the Sherpas I had already worked with on two previous research projects. The reality when I arrived was that the Tamangs, while highly visible (i.e. living near the main trekking path through the area) comprised only 11 percent of the population in one of the villages to be studied and .4 percent in the other, while the majority (average of 70 percent) were high caste Hindus and a substantial 15 percent were Untouchables (Sacherer, 1986: 10). This meant that I had to learn something about a religious system unfamiliar to me (Hinduism) as well as the Nepalese national language. The Sherpas and Tamangs with whom I'd worked before were Buddhist and spoke Tibetan dialects which were not even in the same language family as Nepali. Needless to say, this unanticipated extra work at the very beginning of the project was both an unpleasant surprise and a substantial burden.

## Unrealistic Project Designs

My next discovery was that none of the ethnic groups, including the richest and highest castes, were self-sufficient in food for more than nine months of the year (Sacherer, 1986: 26) and child malnutrition rates averaged 72 percent of all children under five in one area and 53 percent in the other (Sacherer, 1986: 287). Many families spent several months in the spring drinking thin millet soup once a day and sleeping through the rest of the day to conserve energy and calories until the corn and millet harvests were in and the spring "starving season" was over. Eventually an old woman I knew personally did starve to death during one of my absences from the village (Sacherer, 1986: 122–128).

The centerpiece of the whole IHDP project was a "feeder" road to connect the area with Kathmandu in order to bring in agricultural inputs such as improved seed and artificial fertilizer and carry local cash crops out. The project design was based on an assumption that part of the region already had a large enough food surplus to enable the local farmers to take the risks of innovation (SATA, 1974, 1978). Therefore my findings were disappointing and embarrassing to say the least and my colleagues' initial reaction was to disbelieve them. This too placed an extra burden on me as I was then obliged to justify my unpopular results. I later discovered that this pessimistic adversary role has been a common experience of anthropologists in other aid projects (Hoben, 1982: 359). For my part, I never would have agreed to work on the project had I known the true situation beforehand.

## Resistance to Structural Change

The next great problem which confronted me after my unwelcome results began to be acknowledged was that most of the expatriates working on the project were a tightly-knit group who had been in Nepal for a number of years under conditions of great hardship and personal sacrifice, and consequently were suffering (in my estimation) severe cases of professional burnout. At the time I was appalled at their emotionalism on the issues yet three years later, after working on the same insoluble problems, I found myself in the same state. In the meantime however, I was in the extremely uncomfortable position of being rejected by the IHDP team that I was supposed to be working with, while on very friendly terms with other non-project members of the general organization (SATA). The IHDP technicians in the field held a rather cynical view toward home office bureaucrats back in Switzerland while these same bureaucrats felt that they had more of an objective view. I felt myself to be caught in the middle.

The IHDP technicians unfortunately, yet understandably, came to feel that any change I might suggest to the head office was a direct criticism of them and their past misunderstood and unappreciated efforts. Although I did specifically note in my final report that I believed all major problems in the IHDP project to be the result of unrealistic expectations in the planning phases rather than weaknesses of any of the participants (Sacherer, 1981: 1-2), 20), I was never able to allay their suspicions and hostilities. Only after the end of my contract, did I learn that the same sorts of problems have been shared by a number of other applied anthropologists (Fetterman, 1983: 215) and I needn't have taken it personally.

### Time Pressures

I was under constant pressure to work quickly because my study results were needed before 8,000 laborers arrived to construct the road. Consequently I neglected my health and eventually had to be hospitalized for tropical parasites, problems which plagued me for two full years after I returned to Europe. Since road construction eventually lagged two full years behind initial estimates and was still many miles from completion when I had finally finished my own study, this was a particularly useless bit of self-sacrifice on my part, and one for which I paid dearly. Looking back, I can't believe I ever felt that my work was that indispensable.

I believe a colleague (Pillsbury, 1985: 6) showed much more realism in responding to the following question during an interview.

"Do you think you've been successful in 'shoring up the field of international development'?"

"No, I soon learned that not even all the wisdom of anthropology could bring peace to the world or rationality to international development."

### Vague and Unrealistic Expectations of the Anthropologist

Once the anthropologist has been called in at the eleventh hour, another problem seems to be that he or she is often expected by the project technicians to offer a panacea. Often the anthropologist's job description is extremely vague (Foster, 1982: 191) or representative of several points of view. In general, the higher administration will be interested in longer-term issues pertaining to policy and the field technicians will be interested in very practical solutions to specific short-term problems. Given the on-going debate among applied anthropologists themselves over the nature, goals, and ultimate usefulness of their work (Hoben, 1982: 366–367), it is not surprising that their employers and co-workers are also confused or have unrealistic expectations of their capabilities.

Take for example, some of the questions on my job description. Some were quite realistic and relevant—"What are the roles of the various ethnic and caste groups? Who is innovative? Correlation with wealth? Are there differences in the nutritional customs of the different groups?" (Sacherer, 1986: 7). Others, however, were basically unanswerable by present day social science methods. "How will the social, economic, cultural, and political behavior of the people of the project be influenced through all the project activities (long-range 20-year objective of the study)?" (Sacherer, 1986; 8) was one such question.

### Ambiguous Job Description

The general confusion about the role and usefulness of an applied anthropologist is nowhere better reflected than in the initial job description. While this confusion may never be resolved, the wise anthropologist will make sure at least that there is a job description and that it is as specific as possible. This ensures that even though employers and co-workers may later end up disgruntled with the anthropologist's performance or results, the applied anthropologist is at least ensured against accusations of dereliction of duty.

My own experience illustrates exactly how not to proceed and the nearly disastrous consequences when confusion is added to ambiguity. In my case, due to time constraints imposed by my crisis hire, I left Switzerland without a job contract, content that the forms awaiting me in Kathmandu were not important since I had experienced such good rapport with the higher level management in Bern. As I understood it, my job was to do a baseline survey along the lines of the detailed academic project proposal which had already been submitted and approved both by Swiss headquarters in Bern and the Research Division of the Tribhuvan University in Kathmandu.

When I did sign my contract upon arrival in Nepal, I found attached to it a list of questions submitted by the various technicians on the IHDP team. I understood these to be a kind of addendum to the major work of the baseline survey. At the time, I was far more interested in the accompanying 50 pages of fine print instructions (in French) which went with the contract. I was assured by office personnel in Kathmandu that all of this verbiage was just a formality but discovered several weeks later, that part of the formalities was a clause forbidding me to make any media statements or publish any data without prior approval until five years after the expiration of the contract.

A year and a half later the IHDP team members called a meeting to discuss the dissatisfaction with my disregard for the true purpose of my job. It was only at this late date, after a number of acrimonious accusations and counter-accusations that we all discovered we were talking about two different job descriptions. They were astounded to hear about the officially approved formal baseline survey and I was equally amazed to discover that they regarded the added-on questions as my main work. This lack of communication was fostered, I might add, by the fact that we all lived in the field one and a half days' hard hike from each other and were only able to keep in contact through human porters and mail runners.

The final result, however, was that I had to devote several extra months to answering their questions, three of those months representing work done after the expiration of my contract. Given the choice of presenting haphazard work on time or a competent professional job several months late, I opted to work the extra time without pay.

In the end, my reports were 150 pages longer than anticipated and included something of everything ranging from pages of essays covering the proposed questions (Sacherer, 1986: 6–142), statistical charts (1986: 186–242 and 243–298), bibliographic documentation (1986: 299–326), and personal practical advice (1986: 143–185) for the next Five Year Plan.

## Generalized Hostility Toward Social Science

Another problem which a well-prepared development anthropologist should anticipate is the frequent hostility toward social science and social scientists held by many (but certainly not all) technical personnel such as engineers, agronomists, foresters, and livestock breeders. Regardless of whether or not this hostility has any rational basis (in fact it often does and this is the point of the second half of this chapter), it is a phenomenon for which the anthropologist should be prepared.

Initially I disregarded this ill-will since I had already been told in the head office back in Europe that many of the bureaucrats there felt the field technicians had too narrow a perspective and were probably working so hard at their individual jobs that they had lost the overall view. Later, I came to realize that the very fact I had been hired by the European office and sent out to do a survey which involved certain questions about project policies and impacts, made me not only perceived as an outsider, but a possible management spy. Obviously (in retrospect), one lone anthropologist was a much easier and safer target for all of the latent hostilities toward the organization hierarchy than forthright criticism of those who held the contractual and financial power. Therefore in my own experience, it will always be impossible for me to assess how much of the hostility generated toward me as a "non-productive academic type" was the antagonism toward the head office, and how much was the result of distrust of social science in general. Certainly, I will never forget being told, "Ah yes, in our country we always say that when you don't know what else to do with your life, you become a social scientist."

In the same circumstances today, I feel that I would deal with the problem more effectively by a combination of better initial relations and an otherwise thick-skinned approach. I think it very important for any potential applied anthropologist to realize that having detractors, even antagonists, is probably an inevitable part of working in such a controversial and stress-filled occupation, and that hostility toward one does not necessarily have anything to do with the personality or performance of the individual anthropologist.

To quote another applied anthropologist with a long-term successful career in the field, "The most demanding part of such work is to reconcile oneself to being in the lonely position of pioneer and if not of pioneer, then at least one of atypicality" (Weidman, 1979: 6).

## Anthropologists as Marginal to Everybody

The socially ambivalent role of the anthropologist has of course, long been recognized with such labels as "marginal natives," (Freilich, 1970) and "strangers and friends" (Powdermaker, 1966). This role becomes immensely more complicated however, for the applied researcher who must relate not only to the villagers but to many different groups of Westerners and to the local elites. Especially in Nepal it is not uncommon to have dinner squatting on a dirt floor by candlelight one night and dine with UN officials and Nepalese government ministers in an old palace several evenings later. The Western officials tend to be concerned about the true motives of the local power structure as well as their perceived inefficiency and possible corruption. The local officials meanwhile, seem to be preoccupied with speculations and conspiracy theories concerning "the real reasons" these crazy Europeans have given up the comforts of home to go and live in a bunch of backward villages. Western diplomats are constantly admonishing the anthropologist not to mention certain inconsistencies between stated policies and local realities in the name of "the big picture" and the "overall good." Local intellectuals on the other hand, frequently beseech him to "finally reveal the truth" whatever the current version of that is.

Although the applied anthropologist's true sympathies will remain with the villagers where they always have been, the complicated layers of both indigenous and expatriate expert bureaucracies can cause many soul-searching dilemmas. While the anthropologist will not enjoy overlooking inefficiency or possible corruption any more than other expatriates, he will have more understanding of the traditional roots of these problems and also unfortunately, more of a vested interest in doing so. Most of the other technicians on the development team have worked in several other countries and can always go to the same sort of job elsewhere if they encounter political difficulties. The anthropologist, however, has often invested years of his life in language learning and specialty studies of a single country. Inevitably I think he will find himself on the more conservative end of the spectrum, boxed in by exactly the same sorts of considerations as the peasants, villagers, and local intellectuals with whom he works.

There inevitably comes a time then, when the applied anthropologist of any sensitivity must ask himself if he hasn't perhaps sold out to reactionary forces in order to maintain his own future contacts and research visas.

There are many things one learns as an applied anthropologist that one would rather not know about one's favorite foreign country and I have personally heard several experienced development anthropologists state that the last place one should try to do applied work is the country of one's original research and emotional commitments.

The fact that the anthropologist's local rapport is the very quality for which he was hired often escapes harassed technicians in the field especially when their conflicting styles yield differential results in the anthropologist's favor. This most frequently happens when both groups approach local officials for bureaucratic paperwork or favors.

A clear example of this occurred in my own case when I went to visit the chief district officer (CDO) of my region shortly after a similar visit by an engineer from our project who had noisily rushed in and demanded an immediate signature on his urgently needed project paper.

Unaware of the CDO's bad reputation among my fellow team members, I acted in normal Nepalese style, introducing myself through my assistant and then ordering tea for everyone while chatting to the CDO about our families, philosophies of life, and mutual interests. After an hour, the CDO asked me to sit in on his daily office routine which resembled a medieval court with its varied petitioners. At the end of a fascinating afternoon, I had a notebook full of information on the political and social life of the entire district. Later while dining privately with his family, I was briefed on all the intricacies of the political factions and feuds of my new area of research. All of my papers were signed, letters of introduction were written, and a police escort was provided back to my guesthouse. Three weeks later, I learned that our project engineer was still waiting for his paperwork to be signed.

## Critiques of the Anthropologist:
## The Development Agency's Perspective

*Inability to Write Concisely*

In speaking with other applied anthropologists, the conflicting desires to do a thorough professional job and the need to keep things brief appear nearly universal. For myself, having spent eight university years learning how to qualify and footnote everything, I was caught offguard when confronted with readers who had neither the time nor the inclination for an academic literary style and it was something which I resented at first. Eventually however, over a two and a half year period, I learned to condense everything and even developed special techniques for doing so.

Major fields of research were divided into separate reports whose titles would appeal to certain specialists but not to everybody ("Agriculture, Horticulture, Livestock, Fuel and Fodder Surveys"). Summaries of the fifteen or twenty major points of each report were made in the very front of the reports before the table of contents. The bibliography became a separate report and was divided up into different specialties such as "Transport and Public Works; Small Scale and Cottage Industry; Women's Work; Bureaucratic Planning and Problems." Also, much of the verbiage was reduced to statistical tables and easy-to-skim lists, charts, and graphs.

These schemata were particularly appreciated since they conformed to the only social science format with which the average development technician is familiar—that of the economists. Personal considerations and anthropological training aside, the same results presented in this style satisfied more people and had more of an effect than pages of carefully thought-out prose. Like it or not, the prose was usually designated as my personal opinions while the statistics were regarded as "fact."

## Over Collection of Data

Here again the training of graduate school appears at odds with applied work as the emphasis shifts from generalized data gathering to specific problem-oriented tasks. The tendency of the anthropologist will be to gather everything possible anyway and then condense out the relevant applied data later. Three problems arise from this academic approach.

First of all, a general hostility toward social science readily predisposes Western technicians and administrators toward the suspicion that one is just a useless ivory tower academic anyway, a prejudice which is all too easily reinforced if one appears to be doing any extraneous data gathering. If one is not very careful, the additional charge will be made that the anthropologist is "just a freeloader" doing private research at company expense. Since personal rapport and status as a trusted insider rather than intellectual brilliance or methodological perfection are the chief criteria for the eventual use of the anthropologist's data by development organizations (Hoben, 1982: 359), it definitely behooves the applied anthropologist to try to avoid this label. Secondly, as the seemingly inevitable hostilities and pressures mount against the anthropologist, the temptation to try to salvage the situation by writing off the applied experience and collecting data for academic use is all too great anyway. Thirdly, the anthropologist who does this risks wearing himself out so completely that he won't be able to do any academic writing for several years. Since job stress and job burnout are already recognized as intrinsic professional hazards for the applied anthropologist (Fetterman, 1983: 221), the neophyte researcher should be especially cautious about adding any extra stress however this might seem like a good idea at the time.

The over-collection syndrome results in large part, I believe, from the general attitude conveyed in graduate school that applied anthropology is on the periphery of "real" anthropology. With this attitude I fear that the "real" anthropologists are in danger of becoming mere collectors and custodians of the mostly extinct, deliberately shutting themselves off not only from influence in international development organizations (Foster, 1982: 192), but also from many of the great humanistic concerns of our times.

Certainly the one thing that applied anthropology is not, is the one most often hoped for in the halls of academe—an easy way to get paid for doing more fieldwork in one's favorite country.

## Bureaucratic Naivete

Anthropologists, myself included, are notoriously inept at dealing with Western administrators (Hoben, 1982: 353–354). While this ineptitude may be the unavoidable result of a clash between the very values necessary for successful fieldwork, successful academic careers, and Third World bureaucratic maneuverings, a great deal of it appears avoidable. Certainly the characteristics which make for a successful fieldworker—individual initiative, general unshockability, and a high tolerance for disorder and ambiguity, are not likely to win any friends in a Western bureaucracy. Nor do the qualities which endear one to Third World bureaucracies—personal relationships based on friendly ties to others outside the organization as well as patient persistence while maintaining good humor. Nevertheless, I shudder to think of how thoughtlessly I irritated the administrators in my own organization and added to my own considerable difficulties by not paying careful attention to rules, regulations, and protocol. Knowing the rules and observing them without making any undue waves is, of course, one of the primary requisites for success in a Western bureaucracy.

Moreover, it is certainly possible for the anthropologist to apply his field methods to the Western bureaucracy he works for. His knowledge of who in his organization is sympathetic to social science and that person's relative power in the bureaucratic scheme of things can prove invaluable. The anthropologist can also use his skills at kinship charts by applying them to the hierarchy of his own organization. This along with a mini-ethnography will help prevent him from being unknowingly co-opted by one or another of the various factions. Clearly, this kind of bureaucratic fieldwork along with a little library research on the types of programs and the styles of past program documents is time better spent than collecting extra data in the field. I cannot emphasize strongly enough that the anthropologist's effectiveness in the aid organization, particularly at decision-making levels, will depend on this.

Finally, my own experience and that of others I have talked with indicates that the anthropologist will do well to make particular friends of the local nationals who work in the administration of his aid organization. Normally they will be especially friendly toward him, seeing him as a bridge between the two cultures, and therefore more sensitive to their problems and concerns. Occasionally however, one of them may lose his or her status as the local "expert" due to the arrival of the anthropologist and this can cause enormous amounts of ill will to be generated against the anthropologist. The anthropologist forewarned of this should pay special attention to this possibility and seek in every way to sooth and disarm such potential hostility.

*Ignorance of Development Theory*

This extremely valid critique of myself and my training was made by the better educated administrators and technicians of my organization, but especially the economists. I agreed at the time and today even more so, that my training for development anthropology should have been a mixture of both anthropological case studies and more general theories and studies of development.

My applied anthropology seminars back in 1972–1973 consisted basically of moralistic and generally pessimistic examinations of the anthropologist-colonialist link, and the nuts and bolts findings of small and highly atypical enterprises such as the Cornell University project in Peru. This pessimistic and perfectionistic approach it turns out, is quite common among applied anthropologists, and has been dubbed the "hypercritical Cassandra syndrome" by development administrators (Hoben, 1982: 354).

If teaching a course on development anthropology today, I would use a mixture of anthropological case studies along with such works as Schumacher's *Small is Beautiful* (1973), Harrison's *The Third World Tomorrow* (1980), and Brandt's *North-South: Program for Survival* (1980). Even a basic text on peasants would be welcome (Wolf: 1966), while more detailed works such as Myrdal's *Asian Drama* (1972), and Hinton's *Fanshan* (1968), could provide alternative political viewpoints.

Ideally, there should be multidisciplinary program,s including graduate degrees in development studies. However, for the anthropology student who is interested in applied anthropology but not yet committed to it as a career, there should at least be provision in departments of anthropology for graduate level reading courses in development theory and practice, or credit given for courses taken in the international economics department.

*Ignorance of Technical Subjects*

Equally important and equally lacking in my training were the fundamentals of some very practical subjects such as tropical agriculture, tropical health and hygiene, basic nutrition, and for my larger project sample—statistics, organizational theory, and personnel management.

Knowledge of these subjects is, of course, extremely useful for anthropological research. Even more important, I feel, is their usefulness in helping to bridge the gap between anthropologists and other development technicians. This gap includes everything from lack of a common technical jargon to lack of understanding on the anthropologist's part of the general theories and assumptions behind the technicians' approaches. These approaches, of course, represent some forty years of hands-on practical experience.

Once this gap is bridged, the anthropologist then finds himself in a position to contribute detailed cultural data which is suddenly meaningful to the individual technician. Often what the anthropologist then has to say is nothing different from advice given all along, only now it is couched in a vocabulary which the technical worker can understand and trust.

## Final Contributions to an Aid Organization

I will begin by saying that despite some of the seemingly unique peculiarities of my own situation, my experiences described in this chapter seem to have fallen completely within the range of others' applied experience (Hoben, 1982: 369–370), and to have contributed accordingly. I personally would agree with Hoben (1982: 370) that applied anthropology's most valuable contribution to development work is "to challenge and clarify, and hence help revise explicit and implicit assumptions made by those responsible for planning and implementing development policies." In this sense, every painful confrontation and controversy served some useful purpose.

As stated earlier, many of my suggestions were already accepted and were in the process of implementation as I left Nepal, with even more in evidence five years later. While I deserve some personal credit for this, most of it should be attributed to the decentralized and innovative nature of my particular organization, and also to the highly significant fact that there was a nearly complete changeover of personnel at the time my final reports were submitted. Only after most of the original project participants including two different project managers had come and gone, were my recommendations seriously considered. As a result, a number of these recommendations were incorporated into the new 1980–1985 IHDP Five-Year plan (SATA, 1979).

Still later, my reports on conditions in the project area were thought important enough by the management of the general aid organization in Kathmandu (SATA) that they were made the subject of a day-long seminar which I presented to some seventy staff members. Since many of the SATA employees and their spouses worked in the capital city and only ventured into the rural areas on holiday hikes to the tourist spots, they had no direct knowledge of conditions or problems in the less glamorous villages of the Integrated Hill Development project. Hence, my seminar also served as a cross-cultural orientation for diverse project members of SATA in general as well as the various Nepalese counterparts and Western technicians.

Finally, my reports were well enough accepted back in the head office in Europe that I was asked to submit another report for a large-scale evaluation of the whole IHDP project (Sacherer, 1981). In the end then, despite my many problems with this particular aid institution, I remained convinced that I had worked for the agency utilizing the philosophy, methods, and proven trial record most suited to my own personal style and value system.

## Final Contributions to the Project Poor

• I think the wisest advice in this regard came from the Nepali foreman with twenty years' experience in development work for our organization. "Have patience, and don't expect to see any village results for many years. Don't even look for them for at least the first five years and better yet, don't come back expecting anything until ten years have passed. Then you will begin to see what you really did and you will probably find that it was not at all what you were expecting."

His advice was stated in a slightly different way by an applied anthropologist about the same time (Weidman, 1979: 6–7) and I find it also worth quoting. "When certain strategies pay off in the form of systematic change over long periods of time, the sense of achievement is all the more rewarding, although not necessarily recognized by anyone other than the person who succeeded in setting the whole process in motion."

There are two changes for which I can claim credit already. The first one is that several farmers are now making a good cash income growing vegetables from seeds that I gave them after they expressed an interest in my demonstration garden. Since these seeds were southern U.S. and Mexican varieties, they proved much more resistant to the monsoon heat and humidity than the European vegetables which have been propagated by aid projects in Nepal so far. The second one is the observation (Eirich, 1980) that many more girls were enrolled in primary school the year after I left. The explanation given for this by the villagers themselves was the example provided by myself and that observer, both of us financially independent women with Ph.D.'s.

## Final Observations and Philosophical Dilemmas

Just as the academic anthropologist believes that development problems involve cultural issues as well as technical solutions, all of the development anthropologists that I have talked to believe that development problems ultimately involve questions of values and political philosophy, particularly when the results of development work often seem to produce the opposite of what was intended (Russell,1985: 82–83).

In my own life these issues have so far evolved around those I label cosmic doubt categories and those which have evolved as purely personal questions. In the cosmic doubt categories, depending on the country, are basic questions about the meaning and worth of the individual human life and the destiny of humankind. How does one eat three meals a day when the neighbors are going to bed hungry? Will the child I save today with antibiotics starve ten years from now? What should be my moral stand if peaceful development fails? What should be my stand if people are too emotionally dulled by malnutrition, physically weakened by hunger, and spiritually sapped by general exploitation and ignorance, to contemplate even peaceful change? Can I in good conscience sit now on the sidelines, living in comfort provided in part by the money I saved while working with the villagers?

In the personal doubt categories have arisen deep questions and dissat-isfactions for the newly-perceived limitations of the liberal, secular, tech-nological, and behavioristic worldview of my own society and chosen profession. These dissatisfactions have been reflected in the fact that I spent the first three years back in the West trying to understand and assimilate my applied experience not by reading anthropology but by reading history, philosophy, and comparative religion.

I feel that I have finally attained a global world view. I feel also that this world view results not so much from my anthropological training as from the fact that I have in some small way shared and tried to alleviate, albeit with many mistakes and insoluble dilemmas, the sufferings and struggles of the destitute majority of humankind.

## Conclusions

In sum, my experience with development anthropology has made it seem far more challenging and frustrating than academic research; problems in this field are myriad although most of my own personal problems were precipitated by misunderstandings between myself and members of my aid organization, particularly the development technicians.

Development work is complex and nerve-wracking for the anthropologist in large part because it is a team effort and anthropologists have traditionally been, both by training and nature, self-sufficient individualists. Difficult as it may be for anthropologists to accept, one's effectiveness in applied work depends more on good personal relations with one's co-workers than on high quality data. Thus, knowledge of the methods, expectations, and institutional requirements of one's co-workers are essential to professional success.

Particularly useful job skills I would emphasize include the importance of having a specific job description, the necessity of a concise writing style, the ability to work well with others within the constraints of a highly politicized bureaucracy, as well as a broad knowledge of both theoretical and technical development subjects. Personal qualities which I think are essential to long-term success in the field include nearly infinite patience, diplomacy, and self-confidence in the face of personal criticism, along with a marked lack of perfectionism and an intact sense of idealism.

Finally, the type of graduate training which I believe would be most useful to prospective development anthropologists and their employers, is a broadly based, multidisciplinary one including a mix of anthropological case studies and both technical and theoretical material from a wide range of other academic fields including economics, public health, and agriculture.

## References

Berreman, G. *Behind Many Masks: Impression Management in a Himalayan Village.* Monograph 4. Ithaca, N.Y.: Society for Applied Anthropology, 1962.

Brandt. W. *North-South: A Program for Survival.* Cambridge: MIT Press, 1980.

Cheesman, A. "Further Comment on Green's Report from Sudan." *Human Organization,* Vol. 41, No. 2, 1982, pp. 186–187.

Eirich, S. Personal communication, 1980.

Evleens, K. "Help We Need But Save Us from AID: A Commentary on Green's Travel Report on Sudan." *Human Organization*, Vol. 41, No. 1, 1982, pg. 90.

Fetterman, D. "Guilty Knowledge, Dirty Hands, and Other Ethical Dilemmas: The Hazards of Contract Research." *Human Organization*, Vol. 42, No. 3, 1983, pp. 214–224.

Foster, G. "Applied Anthropology and International Health: Retrospect and Prospect." *Human Organization*, Vol. 41, No. 3, 1982, pp. 189–197.

Freilich, M. *Marginal Natives: Anthropologists at Work.* New York: Harper and Row, 1970.

Golde, P., ed. *Women in the Field.* Chicago: Aldine Publishing Co., 1970.

Green, E. "Have Degree Will Travel: A Consulting Job for AID in Africa." *Human Organization*, Vol. 40, No. 1, 1981, pp. 92–94.

Harrison, P. *The Third World Tomorrow.* New York: Penguin Books, 1980.

Hinton, W. *Fanshen: Documentary of Revolution in a Chinese Village.* Englewood, N.J.: Prentice Hall, 1968.

Hoben, A. "Anthropologists and Development," in B. Siegel, ed., *Annual Review of Anthropology.* Palo Alto: Annual Reviews, 1982.

Jongmans, D. and P. Gutkind, eds., *Anthropologists in the Field.* New York: Humanities Press, 1967.

Justice, J. "Perspectives on Applied Anthropology in Public Health Planning in Nepal." Seminar, Center for Nepal Asian Studies, Tribhuban University, Kathmandu, 1977.

Middleton, J. *The Study of the Lugbara: Expectation and Paradox in Anthropological Research.* New York: Rolt Rinehart & Winston, 1970.

Myrdal, G. *Asian Drama: An Inquiry into the Poverty of Nations.* (1 vol. abridged ed.), King, S., ed., New York: Pantheon Press, 1972.

Pillsbury, B. "Interview with Barbara Pillsbury," in H. Fisher, ed., "National Association for the Practice of Anthropology." *American Anthropology Newsletter*, November 1985, pg. 6.

Powdermaker, H. *Stranger and Friend.* New York: W. W. Horton, 1966.

Russell, D. "Counterproductive Development." *Human Organization*, Vol. 44, No. 1, 1985, pp. 82–83.

Sacherer, J. "Agriculture, Horticulture, Livestock, Fuel and Fodder Surveys from Two Panchayats in North Central Nepal." Kathmandu: SATA, 1979a, 52 pp.

Sacherer, J. "Suggestions for IHDP Five Year Planning—1980–1985." Kathmandu: SATA, 1979b, 34 pp.

Sacherer, J. "Practical Problems in Development in Two Panchayats in North Central Nepal: A Baseline Survey." Kathmandu: SATA, 1979c, 102 pp.

Sacherer, J. "Health Education, Nutrition, and Family Planning Surveys in Two Panchayats in North Central Nepal." Kathmandu: SATA, 1980a, 45 pp.

Sacherer, J. "Selected Bibliography of Development Literature Utilized in the IHDP Anthropological Surveys." Kathmandu: SATA, 1980b, 15 pp.

Sacherer, J. "Contribution to the Evaluation of the Integrated Hill Development Project, Nepal." Bern: Swiss Federal Department of Humanitarian Aid and Technical Cooperation, 1981, 21 pp.

Sacherer, J. *Collected Anthropological Reports Made to the Integrated Hill Development Project Nepal.* University Microfilms International, Ann Arbor, Mi., Order #L000964, 1986, 326 pp.

SATA (Swiss Association for Technical Assistance). "Integrated Hill Development— Project Outline." Kathmandu: SATA, 1974.

SATA (Swiss Association for Technical Assistance). "The Integrated Hill Development Project." Kathmandu: SATA, 1978.

SATA (Swiss Association for Technical Assistance). "Integrated Hill Development Project Activities for the Sixth Five Year Plan Period 1980–1985." Kathmandu: SATA, 1979.

Schmid, R. *Land Use Mapping in Hill Country, Eastern Nepal: Interpretation of Air Photographs in Compilation of Agricultural Statistics.* Berhamted, Herts, Great Britain: Geographical Publishers Ltd., 1970.

Schmid, R. *Road Feasibility Study of the Tamba Kosi/Khimti Khola Area.* Kathmandu: SATA, 1971.

Schumacher, E. *Small is Beautiful.* New York: Harper & Row, 1973.

Spindler, G., ed., *Being An Anthropologist: Fieldwork in Eleven Cultures.* New York: Holt, Rinehart, & Winston, 1970.

Wax, R. *Doing Fieldwork: Warnings and Advice.* Chicago: University of Chicago Press, 1971.

Weidman, H. "Profile of an Anthropologist." *American Anthropology Newsletter,* Vol. 20, No. 10, 1979, pp. 6–7.

Wolf, E. *Peasants.* Englewood Cliffs, N.J.: Prentice Hall, 1966.

# 17

## Finding Employment in Development Anthropology

*John Mason and Edward C. Green*

### Obtaining Relevant Skills During Academic Training

*Set Sights on Development Career Early*

The consensus among anthropologists currently working in development is that much of their academic training in anthropology was irrelevant to the work they now do. Therefore it is necessary to focus your career goals as early as possible in order to ensure maximum relevance of your graduate education.

It should be noted that while a Ph.D. has become a *sine qua non* for teaching anthropology at the university level, a masters-level degree may be more than adequate for development work. Most development professionals, including many or most in important administrative positions, hold degrees no higher than an MA, MS, MBA, MPh, or MPA. The holder of a Ph.D. may even be regarded as overly-specialized and therefore inflexible and unsuited for promotions to managerial or administrative positions.

In any case relevant, marketable skills along with appropriate experience are more highly valued by development organizations than academic degrees, therefore lack of a Ph.D. is by no means an obstacle to employment. Incidentally, there are very few job descriptions that call for a development anthropologist, or even for a medical or economic anthropologist. They do occur, but probably most development-related jobs in which anthropologists are engaged have more general job titles and descriptions such as "social analyst," "research associate," "project officer," or "technical advisor." Therefore we will talk about employment in development rather than employment in development anthropology.

Graduate curriculum should be designed to include courses that teach generally-useful skills such as applied or operations research methods, evaluation research, statistics, computers, foreign languages, policy analysis, or public administration. (One of the present authors sometimes lies awake at night and wishes he had taken more of these useful courses.) It is also advisable to develop sectoral skills outside the field of anthropology by taking courses in e.g., agricultural sciences, economics, or public health. A single course is obviously better than no course but a concentrated and sustained effort is needed to gain substantive and marketable skills in one of the major sectors of development assistance. There are smaller, less well known sectors of development such as small business enterprise development, community development, or development communications that also offer opportunities for the anthropologist.

Since the bald fact is that anthropology degrees are not very marketable in development work, the anthropologist intent upon a career in development should consider a dual degree or obtaining a masters degree in one of the technical or sectoral areas mentioned above. The anthropologist-*cum*- whatever can thus become more employable and can still bring the full range of anthropological perspective and skills to bear in a development job.

For the anthropologist already holding a PhD, it may be possible to obtain a marketable degree such as an MPh in half the usual time. A year invested thusly can pay substantial dividends in the marketplace as well as provide a range of skills complementary to medical anthropology.

## Study a Language Useful in Development Work

Learning a second or third language can be invaluable for both locating and building a career in development anthropology. The value, if not necessity, of speaking the language of the people one lives with for purposes of study, whether for a masters or doctorate in anthropology, seems obvious. While language competence may at first glance seem somewhat distant from the task of finding and gaining a foothold in development anthropology— all other things being equal (which in practice they never are)—such competence can make all the difference. Say you are competing with another anthropologist for a position (God forbid, it does happen) and for all intents and purposes you are both equally qualified. You both rate equally on possession of experience in research design, quantitative analysis, skills in training host country nationals in social research methods, report writing and briefing skills. However, if you already possess language skills relevant to the job at hand, you will most probably be selected for the position. Often, in fact, competence in a foreign language may in and of itself give you entry to a specific job for which you otherwise would be ineligible.

The languages most currently called for in the development arena (besides English) are: French, used in francophone West and Central Africa, North Africa, and Haiti, among others; Spanish, used in Latin America; Arabic, used in North Africa and the Middle East. Proficiency in any combination of these three languages will give the anthropologist a clear advantage in the marketplace. Sometimes deficiencies in experience or technical skills will be overlooked if the job candidate is strong in the language required by the job.

Concerning level of competence, several points need raising. A U.S. interviewer may break out in the language you profess to know and, awkward as it may seem speaking a foreign language with a countryman, you will have to pass muster. A Foreign Service Institute (FSI) language exam or equivalency rating may be required to justify your stated knowledge of a language. In any case, the best advice is: do not overstate what you know; on the other hand do not be needlessly modest.

## Conduct Dissertation Research in a Developing Country with a Large Assistance Program

To the extent that it is realistic or feasible, plan your master's or doctoral research around a development topic. The topic should be interesting and meaningful to you, acceptable to your academic mentors, and have potential value to the development organizations. If you are planning on future work with AID, including as a contractor with consulting firms dependent upon AID funding, you should consider the advantages of conducting your dissertation research in a country that has an AID program. Curry and Greeley in this volume provide examples of anthropologists who were hired by AID in the countries of their respective dissertation work on the strength of their familiarity with these countries. And if you want to be truly opportunistic, the larger the AID mission and therefore funding levels in a given country, the greater the opportunities for employment with or under AID.

One of the present authors did his dissertation research in a country so small and AID-less that he spent most of his early job interviews explaining where the country is. Interviewers from high-powered development organizations were not impressed that he was fluent in a language spoken by 8,000 people, nor that he had mastered the mysteries of matrilineal fission.

Selection of a topic which is of value to development organizations and at the same time worthy of scholarship is not always easy. Your dissertation advisor may be the leading expert in ethnosemantic analysis of canoe terms and wish you to follow in his footsteps. But if you want to increase your chances of employment in development, you would do well to choose a topic that relates in some way—the more centrally the better—to sectors of development assistance such as agriculture, public health, population, economics, or educational development ("human resources development" in the AID argot).

Some development agencies including AID and the U.S. Department of Agriculture Office of International Cooperative Development (USDA/OICD), have programs with certain universities—land-grant as well as others—to carry out development-related research. Some of that research is specifically socioeconomic, sociopolitical, socioecological and even plainly anthropological in its scope. The realistic or practical-minded student might even choose his or her academic department on the basis of whether it has such a program. Furthermore, if you carry out credible, recognizably usable research, it may just come to the attention of some official in the agency which sponsors it, giving you a possible advantage for future consulting or even permanent hire with that agency.

As we have already noted, relevant practical experience is generally worth more than academic degrees—certainly more than publications or mere research experience—in the development marketplace. Even if you did your dissertation on "Developing Zaire's Private Sector in the delivery of AID-funded Family Planning Services" and have achieved fluency in French, Swahili, and Lingala, you may still be required to have practical experience in order to obtain employment in francophone central Africa. There are several ways to get this experience.

## Obtaining Relevant Practical Experience

### Peace Corps and Other "Volunteer" Work

The Peace Corps may offer hands-on experience in grassroots, community-level development which is difficult to obtain elsewhere. It provides training and on-the-job experience in several of the endeavors important to the development anthropologist such as language and cross-cultural sensitivity training; experience in dealing with host country officials and in living with lower income people; experience with working in a development organization; and getting a taste of development problems and the difficulties of delivering appropriate solutions at local and community levels.

The United Nations has a similar voluntary program, which calls on an individual's specialized skills for use in an ongoing development program of the UN in many countries where it has a presence. Other possible routes to overseas experience are via private voluntary organizations (PVOs) which have developing country programs. Many of these organizations require specific professional experience and remunerate professionals at salaries higher than what one might normally associate with a volunteer position.

### Short-term Contracts with Donor Agencies, Consulting Firms or PVOs

While masters or doctoral research conducted through programs formally linking U.S. development agencies and universities or volunteer work overseas may connect you with a specific agency for the purpose of making a career in international work, those are not the only channels. Short-term consultancies provide another viable introduction to international work. However, these do not come easily, since "prior experience" is usually a prerequisite for obtaining such a position. Unless you possess a unique skill that no one else has and which is pertinent to development work—can you name one?—competitors' overseas experience will often win out. And therein lies the rationale for the initiation rite of voluntary service.

Short-term consulting, despite the difficulties of getting that first chance, is in our opinion one of the most rewarding forms of international work. Our reasoning here is that short-term consultancies put your knowledge, skills and savy on the line. Your ability to communicate cross-culturally, carry out an independent piece of work, effectively brief host government and donor agency officials, be able to "take the heat" for your or a team member's professional judgment, or quickly get a feel for an unfamiliar culture—these are all critical. On the other hand, your capacity to work with others, including high-powered consultants from other, more widely recognized disciplines and still hold your own is equally important. Perhaps our most challenging task as anthropologists is to be able to represent the ideas and preferences of very poor people to elites who may not care very much about the poor in their countries. However, advocacy must be handled with the utmost of care and must often be carried out in some disguised way, usually employing some notion of "cost effectiveness," or "internal rate of return" and other "sophisticated" measures of socioeconomic soundness.

## Training, Experience, and Catch-22

Since much of the social anthropologist's training is carried out in that great ethnographic laboratory known as the world, the distinction between training and experience is not as clear as it is in many other disciplines.However, fieldwork experience consisting of research is rarely sufficient. Development organizations usually require hands-on experience relating to a development project or program as a prerequisite for a field assignment. Skills or capabilities that may be sought by the organization include: languages, research design, data analysis, writing, management, negotiation, team building, project design or evaluation, and, equally important, skills more specific to sector work in agriculture, health and population, education and training, urban planning, or private enterprise development. Some of these skills can be acquired through education and training, but many of them can only come from work in a development organization. Since there are many more job-seekers around with excellent educational qualifications than with hands-on development experience—and more graduating from universities every year—practical experience has come to be more highly valued than academic skills. The trick for the would-be development anthropologist is how to overcome the "catch-22" of no experience, no job/no job, no experience.

One of the distinct differences between development anthropologists and other specialists is that an important part of our tool kit is the very kind of knowledge and understanding that one obtains almost exclusively from being in the place one is supposed to "know" about. One way to overcome catch-22 is to have such good knowledge of the country of interest to a development organization that it is willing to overlook lack of specific development experience. Sometimes an anthropologist is hired by such an organization when the anthropologist is already in the country of interest, thereby saving the organization travel costs. If you find yourself presented with the opportunity of a short-term or other assignment with a donor agency or with a reputable consulting firm while in the field, our advice is to take it since practical experience is so highly valued yet hard to obtain when starting in this profession.

## Preparing for Employment

### Self-Assessment and Setting Objectives

It is important that you ascertain your true inclination and interests in doing development work overseas. For this purpose you will need to know something about your own character and temperament (see next section) and to learn how to target your goals and objectives. It is useful to hierarchically list your career and related goals over a period of several years. How much time will you devote to getting overseas experience as a prerequisite to remunerative development work? How much time will you give to language study? Are you willing to take the risks of being a freelance consultant, at least for a time? After what period of time would you expect a permanent job with a firm or organization? How many years in a consulting position would make sense before returning to academia (if that is your interest)? What kinds of professional papers or publishable articles do you intend to write and in what timeframe? This might help you comprise a partial list of objectives. Your goals would be broader in scope than your objectives and might include such basic questions as whether you will plan a consulting, government, teaching or other career with an international focus. Several books and articles are available for practical planning and target setting (e.g., Tec, 1980).

### The Résumé

There are many guides to resume preparation, not only written but in the form of resume consultants that advertise their services in newspapers and journals. Therefore we will keep our advice brief and tailored to the needs and interests of development organizations.

The qualifications most sought by such organizations have already been discussed: relevant practical experience (preferably in-country, that is in the country or region relating to the position to be filled), technical expertise (for which an academic degree is a major, but not the only, qualification), and language skills. Obviously these should jump out of your resume and catch the attention of the reader. Often resume reviewers have scores of resumes to go through within a brief time period, so whatever qualifications you have should be easy to spot on your resume. A Summary of Experience, a brief paragraph in length and located after your name and address at the top of the page, is a good way to highlight your qualifications.

Access to a word processor makes possible tailoring your resume to the organization or to a specific job opening. For example, your Summary of Experience can be modified to highlight certain country or sectoral experience relating to a particular job, then be changed back to the way it usually reads after printing the page.

Unlike an academic curriculum vitae, your resume should emphasize skills and relevant employment history. It should deemphasize nonrelevant employment history (little if any detail is needed in listing an academic job), publications and presented papers, "community service," and membership to professional organizations. Of course there are exceptions. If you are applying for a research position then a list of research publications— perhaps a brief, edited list—would be appropriate.

## Aiming at International Work

Target setting is integral to developing your areas of expertise and potential marketing in the international arena. As noted above, agriculture and rural development, health and population, and education and training—in that order—are the "sectors" of greatest importance to AID as well as generally to other major donor agencies. Some of these sectoral programs have topical foci, such as AID's Women in Development program, UNICEF's focus on children's health and growth, AID's small business development program, or UN HABITAT's concentration on human settlements.

In addition to the above major sectoral interests of international donor agencies, there are numerous sub-programs and special interests. A look through the office directories of such agencies for the regional and program headings will give you an idea of the program based funding areas. In the AID directory, for example, Food for Peace and Voluntary Cooperation is named as a "bureau" whose foci are food distribution and cooperative development, including the formulation of cooperative organizations. The Science and Technology Bureau has among its many interests rural development, small enterprise programs, and a newly evolving field (which is actually a new version of a former concern) known as "development administration." This last may hold special interest to some anthropologists since its thrust is the workings of developing country bureaucracies in managing their development programs (which includes much of such governments' endeavors). Success in this area, which is important since institutional development is critical to the sustainability of development programs, has come to those with an expertise in management organization, corporate culture and related concerns. Development administration, because of its role in channeling funds, is of major import to AID as well as to donor agencies. It, along with improved public management of development programs and projects, may comprise an area of interest which has a potential for increased input from anthropologists with an expertise in intermediate and micro social and bureaucratic organization.

Whatever the selected sector or area of interest to the development anthropologist, it is important for you to target it in terms of your own expertise as well as the market for that particular kind of work.

## Interests, Habits, and Temperament

It is important that you have a fairly good idea of what you are willing and unwilling to do and what you like and dislike, before embarking on a career track in development. Rather than try to do deep analyses of individual character and temperament types and their relation to the range of development work conditions and situations, it is probably best to ask you to raise questions with yourself in order to determine your suitability to development work. First, ask yourself if you can cope with situations characterized by great uncertainty as well as considerable ambiguity and contradiction. Can you help mediate contrary points of view, even if you concur with only one side? Can you compromise your own high standards of research in order to have at least some impact on the outcome of an issue? Are you willing to accept a "quick and dirty" approach to a problem, which under normal academic conditions might permit a leisurely, more elaborate approach? Can you carry out a consultation even if the client group comprises elites who may disdain the "poor majority" among whom you are carrying out research? Can you afford to be overseas for weeks, months, or years in relation to your interests which remain behind? Can you operate between the fine lines separating the multilayered clients and interests in the interest of solving a great problem? Do you have good work habits so that you can work independently, if necessary, and deliver required products on time? If you answer no to one or more of these questions, it would be useful to discuss these issues in some depth with someone who has been doing development for a while.

It may also be useful to take a standard, self-administered test to arrive at a fuller understanding of your character and temperament, especially as these shed light on your potential for getting along with types of people different from yourself. One such test which one of the author's has found quite useful in this respect is the Keirsey Temperament Sorter, a short form of the better known Myers-Briggs Type Indicator. The self-administered form is readily available in paperback (Keirsey, 1978).

## Where to Find Employment in Development

### United Agency for International Development (USAID)

As of April 1986, AID resumed limited hiring—after an employment freeze of over a year. Hiring recommenced for Foreign Service Officer (FSO) positions as well as the Agency's International Development Intern Program (IDI). That program was reactivated and expanded to include mid-level as well as entry-level applicants. Recent information from AID's recruitment division indicates that hiring will continue to be limited but since this Agency possesses good opportunities for development anthropologists, it is recommended that you consider applying.

AID as of mid–1986 was requesting applications for the following "targeted" positions:

- administrative management officers
- accountants
- contract specialists
- education/human resources development officers
- health/population/nutrition officers
- housing/urban development officers
- program economists
- project development officers

On this list there are several places for the development anthropologist. Particularly relevant are the "substantive" positions: health, education, and housing; also open to anthropologists is the project development officer position.

Graduate degrees and two or more years of pertinent professional experience are required. Any foreign language is useful for qualifying. For information on these programs write: Recruitment Division, MIPM/R, Agency for International Development, Washington, D.C. 20523.

*Other Major Donor Organizations*

Although AID may be the most obvious place of employment for development anthropologists, there are several other appropriate organizations you should consider.

Within the United Nations organization, to begin with another well known development body, there are numerous agencies which utilize our kind of expertise. Some of these are:

- United Nations International Childrens and Education Fund (UNICEF). Headquarters: New York
- United Nations Development Program (UNDP). Headquarters: New York
- Food and Agriculture Organization (FAO). Headquarters: Rome
- United Nations Center for Human Settlements (HABITAT). Headquarters: Nairobi
- United Nations Environment Program (UNEP). Headquarters: Nairobi
- United Nations Industrial Development Organization (UNIDO) Headquarters: Vienna
- United Nations Education, Science and Culture Organization (UNESCO). Headquarters: Paris
- United Nations Department of Technical Cooperation and Development (UNDTCD). Headquarters: New York
- United Nations International Labor Organization (ILO). Headquarters: Geneva
- United Nations World Health Organization (WHO). Headquarters: Geneva

- World Bank, International Bank for Reconstruction and Development (IBRD), and International Finance Corporation (IFC). Headquarters: Washington, D.C.

Employment in any of these agencies of the UN is theoretically obtainable through an agency of the U.S. government. Several departments of the federal government, such as Departments of State, Education, Agriculture, and Labor, keep current listings of openings in the UN and seek to place Americans in those positions. This placement system is tied to the number of positions "allotted" to the U.S. based on its level of funding.

One of the authors found this system to be basically ineffectual, in that it takes much wheel spinning and paper pushing to obtain the support of the relevant federal department. If you happen to gain such support and a case is made on your behalf to the hiring agency, then your choices of being hired may be enhanced. However, it must be understood that each country participating in the UN has its interest in promoting its own candidates for positions. Therefore, searching out positions in the agencies, either through the representative office in New York or in the headquarters offices, if you happen to be there, is probably the best approach. Networking, accompanied by the agency directory, to find a relevant position and hiring official seems to be more workable than the U.S. "patronage" system.

Besides the United Nations family, there are also such regional multi-or bilateral donor institutions as the Interamerican Development Bank (IDB); African Development Bank (ADB); Asian Development Bank (ADB) Arab Development Bank; Overseas Development Association (ODA-British); Canadian International Development Association (CIDA); Swedish International Development Association (SIDA); German Development Bank (KfW); and many other, less well known agencies. Access to these institutions must be networked and researched on an individual basis.

It is worth mentioning that techniques which anthropologists use in researching communities, organizations, and associations should be used in approaching these major donor institutions. That is, we should apply the same techniques in learning about the corporate cultures of potential clients as we use in our research, to uncover such features as core values, rules and regulations, special language patterns (jargon), and hierarchical configurations, among others.

## Private Consulting Firms

Private organizations, both profit and non-profit, offer an important source of employment for development professionals. In this case, development anthropology is not given special emphasis—the same applies to the donor agency category—principally because the use of that nomenclature *per se* may not be of particular help in defining yourself. Many consulting firm officials know what development anthropology refers to but not all are aware of its precise meaning. It is perhaps more effective to define your skills in terms of what you can do for them specifically, e.g., carry out a social soundness analysis of an integrated rural development project, evaluate a family planning project, produce a physical development plan for an urban squatter community, design a small enterprise development project for villagers, or analyze the administrative structure of a government development agency.

Finding a consulting firm which hires consultants with our skills is not difficult in and of itself. Finding one which will employ *you* is another question. Here networking is the key.

Start by talking to anyone and everyone you know working in the international consulting business. Obtain lists of the firms or organizations which hold Indefinite Quantity Contracts (IQCs) with AID to respond to "requests for service" or "requests for proposal" to carry out work in AID's sectors. Each of the sectors, such as agriculture, health and population, education and training, or housing, among others, has lists of firms specialized in the work of that sector and with which AID has an IQC. These firms usually keep rosters of specialists in their work. Many firms have computerized data banks containing literally thousands of consultants organized around a data base which disaggregates according to discipline, language(s), previous experience, consulting reports produced. Getting into such a data bank is relatively routine, once you determine which firms are appropriate for your services. Obtaining an interview may also be somewhat routine, although sometimes easier said than done, even for seasoned consultants.

One of the keys to being in the right place at the right time is to know when a request for proposal (RFP) is coming down and who the likely bidders on the contract may be. Then try to get hold of the Terms of Reference (TOR) or scope of work called for in the RFP from the appropriate project manager in AID. Next, contact the firms most likely to bid on the contract and present your two to three page tailored resume which stresses your experiences relevant to the proposed work. Information on the interviewing process is covered later in this chapter.

### Church and Voluntary Organizations

These potential employers are lumped together mainly for convenience, since the range of such organizations is considerable. Both of the authors have worked for private voluntary organizations (PVOs), most of which are very serious about their contributions to development, but some of which operate much more like consulting firms than others. The differences are mainly seen in their relationship to the client (namely degree of independence in shaping a development project) and their cost of doing business.

Most church-based organizations (which are classified as PVOs) and many non-church based PVOs contrast with a typical consulting firm in that they are not in business for the "profit," but rather for altruistic purposes, hence the appelation "voluntary." Nevertheless, these organizations must cover their costs and make some attempt to hedge their bets for the future, that is to develop new projects. "Development costs" must somehow be charged for, so the notion of "not for profit" is somewhat illusive. In any case, working for a PVO can be intellectually and personally very rewarding (see DiBella, this volume), especially with such organizations known to the authors as American Friends Service Committee (AFSC), the Mennonite Central Committee, Foster Parents Plan International, Catholic Relief Services, Save the Children Fund, Agriculture Cooperative Development International (ACDI), and Oxfam, among others. Lists of PVOs involved in development work are available.

### USDA and Other Federal Agencies

It should be mentioned that anthropologists may also work in development-related jobs for federal agencies other than AID. The U.S. Department of Agriculture is one such agency. Both the National Association of Practicing Anthropologists (NAPA) and the Washington Association of Professional Anthropologists (WAPA) publish directories of members that list places of employment. A good way to begin a job search in any federal agency is to contract a fellow anthropologist working in that agency. A good general guide for anthropologists seeking federal employment is the WAPA publication, *Stalking Employment in the Nation's Capital* (1982 ).

## How to Find Employment in Development

### Broadcasting your Resume and Accessing Data Banks

Mention has already been made about getting your name "out on the street" by placing your name in the numerous data banks of consulting firms and PVOs. Networking can be a systematic approach to disseminating your name and credentials in the market, that is following up every lead you obtain. Once your reputation begins to develop, especially in consulting where this is so critical, it will tend to snowball. The reason for this is that "good" consultants who have an ability to "hit the ground running" and consistently produce quality work are hard to come by.

In any case, get your name into the data banks of all possible sources of employment. Follow-up every contact with a note as a reminder of your conversation or meeting, or accompanying your mailed resume. Communicating with your contact within thirty days is advisable lest your contact assume that you have obtained the job you were looking for.

### Personal Interviews

Assuming you have followed most of the above suggestions, your next task is to obtain personal interviews. While this does not, of course, guarantee a position, it gets you that much closer to one. Because the interview provides the employer with a level of knowledge about you beyond that of your resume, you must make the very best of it. You are often being compared with other candidates for the same position, so you need to act in ways that give you the edge.

First, as suggested earlier, do a mini ethnography of the organization: How are they organized? Who funds them? Where are their strengths and weaknesses? What are their biases? How do they think, speak, dress? Plan your interview ahead of time by doing your homework: review your notes on the organization, its funding sources, its projects, programs, and evaluations of its work, determining voids where your contribution could make a difference. Second, once in the interview, engage the interviewer in dialogue, make your points about what you have done without exaggerating your capabilities, find out key points about the service or skills required, demonstrate a familiarity with the organization's work by using words and phrases which make you seem knowledgeable and in sympathy with the organization's aims and values. Third, do not talk about money on initial interviews. Instead talk about your professional abilities and establish a sense of rapport with the interviewer.

It is important to mention that many employers do not, in fact, know how to interview candidates, particularly one whose background or discipline is distant from the interviewer's. Therefore, it is crucial for you to steer the interview in such a way that you manage to provide all of the essential information about yourself. Do not allow yourself to linger too long on small talk or personal reminiscences, since the interviewer will usually recall those points relevant to the job, and few of the more casual pieces of information. In later comparing you with other interviewees, the interviewer may be pressed by his or her colleagues to defend his or her choice based on the information you have provided.

### Getting a Foot in the Door:
### Proposal Preparation,
### Volunteer Work, Design, and Evaluation

Consulting firms and PVOs are always preparing proposals and competing for contracts and awards that enable them to carry out their work. Anthropologists may well have the requisite writing and analytic skills, as well as country or regional familiarity or sectoral expertise, to prepare a winning proposal. By reading the *Commerce Business Daily* at a library, or by word of mouth, you can find out which requests for proposals from AID or another federal agency are current and then present yourself at firms likely to bid on these contracts. Bring along samples of relevant writing and offer to bring whatever special expertise you have to sections of the proposal to be prepared. You should be paid for this work, so have a daily rate in mind.

Some firms located in cities such as Boston or Washington have so much talent to draw upon that they may expect some proposal writers to volunteer their services. If volunteering means a place in a proposal that has a reasonable chance of being selected, your investment may pay off. And if it is not selected, you may still have established a reputation for being able to write well, think creatively, and get along with the employees of a firm or other organization. However, aspiring development anthropologists have to eat and pay rent. We know some development hangers-on who started by volunteering their time and several years later have not progressed beyond this.

Other modes of entree are to offer low-cost service to an organization—including AID directly—in carrying out some aspect of project design and evaluation. A fresh eye, especially if inexpensive, is often desirable in working out ideas for a project design or in planning a project evaluation. If such jobs are overseas, the anthropologist can gain extremely valuable hands-on field experience in a wide variety of enterprises and activities, including general ones such as working on a multi-disciplinary team and more specific ones such as those that relate to a sector or subsector like health or community development (see Robins, this volume).

### Internships

Some development agencies, firms, and voluntary organizations offer internships for aspiring development professionals. In anthropology, internships may be offered at the graduate level, and less often at the bachelor's, through universities. Hopefully your academic department has an internship program. If not, internships are still possible if you know professors with good networks for placing students. Otherwise you will have to do the networking yourself, as described earlier.

The internship provides a kind of "rite de passage" for the inexperienced development specialist. It offers a unique approach to learning an organization's way of doing development business. It also offers an opportunity to learn about the client—the agency which is promoting a specific project or program—and, importantly, about the host country and beneficiary population being served. The internship may or may not remunerate you for your work.

While the perspective of the organization in which the internship occurs may be unique to the specific setting and to the sector in which that organization works, the internship still teaches invaluable lessons about working in an office, dealing with the client—usually a development agency—and about the range and complexity of the problems faced by developing countries.

### Opportunities for Academic-based Anthropologists

Many academic-based anthropologists additionally play consulting roles in the development field. Some have established excellent reputations with such agencies as AID, World Bank, or Inter-American Development Bank, as well as with consulting firms. They usually have knowledge and experience in such specialized and complex areas as resettlement, health and family planning, urban planning, development administration, as well as in research evaluation, and/or project design. In addition to their technical contributions, these anthropologists may lend a ceratin aura of respectability to an agency's reputation as a body that knows how to grapple with the sociocultural reality and exigencies of development.

Several important ingredients go into the makeup of a successful anthropologist who moves back and forth between academia and the development consulting environment. First is development experience, either through fieldwork or other research relating to a development problem in a developing country Second is the ability to translate knowledge into usable forms for development agencies or consulting firms. Included in this second factor is a capability to speak the language of the development organization in such a way that you (1) make sense to development officials, (2) bring them something that they do not already know about the development process (such as counterintuitive social knowledge), and (3) provide these officials a compelling rationale for their programs and projects. Third is a clear competence to write reports that fit their requirements for reporting, which often means assisting the agency or firm in promoting a particular program or project.

What is clear about the commuting of anthropologists back and forth between academia and consulting is that it often means sacrificing a purely intellectual approach to the definition, study and solution of problems. This is not to say that intellect *per se* is not respected—it is. However, long, theoretical academic studies or analyses are basically unacceptable, both from the point of view of time, which is also money, and comprehensibility. Development officials most often need information, reports, proposals—all "yesterday," a situation which has led to the growth of such descriptors as "quick and dirty" studies and "windshield" surveys. A work environment predicated on abbreviated kinds of research and analysis is by no means every anthropologist's preferred model. Care must therefore be given to selection of such an environment.

### Networking with Development Anthropologists

While the market in international development is somewhat limited for development anthropologists, it is nevertheless very important to develop and maintain a strong network among fellow practitioners. The interlocking connections among development agencies, consulting firms, voluntary organizations, and universities, among others, are considerable. Therefore, keeping open ties with those in our discipline is critical from the perspective of developing our reputations, for it is in the surprisingly small world of development specialists (where meeting one another in airports, hotels, restaurants, or government ministries overseas, is quite common) that we become known as credible, valuable or their converse, as the case may be.

There are both informal and formal networks for interacting with development anthropologists. Both are equally important, in the eyes of the authors, since each of these networks offers different benefits. The informal, based on personal relationships formed as a result of your private initiative, may offer fresh, immediate information on leads for work. Formal networks offer the possibility of sustained contacts based on associations of anthropologists organized for a variety of purposes.

The American Anthropological Association (AAA) and the Society for Applied Anthropology (SfAA) are national organizations which offer membership for anthropologists of many different stripes, including development types. Their resources for employment generation in the development field are limited, in part by the fact that these associations mainly support academic endeavors, in contrast to serving the needs of non-academic, practicing anthropologists. In an attempt to take advantage of the increasing market for non-academic anthropologists, the AAA has recently organized within its jurisdiction the National Association of Practicing Anthropologists (NAPA). NAPA, whose membership includes both university based as well as non-university based anthropologists, is presently developing its identity as a national level organization.

One organization which actively promotes the work of development anthropologists as well as other practitioner anthropologists is the Washington Association of Professional Anthropologists (WAPA). Geared to serving anthropologists in the District of Columbia area yet with a large membership around the country (total number of members is 256), WAPA is well adapted to serving the needs of the development community, since a significant number of that community resides in or around the District. Besides offering a general employment service to its members, WAPA provides a networking mechanism which is next to none in its success in linking development anthropologists to one another, to development agencies and organizations, consulting firms and, ultimately, to jobs.

## References

Keirsey, David and Marilyn Bates. *Please Understand Me: Character and Temperament Types*. Delmar, Ca.,: Prometheus & Nemisis Books, 1978.

Tec, Leon. *Targets: How to Set Goals for Yourself and Reach Them*. New York: Harper and Row, 1980. USAID. "Opportunities Overseas." Washington, D.C., March 1986.

WAPA. "Stalking Employment in the Nation's Capital." Iles Minoff, ed., Washington, D.C., 1982.

# About the Contributors

**John J. Curry** is an Economic Anthropologist who has spent five of the last six years working on agricultural and livestock development projects in Subsaharan Africa. He is currently the Socioeconomist for the Cropping Systems Research and Extension Training Project at Malkerns, Swaziland. A native of Washington, D.C. and its environs, he attended the University of Maryland, College Park, where he earned a B.A. in History, and an M.A. in Sociology/Anthropology. He received his Ph.D. in Anthropology in 1984 from the University of Massachusetts, Amherst. His dissertation topic examined the relationships between local agricultural production and regional commerce in a Hausa village in the Niger Republic, where he lived for three years. A traditional Irish musician, Dr. Curry plays the flute, the fiddle, the tin whistle and the uileann pipes for cultural and therapeutic reasons.

**Anthony J. DiBella** was born and bred in Boston. He received a B.A. in Sociology from Trinity College, and an MA in Applied Anthropology from American University. He has held a variety of social service and applied social science positions. Currently he is Chief of the Evaluation/ Research Unit of Foster Parents Plan International. He received the WAPA Praxis Award in 1985. Last year he was elected to the Executive Committee of the Society for Applied Anthropology.

**Kjell Enge** is an Assistant Professor and Director of the Latin American Studies Program at Dickerson College in Carlisle, Pa. His work in applied anthropology has been extensive, most recently including major roles in a national education sector assessment and studies of bilingual education in Guatemala, as well as the evaluation of health promoters in Peru on which his chapter is based. At present Dr. Enge is the consulting anthropologist to the USAID mission in Guatemala for the national project on oral rehydration therapy and immunization. His dissertation topic, and an ongoing research interest, is rural social organization and small-scale farming and irrigation systems.

**Sam Fujisaka** received his Ph.D. from the University of Oregon in Cultural Anthropology. Since 1982 he has been a Visiting Assistant Professor/ Visiting Scientist at the Program on Environmental Science and Management, University of the Philippines at Los Banos.

**Edward H. Greeley** received his Ph.D. from The Catholic University of America.His dissertation topic was on population change in the Kenya Highlands. He worked in the AID Regional Office (REDSO) in Kenya from 1977 to 1981 as a Behavioral Science Advisor, working in fifteen countries in East and Southern Africa. From 1981 through 1984 was Project Officer for the AID mission in Nairobi. He is currently working in the Office of Development Planning, Africa Bureau, USAID.

**Edward C. Green** is currently Senior Research Associate with John Short and Associates of Columbia, Md. After two years of dissertation fieldwork among the Maroons in Suriname, he spent five years teaching anthropology before beginning a career in development anthropology in 1980. He has since worked primarily in health and population in Africa. He received two Praxis awards from WAPA for his policy-related research in Swaziland. Like Dr. Curry, Green also performs folk music on several instruments. In fact, he and Curry sometimes perform together.

**David J. Groenfeldt** is staff anthropologist with the International Irrigation Management Institute in Sri Lanka. His dissertation research was in Northwest India where he studied village level effects of irrigation development. More recently he has worked on issues of farmer organization and irrigation bureaucracies in South and Southeast Asia.

**Polly Harrison** is presently a Senior Staff Associate in the Primary Health Care Technologies Project of Management Sciences for Health. She has specific responsibility for the Central American Regional Child Survival Project and carries out a variety of evaluative and project design work, as well as anthropological research and analysis. Most recently she has led teams which evaluated innovative private sector health delivery projects in Haiti and designed a national ORT program for Guatemala. This year's anthropological activity will include design of national protocols for appropriate child feeding practices, development of a methodology for analysis of the health provider-client interface, and research into the differences between the users and non-users of health services.

**John P. Mason,** Director, Development Studies Program, AID/University Southern California in Washington, D.C., is a development anthropologist with eighteen years experience in development, including North Africa, the Middle East, Subsaharan Africa and the Caribbean, and author of *Island of the Blest: Islam in the Life of a Libyan Oasis Community.*

**Robert E. Rhoades** is a native of rural Oklahoma. Before receiving his Ph.D. in Anthropology in 1976, he studied agriculture and sociology. He has conducted agricultural anthropological research in a dozen countries of Asia, Europe, and Latin America. Since 1979 he has been with the International Potato Center (CIP) in Lima, Peru. He is now Leader of Food Systems Research, one of CIP's ten research thrusts.

**Edward Robins** is Professor of Anthropology at the University of Wisconsin—River Falls. From 1983 to present he served as Social Science Advisor to USAID in Rwanda as one of the first participants in AID's innovative Joint Career Corps program. In addition to his work as an applied anthropologist in Africa, Professor Robins has studied inter-ethnic relations in Israel and the social impact of rice intensification in Indonesia. He received his Ph.D. from Tulane University in 1972.

**Janice Sacherer** has lived and worked in Asia and Europe since completing her dissertation research in Nepal. She is currently a lecturer in the University of Maryland's University College Asian Division, stationed in Okinawa.

**Ruth Ann Sando** received a B.A. degree from the George Washington University and an M.A. and Ph.D. from the University of Hawaii. She has been a consultant to the California Department of Parks and Recreation, State Archeology Lab; Senior Analyst in the Research and Development Department, American Savings & Loan Association; and is currently with the Corporate Management Systems Division of Blue Cross of California.